GOD AT WAR

GOD AT WAR

Power in the Exodus Tradition

THOMAS B. DOZEMAN

New York   Oxford
OXFORD UNIVERSITY PRESS
1996

Oxford University Press

Oxford   New York
Athens   Auckland   Bangkok
Calcutta   Cape Town   Dar es Salaam   Delhi
Florence   Hong Kong   Istanbul   Karachi
Kuala Lumpur   Madras   Madrid   Melbourne
Mexico City   Nairobi   Paris   Singapore
Taipei   Tokyo   Toronto

and associated companies in
Berlin   Ibadan

Published by Oxford University Press, Inc.
198 Madison Avenue, New York, New York 10016

Oxford is a registered trademark of Oxford University Press, Inc.

Library of Congress Cataloging-in-Publication Data
Dozeman, Thomas B.
God at war : power in the Exodus tradition / Thomas B. Dozeman.
p. cm.
Includes bibliographical references.
ISBN 0-19-510217-7
1. War—Biblical teaching. 2. Power (Social sciences)—Biblical
teaching. 3. Bible. O.T. Exodus—Criticism, interpretation, etc.
I. Title.
BS1245.6.W2D68   1996
222'.1206—dc20   95-12579

1 3 5 7 9 8 6 4 2
Printed in the United States of America
on acid-free paper

For my parents,
Lucille Mulder Dozeman
and Milton Dozeman

Preface

Many colleagues, friends, and institutions have influenced and assisted me in researching and writing this book. The Pentateuch Seminar of the Society of Biblical Literature provided an important context for me to listen to other researchers in the field and to raise new questions about the formation of pentateuchal literature. I would like to thank the members of the seminar and, in particular, the chairpersons (Professors John Van Seters, Rolf Knierim, and George Coats) for their responses to papers and for a lively exchange of ideas during the years 1986–1991. Papers presented at the Catholic Biblical Association in 1991 and 1993, at Hebrew Union College-Jewish Institute of Religion in Cincinnati in 1992 and at the Society of Biblical Literature in 1993 on topics of the exodus, wilderness, and law have also provided me with important forums of exchange that have influenced my interpretation of the exodus. I would like to thank these institutions and individuals for their interest in my research and for their critical response.

Much of the research for this book was undertaken while I was on sabbatical leave in Münster, Germany, during the 1992–1993 academic year. I would like to thank my home institution, United Theological Seminary, for approving my leave, and Professor Walter Beyerlin of the Evangelische-Theologische Fakultät of the Westfälische Wilhelms Universität for sponsoring my stay in Germany. The sabbatical was made possible, in part, by a Theological Scholarship and Research Award from the Association of Theological Schools in the United States and Canada (ATS). I would like to thank the ATS for its support, as well as Professors John Van Seters and Rolf Rendtorff for acting as senior mentors in connection with the grant.

Books are slow in coming and their content is influenced by the everyday exchange with colleagues over long periods of time. Many conversations with Professor Kathleen Farmer, my Old Testament colleague at United Theological Seminary, have certainly found their way into the pages of this book. The theoretical work on power is a gift from my colleague in theology, Professor Tyron Inbody, and my wife, Professor Mary R. Talen, whose research in Family Systems Theory is not as far afield as I once thought.

My intention in writing this book is to contribute in some small way to an understanding of divine power in our world at least as it has been glimpsed and codified in the formation of the Pentateuch. I wish to dedicate this effort to my mother, Lucille Mulder Dozeman, and to the memory of my father, Milton Dozeman (1917–1994).

Dayton, Ohio   T. B. D.
Epiphany 1995

Contents

Abbreviations

ETL	*Ephemerides theologicae lovanienses*
EvT	*Evangelische Theologie*
ExpTim	*Expository Times*
FRLANT	Forschungen zur Religion und Literatur des Alten und Neuen Testaments
GKC	Gensius' Hebrew Grammar, ed. E. Kautzsch, tr. A. E. Cowley
HAT	Handbuch zum Alten Testament
Hen	*Henoch*
HS	*Hebrew Studies*
HSW	Harvard Semitic Monographs
HUCA	*Hebrew Union College Annual*
IB	*Interpreter's Bible*
IBS	*Irish Biblical Studies*
ICC	International Critical Commentary
IDB	G. A. Buttrick (ed.), *Interpreter's Dictionary of the Bible*
IDBSup	*Supplementary volume to IDB*
Int	*Interpretation*
JANESCU	*Journal of the Ancient Near Eastern Society of Columbia University*
JAOS	*Journal of the American Oriental Society*
JBL	*Journal of Biblical Literature*
JHNES	Johns Hopkins Near Eastern Studies
JNES	*Journal of Near Eastern Studies*
JPOS	*Journal of the Palestine Oriental Society*
JQR	*Jewish Quarterly Review*
JSOT	*Journal for the Study of the Old Testament*
JSOTSup	Journal for the Study of the Old Testament-Supplement Series
JSS	*Journal of Semitic Studies*
JTS	*Journal of Theological Studies*
NCB	New Century Bible
NICOT	New International Commentary on the Old Testament
NRSV	New Revised Standard Version
OBO	Orbis biblicus et orientalis
ÖBS	Österreichische biblische Studien
OBT	Overtures to Biblical Theology
Or	*Orientalia*
OTL	Old Testament Library

OTS	*Oudtestamentische Studiën*
PJ	*Palästina-Jahrbuch*
RB	*Revue biblique*
RevExp	*Review and Expositor*
RTL	*Revue théologigue de Louvain*
SBLASP	Society of Biblical Literature Abstracts and Seminar Papers
SBLDS	SBL Dissertation Series
SBLMS	SBL Monograph Series
SBS	Stuttgarter Bibelstudien
SEÅ	*Svensk exegetisk årsbok*
SJLA	Studies in Judaism in Late Antiquity
SJT	*Scottish Journal of Theology*
ST	*Studia theologica*
Tbü	*Theologische Bücherei*
TDNT	*Theological Dictionary of the New Testament*, G. Kittel and G. Friedrich (eds.)
TDOT	*Theological Dictionary of the Old Testament*, G. J. Botterweck and H. Ringgren (eds.)
TynBul	*Tyndale Bulletin*
TZ	*Theologische Zeitschrift*
UF	*Ugarit-Forschungen*
VT	*Vetus Testamentum*
VTSup	Vetus Testamentum, Supplements
WBC	Word Biblical Commentary
WMANT	Wissenschaftliche Monographien zum Alten und Neuen Testament
ZAW	*Zeitschrift für die alttestamentliche Wissenschaft*
ZDPV	*Zeitschrift des deutschen Palästina-Veriens*
ZTK	*Zeitschrift für Theologie und Kirche*

GOD AT WAR

1

Divine Power in the Exodus

The destruction of the Egyptian army is the primary story of salvation for Israel, and central to it is the portrait of God in combat. So important is this image of divine power that the annihilation of the enemy by Yahweh marks the moment of salvation for Israel and prompts its victory hymn of celebration in Exod 15:3, "Yahweh is a warrior!" The war cry underscores how salvation is an event of divine warfare, in which the destruction of the enemy is victory for God and liberation for Israel. The mythology of the story has powerful religious and social consequences.

This study will interpret the influence of militaristic imagery in the exodus on Israel's understanding of God, with special attention directed to their conception of divine power. The militaristic imagery has long caught the attention of scholars. Noting how enmeshed salvation and war are throughout the exodus, Julius Wellhausen remarked that perhaps the war room should be considered Israel's first sanctuary, since it looks to be the cradle of the nation and the place where humans and the divine most clearly met.[1] The observation by Wellhausen raises a number of important questions that will frame the present study. Is the Judeo-Christian tradition of salvation a complex attempt to deify a kingdom by making its wars holy? If the account of the exodus is not simply religion masking as nationalism, how did it overcome its origins? These questions presuppose a more fundamental one: How does divine power function in the exodus?

The destruction of the Egyptians is a story of holy war.[2] The aim of this study is to address the theological problem of divine power implicit in holy war and at the heart of the exodus story. The primary means for achieving this goal will be an interpretation of character and plot in the story of the exodus. Thus what follows is essentially a literary study, but one that is adapted to the character of pentateuchal narrative, with its close ties to Israelite cultic tradition and hence its tendency to undergo transformation as the worship practices of Israel changed.[3] It will become clear that the exercise of divine power in holy war is not a static concept in Israel's theological reflection but one that was open to critical evaluation and to dynamic reformulation, which in the end has given rise to a history of tradition. Interpreting the influence of the militaristic imagery in the exodus on Israel's understanding of God will lead to a more broadly based study that includes not only transformations in the cultic life of Israel and, with it, literary changes in the account of the exodus, but also the rise of salvation history in the formation of the Pentateuch.

The exile signifies the clearest point of change in Israel's understanding of divine power, and this study is structured to reflect this development. Chapters 2 through 4 present an interpretation of the narrative liturgies of the exodus as they are preserved in the Book of Exodus. Chapter 2 examines the preexilic cultic tradition of the confrontation between Yahweh and Pharaoh in the sequence of events that begins with the plagues and continues through the expulsion of Israel from Egypt. Chapters 3 and 4 explore the effects of the exile on Israel's reformulation of the exodus, paying particular attention to the presentation of divine power. Chapter 5 interprets the poetic accounts of the exodus in Exodus 15. Here my aim is to interrelate the distinctive poetic voices of Moses and Miriam with the narrative accounts outlined in chapters 2 through 4. Chapter 6 broadens the scope of this study in order to raise larger questions concerning the formation of the Pentateuch and possible future directions for pentateuchal theology.

Pentateuchal studies are on the move.[4] Long-standing debates over the historical origins of ancient Israel as compared to the pentateuchal story and the implications of this tension for interpreting ancient Israelite religion are increasingly spilling over into a reevaluation of pentateuchal literature itself. As a consequence, new questions are being raised concerning the dating of the literature, the character and function of independent literary traditions, as well as the rise of historiography in ancient Israel and its influence on the formation of the Pentateuch.[5] Nowhere do these questions come into sharper focus than in the exodus.

My aim in this study is to address these larger questions concerning the formation of the Pentateuch through a narrower study of the exodus tradition as it has evolved within the changing cultic traditions of Israel. What follows, then, is not a history of ancient Israel but a history of literature in its cultic setting. The formation of the exodus tradition is interpreted as a process of supplementation in which the story is transformed from a preexilic liturgy celebrating the holy-war victory of Yahweh at the sea to an extended and incomplete account of salvation history. I intend to demonstrate that problems surrounding divine power remain a prominent feature of the exodus and that reinterpretations of divine power influence both the characters and plot structure of the story of the exodus. A brief examination of character and plot in the exodus will provide a more precise methodological and theological focus.

DIVINE POWER AND CHARACTER IN THE EXODUS

Divine power presents a problem of character. The literary structure of the story illustrates the point. The story of salvation is presented as a holy war against Egypt, which is meant to probe conflict between Yahweh and other powers concerning the divine claim on Israel. Thus, characterization is central to the exodus, since the story is about divine power and how it affects other cosmological powers (the sea), other nations (Egypt), and Israel. In fact, it is only through God's exerting power that other characters acquire a place in the story as either opponents or allies of God.

The importance of divine power in defining characters cannot be underestimated. Even though all characters exercise a certain degree of power in relation to Yahweh, it would be a mistake to read the story of the exodus from the perspective of any of the secondary characters (sea, Egypt, or Israel). On the contrary, the exodus must be read from God's point of view. Only then does the reader engage a central literary problem for interpreting the text: whether any of the secondary characters emerge with real personality (and hence causality) either over against or in conjunction with God. The literary problems of character and causality are anchored in a theological problem concerning the nature of divine power, since they raise the troubling question of whether the God of the exodus is, in the end, a despot, who manipulates others through events that are already predetermined.[6]

A central thesis of this study is that the character of Yahweh undergoes change as divine power is redefined by Israel. And once divine power is transformed, there is also change in the way characters interact in the story of the exodus. To trace such changes in the characterization of God requires a definition of divine power that is broad enough to incorporate Israel's emerging understanding of salvation in light of their ongoing social and religious experience, which included the tragedy of the exile. The distinction between unilateral and relational forms of power will provide a heuristic tool for achieving this goal. This distinction has arisen within the process-relational school of contemporary American philosophical theology, of which Bernhard Loomer was a leading figure. His work will provide a framework for making tradition-historical distinctions in Israel's emerging understanding of divine power within the exodus.[7]

Loomer defined unilateral power as "the ability to produce intended or desired effects on the other."[8] This definition underscores how a relationship between two persons is essential for unilateral power, since strength can be measured only by the ability of one person to actualize his or her purposes on another.[9] Yet the relationship itself is not the point of focus. Instead, unilateral power focuses exclusively on the personal goals of one of the two subjects. Such a view of power, therefore, is one-directional and it measures only active force.[10] Loomer describes this view of power as being *either/or*, since a compromise between two persons would signal weakness in the person under study: *Either* individuals are able to exercise their will on another (and hence be powerful) *or* they must seek a compromise (because they lack enough power to achieve their goals).[11] When such a view of power is applied to God, the same guidelines for measuring power apply, but on a larger scale.[12] In such a framework God is static and unchanging and must be seen in an either/or relationship with all other powers in the world. God must be able to dominate and to control these powers by bringing them into conformity with the divine will.[13]

Relational power is defined as "the ability both to produce and to undergo an effect."[14] As in unilateral power, relationship remains essential, but it functions very differently. The starting point of relational power "lies in the constitutive role of relationships in the creation of individuals and societies."[15] With such a starting point it is the relationship between two persons that becomes the point of focus in the study of power, rather than one of the two parties. Relational power, therefore, is bidirectional and it includes both active and passive force, with the result that strength is measured by the range of internal relationships that can be maintained instead of by one's ability to control another.[16] Loomer describes this view of power as being *both/and,* since its exercise must include *both* an active exertion to produce an effect *and* the more passive ability to undergo an effect. He writes: "[relational power] has as one of its premises the notion that the capacity to absorb an influence is as truly a mark of power as is the strength involved in exerting an influence."[17] When such a view of power is applied to God, the same guidelines for measuring power apply, but on a larger scale. In such a framework God is no longer a static and unchanging force independent of the world and seeking to bring it into conformity with the divine will through active domination. Instead, relationship also becomes central to the divine character. Thus God too is in a both/and relationship with the world—in the sense that divine power consists of producing active effects and of undergoing effects. One implication is that the capacity to change becomes constitutive of God.[18]

Unilateral and relational views of power contrast in how they view an opposing party, "the other." When divine power is viewed unilaterally, all other powers tend to be viewed abstractly and impersonally as groups, stereotypes, or classes that function over against God as gauges to measure divine strength. This is true not only for powers that oppose God, but also for powers that function in conjunction with God.[19] Relational power, by contrast, allows other characters to be viewed personally and concretely as independent forces that interact with God.[20] We will see in chapter 2 that a unilateral view of divine power dominates in the account of the exodus from the monarchy period. The result is that neither the Israelites nor the Egyptians develop as genuinely independent characters. The Israelites function as a mirror or extension of divine power, while Pharaoh and the Egyptians must be either transformed into the exact image of the people of God or destroyed. In either case all powers other than God remain impersonal abstractions for the purpose of measuring divine strength. Chapters 3 and 4 will explore how the development of secondary characters, who function over against or in conjunction with God, signals a transformation in Israel's understanding of divine power, and that the change is more characteristic of relational power. The result is that other characters begin to influence divine action, and with it the outcome of the story of the exodus. This shift in perspective occurs in exilic and postexilic deuteronomistic and priestly tradition.

Unilateral and relational views of power also yield different tolerances for inclusion. The abstract character of other powers or persons in unilateral power tends to support a more exclusive and nationalistic theology. Distinctions between groups remain absolutely clear, while the "other" never emerges beyond a stereotype to be transformed into the image of the self.[21] Chapter 2 will illustrate the tendency in the preexilic interpretation of the exodus to support a theology of the kingdom. This account maintains clear boundaries between Israel and Egypt, because it presupposes a static and unilateral view of divine power. Chapters 3 and 4 will explore how relational views of divine power critically evaluate the theology of early exodus tradition, and how the transformation of characters in the story of the exodus is one means for achieving this goal.

DIVINE POWER AND PLOT IN THE EXODUS

Different conceptions of divine power also influence the plot structure of the exodus, because they produce varying outcomes to conflict. The most striking difference between unilateral and relational views of power is the contrast between orderly versus ambiguous results from actions. Unilateral power does not tolerate ongoing ambiguity. Such ambiguity would signal a weakness in God, since it would imply a lessened degree of divine influence both over the people of God and over other opposing powers.[22] Relational power, by contrast, implies ambiguity because the specific outcome of events can take shape only in the concrete interaction of characters. Such a striking contrast in the outcome of conflict will have profound effects on the plot structure of the exodus. Thus, as the divine character undergoes change in the transmission of the exodus, so also does the plot structure evolve from an orderly story with a clear ending to a more ambiguous story that looks to the future for its ending. I will argue in this study that the transformation in the plot of the exodus gives rise to salvation history.[23]

I will also argue that the wilderness is not an original component to the plot structure of the exodus, but a later addition by deuteronomistic tradents, and that it is the most significant addition to the plot of the exodus. Its emergence into pentateuchal tradition separates the exercise of divine power (in the events of the exodus) from its intended outcome (of

Israel's possession of the land). Hence the wilderness signals transformation in the plot of the exodus from an orderly story, in which Israel's liberation from Egypt is celebrated from the perspective of the land, to an
account of salvation history, in which Israel is presented as journeying
toward a land that is only promised. Once the framework of salvation history is in place, the outcome of events can emerge only through concrete
interaction of characters as they journey through the wilderness. Thus, as
the transitional setting between exodus and land, the wilderness symbol-
izes the ambiguity of relational power,[24] and it is this view of power that
has come to dominate the present form of the Pentateuch, where the wilderness setting extends from Exodus through Deuteronomy.[25]

The argument for the late development of the wilderness as an immediate outcome of the exodus runs counter to current interpretations, in
which both the wilderness tradition and a salvation history perspective are
judged to be original to the story of the exodus. Current evaluations of the
role and significance of the wilderness in the Pentateuch are influenced
most strongly by the work of Martin Noth, specifically *A History of Pentateuchal Traditions*.[26] Noth argued that the exodus was the kernel
of the entire Pentateuch.[27] He traced the tradition-historical development
of the exodus by describing how it branched out immediately to join with
the theme of the land, which, according to Noth, was already implicit in the
exodus theme.[28] The wedding of the exodus and the land themes required
the wilderness as a bridge at the earliest stages in the formation of the
Pentateuch. Such a view of tradition supported the hypothesis of a desert or
nomadic ideal at the origin of Israelite Religion.[29] Yet, because of its subordinate role as bridging together the more significant themes of exodus and
land, the wilderness never played an important role in Noth's interpretation
of the Pentateuch. In fact Noth wrote concerning the wilderness: "[I]t is
. . . obvious that this is not a very important or really independent theme. It
presupposes in every instance the themes 'guidance out of Egypt' and 'guidance into the promised land' and depends on both of these."[30]

Two hypotheses are central to the work of Noth, and they have strongly
influenced contemporary interpretations of the plot structure of the exodus and even theories concerning the formation of the Pentateuch as a
whole.[31] First, Noth assumed that the genre of historiography was present
at the earliest stages in the formation of the Pentateuch. Second, because
the wilderness was already present in a subordinate role in Israel's earliest
formulations of the exodus, Noth never entertained the possibility that the
wilderness might represent a significant transformation in Israel's interpretation of the exodus. What becomes clear from the review of Noth's work
is that an interpretation of the wilderness as representing a later change in
the plot of the exodus will bring the present study in conversation with
larger issues regarding the place of salvation history in ancient Israelite
cultic tradition and the influence of this perspective in giving rise to historiography in the Pentateuch.[32]

A study of plot in chapters 2 through 4 will illustrate how the inter-weaving of the wilderness with the exodus creates salvation history. Chapter 2 is an interpretation of the exodus without a wilderness wandering. The absence of the wilderness results in an orderly story that is closed off and finished in its celebration of Yahweh's present kingship in the land as the Day of Yahweh. It neither is historiographic nor does it present a theology of salvation history. Such an account of the exodus conforms to the argument of Rolf Rendtorff that early traditions of the Pentateuch (like the exodus) must be interpreted independently of their adjacent themes.[33]

The effects of the exile on the plot of the story will be explored in chapters 3 and 4 through interpretation of deuteronomistic and priestly supplements to the exodus. A common feature of these theologically distinct traditions is the important role of the wilderness as the immediate outcome of the exodus from Egypt. The introduction of the wilderness within both traditions introduces the motif of journey, which requires that the cultic kingship of God in the land be reinterpreted as a future hope and not a present reality. I will argue that such restructuring of the plot of the exodus creates salvation history in the Pentateuch. John Van Seters provides an avenue for reevaluating the transformations in the plot of the exodus with his research in historiography. His argument that ancient Israelite history writing is a late development within deuteronomistic tradition will provide the point of departure for exploring how the exodus and wilderness themes were interrelated in the development of the Pentateuch, and how this interrelationship is part of a larger historiography that recounts the origins of Israel.[34]

A study of the exodus potentially relates to nearly every aspect of study concerning the history, culture, and religion of ancient Israel. Thus it is important to underscore the narrow focus of the present study as a history of literature in its cultic setting. The method of study is supplementation rather than source criticism. My theological aim is to demonstrate the prominent role of divine power in the story of the exodus and how it undergoes significant reinterpretations that influence both the characters and plot structure of the story. Chapters 2 through 5 will trace the evolution of the exodus from a holy-war confrontation at the sea to an incomplete story of salvation history. The first section of chapters 2 through 5 will explore literary changes in the story of the exodus that result from supplementation, while the second section of each chapter will focus on the implications of the changes for interpreting divine power. In the process it will become clear that God acquires the ability to change as secondary characters take on more prominent roles in the unfolding story of the exodus, while transformations in the plot structure of the exodus—especially the incorporation of the wilderness tradition—give rise to historiography in ancient Israel along with a theology of salvation history. The result is a reinterpretation of divine power from being unilateral to being relational. Chapter 6 will conclude the study by raising a larger question concerning the relationship between the exodus and Sinai traditions in the formation of the Pentateuch.

Notes

1. J. Wellhausen, *Israelitische und Jüdische Geschichte*, (5th ed. (Berlin: Georg Reimer, 1904), 25-27.

2. F. Schwally (*Der heilige Krieg im alten Israel*, Semitische Kriegsalter-tümer 1 [Leipzig: Deiterich, 1901]) inaugurated the study of holy war with his argument that Israelite warfare was holy because ancient Israel saw itself as a fed-eration constituted around the warrior God Yahweh. As a consequence, Israel waged war as Yahweh's military host, which meant that war became an impor-tant feature of the cult, while warfare itself took on sacrificial characteristics. In more recent times G. von Rad (*Holy War in Ancient Israel*, trans. M. J. Dawn [Grand Rapids: Eerdmans, 1991], 39-134) argued that holy war was a polit-ical and military activity based in the cultic institution of the amphictyony. Sub-sequently R. Smend (*Yahweh War and Tribal Confederacy: Reflections upon Israel's Earliest History*, 2d ed. [trans. M. G. Rogers [Nashville: Abingdon, 1970], 13-25) critically evaluated von Rad's theory by arguing that holy war must be separated from the cultic institution of the amphictyony and thus be seen as a profane military action. One result of the work of Smend was that the term "Yahweh war" (the actual practice of Israelite warfare) was dissociated from "holy war" (later theological reflection on warfare). The present study will follow the lead of Smend by using "holy war" to mean theological reflection on war for cultic purposes. For additional discussion see Gw. H. Jones, "Holy War or Yahweh War?" *VT* 25 (1975): 642-658.

3. The assumption that pentateuchal narrative is closely related to Israel's cultic tradition takes its starting point from J. Wellhausen (*Prolegomena to the History of Ancient Israel*, trans. Menzies and Black [New York: Meridian Books, 1957], 17-164). This assumption demands that the cultic history of the exodus be undertaken in conjunction with a literary reconstruction of the tradition.

4. The phrase comes from R. Rendtorff, "Pentatuechal Studies on the Move," *JSOT* 3 (1977): 43-45.

5. Recent developments in pentateuchal studies with regard to method have been more than adequately reviewed by a number of scholars, including: A. de Pury and T. Römer, "Le pentateuque en question: Position du problème et brève histoire de la recherche," in *Le pentateuque en question: Les origines et la com-position des cinq premiers livres de la Bible à la lumière des recherches récentes,* ed. A de Pury, Le monde de la Bible (Genève: Labor & Fides, 1989), 9-80; J. Blenkin-sopp, *The Pentateuch: An Introduction to the First Five Books of the Bible,* The Anchor Bible Reference Library (New York: Doubleday, 1992), 1-30; and C. Hout-man, *Der Pentateuch: Die Geschichte seiner Erforschung neben einer Auswer-tung,* Biblical Exegesis and Theology 9 (Kampen: Kok Pharos Publishing, 1994).

6. See J. Kegler, "Zu Komposition und Theologie der Plagenerzählungen," in *Die Hebräische Bibel und ihre zweifache Nachgeschichte: Festschrift für Rolf Rendtorff,* ed. E. Blum et al. (Neukirchen-Vluyn: Neukirchener, 1990), 55-57. For a review of past research on the topic of power, see especially N. Lohfink, "Lit-eraturverzeichnis," in *Gewalt und Gewaltlosigkeit im Alten Testament*, ed.

N. Lohfink, Quaestioines Disputatae 96 (Freiburg: Herder, 1983), 15-50; and J. P. M. Walsh, *The Mighty from Their Thrones: Power in the Biblical Tradition,* OBT 21 (Philadelphia: Fortress Press, 1987).

7. See the summary of this school by Tyron Inbody, "History of Empirical Theology," in *Empirical Theology: A Handbook,* ed. R. C. Miller (Birmingham: Religious Education Press, 1992), 11-35.

8. B. Loomer, "Two Kinds of Power," *Criterion* 15 (1976): 14.

9. Loomer, "Two Kinds of Power," 15.

10. Loomer, "Two Kinds of Power," 14.

11. Loomer, "Two Kinds of Power," 14.

12. See Loomer ("Two Kinds of Power," 14-15, 28) for a discussion of scale and size.

13. See A. Case-Winters (*God's Power: Traditional Understandings and Contemporary Challenges* [Louisville: Westminster/John Knox, 1990], 63-93 and passim) for a detailed discussion of how unilateral views of divine power lead to social domination and control. See also Loomer, "Two Kinds of Power," 16-18.

14. Loomer, "Two Kinds of Power," 20.

15. Loomer, "Two Kinds of Power," 21-23.

16. Loomer, "Two Kinds of Power," 23.

17. Loomer, "Two Kinds of Power," 14.

18. For a more detailed discussion see Case-Winters, *God's Power,* 129-170, 206-232.

19. Loomer, "Two Kinds of Power," 17.

20. Loomer, "Two Kinds of Power," 18, 23-25.

21. Loomer, "Two Kinds of Power," 15-18.

22. Loomer, "Two Kinds of Power," 17-18, 25-26.

23. Salvation history designates both a contemporary hermeneutic for constructing biblical theology and an ancient hermeneutic for viewing the past. Although it is difficult to separate these two meanings completely, the emphasis in the present study is on developments in Israel's cultic tradition in which religion and history merged, giving rise to a "canonical history" (see G. von Rad, *Old Testament Theology,* vol. 1, trans. D. M. G. Stalker [New York: Harper & Row, 1962], 126, 129). Salvation history therefore designates the emergence of a fixed pattern of divine activity in Israel's past, in which the promise to the ancestors, exodus, wilderness wandering, revelation at Sinai, and life in the land are interwoven into a theologically motivated historiographic framework. The essential feature of salvation history is not that the divine acts in human affairs, nor is it the uniqueness of Israel as the object of divine action. These features are characteristic of the earliest forms of the exodus tradition. Rather the essential component in the construction of salvation history is that the weaving together of a sequence of episodes into a canonical history introduces promise and hence incompleteness to the story. As a result, salvation history has a future orientation that was not always characteristic of the earliest forms of the exodus. For an overview of the problems associated with salvation history see R. Gnuse, *"Heilsgeschichte" as a Model for Biblical Theology: The Debate Concerning the Uniqueness and Significance of Israel's Worldview,* College Theology Society Studies in Religion 4 (Lanham: University Press of America, 1988); and T. L. Thompson, "Historiography [Israelite]," in *The Anchor Bible Dictionary,* vol. 3, ed. D. N. Freedman (New York: Doubleday, 1992), 209-210.

24. For definition of the "wilderness" (Hebrew מדבר) as a symbolic location between the exodus and land, which represents a rite of passage, see S. Talmon, "The 'Desert Motif' in the Bible and in Qumran Literature," in *Biblical Motifs: Origins and Transformations,* ed. A. Altmann, Philip W. Lown Institute of Advanced Judaic Studies, Brandeis University Studies and Texts, vol. 3 (Cambridge: Harvard University Press, 1966), 31–63; and "Wilderness," in *IDBSup,* ed. K. Crim (Nashville: Abingdon, 1976): 946–949. This temporal meaning of wilderness as a rite of passage is often used in conjunction with a more spatial meaning in which wilderness signifies the "drift"—a borderland between civilization and chaos. As such the motif of the wilderness in Israelite tradition is never an ideal with intrinsic value, according to Talmon, but a place of transition. For a similar discussion using the anthropological research of Victor Turner with regard to ritual see R. L. Cohn, *The Shape of Sacred Space: Four Biblical Studies* (AAR Studies in Religion 23 [Missoula: Scholars Press, 1981], 7–23), where he discusses the concept of liminality (the marginalizing that takes place at times of transition) in relationship to the wilderness.

25. The wilderness is the primary setting of the Pentateuch. Defined as broadly as possible, the wilderness begins in the middle of the events of the exodus (Exod 13:17) and it remains the setting for all subsequent events through the Pentateuch. See G. W. Coats, "A Structural Transition in Exodus," *VT* 22 (1972): 129–142; and "An Exposition for the Wilderness Tradition, *VT* 22 (1972): 288–295.

26. M. Noth, *A History of Pentateuchal Traditions,* trans. B. W. Anderson (Chico: Scholars Press, 1981).

27. Noth (*A History of Pentateuchal Traditions,* 47–51) concluded that the exodus was the oldest of the four themes—promise to the ancestors, exodus, wilderness, land—which merged to form the historical credos, and that, as the primary confession of Israel's faith, the exodus was the kernel of the entire Pentateuch. Furthermore, the event at the heart of this theme was the destruction of the Egyptians at the Red Sea. Noth concluded, therefore, that the poetic couplet in Exodus 15:21b celebrating this event was the nucleus of the Pentateuch and that it could stand alone as an "all Israelite" confession of faith without further supplementation.

28. Although the exodus theme could stand alone, Noth concluded that it didn't for very long. In fact Noth spends almost no time in describing how the exodus theme might have developed independently. Instead he traces its tradition history by describing how it branched out to join with the theme of the land. He writes that the "leading out" of the confessional statement ("Yahweh, who led Israel out of Egypt") certainly did not mean "a 'leading out' into the unknown or into vacant space but precisely into the state of free fullness of life which Israel now enjoyed on her own soil." See Noth, *A History of Pentateuchal Traditions,* 50 n. 167; and *Exodus: A Commentary,* OTL, trans. J. S. Bowden (Philadelphia: Westminster, 1962), 104–105.

29. For literature on the "desert ideal," see K. Budde, "Das nomadische Ideal im Alten Testament," *Preussische Jahrbücher* 88 (1895): 57–79; and J. W. Flight, "The Nomadic Idea and Ideal in the Old Testament," *JBL* 42 (1923): 158–226.

30. Noth, *A History of Pentateuchal Traditions,* 58.

31. The influence of Noth runs deep in contemporary pentateuchal studies. For example, the tradition-historical analysis of the exodus as a holy-war event intimately tied to the land was expanded upon by von Rad in *Holy War in*

Ancient Israel and by the Albright School, especially through the work of F. M. Cross and D. N. Freedman in *Studies in Ancient Yahwistic Poetry,* SBLDS 21 (Missoula: Scholars Press, 1975) with their thesis that the entire poem in Exodus 15 is ancient and part of an early epic that included poetry about life in the land, like Judges 5. In this regard see also the work of P. D. Miller, Jr, *The Divine Warrior in Early Israel,* HSM 5 (Cambridge: Harvard University Press, 1973), 113-117, 166-170. The same model is also evident in Norman K. Gottwald's sociological study, *The Tribes of Yahweh: A Sociology of the Religion of Liberated Israel, 1250-1050 B.C.E* (Philadelphia: Fortress Press, 1979). Like Noth, he concludes that the exodus and land are the "fundamental themes," that these "two basic themes fuse into a conceptual whole which forms the minimal starting point for the cultic-ideological consciousness of Israel," and that the wilderness is a subordinate theme whose function is merely to provide a bridge between exodus and land (pp. 79- 80). The fusion of the exodus and land is also constitutive for contemporary theologies of liberation. J. Severino Croatto provides illustration when he writes in *Exodus: A Hermeneutics of Freedom* (trans. S. Attanasio [Maryknoll: Orbis Books, 1978], 25): "[T]he Exodus event is interpreted from the vantage point of the fulfillment in the promised land: the two moments of the "departure" (from Egypt) and of the "entry" (into the promised land) are correlates. . . . The 'song of the sea' of Exodus 15 celebrates the God of the Exodus at the very moment of the liberation . . . but from the perspective of the full gift of the land. . . ." In all of these instances the genre of historiography is presumed to lie at the root of the formation of the Pentateuch, with the wilderness providing the necessary connection between the more significant traditions of exodus and land.

32. The definition of "historiography" in biblical literature is in debate because of conflicting standards in Israel and Greece. A. Momigliano (*The Classical Foundations of Modern Historiography,* Sather Classical Lectures 54 [Berkeley: University of California Press, 1990], 18-21) notes how reliability of evidence and trustworthiness of research are essential to Greek historians. As a result the "choice between what is true and what is untrue, or at least between what is probable and what is improbable, was inherent in the profession of the historian as the Greeks understood." Momigliano notes how the criterion of reliability was different for the ancient Israelite historian, because history and religion were one. As a consequence, reliability "coincides with the truthfulness of the transmitters and with the ultimate truth of God in which the transmitters believe." It could never be verified according to objective criteria.

If the emphasis in defining historiography is on the recounting of the past for the purpose of present identity, then the formation of the Pentateuch into an overarching story of origins can be defined as being historiographical. See, for example, J. Van Seters, *In Search of History: Historiography in the Ancient World and the Origins of Biblical History* (New Haven: Yale University Press, 1983), 1-6. If the emphasis in defining historiography rests on the reliability of the evidence, then the Pentateuch is not historiography. See T. L. Thompson, *Early History of the Israelite People: From the Written and Archaeological Sources,* Studies in the History of the Ancient Near East 4 (Leiden: E. J. Brill, 1992), 372-383; and "Historiography [Israelite]," 206-212. The term "historiography" is being employed in the present study because the emphasis is on Israel's interpretation of its past rather than on the reliability of the sources. Such an emphasis corresponds with the earlier conclusion that the cult is the proper *Sitz im Leben* for interpreting the formation of the exodus tradition. In this regard see G. W. Ahlström, *The History of Ancient Palestine* (Minneapolis: Fortress Press, 1993), 26-30, concerning "mythological historiography."

33. R. Rendtorff, *Das überlieferungsgeschichtliche Problem des Pentateuch*, BZAW 147 (Berlin: A. Töpelmann, 1976), 82-145. Even the use of the word "exodus," with its imagery of Israel's journeying from Egypt to Canaan, may be an anachronistic description of the earliest stages of the tradition.

34. Van Seters, *In Search of History*, 8-54, 209-248. Although the present study is building off Van Seters's more general work in historiography, it diverges from his tradition-historical interpretation of the Tetrateuch by describing the earliest historiography as deuteronomistic rather than as an exilic Yahwist and by anchoring the formation of the tradition in Israel's cult. The first distinction may be little more than terminological; the second, however, is potentially more substantive since it raises the question of the institutional setting for the rise of historiography in the Tetrateuch/Pentateuch. See chapter 3 for a more detailed discussion.

2

Exodus and Kingship

The preexilic liturgy of the exodus is a holy war between Yahweh and Pharaoh that culminates in divine victory on the Day of Yahweh. A preexilic setting for such a liturgy is hardly innovative, since most scholars have argued for some form of a Yahwistic or JE account to the plague cycle and exodus.[1] What is innovative is that the liturgy of the exodus described in this chapter lacks ties to the wilderness, Sinai, or conquest traditions.[2] It is independent and thus not an episode of a larger history of salvation. For this reason, the term "Yahwist" will be avoided throughout the chapter, since this term has tended in the past to designate a preexilic account of salvation history.[3]

YAHWEH'S DEFEAT OF PHARAOH AND ISRAEL'S EXPULSION FROM EGYPT

The preexilic liturgy of the exodus focuses on two distinct (but related) actions, which take place in a single evening from midnight to dawn: the death of the Egyptian firstborn at midnight and the destruction of the Egyptian army at dawn. These two central events are interrelated by the account of Israel's expulsion from Egypt during the night,[4] and they are introduced by a series of conflicts between Yahweh and Pharaoh in the cycle of plagues. What follows is a description of this liturgy.

The Plague Cycle

The plague cycle is firmly anchored in the preexilic liturgy of the exodus. Excluding, for the moment, darkness and any of the events of the exodus,

(margin notes, left side)
cycle is from J/E → p. 27 n. 1

וְעַבְדֻנִי (אֶת-)עַמִּי שַׁלַּח → p. 29 n. 9

cf. Dozeman, Exodus (2009) 192.

	Initial Encounter 5:1–6:1*	Blood 7:14–24*	Frogs 7:25–8:11*	Flies 8:16–28*	Cattle 9:1-7	Hail 9:13–35*	Locust 10:1–20*
Introduction	בוא (go)	נצב (stand)	בוא (go)	יצב	בוא	יצב	בוא
		בקר (morning)		בקר		בקר	
Messenger Formula	כה אמר יהוה (Thus says Yahweh)	X	X	X	X	X	X
Condition	—	שלח (send) עבד (worship)	X	X	X	X	X
Plague	—	X	X	X	X	X	X
Concession	—	—	X	X	—	X	X
Intercession	—	—	X	X	—	X	X
Reversal	—	—	X	X	—	X	X
Conclusion	—	חזק (harden)	כבד (heavy)	כבד	כבד	כבד	חזק
				לא שלח (not send)	X	X	X

(*) Signifies that the boundaries of the cited text include more than the earliest account. (X) denotes the presence of a motif and (—) its absence.

this early form of the plague cycle contains six plagues: blood, frogs, flies, death of cattle, hail, and locust.[5] Its structure can be outlined in the accompanying chart.[6]

    The outline provides the backdrop for several conclusions concerning the design of the plague cycle. Although there is variation of motifs throughout the six plagues, they nevertheless, tend to follow a set pattern, which includes the announcement with conditions, plague, concession, intercession, reversal, and conclusion.[7] Throughout this process, divine communication is channeled through Moses, whose role as mediator is underscored by the use of the messenger formula, "Thus says Yahweh," to announce an impending action by God.[8] The announcement by Moses for Pharaoh to "send out" Israel for the purpose of "worshipping" or "serving" God always includes the presentation of a condition to Pharaoh.[9] Pharaoh's negative response is described as a hardening of his heart, in which the word "to harden" in the initial plague of blood and final plague of locust frames the word "to be heavy" in the middle four plagues of frogs, flies, cattle, and hail. Pharaoh's hardening results in his refusing "to send out" Israel. The conclusions to the individual plagues signal development in the story from Pharaoh's at first hardening his own heart in the plague of blood to the point where God finally hardens his heart in the plague of locust.[10]

Most important are the introductions. A comparison of them illustrates that the six plagues are structured in pairs:[11] (1) blood and frogs, (2) flies and cattle, (3) hail and locust. The first plague in each of the initial three pairs (blood, flies, hail) is introduced with the divine command to Moses that he "stand" or "station himself" (יצב/נצב) before Pharaoh in the "morning" (בקר), while the second plague (frogs, cattle, locust) is clearly separated in each case from the first with the more abrupt divine command that Moses "go" (בוא) to Pharaoh.[12] This sequence of paired actions provides insight into the overall plot structure of the exodus, which will be examined momentarily.

But first the problems of interpretation must be examined with regard to the plague of darkness. This plague shows few of the characteristics of the previous plagues. As Rudolph has noted, darkness functions more as a divine wonder than a plague, since there are no conditions by which it could be stopped.[13] Kohata and Schmidt have noted further problems of form in that Moses is not really sent to Pharaoh, nor does he present any message.[14] The plague of darkness also lacks the expected introductory divine command to Moses that he "stand" before Pharaoh in the "morning," or, for that matter, the more abrupt command that he simply "go" to Pharaoh. The lack of any real conditions in the confrontation between Moses and Pharoah, along with the emphasis on divine wonder rather than a more specific plague, have prompted some scholars to attribute all or most of this event to priestly tradition.[15]

The problem with attributing the plague of darkness to priestly tradition is that it lacks the motifs that are so clear in the other priestly additions: Aaron, his staff, the magicians, and the concluding formula that describes Pharaoh's negative response as one of not "listening" (שמע) to the words of Moses or Aaron.[16] Moreover, the motifs of sight[17] and of Moses' role in instigating a plague with an action of his hand,[18] and the description of Yahweh's hardening Pharaoh's heart with the result that he would not send Israel from Egypt,[19] all fit well into the larger plague cycle. In view of this, the plague of darkness would appear to be a part of the earliest formation of the plague cycle.[20] The many departures in form as well as the absence of a clear introductory formula favor an interpretation of darkness as providing an introduction to the death of the Egypt firstborn at midnight rather than as being an independent event in the cycle.

The introductory role of darkness for the events that follow, in conjunction with the tendency of the account to structure plagues in pairs, provide the central clues to the plot structure of the exodus. As an introduction, darkness signals transition and reversal in the plague cycle and hence the culmination of the sequence. The previous three pairs of plagues have established a series of expectations in the reader that are disrupted by darkness. These expectations include: first, plagues occurring in pairs signaled by set introductory words to Moses that he "stand" before Pharaoh in the "morning" or that he simply "go" to him; second, manifestations of divine power occurring at dawn; and, third, real conditions being presented to Pharaoh through a mediator whose message always provides guidelines for averting a plague. Darkness departs from all of these expectations, and in so doing it introduces a reversal in which action commences at midnight and progresses through the night until dawn.

The exodus consists of the death of the Egyptian firstborn at midnight and the destruction of the Egyptian army at dawn. Closer examination of the text illustrates the care with which temporal reversal of the plague cycle has been constructed. Not only do the events of the exodus begin in darkness rather than dawn, but darkness itself is intensified as being "midnight" (Exod 11:4; 12:29). In addition the internal structure of the death to the Egyptian firstborn undergoes change from the plague cycle, signaling further intensification. Most notable is the elimination of Moses, the mediator, who had presented Pharaoh with real conditions through the plague cycle. Such negotiation is replaced by the announcement of an inevitable and direct divine action when God states to Moses in Exod 11:1, "I will bring [בוא] one more plague. . . ." The use of the hiphel form of the verb "to go" in the introduction is itself a reversal, since this verb had been used to introduce the *second* plague of the three previous pairs. Dawn remains a central setting in the sequence of the exodus, but this time it signals the second event; the defeat of the Egyptian army is carefully delineated as taking place at the break of day, thus completing the reversal.[21] And, as in the death of the Egyptian firstborn, Moses also recedes in the confrontation at the sea, when Israel is commanded "to stand firm" (14:13, יצב) in the midst of the manifestation of divine power at dawn. The careful structuring of the story, with its movement from the death of the Egyptian firstborn at midnight to the destruction of the Egyptian army at dawn, points to the Day of Yahweh as the cultic setting of this story. It is a liturgy for celebrating the Day of Yahweh. The plot structure of this liturgy can be outlined in the following manner:[22]

Initial Plagues (3 Pairs)							Salvation from Egypt			
A	B	A	B	A	B	Intro	B	Link	A	Conclusion
Blood	Frog	Flies	Cattle	Hail	Locust	Darkness	Death	Exodus	Sea	Hymn
נצב	בוא	יצב	בוא	צב	בוא		בוא		יצב	
(stand)	(go)	(stand)	(go)	(stand)	(go)		(go)		(stand)	
בקר		בקר		בקר					בקר	
(morning)		(morning)		(morning)					(morning)	

The Death of the Egyptian Firstborn

The death of the Egyptian firstborn is an epiphany of darkness. It begins with the divine announcement in Exod 11:1 that there would be one additional plague of death. Yahweh informs Moses that after the plague of death Pharaoh and the Egyptians would not only send the Israelites out of Egypt but actually drive them out. So much is clear, but problems of interpretation arise with vv. 2–8.

The central problem in interpreting Exod 11:2–8 is to determine to whom Moses is speaking. Clearly, there is a history of tradition in the text, because even though Moses is told to instruct Israel in vv. 2–3, when Moses finally conveys the divine message concerning the last plague in vv. 4–8, Pharaoh rather than Israel is the object of the speech.[23] The confusion in the present form of the text has prompted debate concerning which speech is a later addition, the instructions for Israel in vv. 2–3 or the announcement by Moses in vv. 4–8. Interpretation will follow the lead of Childs, who argued that the instructions to Israel (with the motif of despoiling) are later, and that they have displaced the speech of Moses in vv. 4–8.[24] Yet even when interpretation is narrowed to vv. 1, 4–8, debate remains whether the speech of Moses in vv. 4–8 was originally intended for Israel or for Pharaoh,[25] especially when we note that the concluding notice in v. 8b—of Moses' angry departure from Pharaoh—is best read as a later addition.[26] Comparison of Exod 11:4–8a with the six other instances in the plague cycle where Moses employs the messenger formula ("Thus says Yahweh," Exod 7:17, 26; 8:16; 9:1, 13; 10:3) underscores that all messenger formulas are addressed to Pharaoh, which suggests that he rather than Israel is the intended audience also in vv. 4–8a.

After the initial divine announcement to Moses in 11:1, the death to the Egyptian firstborn has a compact structure which consists of a series of repetitions between the announcement of Moses (vv. 4–7a, 8a) and the description of the event (Exod 12:29–30). Moses predicts the *time* (midnight, v. 4), *content* (death of Egyptian firstborn, v. 5a), *scope* (from Pharaoh to Egyptian servants and cattle, v. 5b, but not Israelites, 7a) and *outcome* of the plague (a great cry, v. 6, and a request for Israel to leave, v. 8a). Then his announcement is followed by the plague itself in Exod 12:29–30, which presents a series of repetitions concerning the *time* (midnight, v. 29a*a*), *content* (death of Egyptian firstborn, v. 29a*b*), *scope* (from Pharaoh to Egyptian prisoners and cattle, v. 29b), and *outcome* of the event (a great cry, v. 30, and the exodus event, vv. 31–34, 39b).[27] These repetitions provide one criterion for determining the boundaries of the story at this stage of the tradition. The content of the story is a confrontation between Yahweh and Pharaoh (Exod 11:1, 4–7a, 8a), in which Israel is absent (vv. 2–3). The statement that Pharaoh will "know" that God distinguishes between Israelites and Egyptians (v. 7b)[28] and the

for chart
→ pp. 32–
33 n. 27

angry departure of Moses (8b) may be later additions. The motifs of departure from Egypt in the introductory divine speech of 11:1 ("to send out," שׁלח, and "to drive out," גרשׁ) indicate that the death of the Egyptian firstborn is not an independent story but is inextricably interwoven with the exodus from Egypt.

The Exodus from Egypt

The act of leaving Egypt in Exod 12:31–34, 39b is more an expulsion than an escape or journey. Pharaoh summons Moses during the night and demands that he and Israel leave (vv. 31–32). Pharaoh's demand is then intensified by the Egyptians, who are presented as driving Israel from Egypt, with the result that Israel leaves in haste (vv. 33–34, 39b). As striking as Israel's expulsion from Egypt is, it is important to see that it is not a central feature of the liturgy. The central events are the death of the Egyptian firstborn and the confrontation at the sea, with the act of leaving Egypt (the "exodus motif") providing a transition between the two. One result of the subordinate role of the exodus motif is that it is not possible to make a clear distinction between it and the death of the firstborn. The two events flow together so that the present designation of vv. 31–34 and 39b as constituting a distinct section is artificial and could just as well be reduced to v. 39b, since this half verse makes it clear that, at this stage of the tradition, the exodus consists of Israel's being "driven out" of Egypt as a consequence of the death to the firstborn.

The verb "to drive out" (גרשׁ) occurs four times in the exodus (Exod 6:1; 10:11; 11:1; 12:39b).[29] It is prominent in the introductory divine speech in 6:1, when Moses is told that Pharaoh will not simply send the Israelites out but that he will drive them out. This introductory speech underscores how the motif of Israel's being "driven out" of Egypt must be interpreted in the larger context of the request that Pharaoh "send out" Israel from Egypt for the purpose of worship. The term occurs somewhat ironically as a minor motif at the close of the plague of locust when Pharaoh is described as driving Moses out of his presence (10:11). Then the motif returns in a central position within divine speech in 11:1 in much the same manner as in 6:1.[30] Again Yahweh addresses Moses with a prediction in 11:1 that after the last plague is exercised on Egypt, Pharaoh will not only send out the Israelites, but actually "drive [them] out" (גָּרֵשׁ יְגָרֵשׁ) from Egypt.[31] The motif reappears one last time as fulfillment of the divine announcements in 6:1 and 11:1, when Israel is described in 12:39 as being driven out by the Egyptians after the death of their firstborn. The fact that 12:39b is a causal clause, which emphasizes Israel's hasty departure and the people's inability to make provisions, suggests that the causal situation is the account of how the Egyptians expelled Israel from Egypt in vv. 31–34, and not the motif of despoiling in vv. 35–36, nor the itinerary notice with its distinctive travel motifs in vv. 37–39a.[32]

The action of the Egyptians in v. 33 in expelling (חזק) the Israelites and in sending (שלח) them out in such haste that they leave with unleavened bread is a reversal to the previous concluding formulas of the plague cycle, where either Pharaoh would harden (חזק) his own heart or Yahweh would harden it, which in either case would result in Pharaoh's *not* sending out (שלח) Israel.[33] The action of the Egyptians (vv. 33, 39b), however, does not represent the view of Pharaoh (vv. 31-32),[34] and this separation of viewpoints propels the story to its final confrontation at the sea.

Salvation by the Sea

Transition to the new setting of the sea is accomplished in 14:5-7, 9a, which serves as an introduction to the impending confrontation. Several motifs tie this introduction to the developing story line.[35] That Pharaoh must be informed of the exodus in v. 5 fits in well with the separation of Pharaoh from the Egyptian people in Israel's expulsion from Egypt, as does the combination of the verbs "to send" and "to serve" in the speech of Pharaoh and his servants.[36] The change of mind of Pharaoh and his servants concerning the effect that Israel's absence would have on them provides the occasion for the gathering of an army (vv. 6-7)[37] and the pursuit of the Israelites (v. 9a). Most significant, however, is the new setting of the sea, since it provides an explicit mythopoeic setting for the final event of salvation.[38] The focus of this account is not on Israel's crossing the sea but on Yahweh's controlling the sea to destroy the Egyptians.[39] Twice the sea becomes the object of divine action, when Yahweh first sends an east wind on the sea (v. 21a) and then dries it (v. 21b). And once the sea is the subject of action, when it is described as returning to its natural flow and thus destroying the Egyptian army (v. 27).

The confrontation at the sea is firmly anchored in Israel's holy war tradition, which is made explicit by the central role of a war oracle in 14:10, 13-14.[40] Closer examination shows that the Israelites' fear and their cry to Yahweh at the approach of the Egyptian army in v. 10 provides the occasion for the war oracle by Moses in vv. 13-14.[41] The use of the verb "to cry out" (צעק) with the preposition "to" (אל) signifies a cry for help in a situation of distress,[42] and this is the third occurrence of such a construction. It was used once to describe the intercession of Moses during the plague of frogs (8:8), and most notably it was used twice by Israel—once at the outset of the plague cycle, when the people cried initially to Pharaoh for relief from their oppression (5:8, 15), and again in the present text where they cry to Yahweh. The contrast between Israel's action in Exodus 5 and Exodus 14 shows development in the people, which suggests that their cry to Yahweh is the proper response in such a situation of threat.[43] The use of holy-war language by Moses in v. 13 within the larger context of a salvation oracle supports this interpretation.[44]

The war oracle of Moses in vv. 13–14 includes a word of assurance that the people "not fear" (אל־תיראו), a directive that they "stand firm" (the hithpael of יצב), a basis for the assurance that they would see the salvation of Yahweh, and finally, orders that Yahweh would fight for them, requiring that they be passive or "keep still" (חרש).[45] The directive to stand firm is an important feature of the war oracle of Moses, which can function both in military (2 Chr 20:17–20; Jer 46:3–4) and epiphanic (1 Sam 12:16–18) contexts.[46] And indeed, both contexts enhance interpretation, since the impending military confrontation is intended as an epiphany of divine power.

The epiphanic character of the confrontation is underscored by the larger narrative, where the call "to stand" before Pharaoh has already prompted a series of divine manifestations at dawn throughout the plague cycle. The war oracle, with its call for Israel to stand firm, follows this pattern and signals the culmination of the exodus by preparing the reader for the final manifestation of divine power at dawn (note the double use of "morning" or "dawn" in vv. 24, 27). The confrontation at the sea, however, does not require Israel's participation. On the contrary, the war oracle of Moses is a command for Israel to be passive. Conrad has made clear how the call for passivity in holy war is certainly not deuteronomistic,[47] even though a number of recent scholars have related this text to deuteronomistic tradition.[48] A closer parallel is First Isaiah, where the prophet encourages King Ahaz in Isa 7:4–9 to have confidence in Yahweh by taking a passive stance to the Syro-Ephraimite threat.[49] The correspondence encourages an identification with preexilic Zion tradition.

The announcement of holy war is followed by the event itself. Scholars have long recognized a history of tradition in the narrative account of the confrontation at the sea, because of the many repetitions and conflicting points of view. Examples include the nature of the event at the sea (a strong east wind or the splitting of the sea), the character of divine presence (direct or mediated through Moses), the action of the Israelites during the event (especially noteworthy is whether or not they are described as entering or crossing through the sea), and finally whether or not there is a motif of divine leading in every account of the story, and, if so, what the circumstances of divine leading might be (the angel of Yahweh or the cloud).[50] In spite of the vast overlay of commentary in the present form of the text, there does appear to be a paradigmatic structure to the confrontation that includes Exod 14:15a*a*, 16a*a*, 21a, 24a*a*, 24b-26, 27, 30.[51] Central to this account is the motif of Moses stretching his hand or staff over the sea.[52] It occurs four times (14:16a, 21a, 26a, 27a*a*). The distribution of this motif yields two cycles of action, each of which consists of a divine command (first cycle—14:15a*a*, 16a*a*; second cycle—14:26) and fulfillment (first cycle—14:21a, 24a*a*, 24b-25; second cycle—14:27). In the first cycle the sea is dried up; in the second it is brought back as a destructive force against the Egyptian army. Israel plays no role in this narrative. The structure can be illustrated in the following manner:

First Cycle
Evening to the Morning Watch

Divine Command: Moses to stretch out his hand/staff over the sea (vv. 15a*a*, 16a*a*)

Fulfillment: Moses stretches his hand over the sea (v. 21a)
1. During the night (v. 21a)
   East wind dries the sea
2. At the morning watch (vv. 24a*a*)
   Yahweh's initial action of holy war (vv. 24b-25a)
   The Egyptians recognize the power of God (v. 25b)

Second Cycle
Break of Day

Divine Command: Moses to stretch out his hand over the sea (v. 26a)
   The return of the water (v. 26b)

Fulfillment: Moses stretches his hand over the sea (v. 27a*a*)
3. At break of day (v. 27a*b*)
   Sea returns (v. 27a*b*)
   Egyptian army flees (v. 27a*b*)
   Yahweh destroys the Egyptian army (v. 27b)
   Israel is saved (v. 30)

The temporal sequence of events is carefully orchestrated within the two cycles of action. The confrontation progresses through three stages: (1) During the night (v. 21a, כל־הלילה) Yahweh blows an east wind over the sea, resulting in its drying up.[53] (2) At the morning watch (vv. 24a*a*,b, 25, ויהי באשמרת הבקר)[54] Yahweh throws the Egyptian camp into panic[55] by turning the wheels of their chariots[56] and causing them to drive with difficulty. This action prompts recognition of holy war by the Egyptians, who then try to flee.[57] (3) Finally, at the break of dawn (לפנות בקר)[58] the water returns to its natural flow, killing the fleeing Egyptians. Thus Yahweh shook off the Egyptian army in the sea (v. 27b). The precise temporal sequence certainly has liturgical overtones and it also reinforces how important the progression of action from midnight to dawn is within this account of the exodus.

The destruction of the Egyptian army is more than a plague; it is a salvific event. This is underscored by Moses in the war oracle (v. 13: the Israelites are told that they will see the salvation of Yahweh), it is repeated in the conclusion to the account (v. 30: Yahweh saved Israel that day), and it is a central motif in the hymn (15:2: Yahweh is salvation). Sawyer writes concerning the semantics of the word "salvation" that it "implies bringing help to those in trouble rather than rescuing them from it." As Sawyer goes on to note, "[salvation] is not one of the regular terms used for the exodus."[59] Other images of divine rescue, especially the portrait of Yahweh leading Israel into the wilderness toward a promised land, become more central to the story over time. But such images of salvation history are absent in this more static understanding of the exodus as Yahweh's holy war and victory over Egypt.

A CELEBRATION OF THE DAY OF YAHWEH

The Plot Structure of the Exodus as a Night Vigil

The plot of the exodus is clear. The literary study has demonstrated that the exodus consists of two actions, the death of the Egyptian firstborn and the destruction of the Egyptian army, and that these events are preceded by a series of plagues. This is an orderly story in which everything that is predicted is fulfilled. There is no unfolding of salvation history into an unknown future. Instead the absence of the wilderness tradition (as the immediate outcome of the exodus) and of the conquest tradition (as a more distant future goal) produces a static story, in which the oppression in Egypt and life in the land are pitted against each other. As a result, the destruction of the Egyptians and the present rule of Yahweh in the land are two sides of one action.

The liturgy itself is carefully structured with precise temporal markings. The series of paired plagues provides a prelude to the exodus by emphasizing, first, that Yahweh's intervention on behalf of Israel is destructive, and, second, that manifestations of divine power occur at dawn. The events of the exodus build off of and intensify these expectations through reversal. Darkness provides the setting for a precise sequence of events. The death of the Egyptian firstborn occurs at midnight (11:4; 12:29), inaugurating a night vigil that includes Israel's hasty departure from Egypt with unleavened dough (12:34, 39b).[60] The vigil leads into the confrontation at the sea, where, as we have seen, a series of three events occur. During the night (14:21a) Yahweh creates a strong wind that dries up the sea. Then at the morning watch (14:24aa,b, 25) Yahweh turns the Egyptian camp into a panic, until the events of the exodus conclude at dawn (14:27b) with the destruction of the Egyptian army.

The plot structure brings to light that a night vigil is an important part of the celebration of the exodus in preexilic Israel. The nocturnal setting provides clues into the cultic setting of the liturgy. It suggests that worshippers and/or the king kept vigil for the coming of God's deliverance at dawn.[61] Additional support for such a nocturnal setting is the fact that such imagery is not limited to this text but is also reflected in a number of Israelite psalms, as well as in Canaanite mythology. McKay has demonstrated that psalms such as 17, 27, and 63 describe night vigils,[62] while Ziegler has shown that psalms like 46 associate Yahweh's salvation with break of day.[63] Some form of nocturnal setting for cultic events is also evident in

Canaanite mythology. De Moor has argued that there are several instances in Baal's conflict with Mot which suggest that this mythology may also have served as a nocturnal liturgy.[64] Examples include the growing darkness that surrounds Baal immediately after the construction of his temple, when he sends his couriers to Mot with an invitation to attend a banquet (CTA 4.VII.45-60). Then too throughout Baal's struggle with Mot in CTA 5-6, there is the prominent role of Shapash, the sun god, who even becomes the object of a hymn at the close of the cycle in CTA 6.VI.41-52, where Shapash is celebrated as ruling the shade, the ghosts, and even the dead. Finally, in the details of Baal's struggle with Mot, there are further indications of a nocturnal setting when Shapash journeys to the nether world of darkness to aid Baal and, most likely, to lead him back to light and to life (CTA 6.IV.41-49).[65]

A nocturnal cultic setting in both Israelite psalms and Canaanite mythology provides indirect support to the conclusion that a similar setting in the celebration of the exodus would not be unusual. The nocturnal setting in the Canaanite myth raises the additional question of how extensive its influence on the Israelite cult may have been. In particular, the fact that the entire Baal cycle appears to reflect a seasonal pattern, which may have served as the liturgy for a Canaanite New Year festival, perhaps associated with an epiphany of Baal at dawn,[66] at least raises the question of to what degree the preexilic celebration of the exodus may also be structured around a New Year celebration.[67]

A second significant feature in the liturgy is the emphasis on dawn as the time of Yahweh's manifestation of destructive power. The literary study has underscored that Yahweh's early morning conflict at the sea does not fit any one genre. Instead the account includes motifs of supernatural occurrences (a great wind drying up sea), holy war (the routing of the Egyptian camp into a panic), destruction (the killing of the Egyptians in the sea), and epiphany (the Egyptians' recognition of Yahweh's attack and the appearance of Yahweh at dawn), all of which combine to celebrate Yahweh's present victory over chaotic forces (be they Mot during the night or Yamm and Pharaoh at dawn).

The combination of motifs, in a liturgical setting that progresses from a night vigil to an experience of salvation at dawn, suggests a cultic setting that incorporates most if not all of the fragmentary references to the Day of Yahweh in prophetic literature.[68] For example, when the ironic proclamation of Amos (that the Day of Yahweh is darkness rather than the expected light) is read in the context of this liturgy, it becomes clear that his discourse is not simply a literary trope but a reversal of the entire liturgy of the exodus.[69] See also Joel 2:1 and 3:4 for later examples of this same reversal. Furthermore, when the holy-war imagery of Isaiah 13 is placed in this context, it becomes clear that this text does not indicate a distinct genre for the origin of the Day of Yahweh over against the motifs of light and darkness, as von Rad argued, but simply another aspect of the overall liturgy.[70] The same is true for the destructive character of Yahweh's Day in texts such as Zeph 1:18 or Joel 2:11.[71]

The social context of the preexilic liturgy of the exodus is difficult to locate. The absence of exodus tradition in preexilic southern prophets like Isaiah, as compared to the incorporation of such motifs in Hosea and throughout Deuteronomy and deuteronomistic tradition, points to northern tradition.[72] Yet a firm conclusion is not possible because other aspects of the liturgy point to southern Zion tradition. The proclamation by Moses in Exod 14:13–14 for Israel to stand firm during the early morning epiphany of Yahweh and then to take a passive response to Yahweh's holy war suggests that this particular liturgy for celebrating the Day of Yahweh may be rooted in preexilic Zion tradition.[73] In addition, the motifs in this account also correspond to many of the central features of Zion tradition, including Yahweh's triumph over chaotic waters (Ps 46:3) and over kings and nations (Ps 46:7; 48:5–7), where there is also an emphasis on theophany at dawn (Ps 46:6), with its accompanying terror at Yahweh's approach (Ps 2:1–6) and the resulting destruction (Ps 76:6–7).[74] Whether the liturgy was part of an autumnal New Year celebration in the southern Zion cult or northern tradition is difficult to confirm from the limited information in the text. I have emphasized the Zion cult because of the imagery of the Day of Yahweh, which is closely associated with preexilic cultic practice at Jerusalem.[75]

Two features concerning the celebration of the Day of Yahweh will provide a close to this section. The first is that detailed imagery of enthronement is absent from the narrative. Instead the liturgy ends with a proclamation of Yahweh's victory over chaotic powers. The absence of enthronement imagery is difficult to evaluate, however, since the liturgy of the exodus most likely functioned in combination with enthronement psalms (Pss 47, 93, 96, 97, 98).[76] The second conclusion is that Yahweh's victory is celebrated as a present reality. Thus there is no eschatology in this cultic liturgy signified by a future promise of land. Instead the liturgy of the exodus as the Day of Yahweh is a celebration of Israel's life in the land conceived as divine gift.

The Character of God in the Liturgy

Holy war is central for exploring Yahweh's salvific power in the exodus. Moreover, Yahweh's power in holy war is exercised in a unilateral manner. Throughout the narrative divine strength is measured as a confrontation of wills between Yahweh and Pharaoh. Israel plays no active role in this confrontation, nor is the character of Moses developed in any independent way beyond his stereotyped function as Yahweh's prophetic messenger. The central tension of the story, therefore, is whether Yahweh has the ability to produce his intended effects on Pharaoh. Will Pharaoh be forced into "sending" the Israelites from Egypt so that they might "worship" Yahweh? Divine prediction removes any ambiguity surrounding the question. The plagues are afflictions[77] of growing intensity that Yahweh brings to bear on Pharaoh to overcome his resistance.[78] When the death to the Egyptian firstborn fails to stop Pharaoh, the story culminates in Yahweh's destruction of the Egyptian army, which achieves his desired goals.

This is certainly unilateral power, since throughout this conflict the focus of the story never really leaves Yahweh, whose power is exercised only actively in one direction. Neither Israelites nor Egyptians emerge as complex or independent characters whose own actions might account for their different fates. Instead both provide different perspectives for gauging divine power. As a result, the effects of divine action are predetermined for each group, while the divine character itself undergoes no change through the unfolding events of the exodus. The imagery is certainly mythic and awe inspiring, but static and confining. It is a celebration of the power of a national God, in which death for one group is salvation for another.[79]

NOTES

1. The work of Wellhausen serves as a point of departure for evaluating the literary history of the plague cycle. J. Wellhausen (*Die Composition des Hexateuchs und der Historischen Bücher des Alten Testament,* 3d ed [Berlin: Georg Reimer, 1889], 65-71) suggested the following source analysis: P—snakes (7:8-13), blood (7:19, 20a, 21c, 22, 23), frogs (8:1-3, 11b), gnats (8:12-15), and boils (9:8-12); J/E—blood (7:14-18, 20b, 21ab, 24), frogs (7:25-29; 8:4-10, 11a), flies (8:16-28), cattle (9:1-7), hail (9:13-35), locust (10:1-20), darkness (10:21-29). There is general agreement concerning the literary analysis of the plague cycle, especially with regard to priestly tradition. Most debate has centered on whether the nonpriestly material is J or JE.

Subsequent scholarship has branched off in three basic directions. G. Fohrer (*Überlieferung und Geschichte des Exodus: Eine Analyse von Ex 1-15,* BZAW 91 [Berlin: A. Töpelmann, 1964], 60-79) represents one direction, in which E tradition is identified and more carefully distinguished from J in four places: blood (7:15b, 17b, 20abb, 23), hail (9:22-23aa, 24a, 25b, 35), locust (10:12-13aa, 14aa, 15ab, 20), and darkness (10:21-23, 27). See, among others, B. S. Childs (*The Book of Exodus: A Critical Theological Commentary*, OTL [Philadelphia: Westminster, 1974], 131) and J. P. Hyatt (*Exodus,* NCB [London: Oliphants, 1971], 98-99), who also follow Fohrer at this point.

M. Noth (*Exodus: A Commentary,* 67-71) represents a second trend to eliminate E from the plague cycle in favor of two traditions: P—snakes (7:8-13), blood (7:19, 20aa, 21b, 22), frogs (8:1-3, 11abb in Hebrew; 8:5-7, 15abb in English), gnats (8:12-15 in Hebrew; 8:18-19 in English), boils (9:8-12), hail (9:22, 23aa, 35), locust (10:12, 13aa), and darkness (10:20-22, 27); and J—which consists of substantially the remainder of the text. Others who follow Noth's limitation of the plague cycle to P and J include E. Otto ("Erwägungen zum überlieferungs-geschichtlichen Ursprung und 'Sitz im Leben' des jahwistischen Plagenzyklus,"

VT 26 [1976]: 7 n. 23) and S. I. L. Norin (*Er Spaltete das Meer: Die Auszugsüber-lieferung in Psalmen und Kult des Alten Israel,* ConBOT 9 [Lund: CWK Gleerup, 1977], 13-19). J. Van Seters ("The Plagues of Egypt: Ancient Tradition or Literary Invention," *ZAW* 98 [1986]: 31-32) and E. Blum (*Studien zur Komposition des Pentateuch,* BZAW 189 [Berlin: de Gruyter, 1990], 13-17, 242-256) represent a variation of Noth by limiting the plague cycle to two traditions but by reevaluating the literary character of P as an independent source.

Third, recent work has tended to attribute a more prominent role to subsequent redactors than did Noth. See especially W. Fuss, *Die deuteronomistische Pentateuchredaktion in Exodus 3-17,* BZAW 126 (Berlin: de Gruyter, 1972), and S. Ö. Steingrimsson, *Vom Zeichen zur Geschichte: Eine Literar- und formkritische Untersuchung von Ex 6,28-11,10,* ConBOT 14 (Lund: CWK Gleerup, 1979). See also P. Weimar, *Die Berufung des Mose: Literaturwissenschaftliche Analyse von Exodus 2,23-5,5,* OBO 32 (Göttingen: Vandenhoeck & Ruprecht, 1980), 56 n. 108, and 57; F. Kohata, *Jahwist und Priesterschrift in Exodus 3-14,* BZAW 166 (Berlin: de Gruyter, 1986), 93-129; and L. Schmidt, *Beobachtungen zu der Plagener-zählung in Exodus VII 14-XI 10,* Studia Biblica 4 (Leiden: E. J. Brill, 1990), 4-84.

2. The closest analogy to the character of preexilic tradition described in this chapter is provided by Rendtorff (*Problem des Pentateuch,* 1-28), who uses the term "Yahwist" to describe unrelated complexes in the Pentateuch. For a summary of recent developments in pentateuchal studies see de Pury and Römer, "Le pentateuque en question," 9-80, esp. 55-80.

3. The work of John Van Seters is a significant departure from past scholarship, since for him the Yahwist designates an exilic author. For a recent overview of the different positions and arguments in favor of a more traditional interpretation, especially with regard to the ancestral texts in Genesis, see K. Berge (*Die Zeit des Jahwisten: Ein Beitrag zur Datierung jahwistischer Vätertexte,* BZAW 186 [Berlin: de Gruyter, 1990], 1-11 and passim), who favors the early monarchy period as the date of J.

4. The death of the Egyptian firstborn includes Exod 11:1, 4-7a, 8a; 12:29-32; the expulsion from Egypt includes Exod 12:(31-32) 33-34, 39b; and the confrontation at the sea includes Exod 14:5-7, 9a, 10, 13-14, 15a*a*, 16a*a*, 21a, 24a*a*, 24b-26, 27, 30. The plague cycle is not the boundary of the preexilic account of the exodus, since the liturgy would appear to include some form of Israel's slavery in Egypt from the opening chapters of the Book of Exodus.

5. Three levels of tradition will be identified in the plague cycle. The following is a brief summary of the literary study presented in the next three chapters.

(1.) The preexilic six-plague cycle noted earlier:

blood:	(Exod 7:14-16a,b*a* [minus reference to the wilderness], 17a*a*,b, 18, 20a*b*-21, 22a*b*, 23-24)
frogs:	(Exod 7:25-29; 8:4-6b*a* [minus reference to Aaron], 7-11a*a* [minus reference to Aaron])
flies:	(Exod 8:16-18a, 19-22 [minus reference to Aaron], 23 [minus reference to the three-day journey into the wilderness], 24-28 [minus reference to the wilderness])
cattle:	(Exod 9:1-7)
hail:	(Exod 9:13-14a, 15-16a, 17-28 [minus reference to Aaron in v. 27], 29a,b*a*, 30-35a)

locust: (Exod 10:1a, 3–20 [minus references to Aaron in vv. 3, 8, 16 and the designation of the sea as סוּף in v. 19ab]

(2.) A minimal deuteronomistic editing of at least four plagues (along with additions in the introduction, Exod 5:1, 3), the primary aim of which is to interrelate the plague–exodus cycle to the wilderness tradition. Signs of deuteronomistic editing include:

blood: (reference to the wilderness in Exod 7:16)
flies: (reference to the three-day journey into the wilderness in Exod 8:23, and again reference to the wilderness in v. 24)
hail: (the proclamation of the divine name in the land in 9:16b)
locust: (catechetical instruction in Exod 10:1b–2a, and a more specific name to the sea as the סוּף in v. 19)

(3.) A more thorough priestly editing includes a new introduction (Exod 6:2–7:7), the addition of three more plagues (snakes in Exod 7:8–13, gnats in Exod 8:12–15, and boils in Exod 9:8–12), a redefinition of plagues as signs (מוֹפֵת), the summons to knowledge directed primarily at Pharaoh and his refusal to hear (שׁמע), as well as the addition of Aaron, his staff, and the magicians. The priestly editing includes:

snakes: (7:8–13)
blood: (7:16bb, 17ab, 19–20aa, 22a, bb)
frogs: (8:1–3, 4* [Aaron], 6bb, 8* [Aaron], 11ab, b)
gnats: (8:12–15)
flies: (8:18b, 21* [Aaron])
boils: (9:8–12)
hail: (9:14b, 27* [Aaron], 29bb, 35b)
locust: (10:2b, 3*, 8*, 16* [Aaron])

6. See also L. Schmidt, *Plagenerzählung*, 59–77.

7. See H. H. Schmid (*Der sogenannte Jahwist: Beobachtungen und Fragen zur Pentateuchforschung* [Zürich: Theologischer Verlag, 1976], 44–53) for an additional study of the internal structure of the plagues.

8. The messenger formula in the plague cycle has raised discussion concerning the relationship of the plagues to Israel's larger prophetic tradition. See Childs (*Exodus*, 144–149) and compare Schmid (*Der sogenannte Jahwist*, 44–53).

9. Note how the stereotyped phrase שׁלח אֶת־עַמִּי וְיַעַבְדֻנִי ("Let my people go that they may serve me") occurs in the plagues of blood (7:16), frogs (7:26), flies (8:16), cattle (9:1), hail (9:13), and locust (10:3).

10. For discussion of the hardening motif see R. R. Wilson, "The Hardening of Pharaoh's Heart," *CBQ* 41 (1979), 18–36; and D. M. Gunn, "The 'Hardening of Pharaoh's Heart': Plot, Character and Theology in Exodus 1–14," in *Art and Meaning: Rhetoric in Biblical Literature*, JSOTSup 19, ed. D. J. Clines, D. M. Gunn, and A. Hauser, JSOTSup 19 (Sheffield: JSOT Press, 1982), 72–96.

11. This observation is limited to the introductory formulas. For a more detailed discussion of pairing in the early formation of the plague cycle see U. Cassuto, *A Commentary on the Book of Exodus*, trans. I Abrahams (Jerusalem: Magnes Press, 1967), 93; and L. Schmidt (*Plagenerzählung*, 58–77), who argues that the six-plague cycle consisting of three pairs is the result of two stages of

tradition: J (four plagues consisting of two pairs: pollution of the Nile—frogs, and flies—locust) and a JE supplementation (the death of cattle and hail along with extensive editing throughout).

12. See also F. Michaeli, *Le livre de l'Exode,* CAT 2 (Paris: Delachaux et Niestle, 1974), 80.

13. W. Rudolph, *Der "Elohist" von Exodus bis Josua,* BZAW 68 (Berlin: A. Töpelmann, 1938), 21.

14. Kohata, *Jahwist und Priesterschrift in Exodus 3-14,* 104; and L. Schmidt, *Plagenerzählung,* 45-50.

15. Norin (*Er Spaltete das Meer,* 18) attributes the tradition to P. Compare Kohata (*Jahwist und Priesterschrift in Ex 3-14,* 103) and L. Schmidt (*Plagenerzählung,* 45-50), who attribute the story to an even later redactor of priestly material.

16. See note 5 for an overview of the literary boundaries of priestly tradition.

17. The motif of sight (ראה) from the plague of darkness (10:23, 28-29) also appears in the plagues of frogs (8:11), hail (9:16, 24), and locust (10:5, 6, 10).

18. In addition to the plague of darkness (10:21-22), Moses' role in instigating a plague with an action of his hand also occurs in the plagues of blood (7:20), hail (9:22-23), and locust (10:12-13). The use of hand and staff apear to be interchangeable. Divine commands for Moses to raise his hand (Exod. 9:22, 10:12) are followed by descriptions of Moses raising his staff (Exod. 9:23, 10:13).

19. The description of Yahweh's hardening (חזק) Pharaoh's heart with the result that he would not send (שלח) Israel from Egypt (10:27) follows directly from the intensification of this motif in the plague of locust (10:20), which was the first instance of Yahweh's hardening Pharaoh's heart. The term חזק was used only one other time to describe an action of Pharaoh: in the opening plague of blood (7:22). The word כבד is used in the four intermediate plagues (frogs, flies, cattle, hail) to describe an action of Pharaoh. Thus there is design and intensification with the hardening motif.

20. A number of scholars have argued that Exod 10:21-29 is a conflation, in which the plague of darkness in 10:21-23 and the motif of hardening in 10:27 are a continuation of the plague of locust and a tradition distinct from Exod 10:24-26, 28-29. Among those who accept this separation of traditions there is debate whether the distinct traditions are J (10:24-26, 28-29) and E (10:21-23, 27) (so Childs, *Exodus,* 131); J (10:24-26, 28-29) and P (10:21-23, 27) (so Noth, *Exodus,* 83; and Van Seters, "The Plagues of Egypt," 32, nn. 8, 9, 12); or J (10:24-26, 28-29) and R (10:21-23, 27) (so L. Schmidt, *Plagenerzählung,* 45-50). The motifs that occur throughout Exod 10:21-27 favor a more unified interpretation of the plague of darkness, even though individual motifs like the reference to three days in 10:22, 23 may be the result of later priestly editors.

21. For designation of dawn see Exod 14:24a, "at the morning watch" (ויהי באשמרת הבקר); and Exod 14:27, "at dawn" (לפנות בקר).

22. For examination of the hymn in Exodus 15 as providing a possible conclusion to the liturgy see chapter 5.

23. Wellhausen (*Composition,* 70) saw the problem and attributed Exod 11:1-3 to E and vv. 4-8 to J, with vv. 9-10 being P. Thus according to Wellhausen vv. 4-8 was a speech directed to Pharaoh that continued from 10:29. The only point of consensus to follow Wellhausen's study was the designation of vv. 9-10

to P. Variations of Wellhausen's interpretation of J (as a speech directed to Pharaoh) have continued. See, among others, H. Gressmann (*Mose und seine Zeit: Ein Kommentar zu den Mose-Sagen,* FRLANT 1 [Göttingen: Vandenhoeck & Ruprecht, 1913], 97 n. 13), who interprets the J account of Exodus 11 as a speech addressed to Pharaoh but limited to vv. 1, 4, 5a; J. C. Rylaarsdam (*The Book of Exodus,* IB 1, cd. G. A. Buttrick [Nashville: Abingdon, 1952], 911) and Childs (*Exodus,* 131, 160-161) follow Wellhausen's source-critical analysis by attributing vv. 1-3 to E and vv. 4-8 to J, with the latter verses providing a conclusion to Moses' last interview with Pharaoh in 10:29. Fohrer (*Überlieferung und Geschichte des Exodus,* 81-82) limits E to vv. 2-3 and assigns v. 1 to N, but still interprets vv. 4-8 as continuing the confrontation of Pharaoh and Moses.

Noth (*Exodus,* 88, 92-93) offered a different solution, which has influenced many of the more recent studies of this material. Even though he attributed all of vv. 1-8 to J, he concluded that vv. 7b-8 were a later addition which changed the focus of an original speech to Israel into a speech to Pharaoh. At the heart of Noth's interpretation is his hypothesis that the passover is central to the Yahwistic account of the death of the Egyptian firstborn. Thus, according to Noth, Moses' speech to Israel in vv. 4-6 was to prepare the people for the passover instructions in 12:21-23. Noth's argument has influenced a number of more recent studies, whose common thread is the assumption that the speech of Moses in Exodus 11 was originally addressed to Israel. See, for example, Otto, "Plagenzyklus," 7-13; Steingrimsson, *Vom Zeichen zur Geschichte,* 154-156; Weimar, *Die Berufung des Mose,* 56 n. 108, and 57; and Kohata, *Jahwist und Priesterschrift in Exodus 3-14* , 122.

24. Although Childs (*Exodus,* 161) concludes that Moses' speech to Pharaoh in vv. 4-8 "was displaced by the interjection of the instructions for despoiling the Egyptians," he attributes Exod 11:1-3 to an Elohistic tradition rather than to deuteronomistic tradition, as will be argued in the next chapter.

25. Two additional arguments have been used to support an interpretation of the speech of Moses in Exodus 11 as being addressed originally to Israel. According to the first argument, a problem of narrative logic exists if the speech is addressed to Pharaoh, since the death threat to Moses at the end of the plague of darkness (10:28-29) does not appear to allow for an additional confrontation between Moses and Pharaoh in Exodus 11, and the divine speech to Moses in 11:1 also appears out of place (see Noth, *Exodus,* 92, and Otto, "Plagenzyklus," 7). Some have sought to address this problem by rearranging the text. See, for example, F. V. Winnett (*The Mosaic Tradition,* Near and Middle East Series 1 [Toronto: University of Toronto Press, 1949], 12), who suggests that the original sequence was 11:1-8a; 10:28-29; 11:8b; 12:29-36; and see Van Seters, "The Plagues of Egypt," 32 n. 9. But as Childs (*Exodus,* 130, 160) has noted, the death threat in 10:28-29 can also be read as an ironic pun, since the reader has already been told in 10:23 that no Egyptian was able to see another. The death of the Egyptian cattle provides a parallel to the interjection of divine speech (11:1) in a setting where Moses and Pharaoh are both present, which suggests that this speech may be less awkward than has been argued in the past. Note how divine speech is also interjected in 9:5 in a confrontation between Moses and Pharaoh without change of setting.

According to the second argument, there is a change of person in reference to Pharaoh within the speech of Moses in vv. 4-8a; he is referred to in v. 5 in the third person ("Pharaoh") and in v. 8a in the second person ("your servants"). Noth

(*Exodus*, 92) concluded from this that the more direct second-person address to Pharaoh and the third-person references to Yahweh and Israel in vv. 7b–8 were later additions intended to change an original speech to Israel into an address to Pharaoh. Such a change in person, however, need not be judged as a gap in logic signifying different traditions. There are a number of shifts between second and third person in the messenger speeches of Moses, which occur for the most part when the Egyptians are being contrasted with Israelites. The strongest example is the announcement of death to cattle in 9:1–4, which begins in the second person when referring to Pharaoh (vv. 2–3) but shifts to the third person in v. 4 in order to contrast the Egyptian cattle from the Israelite cattle. The shift between the second and third person in reference to Pharaoh in Exodus 11:4–8a is done for the same reason—to contrast Egyptians and Israelites. What is unique about 11:4–8a is that Pharaoh takes such a central role in the contrast by being referred to in the third person (v. 5) along with Egyptian servants and cattle as constituting the group that will experience the plague. A number of scholars have noted how the plagues progress in intensity (see, for example, Michaeli, *L'Exode*, 96–99; J. I. Durham, *Exodus,* WBC 3 [Waco: Word Books, 1987], xxii and passim; Hyatt, *Exodus,* 96–101). The inclusion of Pharaoh in the final plague fits this pattern by enlarging its scope. When the contrast between Egyptians and Israelites is completed after v. 7a, the text shifts back to the second person in making reference to Pharaoh, as we would expect from the other speeches.

26. A number of scholars have argued that v. 8 or at least v. 8b is a later addition to the text, but the primary reason has been that the setting presupposes a conversation between Moses and Pharaoh in a speech that is intended for Israel. See here Noth, *Exodus*, 92. Although the present study is not following Noth's interpretation, it will be argued in the following chapter that the reference to Moses and Pharaoh in v. 8b functions to clarify ambiguity in the setting of vv. 4–8 which has arisen because of the deuteronomistic addition of instructions for Israel in vv. 2–3.

27. The repetitive structure can be outlined in the following manner:

Announcement (11:4–7a, 8a)   Event (12:29–30)

Time

כחצת הלילה (A)   (A') ויהי בחצי הלילה
(midnight)   (midnight)

Content

מת כל־בכור בארץ מצרים (B)   (B') ויהוה הכה בכור בארץ מצרים
(Every firstborn in the   (Yahweh struck down all the
land of Egypt shall die)   firstborn in the land of Egypt)

Scope

מבכור פרעה הישב על־כסאו (C)   (C') מבכר פרעה הישב על־כסאו
(From the firstborn of   (From the firstborn of
Pharaoh who sits on his throne)   Pharaoh who sits on his thone)

עד בכור השפחה   עד בכור השבי
(to the firstborn of the   (to the firstborn of the
female slave)   prisoner)

אשר אחר הרחים   אשר בבית הבור
(who is behind the sawmill)   (who was in the dungeon)

וכל בכור בהמה			וכל בכור בהמה
(and all the firstborn of the livestock)			(and all the firstborn of the livestock)

Outcome

צעקה גדלה	(D)	(D')	צעקה גדלה
(a great cry)			(a great cry)
וירדו כל־עבדיך אלה אלי	(E)	(E')	The exodus event
(Then all these officials of yours shall come down to me)			(vv. 31–34, 39b)

והשתחוו־לי לאמר
(and bow low to me, saying)

צא אתה וכל־העׁ אשר־ברנליך
(Leave us, you and all the people who follow you)

ואחרי־כ אצא
(After that I will leave)

28. See chapter 3 for a discussion of "knowledge" within priestly tradition.

29. גרשׁ occurs eleven times in Exodus in at least three different contexts. In the preexilic account (6:1, 10:11, 11:1; 12:39) "to drive out" functions in the orbit of the exodus from Egypt, since it is used to describe an action by Pharaoh or the Egyptians on Israel, which signifies the latter's salvation.

This first meaning must be distinguished from a later deuteronomistic use of the term in the context of conquest traditions (Exod 23:28, 29, 30, 31; 33:2; 34:11; Josh 24:12, 18; Judg 2:1–7), where Yahweh (or more precisely his messenger) is described as driving out the inhabitants of the land. The deuteronomistic conquest texts are more in line with Canaanite uses of "to drive out" in describing the minor deity Yagrush and the activity of "driving out" illness or enemies (CTA 1.IV.24; 2.IV.12; 16.V.12, 15, 27; 17.I.30) and the Moabite Inscription where Chemosh is described as driving out (גרשׁ) the enemies of the king.

A third context concerns idealizations of Moses. These occurrences arise in the confrontation between Moses, the daughters of Jethro, and other shepherds at the well in Exodus 2. In this story shepherds drive out the daughters of Jethro (2:17), prompting Moses to rescue them, and resulting in a naming aetiology of Gershom (2:22), possibly building off גרשׁ, even though the name has been reinterpreted to mean גר (resident alien) within priestly tradition. The aetiology of Gershom building off the word גרשׁ may also be part of the preexilic account of the exodus. See W. H. Schmidt (*Exodus,* BKAT II/1 [Neukirchen-Vluyn: Neukirchener, 1988], 95–95) for discussion concerning the etymology of Gershom.

30. The repetition of the divine prediction in 6:1 and 11:1 reinforces the point made earlier concerning the structure of the plague cycle, namely that the first six plagues are separated from the events that begin with darkness. In this regard note also that there are two separate occurrences in which the divine prediction is fulfilled. The first six plagues conclude with Moses' being driven (גרשׁ) from the presence of Pharaoh in 10:11, and the death of the Egyptian firstborn concludes with Israel's being driven out by the Egyptians (כי־גרשׁו ממצרים) in 12:39.

31. Steingrimsson (*Vom Zeichen zur Geschichte*, 154-155) has suggested that 11:1 indicates a history of tradition because of the apparent doublet in 11:1ag (אֶתְכֶם מִזֶּה וְשִׁלַּח) and in 11:1b (יְגָרֵשׁ אֶתְכֶם מִזֶּה). He concludes from this that גרשׁ is a later addition to sharpen the interpretation. Steingrimsson is certainly correct that גרשׁ sharpens the interpretation of שׁלח, but such a nuance of meaning need not indicate distinct traditions, especially when the careful distribution of גרשׁ throughout the plague cycle is noted.

32. See chapter 3 for a further discussion.

33. The concluding formulas show the following development: First, כבד or חֹזֶק are used as descriptions of Pharaoh's heart in the first two plagues (blood: חזק in 7:22; frogs: כבד in 8:11). Second, כבד and שׁלח are used in combination to describe Pharaoh's heart and the resulting actions in the next three plagues (flies, 8:28; cattle, 9:7, and hail, 9:34b, 35b). And third, חזק and שׁלח are used in combination to describe divine influence on Pharaoh and the resulting actions in the remainder of the cycle (locust, 10:20; darkness, 10:27; and death of the Egyptian firstborn, 11:10b). For further discussion see L. Schmidt, *Plagenerzählung*, 58-64 and Wilson, "The Hardening of Pharaoh's Heart," 18-36.

34. Two aspects of vv. 31-32 might very well be later additions by priestly tradents. First, the reference to Aaron in v. 31 is certainly priestly in origin. The second is less clear. Pharaoh's request for a blessing in v. 32 is more difficult to locate in the tradition-historical development of the text. The motif of blessing is rare in the Book of Exodus. Furthermore, the few occurrences present are distributed in both deuteronomistic (20:24; 23:35; 32:29?) and priestly (20:11; 39:43) tradition. To complicate matters further, the request by Pharaoh for a blessing in 12:32 does not fit in well with any of the other references in the book. The motif may be part of the preexilic account or later priestly tradition.

35. Noth (*Exodus*, 105) also attributes vv. 5-7 to J, but in contrast to the present study, he limits J to v. 9aa and assigns the description of Pharaoh's army in 9ab to P. Childs (*Exodus*, 220) distributes vv. 5-7 and 9a between J (5b, 6, 9aa) and E (5a, 7). More nuanced readings include Kohata (*Jahwist und Priesterschrift in Exodus 3-14*, 372): J (14:5b, 6), E (5a), R (7), P (9), and P. Weimar (*Die Meerwundererzählung: Eine redaktionskritische Analyse von Ex 13,17-14,31*, Ägypten und Altes Testament 9 [Wiesbaden: Otto Harrassowitz, 1985], 42, 69-70, 108) Oldest Account (5a, 9a), Je (5b-6), Rp (7).

36. The verb "to serve" or "to worship" (עבד) is used in the final two concessions by Pharaoh (locust in 10:8 and darkness in 10:24). It is also a central motif at the outset in each of Moses' messenger speeches in the first six plagues, when Pharaoh is commanded to send (שׁלח) Israel for the purpose of serving (עבד) Yahweh (blood [7:16], frogs [7:26], flies [8:16], cattle [9:1], hail [9:13], locust [10:3]). Note also the same language in the initial divine prediction to Moses concerning the death of the Egptian firstborn (4:31) and in the speech to Pharaoh by his servants in 10:7. For a brief discussion concerning the combination of these verses, see E. Zenger, "Le theme de la 'sortie d'Egypte,'" *Le pentateuque en question: Les origines et la composition des cinq premiers livres de la Bible à la lumière des recherches récentes*, ed. A. de Pury, Le monde de la Bible (Genève: Labor & Fides, 1989), 318.

37. Tradition-historical distinctions on the basis of the description of the Egyptian army have not been followed in the present study for two reasons. First, the army is described in eight different places in the narrative (14:6, 7, 9, 23, 25, 26,

28; 15:19), and although there is variation in terminology with רכב being the only constant term (סוס is limited to 14:9, 23; and 15:19; פרשׁ to 14:9, 23, 28; and 15.19; and חיל to 14:9, 28), the distinctions are not clear enough to provide literary or transmission history. The second problem is that all of the terms with the exception of פרשׁ appear in the hymn in Exod 15:1-12, 18, which may very well be older than any of the narratives and thus influencing the latter's formation at all stages of development. A more controlled criterion for determining distinct traditions requires changing the focus from the description of the army to its actions. It will be argued in the next chapter that the motif of the Israelites walking (בוא ,הלך) into the sea on dry ground (יבשׁה) and of the Egyptian army's entering (בוא) after them (14:22a, 23, 28-29a; 15:19) are deuteronomistic additions, which contrast with the inactive role of Israel camping at the sea (14:5-7) in the present account. But note that even in the cases designated as deuteronomistic, the description of the army varies (e.g., v. 28 does not include reference to horses).

38. See B. F. Batto, *Slaying the Dragon: Mythmaking in the Biblical Tradition* (Louisville: Westminster/John Knox, 1992).

39. The word "sea" (ים) occurs frequently in Exod 13:17-15:21, both in the narrative (in 14:2, 9, 16 [twice], 21 [three times], 22, 23, 26, 27 [three times], 28, 29, 30; 15:19 [twice]) and in the poetry (15:1, 4, 8, 10, 21). The word "water" (מים) also occurs both in the narratives (14:21, 22, 26, 28, 29; 15:19 [three times]) and in the poetry (15:8, 10), as does the designation Red Sea (ים־סוף), once in the narrative (13:18 but see also 15:22) and once in the poetry (15:4).

The occurrences of the sea in the preexilic account can be summarized in the following manner. (1) Six times the sea is used as a definite noun with the preposition (על־הים), taking on a spatial meaning of simple locational (on, upon, over) or contingent locational (at, beside, by): the children of Israel are camped by the sea (v. 9a, חנים על־הים); there are two sequences of divine command and response concerning Moses' stretching his hand/rod on the sea (vv. 16aa, 21a, 27a, על־הים); and the Israelites see the dead Egyptians on the shore of the sea (v. 30b, על־שׂפת הים). (2) Two times the sea is the object of divine action: Yahweh sends an east wind on the sea and dries the sea (vv. 21a, 21b, את־הים). (3) Once the sea functions as the subject, when it is described as returning to its natural flow (v. 27b, הים). (4) And only once is the definite noun used with the preposition (בתוך הים), taking on a spatial meaning within a domain: Yahweh shook off the Egyptians in the midst of the sea (v. 27b).

Further study in chapters 3-4 will show that the sea continues to play a central role in both the deuteronomistic and priestly traditions. Deuteronomistic tradents refer to the sea with the prepositions ב and בתוך, signifying spatial meaning within a domain, and they combine these prepositions with the verbs בוא and הלך in order to signify movement into the sea by both Israel and the Egyptians (e.g., 14:16b, 28a; 15:19); they also interrelate the sea with Israel's wilderness travels in their use of ים־סוף (13:18 and 15:22), and twice they use the word "water" (המים), perhaps to demythologize the return of the sea on the Egyptians (14:26b, 28a). Priestly tradents use the word "water" (המים) only to describe the splitting of the sea with its subsequent walls (14:21b, 22b, 29b).

40. The remarks by J. L. Ska (*Le passage de la mer: Etude de la construction, du style et de la symbolique d'Ex 14, 1-31,* AnBib 109 [Rome: Biblical Institute Press, 1986], 69) concerning the central role of this discourse in the final form of the text apply equally well to the preexilic version.

41. Scholars are nearly unanimous in reading 14:13-14 as a unified and single tradition, usually attributed to J (see, for example, Noth, *Exodus*, 106; but compare Kohata, *Jahwist und Priesterschrift in Exodus 3-14*, 372; or Weimar, *Meerwundererzählung*, 73, 238). Verse 10, however, is more problematic, especially with regard to the cry of Israel (צעק), because the term is clearly used in priestly tradition (Exod 2:23-25) and is also an important motif within deuteronomistic tradition to describe the actions of both Israel and Moses in the wilderness (e.g., Exod 15:25; 17:4). Noth (*Exodus*, 106) attributed the motif of crying out and the approach of Pharoah to P (14:10a,b*b*), with the description of the Egyptian pursuit to J (14:10b*a*). Yet the term is also central to the earliest account of the exodus, in describing both Israel's initial response to oppression (Exodus 5) and the Egyptian response to the death of the firstborn (Exodus 11, 12), thus providing the criterion for its inclusion in the preexilic account.

42. G. Hasel, "צעק/זעק," *TDOT IV*, ed. G. J. Botterweck and H. Ringgren (Grand Rapids: Eerdmans, 1980), 115. See also R. N. Boyce, *The Cry to God in the Old Testament*, SBLDS 103 (Atlanta: Scholars Press, 1988), 11-12.

43. On the linking together of the verb "to cry out" with "salvation" see Hasel, "צעק/זעק," 120; and Ska, *Le passage de la mer*, 74-75.

44. The holy war motifs include אל-תיראו and לחם. H. F. Fuhs ("ירא," *TDOT VI*, ed., G. J. Botterweck and H. Ringgren [Grand Rapids: Eerdmans, 1990], 304-305) distributes the "fear not" formula in four distinct contexts (everyday life, holy war, oracle of salvation, and theophany). Exod 14:13-14 bridges at least two of these categories. Although it clearly functions as a battle speech, in which the leader encourages the host to be fearless in facing the enemy in holy war, nevertheless, as Ska (*Le passage de la mer*, 74-75) noted, there is no active participation by Israel in holy war. Furthermore, the passive stance of Israel in combination with the explicit language of salvation (וראו את-ישועת in v. 13 and ויושע יהוי ביום ההוא in v. 30) picks up aspects of the oracle of salvation. For discussion of the salvation oracle see J. Begrich, "Das priesterliche Heilsorakel," *ZAW* 52 (1934): 81-92.

45. See E. W. Conrad (*Fear Not Warrior: A Study of "al tira" Pericopes in the Hebrew Scriptures*, BJS 75 [Chico: Scholars Press, 1985], 143-145) for more detailed analysis of this structure and a comparison with other occurrences of the form. See also P. E. Dion ("The 'Fear Not' Formula and Holy War," *CBQ* 32 [1970]: 565-570) for additional discussion.

46. Ska (*Le passage de la mer*, 71-74) in particular underscores the epiphanic character of the narrative over against those who stress the holy war setting, such as von Rad (*Holy War in Ancient Israel*, 88-90). Building on the work of C. Westermann (*Praise and Lament in the Psalms*, 2d ed., trans. K. R. Crim and R. N. Soulen [Atlanta: John Knox, 1981], 93-101), Ska defines "epiphany" as an appearance of God to assist the people of God, in distinction to "theophany," which denotes the appearance of God in general.

47. See Conrad, *Fear Not Warrior*, 143-145; E. Zenger and P. Weimar, *Exodus: Geschichten und Geschichte der Befreiung Israels*, SBS 75 (Stuttgart: KBW Verlag, 1975), 57; and especially Ska ("Ex xivcontientail un récit de 'guerre sainte', de style deutéronomistique" *VT* 33 [1988]: 454-467), who concludes concerning the language of Exod 14:13-14 that "[s]on vocabulaire est en général indépendant de celui des text Dt. -Dtr., et plutôt anterieur."

48. See, for example, Schmid, *Der sogenannte Jahwist*, 54-60; F. Stolz,

Jahwes und Israels Kriege: Kriegstheorien und Kriegserfahrungen im Glauben des alten Israels, ATANT 60 (Zürich: Theologische Verlag, 1972), 90-97; and Blum (*Studien,* 30-31), who assigns the text to a D-Komposition.

49. See Conrad, *Fear Not Warrior,* 53-56.

50. Past scholarship on Exodus 14 can be summarized in the following manner. Although there has been general agreement concerning a history of tradition in Exodus 14, debate has centered primarily on the number and character of the sources. Wellhausen (*Composition,* 77-79) departed from Nöldeke in attributing a minor role to P (13:20; 14:1,2, 4 ("and they did so"), 8b, 9 (with the exception of the place names), 10 (motif of crying out), 16*, and perhaps v. 28. He concluded that the narrative consisted primarily of E (13:17f, 19; 14:3, 4*, 7, 8a, 9*, 10*, 15, 16-18, 19a, and perhaps 20b) and J (13:21f; 14:5, 6, 10*, 11-14, 19b, 20*, 21, 22, 24, 25, 30-31). (*) Asterisk indicates that only part of a verse or section is included with in a particular tradition. Source-critical debate has gone in two directions. One is the elimination of P altogether from the account (see Fohrer [*Überlieferung und Geschichte des Exodus,* 97-116], who distributes the material between J, E, and N with some additions). The second is assigning a larger role to P, and here the arguments bifurcate between those who argue exclusively for two traditions—J and P (e.g., Rudolph, *Der "Elohist" von Exodus bis Josua,* 28-31)—and those who attribute minor fragments to E (e.g., Noth, *Exodus,* 104-106). Source-critical readings have not gone unchallenged. See J. A. Soggin ("Das Wunder am Meer und in der Wüste [Exodus, cc. 14-15]," in *Mélanges bibliques et orientaux en l'honneur de M. Mathias Delcor,* AOAT 215, ed. A. Caquot et al. [Neukirchen-Vluyn: Neukirchener, 1985], 379-385), who identifies five fragmentary accounts of the sea event in Exodus 14-15; or Weimar (*Meerwundererzählung*), who advocates a combination of sources and redactions, including an original account, incorporated by a Yahwist (J), where the salvation at the sea is related to the Abrahamic promise. The Yahwist is expanded by a Yahwistic redaction (Je), perhaps during the time of Hezekiah's reform, which links the exodus to the wilderness and murmuring traditions, before this tradition is expanded still further by a deuteronomistic redaction during the exile, which emphasizes the wilderness wandering by adding the motif of the cloud. A second development is the independent source P and its integration into the other complex by a final pentateuchal redactor (Rp). Blum (*Studien,* 256-262 esp. 257) offers a more efficient two-part development of tradition: a KD (prepriestly composition within deuteronomistic tradition) and a KP (priestly composition), but he does not focus on preexilic exodus tradition.

51. Three levels of tradition will be described in the present study. The following is a brief overview of the literary study presented in the next three chapters. The first level involves a preexilic account of the death of the Egyptian army at the sea as a holy-war event, providing a conclusion to an independent exodus tradition (14:5-7, 9a, 10, 13-14, 15a*a*, 16a*a*, 21a, 24a*a*, 24b-26, 27, 30).

The second level involves a deuteronomistic supplementation which has as its general aim the linking of the exodus with the wilderness in order to incorporate it into a larger historiography. This redaction adds the motif of travel into the wilderness, an itinerary notice, as well as the motifs of crossing the sea, the messenger of God, and faith in Moses (13:17-18a, 20; 14:11-12, 15a*b*,b, 16b, 19a, 20a*a*, 22a, 23, 28-29a, 31).

In the third level, priestly tradents incorporate their own itinerary into the account, as well as the motifs of the cloud, the hardening of Pharaoh's heart, the recognition formula, and the splitting of the water into walls (13:18b, 19, 21-22; 14:1-4, 8, 9b, 16ab, 17-18, 19b, 20ab,b, 21b, 22b, 24ab, 29b).

52. Most scholars attribute the motif of Moses stretching out his hand or rod to P. The reason is that this motif is prominent in P's additions to the plague cycle, where Aaron produces wonders with his rod or outstretched hand (snakes, 7:10; blood, 7.19, frogs, 8.1-2, and gnats, 8.12-13). Yet as Hyatt (*Exodus*, 155) has noted, "Aaron does not appear at all in the narrative of the crossing of the sea." The absence of Aaron raises questions about attributing this motif to P. Coupled with this reservation is the fact that the motif is also firmly anchored in the preexilic account of the plagues, where Moses is described as stretching out his rod or hand in the plagues of hail (9:22-23), locust (10:12-13), and darkness (10:21-22).

53. Three words are used to describe God's action on the sea. In the preexilic account the east wind dries it up (חרבה) and there is no description of Israel's crossing. In the deuteronomistic account Israel is described as entering (בוא, הלך) into the midst of the sea on dry ground (יבש), and in the priestly interpretation Moses splits (בקע) the sea, which is then described as walls of water. חרבה is also included in deuteronomistic tradition, where it is combined with the motif of crossing to describe Israel's action at the Jordan (Josh 3:17; 4:18) and a similar event with Elijah and Elisha (2 Kgs 2:8). Note, however, that the confession concerning the crossing of the Jordan in Josh 4:22 uses the word יבש to describe the event.

54. See Noth (*Exodus*, 117), who writes, "the 'morning watch' is the last of the three 'watches,' i.e. watching periods, into which the night is divided. . . ."

55. The central role of holy war continues throughout this section. המם is frequently used on the context of holy war to describe the confusion or panic of Yahweh's (and Israel's) opponents (e.g., Exod 23:27; Deut 2:15; Josh 10:10; Judg 4:15; 1 Sam 7:10; 2 Sam 22:15).

56. The exact description of events is difficult to determine. Confusion over the meaning of סור begins in the different textual traditions. The Samaritan, LXX, and Syriac texts use a different verb "to bind," which is reflected in the NRSV translation, "He clogged their chariot wheels. . . ." The present interpretation has followed the MT, but ambiguity still remains since the form ויסר could be read as qal ("to turn aside") or hiphil ("to remove"). In either case it is clear that Yahweh has taken over control of the Egyptian army and that they recognize this fact.

If the events in 14:25 are read in the larger context of the plague cycle, then the qal reading "to turn aside" is preferred (at least in the present form of the text), since the use of סור brings to conclusion a motif that was introduced in the plague cycle. Three times Pharaoh had requested of Moses that he pray (עתר) to Yahweh to turn back (סור) a plague (frogs, 8:4, 7; flies, 8:25, 27; and locust, 10:17), which Moses was able to do through intercession. Whether this reading is the result of deuteronomistic supplementation or original to the exodus liturgy depends on when the motif of intercession by prayer entered the text. For further discussion of סור see Zenger and Weimar, *Exodus*, 66-67 and n. 19, and most recently, J. H. Stek ("What Happened to the Chariot Wheels in Exodus 14:25?" *JBL* 105 [1986]: 293-294), who favors the root אסר with the meaning "jammed."

57. Noth (*Exodus*, 117) writes that v. 25a "occurs too early, as it already presupposes the flight of the Egyptians, to which they resort only in v. 25b." See also Hyatt, *Exodus*, 154-155. But compare Weimar (*Meerwundererzählung*, 73), who

סור
in
14:25

includes 14:25a with the oldest account and v. 25b with a Yahwistic redaction meant to accentuate the Egyptians. It is difficult to see any gap in logic between vv. 25a and b, since the actions of Yahweh in v. 25a clearly indicate holy war (see especially the discussion of המם as a holy-war term), which provides the appropriate context for the statement by the Egyptians in v. 25b, with its repetition of להם from 14:14.

58. For similar usage see Judg 19:26 and Ps 46:6.

59. J. F. A Sawyer, "ישׁע," *TDOT VI,* ed., G. J. Botterweck and H. Ringgren (Grand Rapids: Eerdmans, 1990), 445.

60. The question remains whether *massot* is present in the preexilic account of the exodus. There certainly is some form of liturgical action during the night with unleavened dough in Exod 12:34, 39b, and this action is indeed interpreted as *massot* by later deuteronomistic tradents (see Exod 12:39a and 13:1-16). The present study, however, has not stressed an interpretation of *massot* as part of the preexilic liturgy, for several reasons. First, the term *massot* is absent in Exod 12:34, 39b. Second, an autumn setting for the preexilic celebration of the exodus conflicts with the spring setting that is normally attributed to *massot* (see Exod 23:15). For a discussion see R. Martin-Achard, *Essai biblique sur les fêtes d'Israël* (Genève: Labor & Fides, 1974), 33-34; and R. de Vaux, *Ancient Israel,* vol. 2 (New York: McGraw-Hill, 1965), 484-493.

Lastly, the liturgical structure of the text, which requires that all action be complete in one night, would not allow for a seven-day observance, as is normally associated with *massot.* Note, however, that when *massot* is included by deuteronomistic tradents, their additions in Exod 12:37, 38a, and 39a break the tightly woven liturgical structure of the predeuteronomistic narrative. In their reading, Israel journeys to a particular location (Succoth in v. 37) and then stops to bake unleavened bread (v. 39a). With this change of structure the time frame becomes blurred, thus allowing for a seven-day observance at Succoth. For arguments against a seven-day observance in early celebrations of *massot* see B. N. Wambacq, "Les Massot," *Bib* 61 (1980) 36. For arguments locating massot in northern preexilic tradition see A. Cooper and B. R. Goldstein, "The Festivals of Israel and Judah and the Literary History of the Pentateuch," *JAOS* 110 (1990): 19-31, esp. 21-22.

61. See J. Pedersen (*Israel: Its Life and Culture,* trans. A. I. Fausbøll [Copenhagen: Dyva & Jeppesen, 1940], 730) for a discussion of a nocturnal cultic setting for the exodus, which progresses until "the morning watch" when "the contest of the night in the renewed experience in the cult has been brought to an end, and the song of triumph forms its termination." Pedersen's focus, however, is on the final form of the text, which means that this festival, for him, is a celebration of Passover.

62. J. W. McKay ("Psalms of Vigil," *ZAW* 91 [1979] 229-247) examines Psalms 5, 17, 27, 30, 57, 63, and 143 as examples of psalms of vigil.

63. J. Ziegler, "Die Hilfe Gottes 'am Morgan,'" in *Alttestamentliche Studien: Friedrich Nötscher zum 60. Geburtstag,* BBB 1, ed. H. Junker and J. Botterweck (Bonn: Peter Hanstein, 1950), 281-288. Ziegler examines Psalms 5, 46, 59, 73, 88, 90, 92, 143, etc., as well as other texts such as Isaiah 17, 33, 38, etc. For discussion of the exodus narrative see pp. 286-287.

64. J. C. de Moor, *The Seasonal Pattern in the Ugaritic Myth of Ba'lu,* AOAT 16 (Neukirchen-Vluyn: Kevelaer/Neukirchener, 1971), 243-244; and *New Year with Canaanites and Israelites,* vols. 1-2 (Kampen: J. H. Kok, 1972), 1, 5-6; 2, 5-7.

65. For a recent review of the research on the influence of solar imagery in the Yahwistic cult see H.-P. Stähli, *Solare Elemente in Jahweglauben des Alten Testaments,* OBO 66 (Fribourg: Universitätsverlag, 1985). Note also the review by M. S. Smith (*JBL* 106 [1987]: 513-515) and his own analysis in *The Early History of God: Yahweh and the Other Deities in Ancient Israel* (San Francisco: Harper & Row, 1990), 115-124.

66. For discussion and further bibliography see, among others, de Moor, *Seasonal Pattern,* 55, 77, and passim; *New Year with Canaanites and Israelites,* 1, 5; T. H. Gaster, *Thespis: Ritual, Myth, and Drama in the Ancient Near East,* 2d ed., The Norton Library (New York: Norton, 1953), 23-106 and passim; J. Day, *God's Conflict with the Dragon and the Sea: Echoes of a Canaanite Myth in the Old Testament,* University of Cambridge Oriental Studies 35 (Cambridge: Cambridge Universtiy Press, 1985), 8-18, esp. 9, and 17-18.

67. A number of scholars have constructed elaborate cultic New Year ceremonies involving a night vigil, the participation of the king, and a celebration of divine salvation at dawn. See, for example, J. Morgenstern, *The Fire Upon the Altar* (Leiden: E. J. Brill, 1963); and "The Gates of Righteousness," *HUCA* 6 (1929), 1-37; and A. R. Johnson, *Sacral Kingship in Ancient Israel,* 2d ed. (Cardiff: University of Wales, 1967). Yet caution is required, since the degree to which the Canaanite myth is influencing the liturgy of the exodus is difficult to say, especially in light of the limited scope of the present study, and thus this avenue will not be pursued further. For a recent review see J. H. Eaton, *Kingship and the Psalms,* 2d ed., The Bible Seminar (Sheffield: JSOT Press, 1986), 87-110.

68. The references to the יום יהוה include Amos 5:18; Isa 13:6, 9; Ezek 13:5; Obad 15; Zeph 1:17, 18; Joel 1:15; 2:1, 11; 3:4; 4:14. For a somewhat expanded list of references see P. L. Cerny, *The Day of Yahweh and Some Relevant Problems,* Facultas Philosophica Universitatis Carolinae Pragensis 53 (Prague: Nákladem Filosofické Fakuty University Karlovy, 1948), Appendix 1. For a recent summary of scholarship see R. H. Hiers, "Day of Judgment," in *The Anchor Bible Dictionary,* vol. 2; ed. D. N. Freedman (New York: Doubleday, 1992), 79-82; and "Day of the Lord," in *The Anchor Bible Dictionary,* vol. 2, 82-83; and K. J. Cathcart, "The Day of Yahweh," in *The Anchor Bible Dictionary,* vol. 2, 84-85. Two comments are necessary. First, the present study has followed S. Mowinckel's methodological starting point (*The Psalms in Israel's Worship,* vol.1, trans. D. R. Ap-Thomas [Nashville: Abingdon, 1962], 23-41) that the cult is most likely the unifying context for the fragmented prophetic references. See also T. N. D. Mettinger, *The Dethronement of Sabaoth: Studies in the Shem and Kabod Theologies,* ConBOT 18 (Lund: Gleerup, 1982), 70; and B. Halpern, *The Constitution of the Monarchy in Israel,* HSM 25 (Chico: Scholars Press, 1981), 105-106. Second, there is development in the prophetic use of the Day of Yahweh toward an ever-increasing eschatological focus (e.g., Zeph 1:18), which certainly moves beyond the cultic setting of the preexilic account of the exodus (i.e., a cosmological future event is not envisioned in the exodus, nor is there a universal perspective in which all nations are included).

69. The expression "Day of Yahweh" may be an innovation in Amos, since the term does not appear in the exodus liturgy. Yet the cultic event is certainly well-known to the audience of Amos. For review of the arguments see Y. Hoffman, "The Day of the Lord as a Concept and a Term in the Prophetic Literature," *ZAW* 93 (1981): 37-50.

70. G. von Rad, "The Origin of the Concept of the Day of Yahweh," *JSS* 4 (1959): 97-108; *Old Testament Theology 2*, 119-125; and H. W. Wolff, *Joel and Amos,* trans. W. Janzen et al., *Hermeneia* (Philadelphia: Fortress Press, 1977), 33-34. For a criticism of von Rad's view see J. Gray, "The Day of Yahweh in Cultic Experience and Eschatological Prospect," *SEÅ* 39 (1974): 5-37.

71. See especially Cerny (*The Day of Yahweh*, 59-83) for a discussion of the destructive aspect of the Day of Yahweh.

72. See Schmid (*Der sogenannte Jahwist*, 19-60) for examples of the literary relationship between prepriestly exodus tradition in the Pentateuch and deuteronomic-deuteronomistic tradition.

73. Compare Conrad (*Fear Not Warrior*, 144-145), who argues that Exod 14:13-14 is addressed to the community rather than to the king; it reflects more the transformation of Zion tradition in Second Isaiah, where the passive stance was meant "to celebrate Yahweh's coming victory as heralds of good tidings." The focus certainly is on the community in Exod 14:13-14, yet it is very difficult to see such an eschatological perspective in the larger context of the preexilic account of the exodus as the one emerging in Second Isaiah, especially with the absence of wilderness and conquest traditions.

74. For a summary of Zion tradition see, among many others, B. Ollenburger, *Zion, The City of the Great King: A Theological Symbol for the Jeruselam Cult*, JSOTSup 41 (Sheffield: JSOT Press, 1987), 23-52; Mettinger, *Dethronement of Sabaoth*, 1-19; Day, *God's Conflict with the Dragon and the Sea*,18-38; J. D. Levenson, "Zion Traditions," in *The Anchor Bible Dictionary*, vol. 6, ed. D. N. Freedman (New York: Doubleday, 1992), 1098-1102.

75. Mowinckel, *The Psalms in Israel's Worship*, vol 1, 106-192; de Moor, *New Year with Canaanites and Israelites*, vol. 1, 12-29; Day, *God's Conflict with the Dragon and the Sea*, 18-38; Halpern, *The Constitution of the Monarchy*, 51-109, esp. 98; Eaton, *Kingship and the Psalms*, 87-134, esp. 102-105.

76. See Ollenburger, *Zion, The City of the Great King*, 24-52; Halpern, *The Constitution of the Monarchy*, 52-109; Eaton, *Kingship and the Psalms*.

77. Note the motifs נכה, נגף.

78. Note the motifs לא שלח, חזק לב, מאן לב.

79. The absolute distinction between Egyptians and Israelites is maintained throughout the narrative. An overview of the narrative illustrates the point. In the six-part plague cycle Israelites and Egyptians are affected equally in the first (blood and frogs) and third (hail and locust) pairs of plagues. Distinctions are maintained in the second pair (flies and cattle) and in the events of the exodus (darkness, death of firstborn, and destruction at the sea). The sequence of action in the places where clear distinctions are maintained (the second pair of plagues—flies and cattle—and the events of the exodus) is particularly noteworthy, for they progress in the same manner: first there is a distinction between Egyptians and Israelites with regard to geography (flies [8:18] and darkness [10:23]—Egypt versus Goshen), and then in each series there follows a plague of death, which makes a more fundamental distinction between groups (death of Egyptian cattle in the plague cycle and death of Egyptian firstborn in the sequence of the exodus).

3

Exodus and Conquest

The aim in this chapter is to demonstrate how deuteronomistic tradents refashioned the liturgy of the Day of Yahweh into an account of salvation history during the exilic period. Such a hypothesis is not without debate. Although there is a broad consensus that the Tetrateuch contains material that resembles Deuteronomy, there is debate concerning the extent of such literature in the Tetrateuch, and concerning its relationship to Deuteronomy and the deuteronomistic history (Joshua–2 Kings).[1] Is such literature proto-deuteronomic,[2] indistinguishable from deuteronom(ist)ic literature,[3] or postdeuteronomistic?[4] And is the extent of such literature sporadic and minimal,[5] an extensive reworking of the Tetrateuch,[6] or perhaps even the creation of it?[7] I will argue that deuteronomistic tradents worked by means of supplementation to reinterpret the exodus[8] and that their reinterpretation results in an account of salvation history including, most likely, some form of Genesis through Kings.[9]

SALVATION INTO THE WILDERNESS
AND THE PROMISE OF LAND

Deuteronomistic tradents transformed the exodus from a self-contained story of Yahweh's victory over Egypt and present rule in the land into an account of salvation history, where divine rule in the land becomes a future hope. What makes this larger story possible is that the wilderness becomes the immediate outcome of the exodus and thereby it provides the connection between Egypt and Canaan. The introduction of the wilderness, therefore, is a significant feature of the deuteronomistic reinterpretation of the exodus, and a description of how it is merged into the story is a major goal of this chapter.[10]

The wilderness provides much more than a new setting for the outcome of the exodus; it embodies a cluster of related motifs, which accen-

tuate the Israelites' more active participation in the story and their need
to journey with God toward a promised land. These motifs include the command that they take valuables from the Egyptians (the "despoiling motif"),[11]
geographical stopping points in their trek from Egypt (the "itinerary
notices"),[12] the confession of divine leading in the phrase, "Yahweh who
brought Israel out of Egypt" (the "exodus motif"),[13] the future promise of
the land as a divine oath,[14] a series of catechisms in which elders teach
their children about the exodus as they journey through the wilderness,[15]
and the reinterpretation of the sea to include both the destruction of the
enemy and the need for Israel to cross the Red Sea (Exodus 14) and the
Jordan River (Joshua 3-5). These motifs work in consort to achieve a new
rendering of the Exodus as a story of salvation history. Further study will
illustrate that salvation in the deuteronomistic version begins in Egypt with
the account of the death of the firstborn and the institution of passover,[16]
that it traces the Israelites' exodus from Egypt to Succoth, where additional
legislation concerning *massot* and Yahweh's claim on the firstborn is promulgated,[17] and finally, that the confrontation at the Red Sea propels the
Israelites on a wilderness journey,[18] which is not complete until they cross
the Jordan River.

The Plague Cycle

There is little editing of the plague cycle by deuteronomistic tradents. Possible minor additions include the proclamation of the divine name in the
land in the plague of hail (9:16b),[19] the instruction at the outset of the
plague of locust (10:1b-2a),[20] and the naming of the sea as the Red Sea at
the close of this plague (10:19).[21] The recent work of Aurelius on the
intercessory role of Moses in deuteronomistic tradition raises the question
of whether some of the motifs of intercession, such as his crying out
to God or his intercessory prayer in the plagues of flies (8:24b-26), hail
(8:28-30), and locust (10:28) might not also be signs of deuteronomistic
editing.[22] The role of Moses as intercessor is certainly important in deuteronomistic tradition, especially in relation to the murmuring motif in
the wilderness, which is also woven into the exodus story in 14:11-12.[23]
Whether the intercessory role of Moses is also expanded in the plague cycle
is difficult to confirm, but a decision on this issue is not essential to the
goal of this study.

The most important evidence of deuteronomistic editing for this
study occurs at the outset of the plague cycle, where, in his opening speech
to Pharaoh, Moses introduces the wilderness as the location where Israel
must worship God (5:1).[24] Within this same speech a more precise location for worship is given in 5:3, when Moses tells Pharaoh that Israel must
travel three days into the wilderness in order to sacrifice to Yahweh.[25]
Yahweh's requirement that Israel worship in the wilderness is included
one other time, at the outset of the plague of blood (7:16), and the refer-

ence to the three-day journey also reappears one other time, in an exchange between Moses and Pharaoh in the plague of flies (8:23).[26]

The introduction of the wilderness into the plague cycle places the exodus in a new and larger literary context. The divine requirement that Israel worship at a location three days in the wilderness introduces a point of tension into the story that can no longer be resolved simply with the destruction of the Egyptian army in the sea, as was the case in the older narrative.[27] Instead, the deuteronomistic reading requires that the exodus be extended at least to the point where this motif is fulfilled in the wilderness of Shur (15:22–27), since this location is precisely three days into the wilderness. Thus, although the wilderness is only loosely woven into the plague cycle,[28] its insertion certainly changes the boundaries and plot structure of the exodus.

Once the wilderness is the immediate goal of the exodus, the internal structure of the tradition is also transformed with the introduction of itinerary notices, which are meant to provide the framework for the three-day journey. Four such forms occur in Exodus 11–15. It is noted in 12:37 that Israel journeyed from Ramses to Succoth. Exod 13:20 underscores that their travel continues from Succoth to Etham. Travel is disrupted in 14:2 when God commands Moses to reverse the direction of their march momentarily in order to camp at Pihahiroth. And in 15:22 it is noted that Israel traveled from the Red Sea to the Wilderness of Shur. This overview illustrates that the itinerary notices follow a set form that includes descriptions of Israel's travel from one location to another, and that Exod 14:2 has departed from this pattern. Not only is it distinct in form (a divine speech rather than simple narration of travel from one point to another), but also it has no relation to the preceding notice. Such isolation suggests that it is not part of the sequence of action that results from Exod 12:37; 13:20; 15:22. The function of this insertion must be explored later within the context of priestly tradition.

Yet even when the priestly itinerary notice is removed, the sequence of action is still somewhat blurred. The primary reason is the role of the Red Sea in Exod 15:22 as the point of departure for the journey to Shur, rather than Etham, as we would expect from Exod 13:20. This change alerts us to the fact that with the introduction of the itinerary notices the sea (now renamed the Red Sea) has acquired geographical significance that it did not have previously. Its geographical significance is especially important in relationship to the wilderness. Indeed, a reexamination of the itineraries underscores that references to either the Red Sea or the wilderness occur in Exod 13:20 and 15:22. And when we broaden our view to include Exod 13:18a, the Red Sea and the wilderness are even merged. The close interrelationship between itinerary notices, Red Sea, and wilderness would suggest that it is necessary to include Exod 13:18a into this sequence. The distribution of the three itinerary notices (12:37; 13:18a, 20; and 15:22) results in (1) a story that begins in Egypt at Ramses with the death of the firstborn at midnight, prompting Israel's initial journey to Succoth (12:37); then (2) Israel moves along the way of the Red Sea (13:18a) to the edge of the wilderness at Etham (13:20), where the confrontation at the Red Sea takes place, and (3) Israel's deliverance at the Red Sea eventually leads to Shur located three days into the wilderness (15:22).

The work of Davies provides transition to a more tradition-historical study of the itinerary notices through the Tetrateuch and the deuteronomistic history. After evaluating the larger structure of the itinerary framework, Davies concluded that there were two such frameworks: a priestly itinerary spanning Exodus and Numbers (Exod 14:1–4*; 19:1; Num 10:12; 20:1a*; and 22:1), and a prepriestly itinerary connecting Exodus and Numbers with the deuteronomistic history (Exod 12:37; 13:20; 15:22; 19:2b; Num 10:33; [21:4a*]; 21:12–20; 25:1; Josh 3:1; 4:19).[29] After comparing these itineraries to Numbers 33,[30] Davies argued that the formation of the prepriestly itinerary notices is the result of deuteronomistic editors whose purpose was to present the wilderness stories "in the form of a journey."[31] He then went on to note that the deuteronomistic itinerary notices are meant to relate "to the pivotal events of the wilderness narrative (sea, Sinai, Jordan) or [to] serve what seems to be a transitional function between wilderness and conquest narratives."[32]

The more general study of the itinerary notices provides background to describe how the exodus and wilderness traditions are interrelated in the exodus, and furthermore, how such an interrelationship changes the plot structure of the older tradition. In discussing the placement of the first two itineraries (12:37 and 13:20), Davies noted how disruptive they are to their present narrative context. He writes: "This awkwardness could mean that an old written account which lacked precise geographical elements had been worked over by a redactor who was determined to impose his stage-by-stage pattern even on the earliest section of the narrative."[33] Davies is certainly correct on this point, since the insertion of a travel sequence extending over several days breaks down the plot structure of the preexilic liturgy, where salvation took place in one evening from midnight to break of dawn. Yet, as an overview of the itineraries illustrates, their insertion is hardly random. They follow precisely the structure of the older narrative.

Salvation from Egypt into the Wilderness in Deuteronomistic Tradition						
Introduction	Death	Itinerary	Exodus	Itinerary	Sea/Hymn	Itinerary
Darkness	Midnight	1		2	Dawn	3
		12:37		13:18a, 20		15:22

The insertion of the itinerary notices creates tension in the structure of the exodus story. They force a complex sequence of travel over an extended period of time into what had been a single evening of activity progressing from the death of the Egyptian firstborn at midnight to the destruction of the Egyptian army at dawn.[34] The reason for this fragmentation of the older narrative is that the event of the exodus (i.e., the act of leaving Egypt) provides the occasion for deuteronomistic tradents to incorporate travel motifs of divine leading and of Israel's following God. As a result, the precise temporal indicators in the older narrative (that marked events from midnight to dawn) give way to precise geographical locations (that accentuate a journey of days through a number of different encampments). And this gives rise to a new plot structure, because the act of leaving Egypt takes on more significance with the emphasis on geography and travel. Thus, what had been two central events (death of Egyptian firstborn and defeat of the Egyptian army) related by the exodus (the driving out of Israel) in a single night of activity becomes three distinct episodes (the death of the Egyptian firstborn, the exodus from Egypt, and the defeat of the Egyptian army) that take place over many days. The tension underscores at the very least how important it is for deuteronomistic tradents that salvation be conceived as a journey for the people of God, in which the gift of the land becomes a future hope instead of a present reality.

The itinerary notices also raise a question of the relationship between the exodus and wilderness in deuteronomistic tradition. Here Coats provides a point of departure by arguing that the itinerary notices relocate the event at the sea into the wilderness rather than as an event in Egypt.[35] The distribution of the itinerary notices in Exodus 11–15 would certainly support the conclusion by Coats, since the conflict at the Red Sea is placed in the wilderness after the second itinerary in Exod 13:18a; 20. Further study will underscore that the shift in setting is accompanied by a change in focus, from the destruction of the enemy to Israel's safe passage through the water—a perspective that was absent in the older liturgy. The result of this change in structure and in focus is that what had been the final event of salvation in early tradition now becomes Israel's initial event in the wilderness. The restructuring of the plot with the introduction of a wilderness journey reinforces the future orientation of land in the deuteronomistic interpretation of the exodus as the goal of a history of salvation.

The Death of the Egyptian Firstborn

Reinterpretation of the death to the Egyptian firstborn is extensive in deuteronomistic tradition. It includes the motif of despoiling as a sequence of announcement and fulfillment in 11:2–3 and 12:35–36, an insertion about the anger of Moses in 11:8b, and the new cultic setting of passover in 12:21–27.[36] These additions introduce Israel into the story as functioning more actively than in the earlier narrative, where the focus tended to be on Yahweh and Pharaoh. The shift in focus is important, since active participation by Israel in Yahweh's salvation becomes a central component to the deuteronomistic reading of the exodus.

Despoiling the Egyptians

The motif of despoiling can be summarized in the following manner: Exod 11:2-3 is divine instruction that Israel "request" or perhaps even "demand" vessels of silver and vessels of gold from the Egyptians.[37] Along with the demand the narrator also informs us that the Israelites would succeed in their request because God would "give them favor in the eyes of the Egyptians."[38] The announcement is fulfilled in 12:35-36 when Israel requests vessels of silver, vessels of gold, and clothing after the death of the Egyptian firstborn, which they are given because of their favored status.[39] This process is described as the despoiling of the Egyptians.[40] The verb "to despoil" (the piel form of נצל) is not limited to the immediate context of the exodus, but also occurs in the events leading up to the exodus in the call of Moses (3:22) and after the events of the exodus, where, in the setting of the wilderness, Yahweh demands that the Israelites take off their jewelry because of their construction of the golden calf (Exod 33:1-6).[41]

This overview underscores that the despoiling motif is a planned theological insertion and that it is most likely the result of a single tradent.[42] The unified character of the insertion comes to light when one recalls that the death to the Egyptian firstborn consisted of announcement (11:4-7a, 8a) and fulfillment (12:29-33) in the older narrative.[43] The insertion of the despoiling motif in Exod 11:2-3 and 12:35-36 follows this pattern of announcement and fulfillment. Yet in so doing, these insertions also disrupt their immediate narrative contexts.[44] The insertion of a speech to Israel in 11:2-3 in the midst of a speech to Pharaoh creates confusion that is resolved only with the addition of v. 8b, where it is specifically stated that Moses is, indeed, in conversation with Pharaoh and not with Israel.[45] The problems with context continue into 12:35-36, where the despoiling motif is accompanied by a request for coats, whereas, in the older narrative Israel is already packed and leaving Egypt (12:33-34) with possessions wrapped in their coats.

Disruption of context prompts new interpretation. The despoiling motif reinterprets the death of the Egyptian firstborn as an instance of holy war.[46] The power of God to be victorious in holy war is indicated by the peculiar form of the motif of Israel's favored status. The motif does not occur in its expected form that "Israel found favor in the eyes of the Egyptians." Instead, it states that "Yahweh gave Israel favor in the eyes of the Egyptians."[47] The emphasis in this unexpected form is not so much on the relationship between Israelites and Egyptians as it is on the power of God to bring about reversal in the event of liberation.[48] The use of the verb "to despoil" to describe how the Egyptians were dispossessed of their valuables further underscores how the exodus is meant to emphasize holy war. This meaning is reinforced by 2 Chr 20:25, which is the only other text where the piel form of the verb occurs. 2 Chronicles 20 is also about holy war, and in 2 Chr 20:25 the taking of booty from a defeated enemy is described as despoiling.[49] The despoiling motif in Exod 11:2-3 and 12:35-36 presupposes the same context of conflict, since, in the preexilic account, the Israelites were driven out in Exod 12:33-34 following the death to the Egyptian firstborn. Given this situation, it is unlikely that Israel's request for possessions indicates a desire to borrow the objects.[50] Rather, it is a demand for booty, which fulfills the divine prediction given to Moses in Exod 3:22.[51] The despoiling motif is far removed from the passive stance toward holy war that was advocated in the older narrative. Despoiling requires the Israelites' active participation if they are to leave Egypt as victors from a battle.[52] And the Israelites' own self-despoiling after the incident of the golden calf indicates how quickly they can lose the spoils of the exodus in the wilderness.

Passover

Deuteronomistic tradents also accentuate Israel's role in the narrative with the introduction of passover in Exod 12:21-27. In vv. 21-23 Moses addresses the elders of Israel and describes the rite of passover as a family festival. The ritual procedure is followed by parenetic instruction in vv. 24-27 concerning the teaching of passover to future generations. The two parts of the text require separate commentary.

Exod 12:21-23 belongs to predeuteronomistic tradition. The focus on the family does not correspond to Deuteronomy 16, where passover is interpreted as a national festival to be observed at a central sanctuary.[53] Just how ancient the passover legislation in vv. 21-23 may be is difficult to say. Scholars have argued for its antiquity on the basis of motifs in the text[54] and from comparison to other ancient Near Eastern nomadic cultures.[55] What is clear is that regardless of how ancient the passover legislation in vv. 21-23 may be, it is not part of the preexilic account of the exodus and thus did not have the association with the exodus that is implied in v. 23.[56] The instruction for the Israelites to remain in their houses until morning in Exod 12:22b disrupts the chronology of the older account, where it is stated that the exodus occurred during the night in the wake of the final midnight plague of death.[57] Reference to the destroyer in Exod 12:23b as the divine force bringing the plague contrasts with the earlier announcement by Moses in Exod 11:4 that Yahweh himself would bring the final plague.[58] The social intermingling of Israelites and Egyptians in the same location in Exod 12:23 conflicts with what had been the clear separation of Israelites in Goshen (Exod 8:19; 9:26).[59] This clear distinction between groups is also contradicted by the apotropaic character of the blood rite.[60] And finally, the attention given to the Israelites, along with the demand that they actively participate in avoiding the plague of death, does not fit the older narrative, with its more limited focus on a confrontation between Yahweh and Pharaoh.

The instruction by a heroic leader and the call to observe law in Exod 12:24-27 look to be deuteronomistic. Noth saw this and designated vv. 24-27a as a deuteronomistic supplement, to which v. 24b was an even later addition.[61] But subsequent comparisons between the language and style of vv. 24-27a and (primarily) the Book of Deuteronomy have caused some to question Noth's conclusion. Lohfink noted that vv. 24-27a lack the lengthy style of fully developed deuteronom(ist)ic rhetoric with its tendency for repetition and elaborate syntax,[62] and that in eight places the language is either clearly not deuteronom(ist)ic or at least not characteristic of fully developed deuteronom(ist)ic style.[63] The key argument for the nondeuteronomistic character of Exod 12:24-27a is the cultic use of עבדה ("service" or "worship") in vv. 25 and 26, which occurs only once in Deut 26:6 as "forced labor."[64] Lohfink concluded that vv. 24-27a were an early independent speech (protodeuteronomic), whose similarity to deuteronom(ist)ic tradition arises from their use in a similar cultic sphere.[65] More recently Boorer has used the partial similarity between vv. 24-27a and priestly language to argue that 12:21-27 is an addition occurring sometime after Deuteronomy and before priestly tradition.[66]

The present study has not followed either Lohfink or Boorer at this point but instead has attributed the insertion of passover in 12:24-27a to deuteronomistic tradition.[67] A variety of literary arguments support such an interpretation. Parenetic speeches by heroic characters or leaders (especially at transitional points in a story) are a common literary trait of deuteronomistic editors.[68] The passover instructions are addressed in v. 21 to the "elders of Israel," who tend to play a prominent role throughout deuteronom(ist)ic tradition.[69] The emphasis on intergenerational teaching in the question-and-answer format is best explained as a literary trope within deuteronomistic tradition (most likely with older cultic roots).[70] And as Noth observed, much of the language is attributed most easily to deuteronomistic tradition, regardless of nuanced comparisons in form or syntax. Examples include the command "to observe a statute forever" in v. 24[71] and the reference to the land as a future gift from Yahweh in v. 26.[72]

Many of the motifs in 12:21-27 that are unique or at the very least peculiar to deuteronom(ist)ic tradition are also accountable when this unit is read within the particular context of the exodus. The literary tensions noted between the passover instruction in vv. 21-23 and the preexilic narrative actually reinforce the overall perspective of the deuteronomistic editors. The disruption of the chronology that occurs when the Israelites are instructed to remain in their houses until morning (12:22b) fits in well with the restructuring of the exodus as an event that extends for several days at a variety of locations. The intermingling of Israelites and Egyptians in the same location (12:23) adds to the theme that Israel must be an active participant in the events of the exodus. And, when deuteronomistic tradition is viewed as a supplementation to create a history of salvation, the contradiction between the passover instruction in 12:21–23 and Deuteronomy 16 with regard to the focus on the family becomes less of an obstacle for attributing the incorporation of 12:21–23 to deuteronomistic tradents. A centralized celebration of passover is hardly fitting in the aetiological story, and, indeed, is superseded in the larger history by Deuteronomy 16 before it is repeated as a centralized feast at Gilgal upon Israel's entry into the land (Josh 5:10–12).[73]

Given the poetic license in the way that older tradition is incorporated by deuteronomistic tradents, it should also not be surprising that more traditional deuteronom(ist)ic language is refashioned to fit particular literary contexts, or that language from older traditions reappears in the deuteronomistic additions. Thus, even through the more common phrases in deuteronom(ist)ic tradition are that one observes commandments, statutes, testimonies, or judgments,[74] the singular form of "statute" that has prompted some scholars to place this unit outside the scope of deuteronomistic tradition may simply be the result of the context, where only one piece of legislation is being discussed. Or, with regard to more problematic language in 12:24–27a, one suspects the influence of predeuteronomistic exodus tradition. The use of "service" (עבדה) as the designation of a festival is not so problematic within deuteronomistic tradition when we note that it occurs only in legislation within the story of the exodus,[75] where the use of "service" to designate a festival fits in well with the older narrative. Yahweh repeatedly demanded that Pharaoh let the Israelites go so that they might serve God.[76] The interplay between traditions with regard to "service" lays the groundwork for a theological conclusion. By using this unexpected term, deuteronomistic tradents underscore that both passover (12:25, 26) and *massot* (13:5) signify not so much freedom as transferred slavery for Israel from Egypt to Yahweh.[77]

Our interpretation has emphasized that deuteronomistic tradents are working from the structure and imagery of the preexilic account of the exodus. Yet it is also clear that deuteronomistic tradents do not hesitate to develop their own unique story. They have fashioned a new structure to the exodus, in which the death of the firstborn must be interpreted as the decisive defeat of Pharaoh and the Egyptians. The imagery of Israel participating in the spoils of war in 12:35–36, the framing of this action as being a fulfillment of 11:2–3, and the instruction of passover in 12:27, where Yahweh's striking of the Egyptians and Israel's deliverance are closely interrelated, suggest that the drama of the exodus (as a confrontation between Yahweh and Pharaoh) is concluded for deuteronomistic tradents at this point in the story. This interpretation is reinforced by the introduction of an itinerary notice in 12:37, which provides a clear boundary between salvation in Egypt and Israel's subsequent journeying with God outside of Egypt.

Deuteronomistic tradents have also shifted the focus away from an exclusive confrontation between Yahweh and Pharaoh by accentuating the roles of both Moses and Israel in the narrative. The character of Moses is expanded through his angry departure from Pharaoh (11:8b) and his extended parenetic instruction with regard to passover (12:21-27). The despoiling motif emphasizes that Israel must participate in Yahweh's holy war against Egypt, and the instruction of passover underscores that this ritual is not so much a celebration of the death to the Egyptian firstborn as it is a commemoration of Israel's protection from the plague. Thus the passover instruction, like the despoiling motif, makes Israel an active participant in the exodus, only this time its action is one of self-protection.

The Exodus from Egypt

Geography, the Exodus, and the Promise of Land

Expulsion from Egypt during the night becomes an extended journey into the wilderness for deuteronomistic tradents with the addition of Exod 12:37-39a and 13:1-16. It is a journey that does not end until Israel crosses the Jordan River in Joshua 3-5. The transition from a single event to a wilderness trek is brought about by the insertion of three new motifs: geographical locations marking the stages of Israel's departure from Egypt (the itinerary notices), the imagery of divine leading (the exodus formula), and the future promise of land. Each of these motifs requires interpretation.

The expulsion of Israel from Egypt (12:39b) was a subordinate motif in the older account of the death to the Egyptian firstborn (12:29-34). In fact, the two events were nearly merged into one. Deuteronomistic tradents separate the two events with the addition of an itinerary notice in 12:37.[78] The geographical notice makes it clear that the death of the Egyptian firstborn takes place at Ramses, whereas the exodus from Egypt brings Israel to Succoth. As a result, the blurring between the death of the Egyptian firstborn and the exodus that had characterized the older narrative is eliminated, so that each event receives attention in its own right at a separate location with a distinct cultic festival. Passover at Ramses commemorates the death of the Egyptian firstborn, while *massot*/firstlings at Succoth commemorates the exodus.[79] The insertion of more precise stopping points turns Israel's expulsion from Egypt into a journey. And the imagery of journeying is enhanced by the confessions of divine leading and future promise of land.

The confession of divine leading from Egypt (the exodus motif) consists of the phrase, "Yahweh brought us out of Egypt." This confession uses stereotyped language that includes the causative form of the verb "to go out" (יצא) with Yahweh as the subject and Israel as the object.[80] The non-causative form of the verb "to go out" can be a technical term for the going out of a slave, while the causative form of the verb can express release from prison.[81] Thus the exodus motif has overtones of social oppression, and probably "expresses a strict liberation from slavery."[82] There may be some hints of such imagery in the early narrative of the exodus, when God announces the attack on the Egyptian firstborn in 11:4 with the words, "About midnight I will go out through Egypt. . . ."[83] Liberation becomes a common motif in the deuteronomistic interpretation of the exodus. Four times Israel is described as "going out" from Egypt (the noncausative form of the verb in Exod 12:39a; 13:3, 4, 8) and four times the exodus is described as a divine liberation (the causative form of the verb in Exod 13:3, 9, 14, 16).

Salvation as divine liberation may have deep roots in Israel's cultic practice.[84] Emerging forms of the motif occur in older poetry such as the "March in the South" theophany tradition (Ps 68:8)[85] and the so-called "Psalm of David" (2 Sam 22:49) to signify how God brought about a reversal (usually in the context of war), which is then celebrated as a liberating act of salvation. Ps 68:8 describes God as "going out" in the imagery of a military march, which occurs in the larger context of a theophany in v. 9: "the earth quaked, the heavens poured down rain at the presence of God."[86] Second Sam 22:49 takes the imagery a step further by employing the causative form of the verb to signify salvation from an enemy, and it further describes this action as both an exaltation and a deliverance.[87] And the Balaam oracles may even contain an early use of liberation imagery with regard to the exodus, since, in Num 23:22 and 24:8, Balaam describes Yahweh as the "God who brought out or liberated (either the king or Israel) from Egypt."[88]

The exodus motif is a central theologoumenon within deuteronomistic tradition for interpreting the exodus as a past event of holy war, which provides motivation for observing deuteronomic law in the present time.[89] The formula occurs frequently and in a variety of contexts throughout Deuteronomy in association with the exodus. Many of the uses are instrumental: Yahweh is described as "having brought out" Israel with a strong hand,[90] with a strong hand and an outstretched arm,[91] and with his presence and with great power.[92] Other uses of the motif are in describing the place or situation from which Israel was rescued: Israel was "brought out" from the iron furnace,[93] from slavery,[94] from the hand of Pharaoh,[95] from the Egyptians,[96] and from the land of Egypt,[97] all of which are characterized as a state of slavery.[98] Israel's past liberation from Egypt then provides the basis for the promulgation of deuteronomic law in the wilderness.[99]

The important role of the exodus motif in Deuteronomy is also carried over into the story of the exodus. The motif provides the content of the commission of Moses in Exodus 3. He is "to bring Israel out of Egypt" (3:10).[100] The risk implied in the future orientation of this commission prompts rejection by Moses (3:11) and then divine reassurance (3:12). The motif returns in Exodus 13 during the promulgation of *massot* and firstlings to signify that the exodus is now a past event. The past orientation of the motif underscores the initial success of Moses in fulfilling his commission.[101] In spite of his success, the exodus motif returns one last time in 14:11 as a complaint by Israel against Moses in the setting of the wilderness.[102] The reappearance of the motif at the outset of the wilderness murmuring tradition (14:11) signifies conflict between Moses and Israel with regard to his commission because of the absence of land.[103] Here the Israelites state that slavery in Egypt is better than their present liberation into the wilderness. Such doubt on the part of Israel has the potential of stopping the story, and it underscores how important it is to deuteronomistic tradents that, as a by-product of God's liberation, Israel have the faith to journey with God through the wilderness.[104] Thus four times Israel is encouraged through parenetic instruction to participate actively in Yahweh's liberation (the causative form of the verb "to go out") by journeying with Moses from Egypt (the noncausative form of the verb in Exod 12:39a; and esp. 13:3, 4, 8).[105] The changing temporal perspective in the placement of the exodus formula in Exodus 3, 13, and 14 suggests that it should be narrowly defined in scope in relation to the specific motif of Israel's "going out" from Egypt and that it does not refer to the conquest of the land.[106]

The promise of the land is separated from the exodus. It is introduced as a distinct motif in Exod 13:5, 11. The promise of land consists of the causative form of the verb "to enter" (בוא) to indicate the divine leading into the land, the verb "to give" (נתן) to signify the divine gift of the land, and the verb "to promise" or "to swear" (נשבע) to underscore how the land is the fulfillment of a divine promise to the ancestors.[107] The confession has a future orientation, which can be translated in the following manner: "When Yahweh brings you into the land . . . which he swore to [you and] your ancestors to give you."[108] Boorer has demonstrated that the uneven distribution of the promise of land as oath signals its importance in deuteronom(ist)ic tradition, and this work need not be repeated here.[109] What is noteworthy is that the verb "to enter" (בוא) with future meaning signals that the land is not a natural or inevitable result of Israel's liberation from Egypt, but a distant and (as yet) unrealized goal.[110] This is a significant departure from earlier interpretations of the exodus, which presupposed the gift of the land in the very act of liberation from Egypt. The separation provides the framework for salvation history.

The salvation history perspective is enhanced when the exodus motif and the promise of land are read together. The verbs used in the two confessions encourage such a reading, since they both convey motion and are often paired as opposites, with the verb "to go out" (יצא) designating a point of departure and the verb "to enter" (בוא) being the goal.[111] Thus the two verbs convey different points of view on a given journey. The deuteronomistic refashioning of the exodus is built around this difference and it

is even enhanced by an additional temporal contrast. The "going out" of
Israel is celebrated as a completed, past event, which the Israelites are called
upon to remember through signs and through teaching, while their
"entering" into land remains a future hope. The wilderness is the vantage
point from which this difference is noted. It is the setting for bringing the
two confessions together into a single story of salvation history. Israel's
active memory of the exodus in the wilderness will provide the assurance
that the future promise of the land is secure.

A Catechism of Salvation History

Deuteronomistic tradents make the perspective of salvation history even
more explicit by bringing the exodus motif and the future promise of land
together with a catechism (Exod 13:8, 14-15) and by repeating similar
catechisms at significant points in Israel's history of salvation through
speeches by Moses and Joshua. The catechisms occur in conjunction with
passover (Exod 12:25-27a), *massot*/firstlings (Exod 13:8, 14-15), the promulgation of law in the wilderness (Deut 6:20-25), and the crossing of the
Jordan into the promised land (Josh 4:6b-7a, 21-24).[112] The distribution
makes it clear that the catechisms are intended to relate the exodus to the
conquest of the land. Yet within this sequence the exodus motif and promise of land are unevenly distributed. The exodus motif is absent from the
passover legislation, and both the exodus motif and promise of land play
no role in the crossing of the Jordan River. Additional study will illustrate
how the uneven distribution of these motifs encourages one to read the
exodus and conquest as one continuous story of salvation history. Interpretation will begin with the catechisms of *massot*/firstlings and deuteronomic law, since both of these are associated with the wilderness and
both contain the exodus motif and promise of land.[113]

Massot *and Firstlings*

Deuteronomistic tradents provide a new interpretation of the exodus by
introducing the instruction regarding *massot* and firstlings in Exod 13:1-16.
After a superscription in vv. 1-2 in which God demands the firstborn,[114]
the remainder of the text shifts to parenetic instruction by Moses. The text
most likely includes older cultic material which has been incorporated by
later tradents.[115] The catechism is held together with a variety of phrases
that are best characterized as being deuteronomistic.[116] These phrases
include the listing of the nations that occupy Canaan (13:5),[117] the description of Egypt as being the "house of slavery" (13:3, 14),[118] the call for Israel
"to remember" (13:3),[119] the description of the land as "flowing with milk
and honey" (13:5),[120] the "strong arm" of God (13:9),[121] the older Canaanite
calendrical reckoning with the month of Abib (13:4),[122] as well as specific
references to phylacteries (13:9, 16).[123] The present form of Exod 13:3-16

divides almost symmetrically between *massot* (3-9[10]) and firstlings (11-16). Each section contains the promise of land (vv. 5/11), instruction (vv. 8/14-15), a sign (vv. 9/14), and the exodus motif (vv. 9/16).[124]

The instruction is presented in 13:8, 14-15 as a question and answer between a child and an adult.[125] Soggin has clarified how the exchange is not simply about a child's curiosity, but rather cultic ritual.[126] The aim is to provide an aetiology for the cultic practice of firstlings as a result of Israel's salvation from Egypt.[127] Long, building on the work of Soggin, has demonstrated that the larger context of firstlings in 13:11-16 has been fashioned in such a way that its aetiological function is expanded, both with the addition of a sign formula (v. 16)[128] and with a larger framework (vv. 11-13, 16), which he identifies as a sign schema consisting of three parts: the identification of X (vv. 11-13), X as a sign (v. 16a), and the meaning of X as a sign (v. 16b).[129] Long has also argued that the provision for instruction to future generations in Exod 13:8 should be interpreted as an abridged form of the instruction in 13:14-15, even though it lacks the complete sequence of question and answer. He notes the obvious similarities between 13:8 and the answer in 13:14b,[130] and the parallels extending further to include the same three-part sequence of a sign schema when the larger context of 13:3-9(10)[131] is brought into focus: the identification of X (vv. 5-7), X as a sign (v. 9a), and the meaning of X as a sign (v. 9b).[132]

Several aspects of Exod 13:1-16 stand out as a result of the work of Soggin and Long. Soggin has clearly underscored the aetiological and cultic character of the catechism in Exod 13:14-15. Long has illustrated how the catechism actually repeats in Exod 13:8 and 14-15, and his form-critical analysis has underscored that the catechisms are interrelated with larger literary structures. What is missing in these studies is the important role of the future promise of the land as an independent element within this symmetrical structure. When the future promise of land is separated out and added as a distinct feature, Long's interpretation yields the following two-part structure to Exod 13:3-16, including elements of a future promise of land, a sign formula, instruction, and the three-part sign schema in which the meaning of the sign is clarified by the exodus motif.

Massot	Firstlings
(The promise of land): v. 5a	(The promise of land): v. 11
(1) Identification of X—Massot: vv. 5b-7	(1) Identification of X—Firstborn: vv. 12-13
(Catechetical instruction): v. 8	(Catechetical instruction): vv. 14-15
(2) X as a sign: v. 9a Sign formula	(2) X as a sign: v. 16a Sign formula
(3) Meaning of X as a sign: 9:b Exodus motif	(3) Meaning of X as a sign: v. 16b Exodus motif

Exod 13:3–16 alerts us to the possibility of a large pattern of repetition
between the catechisms in Exod 12:21–27; 13:1–16; Deut 6:4–25; and Joshua
4. This larger pattern includes (1) a double occurrence of the catechism,
(2) its aetiological function, which is reinforced by a sign formula as well as
a sign schema, (3) the future promise of land, and (4) the exodus motif.

Deuteronomic Law

Deut 6:4–25 is a parenetic speech by Moses, which is meant to provide an
aetiology for the promulgation of deuteronomic law toward the end of
Israel's wilderness wandering.[133] Although Deut 6:4–25 may have gone
through a history of composition,[134] in its present form it comes closest to
repeating the central motifs from Exod 13:1–16, where *massot*/firstlings
were promulgated at the outset of Israel's wilderness journey. Weinfeld
has gone so far as to conclude that Deut 6:4–25 is patterned after Exod
13:1–16.[135] Comparison of the four features from Exodus 13:1–16 supports
his conclusion. All of the motifs repeat. Deut 6:4–25 includes a double
occurrence of the catechism (an abridged form in Deut 6:7 and the complete form in 6:20–25), a sign formula (Deut 6:8–9), the future promise of
land (Deut 6:10 and perhaps also 17, 23), and the exodus motif (Deut 6:12,
21, 23). In spite of the strong parallels between the two texts, Deut 6:4–25
contrasts to Exod 13:1–16 by focusing on law rather than a specific cultic
rite, and by being structured into a somewhat different pattern.[136] The difference in structure becomes evident when one looks for the sign schema.
Although present, it is less clear than in Exod 13:1–16,[137] possibly as the
result of the less specific nature of law as forming the basis for the
aetiology.[138] The more general focus on law, in turn, lends itself better to
the structuring elements of the covenant-treaty form.[139]

Two points of similarity between Exod 13:1–16 and Deut 6:4–25 are
of particular interest for interpreting the function of the catechisms throughout the deuteronomistic history. The first is that Yahweh's liberation of
Israel from Egypt has a prominent role in the text (Deut 6:12, 21, 23) as it
did in Exod 13:1–16 (Exod 13:3, 9, 14, 16). Moreover, in both texts the
exodus motif must be narrowly defined as referring only to Israel's "going
out" from Egypt, which functions as a past event giving authority to
the promulgation of legislation in the present time.[140] The second point of
similarity is the future promise of land. Both the promulgation of *massot*/
firstlings at the outset of the wilderness journey and deuteronomic law
at its close have a future orientation, which is underscored by syntax:
"When Yahweh (your God) has brought you to the land . . . as he promised. . . ."[141] When read together, Exod 13:1–16 and Deut 6:4–25 provide
aetiologies for celebrating *massot*/firstlings and for observing deuteronomic
law, both of which are aimed at Israel's future life in the land and made
possible initially by Israel's exodus from Egypt. The former text focuses
on specific cultic rites, while the later explores the more general role of
deuteronomic law within the framework of the covenant-treaty form.

Passover

The passover instruction in Exod 12:21-27 presents strong points of simi-larity to both Exod 13:1-16 and Deut 6:4-25. The instruction is promul-gated as parenesis by Moses, it includes instruction in the question-and-answer format (vv. 26-27), and it emphasizes the future orientation of the legislation by placing the observance of passover in the land.[142] In addi-tion, Long has argued that the text exhibits a variety of aetiological functions.[143] Yet there are also differences. Most significantly, the exodus formula is absent. But the double occurrence of the catechism is also miss-ing. In addition the form of the promise of land has Israel (rather than Yahweh) as the subject of the verb "to enter," which occurs here in the noncausative form. Finally, in spite of the clear aetiological function of the text, there is no specific sign formula in association with the blood of the passover sacrifice or with any other specific cultic object or observance. Thus, when interpretation is restricted to Exod 12:21-27, parallels to the instruction from Exod 13:1-16 are limited to three of the four features—the catechism, the future promise of land, and the aetiological function of the text—while within each of these, differences remain.

Some of the differences can be accounted for by the place of passover within the deuteronomistic interpretation of the exodus.[144] Passover occurs in Egypt at Ramses and is separated from the promulgation of *massot*/firstlings at Succoth. This geographical separation indicates that passover is not a festival about the exodus. Rather it commemorates Israel's escape from the plague of death in Egypt.[145] The absence of the exodus motif reinforces this conclusion. The exodus motif is defined narrowly in deuteronomistic tradition in relationship to Israel's march out of Egypt—so narrowly, in fact, that its introduction into the larger story of the exo-dus has even been separated geographically from the passover legislation. The absence of the exodus motif has, in turn, influenced the form of the promise of land, which at this point does not emphasize divine leading into the land (the causative form of the verb "to enter" with Yahweh as the subject), but Israel's obligation to repeat the passover in Canaan (the noncausative form of the verb "to enter" with Israel as the subject). The fulfillment of this obligation takes place at Gilgal in the deuteronomistic history.[146]

The placement of passover at Ramses in Egypt raises the suspicion that this festival is meant to function in the larger context of the plagues, of which the death of the Egyptian firstborn is the culmination. The instruc-tion in 12:27 reinforces such a suspicion, since it states that passover com-memorates Israel's protection from the plague of death. Once the close relationship between the passover and the larger plague cycle is noted, then the deuteronomistic insertion of instruction at the outset of the plague of locusts (10:1b-2a) also takes on a larger function in relationship with passover (12:21-27). Thematically, these two instances of instruction bind the plagues and passover together as destructive actions aimed primarily at the Egyptians, while structurally the combination brings the plagues/passover into conformity with Exod 13:1-16 and Deut 6:4-25 through the double occurrence of instruction (an abridged form in 10:1b-2a and the full form in 12:26-27),[147] and, perhaps also with the introduction of the motif of signs.[148] When the plagues/passover instruction (Exod 10:1b-2a; 12:21-27) is brought into relationship with *massot*/firstlings (13:1-16) and deuteronomic law (Deut 6:4-25), it becomes clear that all the speeches by Moses share a future orientation because of the reference to the land throughout his instruction.[149]

Crossing the Jordan

The final occurrence of a catechism is in Joshua 4. This instruction is also a parenetic speech, but this time by Joshua.[150] The larger boundaries of this text should include at least Josh 3:1-5:1, since the instruction in 4:6b-7 and 21-24 occurs in the larger context of Israel's crossing the Jordan River.[151] This text presents a far more complicated tradition-historical development than any of the speeches of Moses with regard to the earliest form of the legend and its relationship to cultic practice—including the role of the ark and priests in the story, the role of Joshua in the earliest stages of the tradition, and the process of transmission.[152] When the text is approached with an eye on the catechisms, however, it is clear that there are at least two distinct interpretations of the crossing of the Jordan. Both are meant to provide an aetiology for the twelve stones. In Jos 4:6b-7 the twelve stones signify how the water of the Jordan was cut off (כרת) when the ark of Yahweh crossed (עבר) it, whereas in Josh 4:21-24 the focus shifts to the Israelites, who are described as crossing (עבר) the Jordan on dry ground (ביבשה) as a result of Yahweh's having dried up (הוביש) the river as he had previously done to the Red Sea.

Josh 4:6b-7 is the older of the two catechisms.[153] A comparison of language reveals that its horizon is much more limited than that of the second catechism in Josh 4:21-24. The address of Joshua in Josh 4:6b-7 is narrow in scope, being aimed at his immediate audience (e.g., "when *your children* ask . . ." "say to *them* . . ."). The immediacy of this question is expanded in Josh 4:21-24 with a more abstract statement that now includes many generations (e.g., "when your children ask their parents . . ." "you will inform your children . . .").[154] The broadening of the intended audience is carried over into the instruction which is symbolized by the changing location of the stones.[155] In Josh 4:6b-7 the stones are in the middle of the Jordan at the exact location where the ark has cut off the waters.[156] The stones symbolize the power of God to control the Jordan River, and how such power arose from Yahweh's possession of the land.[157] In the second catechism the stones no longer stand in the middle of the Jordan River but are now erected in Canaan at Gilgal. The new location transforms their symbolic significance. Their horizon is no longer limited to the Jordan River or Yahweh's power simply over the land. Instead, their symbolic significance now reaches all the way back to the exodus in order to include the Red Sea.[158] They symbolize Yahweh's power over Israel's entire history of salvation, conceived as both an exodus and a conquest. The broader perspective also introduces Israel into the story as an active participant. Israel is now described as crossing the Jordan on dry ground, in contrast to the older catechism where the focus was simply on Yahweh or the ark.[159]

Formal similarity to the previous catechisms emerges when the two catechisms are read together in the larger narrative setting of Joshua 4. The crossing of the Jordan is structured around a double occurrence of instruction (4:6b–7; 21–24), and the entire narrative takes on an aetiological function with regard to the meaning of the twelve stones, which is reinforced by a sign formula (4:6a). Additional phrases interrelate Joshua 4 in smaller ways to the language of the other catechisms. The sign of the stones in the midst of Israel, their function as a remembrance, and their enduring significance are expressed in language that occurs in the other catechisms.[160] Yet the similarity only accentuates how the content of Joshua 4 has shifted drastically. The future orientation of the land as a divine promise, which dominated the three speeches by Moses, is absent in the speech by Joshua, as is the exodus motif. In place of these motifs, the imagery of Yahweh's triumph over sea/river now dominates. And as the instruction states explicitly in Josh 4:23, the imagery of divine enthronement is meant to complete the confrontation at the Red Sea, thus providing a basis for Israel's present possession of the land.[161]

Salvation History

The points of similarity and contrast provide the basis for interpreting the overall sequence of the catechisms. Deuteronomistic tradents have used the device of parenetic instruction by Moses and Joshua in order to present their interpretation of the exodus. The uneven distribution of the exodus motif and of the future promise of land underscores that the catechisms are being shaped or edited with an eye on the whole in order to reinforce the restructuring of the exodus into three distinct events: (1) the death of Egyptian firstborn, (2) the exodus from Egypt, and (3) the event at the sea, which extends through the crossing of the Jordan. The content of the catechisms reinforces the structure of salvation history. The passover signifies the death of Egyptian firstborn as a plague which Israel avoided in Egypt, *massot*/firstlings commemorate the exodus at Succoth as being both a liberation from Egypt and the beginning of a wilderness journey, while the stones at Gilgal mark Yahweh's power over sea/river in providing the gift of the land. The instruction associated with deuteronomic law reviews this structure up to Israel's entrance into the land and, in the process, provides the means whereby Israel can journey successfully with God through the wilderness and live a prosperous life in the land in exclusive service to God.

Joshua 4 is the oldest version of the catechisms. Although the instruction concerning passover, *massot*, and firstlings clearly contains predeuteronomistic tradition, there are no indications that either 12:21-27 or 13:1-16 has gone through an overly complex transmission history to reach its present form. The same may not be true of Deut 6:4-25 and is certainly not the case with Joshua 4. There is debate among scholars concerning the literary development of Josh 3:1-5:1 and the degree to which it has been influenced by oral cultic tradition. Yet, even allowing for debate, there is little doubt that this text evinces a more complex history of tradition than the other catechisms. Comparison of Joshua 4 with the other catechisms leads to the hypothesis that the genre was originally anchored in the instruction by Joshua at the crossing of the Jordan River (Joshua 4) and that it was extended backward to include the speeches by Moses in the Tetrateuch (Exod 10:1b-2a; 12:21-27; 13:1-16) and in Deuteronomy (6:4-25). This development leads to the literary hypothesis that in deuteronomistic tradition, the Tetrateuch supplements the history of the kingdoms (Joshua-2 Kings) in order to form a history of salvation.

Salvation by the Sea

The catechism in Josh 4:21-24 has already underscored the preference of deuteronomistic tradents to characterize the sea of the exodus as the "Red Sea" (ים־סוף). This preference is not confined to the deuteronomistic history. Indeed, the following study will illustrate a systematic "Red Sea" reading of Exod 13:17-15:26, in which the confrontation at the sea is historicized in the setting of the wilderness. The effect of this historicizing is that the holy-war character of the event is played down, while the sequence of events is expanded to accentuate that the destruction of the Egyptians also inaugurates Israel's wilderness march. The journey of the Israelites through the wilderness is not complete until they cross the Jordan River to begin the conquest of Canaan.

The Red Sea

The term ים־סוף ("Red Sea") is not an innovation by deuteronomistic tradents, since it already occurs in the Song of the Sea when Pharaoh and his army are described in Exod 15:4 as being destroyed בים־סוף.[162] The meaning of the phrase in the Song of the Sea provides an important starting point for interpreting the development of this term in deuteronomistic tradition, and, indeed, there is a history of debate around this problem beginning even with the translation of the Hebrew. The translation "Red Sea" is based on the LXX, which translates the phrase with the Greek εν ερυθρα θαλασση. A competing translation, "Reed Sea" is also common, going back to such early commentators as Jerome and Rashi, who reasoned that when the Hebrew word סוף is used alone, it designates "reeds" or "rushes."[163] The translation "Reed Sea" received support in more recent scholarship when the Hebrew סוף was considered to be a loanword from Egyptian *twf(y)*, meaning "reed" or "papyrus."[164] The debate over translation has tended to focus on geography in order to determine the route of Israel's exodus, in which case it is argued that the Reed Sea designates a different body of water further north than the Red Sea (i.e., the Gulf of Suez).[165] This debate is not particularly helpful for interpreting Exod 15:4, since the geography of the exodus does not appear to play an important role in the song. As a result, neither translation alone probes the significance of the phrase in its context within the Song of the Sea.

Snaith recognized the problem of focusing too exclusively on geography to interpret the phrase ים־סוף in Song of the Sea, and in view of this problem, he shifted his inquiry to a more mythological approach.[166] He noted that the context of Exod 15:4–5 is not about geography but about creation mythology, especially the fact that creation is conceived as a fight against the monster of chaos. Evidence for this conclusion included the words "the deeps" and "depths" in 15:5, which when read in conjunction with 15:4 results in a progression from "the sea," to the ים־סוף, and finally to the great primeval Sea, which has been "God's enemy since before the foundation of the world."[167] The strongly mythological context of the Song of the Sea provided the basis for Snaith to conclude that the Hebrew ים־סוף means "[t]hat distant scarcely known sea away to the south, of which no [hu]man knew the boundary. It was the sea at the end of the land."[168] The meaning "sea at the end of the land" prompted Snaith to suggest a revocalizing from the word סוף to סף (which in Hebrew means "end").[169]

Batto extended the work of Snaith by demonstrating how the Hebrew word סוף in the Song of the Sea could actually take on the meaning of "end" or "extinction" without revocalization.[170] He argued that the mythological associations in the Song of Jonah explain the presence of ים־סוף in Exod 15:4, where the phrase functions simply as the B word in the poetic pair ים־סוף/ /ים.[171] Batto concluded that the term has no more historical or geographical reference in the Song of the Sea than the A word, ים (= "sea," or as Batto prefers, "sea-dragon"). He went on to suggest that at this stage of tradition ים־סוף should not be translated with the geographical designation "Red Sea," but with the more mythological term "Sea of End/Extinction." The primary meaning of the phrase "Sea of Extinction" in the Song of the Sea is to describe the destruction of the Egyptians.[172]

The ים־סוף was taken up in deuteronom(ist)ic tradition.[173] Deuteronomistic tradents are familiar with the meaning of ים־סוף as signifying mythological water which destroys the Egyptian army. In speeches by Moses (Deut 11:4) and by Joshua (Josh 24:6) this interpretation is recounted.[174] But other uses underscore how its meaning is also expanded. First, the chaos water imagery of the Song of the Sea is extended so that it signifies not only the destruction of the Egyptians but also the salvation of Israel. This new interpretation is evident in Josh 2:10 and 4:23, where ים־סוף is dried up by Yahweh so that Israel could journey through the chaotic waters.[175] In these texts the sea has become a symbol of Israel's salvation (or perhaps better, their birth as a nation) through metaphors of travel, while the destruction of the Egyptians is absent altogether.[176] A second transformation of יְם־סוּף builds off the imagery of travel that was already present in Josh 2:10 and 4:23, but this imagery is taken in another direction. The יְם־סוּף is historicized as the southernmost boundary to the land of Canaan (e.g., Exod 23:31; 1 Kgs 9:26), as a road through the wilderness (e.g., Exod 13:18; Num 14:25; 21:4; Deut 1:40; 2:1), and perhaps even as a location in Israel's wilderness travels (e.g., Exod 15:22; Num 33:10-11; Judg 11:16). This historicizing tendency warrants the LXX translation "Red Sea."[177]

The historicizing of the Red Sea both as water through which Israel passes and as a road into the wilderness provides the hermeneutical key for tracing the deuteronomistic interpretation of Exod 13:17–15:26. References to the Red Sea frame the confrontation at the sea, occurring in travel notices leading up to the event (13:17–18a, 20) and following it (15:22). In both of these instances the setting of the wilderness is stressed. In fact the framing actually transfers the setting of the event from Egypt to the wilderness.[178] In addition, references to the Red Sea both as a road (13:18a)[179] and as a specific location (15:22)[180] indicate that the confrontation at the sea has been historicized, an interpretation that encourages a similar reading of the mythological waters in the Song of the Sea (Exod 15:4). The end result is that the Red Sea becomes a doorway for Israel's journey into the wilderness, rather than the occasion for Yahweh's decisive victory over evil. And this reading prompts reinterpretations within the narrative account.

The confrontation at the sea was structured around a war oracle by Moses, which progressed in the following manner: Israel cried out to Yahweh at the approach of the Egyptian army (v. 10), and Moses responded with a war oracle (vv. 13–14), prompting a divine command that Moses stretch out his hand/staff over the sea (v. 16a*a*). This sequence resulted in the destruction of the Egyptians in the sea. Deuteronomistic tradents accentuate the wilderness and frame both the war oracle and the divine command with new material. The wilderness setting is noted twice in the description of the Israelites' approach to the sea (Exod 13:18a, 20) and then again when they complain to Moses at the approach of the Egyptian army (Exod 14:11-12),[181] inaugurating a pattern that continues throughout the wilderness stories.[182] The war oracle (vv. 13–14) is framed by human (vv. 11–12) and divine complaint (v. 15a*b*), while the command concerning the staff/hand of Moses is framed by travel instructions for Israel (vv. 15b, 16b). This framing yields a new interpretation of events, in which the holy-war character of the war oracle by Moses is played down in order to accentuate that Israel entered the sea on dry ground.[183]

Holy war is already played down in Exod 13:17b, when the reader is informed that Yahweh orchestrated a route that was meant to avoid war, because Israel was not yet ready for such a test of faith.[184] This perspective is developed further when the war oracle of Moses (Exod 14:13-14) is framed by human (14:11-12) and divine (15:ab) complaint. The murmuring of the Israelites in Exod 14:11-12 provides confirmation of the divine apprehension in Exod 13:17b that they were not yet ready for holy war. Their murmuring introduces a new point of tension between the people and Moses/Yahweh that is carried through to the divine complaint (v. 15ab) immediately after the war oracle (vv. 13-14). This complaint has caused problems for interpreters because it does not fit the context nor does it follow the sequence of events in the older narrative.[185] It is as though Yahweh has forgotten the setting and the circumstances of the story, since he addresses Moses (rather than Israel) with a question filled with exasperation—"Why do you cry out to me?"—at the very moment when Moses appears to be an ideal of faithfulness. Yet the overall design of the redaction underscores that Yahweh and Israel are talking to each other through Moses. The divine complaint, therefore, must be read in combination with Israel's previous complaint to Moses. The result is that the divine complaint functions as a modification of the war oracle in Exod 14:13-14 in response to Israel's murmuring.

Modification of the war oracle is also accompanied by a change in focus from holy war against the Egyptians to divine leading of Israel. Framing once again signals the change. The divine command within the older narrative that Moses stretch out his hand/staff over the water (14:16aα) is now couched in travel instructions for Israel to march ahead (14:15b) and to enter the sea (14:16b). Such framing results in the Israelites' acquiring a more prominent role in the story. They no longer stand by passively as Yahweh wages war on their behalf. Instead, they are required to follow God by entering (בוא) or walking (הלך) into the sea (בתוך הים) on dry ground (ביבשה). This language is stereotyped and it repeats no less than four times (Exod 14:16b, 22a, 29a; 15:19),[186] following the command and fulfillment pattern of the older narrative.[187] The overall effect of the insertions is that the action of Moses in stretching his hand/staff on the water has less to do with the holy war between Yahweh and Egyptian than with Israel's escape. As a result Israel's perception of the confrontation at the sea also becomes important to deuteronomistic tradents. Their version of the story ends by underscoring how Israel acquired a fear of Yahweh and faith in Moses from this event (14:31).[188]

The imagery of Israel following God into the sea interrelates the confrontation at the sea with Israel's journey into the wilderness. And as a result, movement becomes a central feature of the story. No longer is the confrontation at the sea a static story in which Yahweh confronts and overwhelms the Egyptian army. Such a stationary view of God gives way to a mobile presentation of the divine. In Exod 13:17-18a God is already described as leading Israel, and such imagery returns in Exod 14:19a with the "Messenger of God" (מלאך האלהים).[189] Although the Messenger of God embodies holy war characteristics especially in relationship to the land,[190] in the setting of the wilderness the attributes of rescue and leading tend to predominate.[191] It is the imagery of leading and rescue that predominates in Exod 14:19a. Movement is also central in the presentation of Israel and Egypt. Both characters are described as entering (בוא) into the midst of the sea. Israel enters the sea to escape the Egyptian army, while the latter are destroyed because they enter (בוא) the sea (אל־תוך הים) in pursuit of the Israelites, an action that results in the water covering (כסה) them.[192] This action is described three times (Exod 14:23, 28; 15:19). Thus, entrance into the sea is two-sided in the deuteronomistic reading. It leads to destruction for the Egyptians but is a rite of passage from Egypt to the wilderness for Israelites.

The Jordan River

The close relationship between the Red Sea and the Jordan River has long caught the attention of scholars. Lauha noted that the beginning and the ending of the wilderness wanderings were framed by parallel events concerning the drying up of water.[193] Coats has built off the work of Lauha by providing a more detailed description of how the drying up of the Red Sea provides a doorway for Israel to march into the wilderness and how this event is recounted, first, in the spy story of Joshua 2, in order to set the stage for the conquest of the land, and then again in the catechism of Josh 4:21–24, where the two events are brought into an explicit relationship through the symbol of the stones.[194] Cross is one of several scholars who has demonstrated that the merging of the Red Sea and the Jordan River goes beyond literary stylistics or poetics and that this pattern reflects the mythological influence of Baal's conflict with Sea (Yamm) and River (Nahar).[195] The research in comparative religion has demonstrated how the power of the deity to control chaotic water, symbolized by Yamm-Nahar, is historicized in ancient Israel to provide the framework for interpreting salvation as an exodus and a conquest.[196] My aim in this section is to explore in more detail the relationship between the exodus and conquest.

There are clear differences between the accounts of the Red Sea and the Jordan River crossing.[197] The crossing of the Jordan River is a story about holy war conceived as a conquest of the land. The central role of the ark makes this point clear.[198] And as an account of conquest, the story has an outward focus. It is aimed toward the nations who dwell in the land in order to instill terror in them.[199] The conquest imagery and outward focus of the narrative are underscored by the verb "to cross over" (עבר). Hulst has noted that the verb "to cross over" takes on theological connotations in Deuteronomy, where it signifies action that must take place if Israel is to achieve the divine promise of the land at the end of their wilderness march.[200] It is not surprising, therefore, that this team occurs frequently in Joshua 1–5. A total of twenty-two times the ark,[201] the people,[202] the leaders of the tribes,[203] the tribes east of the Jordan,[204] and even the cultic stones are described as crossing the Jordan River for conquest.[205]

The prominence of holy war imagery in the crossing of the Jordan River contrasts sharply with the deuteronomistic reading of the confrontation at the sea, where holy war is played down. In this story God leads Israel along the Red Sea road in order to avoid war. The difference is underscored by contrasting verbs. The motif of crossing over (עבר) is avoided completely in the account of the exodus in favor of the imagery of Israel entering (בוא) the sea, while the imagery of divine leading is also reversed. The Messenger of God remains behind the Israelites as they enter the sea, as opposed to leading them in conquest.[206] The contrasts underscore that the Red Sea has less to do with a holy-war confrontation between Yahweh and the Egyptians than with the Israelites' escape from Egypt and their inward transformation. The emphasis on fear and faith in the people at the end of the confrontation at the sea underscores this point.

The differences between the Red Sea and the Jordan River should not obscure the fact that the stories are meant to be read together. Their interrelationship is made explicit in the expanded catechism of Josh 4:21-24. The differences inform the reader that the two stories serve distinct functions. And indeed, when the relationship between the two is pursued a clear chronology of salvation history emerges, in which Israel initially enters (בוא) into the Red Sea upon leaving Egypt and commencing their wilderness march, with the hope that one day they would cross (עבר) the Jordan River to begin their conquest of the land. The chronology brings us back to Lauha's original insight that the wilderness is presently framed by parallel events which accentuate Yahweh's power over sea and river and that this framing is providing the backbone for an interpretation of salvation history.[207]

A CELEBRATION OF SALVATION HISTORY

The Plot Structure of the Exodus as Salvation History

The cult is the institutional setting for the writing of the salvation history.[208] Thus it is the cult that provides the plot structure for the deuteronomistic reinterpretation of the exodus. Mettinger has argued that the deuteronomistic reformation during the late monarchy period and into the exilic period was a Copernican revolution of the Israelite cult. He notes several significant innovations from the time of the Josianic reform onward that combine to inaugurate a process of fragmentation of the unified autumn festival in the Jerusalem cult. These innovations include the emergence of passover as a central pilgrimage festival, and with it a shift to a spring calendar; the introduction of a Name Theology that emphasized divine transcendence over the more imminent theology of the Jerusalem cult; a shift in creation theology from a more primeval focus to the formation of Israel as a people; an emphasis on covenant and law; and a tendency to historicize salvation. The result of these transformations was that the cultic celebration of the exodus became more an a act of remembrance than the previously sacramental experience of the theophanic coming and victory of Yahweh in the Zion cult.[209] Mettinger's broadly based conclusions concerning the deuteronomic reform movement provide the background for probing the cultic setting of the deuteronomistic refashioning of the exodus, and more particularly, how the cultic setting provides the plot structure for salvation history.

The refashioning of the plot structure of the exodus supports the conclusions of Mettinger concerning the tendency of the deuteronom(ist)ic school to fragment the cultic practice of Zion. The introduction of the itinerary notices certainly fragments the more unified cultic liturgy of the preexilic narrative. What had been a compact story with precise temporal markings from midnight to dawn becomes a more extended event in which distinct itinerary stops have been superimposed. The once unified account of the Day of Yahweh is separated into distinct events, which take place at different locations over an extended period of time. The effect on the plot structure of the story is enormous. Israel no longer celebrates the death of the Egyptian army at the break of day. Instead the Israelites are still in Egypt hiding in their houses at sunrise in order to avoid the divine plague of death.[210]

The rejection of the Day of Yahweh, however, does not signify a rejection of the cultic setting of the text, but rather indicates its replacement by passover and *massot*/firstlings. The catechisms, with their focus on intergenerational teaching, underscore how cultic practice has been historicized in deuteronomistic tradition, as an act of remembrance.[211] Passover commemorates how Israel was spared the plague of death, while *massot* and firstlings memorialize the exodus from Egypt and look toward Israel's future life in the land. The historicizing of worship is developed further by precise geographical locations for each event within a new temporal framework. Passover takes place during the night in Egypt at Ramses, where Israel remains until the next morning. The instruction for *massot*/firstlings occurs the next day when Israel journeys to Succoth. The time of these rites is the spring month of Abib and together they require eight days to observe (the night of passover plus the seven days of *massot* which ends in a festival).[212] Even though the festivals of passover and *massot* are clearly interrelated, their separate locations underscore that they are not merged into one unified festival in deuteronomistic tradition.

The geographical distinction between passover and *massot*/firstlings signals two very different points of view with regard to salvation. Passover at Ramses is a cultic act that commemorates Yahweh's salvific intervention from the perspective of Egypt. Thus it is a cultic act about death, which does not celebrate so much the death of the Egyptians as it does Israel's avoidance of it.[213] By locating this cultic action in Egypt, it makes clear that the point of reference for passover is a past divine act and that participation in this ceremony only allows one to escape divine destruction. *Massot* and firstlings at Succoth, on the other hand, commemorate salvation from the perspective of the wilderness and land, and there is a logical order to their arrangement in Exod 13:1-16. The primary focus is on firstlings. This fact is evident by the superscription in vv. 1-2 and by the order of the text, in which instruction concerning firstlings both introduces (vv. 1-2) and concludes (vv. 11-16) the material on *massot* (vv. 3-10). The arrangement of the text is reinforced by the content of the instruction, which is different for *massot* and firstlings. The instruction in 13:8 underscores that *massot* commemorates Israel's exodus out of Egypt,[214] while 13:14-15 turns the readers' attention back to the death of the Egyptian firstborn,[215] thus blurring somewhat the geographical distinction between Ramses and Succoth.

The structure of Exodus 13:1-16 indicates the subordinate role of *massot* in the context of the exodus. It celebrates Israel's journey out of Egypt, and in this sense it is both an extension of passover and a necessary prerequisite for firstlings, but it cannot be an end in itself. *Massot* must culminate in the dedication of firstlings, which can take place only in the future context of the land. Once it is clear that the primary focus in the instruction at Succoth is on firstlings, then it also becomes evident that this event is functioning in relationship to passover. It provides an interpretation of the death of the Egyptian firstborn from the perspective of the land. Firstlings signifies Yahweh's claim on all firstborn in the land.[216] Passover, with its setting in Egypt, and, firstlings, with its projected setting in the land, celebrate two different perspectives on Yahweh's salvific intervention in Egypt. These cultic acts are joined by *massot*, the celebration of Israel's journey from Egypt to the land through the wilderness. Here we begin to see that the cultic acts are themselves the basis for a history of salvation and that the goal of salvation history is a future life in the land.

The Character of God in History

Holy war plays a central role in the past event of the exodus (the death of the Egyptian firstborn and the act of leaving Egypt) and in the future conquest of the land, but it is played down in the present time of wilderness journeying. The despoiling motif emphasized the holy war context of the death to the Egyptian firstborn, underscoring that Yahweh's victory was so overwhelming that Israel left Egypt with booty. The exodus motif also added a dimension of holy war to Israel's departure from Egypt, since the central verb "to go out" signifies divine reversals in the context of war. Yet we have also seen how holy war is played down in the confrontation at the sea. The travel notice in Exod 13:17-18a made it clear that Yahweh orchestrated a route that was meant to avoid war. The reason for the change in focus is the separation of the confrontation at the sea into an exodus and a conquest. Once the separation is in place, it is the future conquest that takes over holy-war imagery in the deuteronomistic history. The shift of holy-war imagery from a present defeat of Pharaoh at the sea to a future conquest is a significant restructuring of the story. Such restructuring of holy war implies a reconceptualization of divine power from being unilateral to a more relational view at least with regard to Yahweh's relationship with Israel.

On a first reading, the deuteronomistic version of the exodus also appears to be unilateral in how it conceptualizes Yahweh's strength. This is especially true if the story is read from the perspective of the preexilic narrative, where the focus was simply a confrontation between Yahweh and Pharaoh and where Israel played no active role. If this narrower perspective is maintained, then the central tension of the story continues to be whether Yahweh has the ability to produce his intended effects on Pharaoh. The lack of editing to the plague cycle, the intensification of the death to the Egyptian firstborn with the holy-war motif of despoiling, and the eventual destruction of the Egyptian army in the Red Sea all reinforce a reading that emphasizes unilateral power in much the same way as does the older narrative.

Where the deuteronomistic redaction significantly departs from the earlier account is in introducing Israel into the story as an active and independent character, who can affect the outcome of events at a number of places. The despoiling motif accentuated Israel's need to participate in Yahweh's holy war against Egypt. The passover underscored that even the people of God were required to seek cultic protection from Yahweh's plague of death. The exodus motif emphasized that Yahweh's act of liberation also required that Israel make a decision to journey with God. And the emphasis on journeying was also carried through in the event at the sea with the new imagery of Israels entering the water as part of Yahweh's salvation. Finally, Israel's important role in shaping the outcome of the story in a potentially negative way was foreshadowed in the confrontation at the sea, where deuteronomistic tradents insert the murmuring motif at the outset of the wilderness stories.

The introduction of the wilderness is the most significant addition to the story in redefining divine power. The wilderness turns the exodus into an incomplete story, requiring Israel to make repeated decisions about whether or not they will journey with God. It is only in the process of their making these decisions that the story of the exodus can continue to take on concrete form. When Israel despoiled the Egyptians, the story moved ahead to an exodus from Egypt. But when they murmured against Moses at the Red Sea, their actions prompted divine complaint. The very different outcomes of the first and second generation illustrate how important the wilderness becomes in the deuteronomistic interpretation of the exodus. Once Israel is confronted with real choices whose outcomes are not immediately apparent to God, then they no longer function as an impersonal gauge for measuring divine strength. They can no longer be passive observers of Yahweh's victory at the sea. Instead, they emerge as an independent and active character in an incomplete history of salvation. The independence of Israel in shaping its history influences the exercise of divine power and even the very character of God. One implication of Israel's more active role is that the relationship between God and the people of God becomes the point of focus for interpreting divine power, rather than the exclusive focus on Yahweh in older tradition. As a consequence, the very conception of divine power shifts from control or dominance over Israel to influence or persuasion.

Persuasion means that power is exercised bidirectionally in deuteronomistic tradition between Yahweh and Israel. To paraphrase the words of Loomer, it means that power is now conceived both as an active exertion to produce an effect and as a more passive ability to undergo an effect. Such a refashioning of power not only propels Israel into a new and more influential role with regard to the course of salvation history, it also transforms the divine character. God can undergo change in relationship to the people of God, depending on what decisions they make. Faithful participation in the risk of salvation prompts divine leading, but murmuring can engender divine complaint. And once the very character of God can undergo change in relationship to Israel's actions, then the future must be seen as remaining open. Relational power, therefore, gives rise to ambiguity, which is symbolized by the wilderness. The setting of the wilderness does not allow salvation history to reach any firm conclusion. As a consequence, the deuteronomistic history lacks the orderliness of the older narrative, in which Yahweh's kingship was celebrated as a present reality, from the perspective of the land. For deuteronomistic tradents, divine rule can be celebrated only as a future hope, realized through the concrete interaction of Yahweh and Israel in the wilderness. The accumulated experience of this concrete interaction is the content of salvation history.

One final result in the transformation of divine power is that the exodus ceases to be a story in support of the kingdom. The setting of the wilderness is itself a rejection of a national cult. Passover further confirms this conclusion. It critically evaluates the meaning of the death to the Egyptian firstborn in the older narrative, where divine announcement predestined an event whose effects were determined by national identity. Passover transforms this story by underscoring that the avoidance of the plague was not automatic for any group. Escape from death required choice and cultic participation. Such a universal requirement at the very least opens the rite to non-Israelites and this possibility eliminates the absolute distinction between Egyptians and Israelites that dominated the older story. The effect is a blurring of national boundaries in deuteronomistic tradition, which is signaled by the intermingling of Egyptians and Israelites in one location and by the "mixed multitude" who left with Israel (12:38). Thus, although deuteronomistic tradition is exclusive in its perspective (since the focus remains primarily on Israel and the Egyptians never acquire an independent role in the story), it is no longer a national story. Passover underscores that the plague of death would not discriminate in an absolute fashion between groups.

NOTES

1. For recent reviews of past scholarship with regard to this problem see S. Boorer, *The Promise of the Land as Oath: A Key to the Formation of the Pentateuch,* BZAW 205 (Berlin: de Gruyter, 1992), 7-33; and J. Van Seters, "The So-Called Deuteronomistic Redaction of the Pentateuch," in *Congress Volume: Leuven 1989,* VTSup 43, ed. J. A. Emerton et al. (Leiden: E. J. Brill, 1991), 58-59; and *Prologue to History: The Yahwist as Historian in Genesis* (Louisville: Westminster/John Knox, 1992), 227-245.

2. See J. Muilenburg, "The Form and Structure of the Covenantal Formulations," *VT* 9 (1959): 347-365; Chr. Brekelmans, "Die sogenannten deuteronomischen Elemente in Gen.-Num.: Ein Beitrag zur Vorgeschichte des Deuteronomiums," in *Congress Volume: Genève 1965,* VTSup 15, ed. G. W. Anderson (Leiden: E. J. Brill, 1966), 89-96; N. Lohfink, *Das Hauptgebot: Eine Untersuchung literarische Einleitungsfragen zu Dtn 5-11,* AnBib 20 (Rome: Pontificio Instituto Biblico, 1963), 121-124; Boorer, *The Promise of the Land as Oath,* 129-188 and passim.

3. Perhaps H. H. Schmid (*Der sogenannte Jahwist,* 56-57, 167-183) represents this position when he concludes that Yahwistic material presupposes the preexilic prophets and appears to belong "in die Nähe der deuteronomisch-deuteronomistischen Traditionsbildung und literarischen Arbeit." Rendtorff (*Problem des Pentateuch,* 168) at least raises the question of a closer interrelationship between the formation of the Tetrateuch and the deuteronomistic history.

4. See Van Seters, *Prologue to History*; A. D. H. Mayes, *The Story of Israel between Settlement and Exile: A Redactional Study of the Deuteronomistic History* (London: SCM Press, 1983); M. Rose, *Deuteronomist und Jahwist: Untersuchungen zu den Berührungspunkten beider Literaturwerke,* ATANT 67 (Zürich: Theologischer Verlag, 1981); and Blum, *Studien,* 101-218.

5. Noth, *History of Pentateuchal Traditions.*

6. Earlier, Wellhausen, *Composition* and *Prolegomena,* and more recently Weimar, *Meerwundererzählung*; E. Zenger, *Die Sinaitheophanie: Untersuchungen zum jahwistischen und elohistischen Geschichtswerk,* Forschung zur Bibel (Würzburg: Echter Verlag, 1971); and L. Perlitt, *Bundestheologie im Alten Testament,* WMANT 36 (Neukirchen-Vluyn: Neukirchener, 1969), 156-238.

7. See Van Seters, *Prologue to History*; Mayes, *The Story of Israel between Settlement and Exile*; and Blum, *Studien,* 101-218.

8. The terms "supplementation" and "redaction" will be used throughout the chapter. Both terms are meant to underscore that the earlier formation of the exodus continues to play an influential role within deuteronomistic tradition. Hence deuteronomistic tradition is not an independent source. Whether "redaction" is the best term is open to debate, especially given its narrow meaning in past scholarship as the work of late, passive tradents. For review of the role of

redactors in past scholarship see T. B. Dozeman, *God on the Mountain: A Study of Redaction, Theology and Canon in Exodus 19-24*, SBLMS 37 (Atlanta: Scholars Press, 1989), 2-12.

9. The determination of the exact boundaries of such a historiography go beyond the present study of exodus tradition. One supposes that it extends at least from the promise to the ancestors (Genesis) through the history of the kingdoms (Joshua-Kings). For a review of the vast amount of literature on the promise of the ancestors as a unifying device in the Pentateuch see, most recently, Boorer, *The Promise of the Land as Oath*, 38-99. On the boundaries of Genesis-Kings for such a historiography see the discussion by D. N. Freedman concerning a Primary History—a sixth-century literary compilation that includes Genesis through Kings, in which Deuteronomy plays a unifying role—in "Pentateuch," in *IDB*, vol. 3, ed. G. A. Buttrick (Nashville: Abingdon, 1962), 711-727; "Canon of the OT," in *IDBSup*, ed. K. Crim (Nashville: Abingdon, 1976), 130-136; and *The Unity of the Hebrew Bible* (Ann Arbor: University of Michigan Press, 1991) 1-40. Compare also Blenkinsopp. *The Pentateuch*.

10. The present collection of wilderness laws and stories most certainly contains material that is older than the formation of a deuteronomistic history spanning Genesis-Kings. My aim is not to isolate such material, but to describe how a wilderness period of journey between Egypt and Canaan became a canonical feature of Israel's account of salvation.

11. Exod 11:2-3; 12:35-36.

12. Exod 12:37; 13:17-18a, 20; 15:22.

13. Exod 12:39a; 13:3, 9, 14, 16.

14. Exod 12:25; 13:5, 11.

15. The catechisms indicate the cultic settings of passover (Exod 12:21-27) and *massot*/firstlings (Exod 13:1-16) in the vicinity of Egypt, the importance of law (Deut 6:20-25) in the wilderness, and finally, Yahweh's power over the sea at the crossing of the Jordan (Joshua 4).

16. Exod 11:2-3, 8b; 12:21-27, 35-36.

17. Exod 12:37-39a; 13:1-16.

18. Exod 13:17-18a, 20; 14:11-12, 15a*b*,b, 16b, 19a, 20a*a*, 22a, 23, 28-29a, 31; 15:13-17, 19, 22-27.

19. Two features of the phrase ספר שמי בכל־הארץ look to be deuteronomistic. The first is the use of ספר to signify the recounting of an event as in Exod 18:8 and 24:3 (see Dozeman, *God on the Mountain*, 53-67). Second, the emphasis on the divine name in the land corresponds well with the deuteronomistic name theology (here see Mettinger, *Dethronement of Sabaoth*, 38-79).

20. The call for intergenerational instruction in 10:1b-2a is repeated by deuteronomistic tradents in 12:21-27 and 13:1-16. For a discussion of 10:1b-2a in the larger context of a *D-Komposition* see Blum, *Studien*, 16-17.

21. For initial discussion of the Hebrew ים־סוף (Red Sea) within deuteronomistic tradition see Norin, *Er Spaltete das Meer*, 13-41, esp. 39-41.

22. Especially noteworthy in this regard is the use of Hebrew עתר. For a discussion see E. Aurelius, *Der Fürbitter Israels: Eine Studie zum Mosebild im Alten Testment*, ConBOT 27 (Lund: Almqvist & Wicksell, 1988), 161-186, esp. 160-167.

23. See initially Aurelius, *Fürbitter*, 141-160, and compare G. W. Coats, *The Murmuring Motif in the Wilderness Traditions of the Old Testament: Rebellion in the Wilderness* (Nashville: Abingdon, 1968), 127-137.

24. The wilderness (מדבר) is traditionally anchored in a preexilic Yahwist regardless of debates concerning the overall structure of the tradition. Such views presuppose the early development of historiography in ancient Israel. See, for example, Wellhausen, *Composition*, 65–71; Noth, *Exodus*, 67–71; or V. Fritz, *Israel in der Wüste: Traditionsgeschichtliche Untersuchung der Wüstenüberlieferung der Jahwisten,* Marburger Theologische Studien 7 (Marburg: N. G. Elwert Verlag, 1970), 40; and most recently, L. Schmidt, *Plagenerzählung*, 58–69. Compare Blum (*Studien*, 13–17), who identifies the prepriestly version of the plagues as a *D-Komposition*. His study does not specifically address the role of the wilderness in the transformation of the plague cycle, or, indeed, how the combination of the exodus and wilderness traditions provide the structure for reinterpreting older tradition.

25. Exod 5:3 reads, נלכה־נא דרך שלשת ימים במדבר. Aurelius (*Der Fürbitter Israels,* 146 n. 79) lists the distribution of references to a three-day journey within the Pentateuch in the following manner: הלך + דרך + שלשת ימים in Exod 3:18; 5:3; 8:23; Num 33:8; only הלך in Exod 15:22b; only דרך or minor variations in Gen 30:36 and Num 10:33a,b. Of particular note is the reference to three days in the instructions to Moses at the mountain in Exodus 3, which illustrates how the wilderness is already woven into the exodus story in the call of Moses.

26. The distribution of the references to the wilderness outlined earlier can be illustrated in the following manner:

Initial Encounter 5:1–6:1*	Blood 7:14–24*	Frogs 7:25– 8:11*	Flies 8:16–28*	Cattle 9:1–7	Hail 9:13–35*	Locust 10:1–20*
במדבר 5:1	במדבר 7:16		דרך שלשת ימים נלך במדבר 8:23		Divine Name 9:16a	Catechetical Instruction 10:1b-2aa
דרך שלשת ימים במדבר 5:3						Red Sea 10:19ab

27. See Coats ("A Structural Transition in Exodus," 129–141; and "An Exposition for the Wilderness Tradition," 288–295) for a discussion of how the introduction of motifs into pentateuchal narrative may create points of tension, whose resolution can be helpful in determining the structure of particular traditions.

28. The literary structure of the plague cycle underscores how loosely the wilderness is actually woven into this cycle. The wilderness occurs two times in the opening address of Moses to Pharaoh as part of the condition in the plagues of blood and frogs. Yet it is absent when the same condition is repeated in the plagues of flies, cattle, hail, and locust. The only other occurrence of the wilderness is in the exchange between Pharaoh and Moses in the midst of the plague of flies. See also Otto, "Plagenzyklus," 6.

29. G. I. Davies, "The Wilderness Itineraries and the Composition of the Pentateuch," *VT* 33 (1983): 2–8. Other solutions include that of Noth (*History of Pentateuchal Traditions*, 220–227, esp. 224–226), who questions whether the itineraries might not be independent but in the end interprets them within the framework of J and P; so does F. M. Cross (*Canaanite Myth and Hebrew Epic: Essays in the History of the Religion of Israel* (Cambridge: Harvard University Press, 1973), 307–321), who also attributes far more texts to P than does

Davies (Exod 12:37a; 13:20; 14:2; 15:22a; 16:1; 17:1a; 19:2; Num 10:12; 20:1a, 22; 21:10; 22:1), with the remainder of references belonging to either E or J. See also M. Haran ("The Exodus," in *IDBSup,* ed. K. Crim [Nashville: Abingdon, 1976], 304–310, esp. 309–310), who separates the itineraries according to classical sources (J, E, D, and P). G. W. Coats ("The Wilderness Itinerary," *CBQ* 34 [1972]: 135–152) and J. T. Walsh ("From Egypt to Moab: A Source Critical Analysis of the Wilderness Itinerary," *CBQ* 39 [1977]: 20–33) both argue for a more independent development to the growth of the itineraries over against narrative sources. They differ, however, in that Coats sees more unity to the itineraries in their present form whereas Walsh identifies three distinct itinerary chains. For analysis of the itineraries from a geographical perspective see G. I. Davies, *The Way of the Wilderness: A Geographical Study of the Wilderness Itineraries in the Old Testament,* (Cambridge: University Press, 1979), 62–93; and H. Cazelles, "Les localisations de l'Exode et la critique littéraire," *Autour de l'Exode,* Sources Biblique (Paris: J. Gabalda, 1987), 189–231. For a review of the itinerary notices in relation to recent archaeology see G. I. Davies ("The Wilderness Itineraries and Recent Archaeological Research," in *Studies in the Pentateuch,* VTSup 41, ed. J. A. Emerton [Leiden: E. J. Brill, 1990], 161-175), who concludes that recent archaeological research does little to support a historical and geographical reconstruction of Israel's wilderness travels.

30. As Davies ("The Wilderness Itineraries and the Composition of the Pentateuch," 6) notes, the parallels between Numbers 33 and the itinerary notices throughout Exodus and Numbers are so close that some form of literary relationship must be presupposed. Scholars differ at this point. M. Noth ("Der Wallfahrtsweg zum Sinai," *PJ* 36 [1940]: 5–28) argued that Numbers 33 is a late compilation of isolated itineraries from Exodus and Numbers. Cross (*Canaanite Myth and Hebrew Epic,* 308–309) argues for just the reverse relationship, that Numbers 33 is the base document for the construction of the itineraries in Exodus and Numbers, and he is followed by G. I. Davies ("The Wilderness Itineraries. A Comparative Study," *TynBul* 25 [1974]: 50–51, 60–70; "The Wilderness Itineraries and the Composition of the Pentateuch," 6-7; "The Wilderness Itineraries and Recent Archaeological Research," 171–174). The difference between Cross and Davies is that for Cross, Numbers 33 is the basis for priestly tradition in Exodus and Numbers, while for Davies, Numbers 33 is the basis for a prepriestly (i.e., deuteronomistic) version of the itineraries in Exodus and Numbers, with priestly influence in Numbers 33 being the result of later redaction. Both Noth and Cross agree that the most likely origin of Numbers 33 concerns a list of pilgrimage stations, while Davies looks instead to royal military records like those of ancient Near Eastern Assyrian archives.

31. Davies ("The Wilderness Itineraries and the Composition of the Pentateuch," 1–12) presents the following argument. First, he notes doublets in Exod 19:1-2 (v. 1 being P and v. 2a non-P) and in Numbers 10 (10:12 being P and 10:33 non-P) in order to establish at least two stages of tradition. Second, he argues on the basis of comparison with Numbers 33 that non-P material is a single tradition that is dependent on Numbers 33 (i.e., the material in Exodus and Numbers has telescoped the larger list in Numbers 33 with such techniques as is evident in Exod 17:1, where Israel is said to have progressed "by stages" in the wilderness). Third, he notes the loose connection between the itineraries and the narratives (especially in Exod 12:37 and 13:20) and concludes that the itineraries are a redactional

addition to the stories. This argument presupposes that the introduction of the itineraries creates the wilderness tradition as it is presently read. And fourth, he argues that nonpriestly itineraries are deuteronomistic. His reasons include differences in interpretation with regard to Israel's travel through (or around) Edom/Moab in Numbers 33, Judg 11:18, and Num 21:10–13, as well as motifs of holy war, journeying, and the role of Yahweh as guide.

32. Davies, "The Wilderness Itineraries and the Composition of the Pentateuch," 8.

33. Davies, "The Wilderness Itineraries and the Composition of the Pentateuch," 10.

34. This tension creates problems with regard to both historical reconstruction of the events and the tradition-historical formation of the text. For an overview of the historical problems see, among others, Hyatt, *Exodus*, 149–150; Cazelles, "Les localisations de l'Exode et la critique littéraire," 189–231; Davies, *The Way of the Wilderness*, 62–93; and "The Wilderness Itineraries and Recent Archaeological Research," 161–175. With regard to tradition-historical problems see Childs, *Exodus* 229–230; or "A Traditio-Historical Study of the Reed Sea Tradition," *VT* 20 (1970): 406–418.

35. G.W. Coats, "The Traditio-Historical Character of the Reed Sea Motif," *VT* 17 (1967): 253–265.

36. The overall design of the deuteronomistic redaction can be illustrated in the following manner (note in particular how the supplementations introduce Israel into the story):

> DTR Announcement to Israel—Despoiling (Exod 11:2–3)
> PRE-DTR Announcement to Pharaoh—Death to Egyptian Firstborn (Exod 4–7a, 8a)
> DTR Instructions to Israel—Passover (Exod 12:21–27)
> PRE-DTR Fulfillment—Death of Egyptian Firstborn (Exod 12:29–34)
> DTR Fulfillment—Despoiling of the Egyptians (Exod 12:35–36)

37. Hebrew שאל.

38. Hebrew ויתן יהוה את־הן העם בעיני מצרים.

39. The objects of despoiling (gold, silver, clothing) repeat only in the deuteronomistic history, once as gifts given to Solomon (1 Kgs 10:25) and once as spoils of war (Josh 22:8). Other near parallel texts include Gen 24:53, where Isaac's servant gives gifts of silver, gold, and clothing (ובגדים) to Rebekah, and 2 Sam 8:10, where silver and gold are again mentioned as spoils of war. For discussion of these objects see G. W. Coats, "Despoiling the Egyptians," *VT* 18 (1968):452; and D. Daube, *The Exodus Pattern in the Bible*, All Souls Studies 2 (London: Faber & Faber, 1963), 56 n. 4. There is also mythological background to this imagery. Twice the defeat of a divine foe is described in the Baal mythology as dispossessing a god of gold. See the speech of the messengers of Yamm in CTA 2.I.18–19, where they demand that the gods give up Baal so that they may possess his gold, and also the speech of Anat in CTA 3.D.43, where she recounts her victory over gods with the imagery of dispossessing them of gold.

40. Hebrew וינצלו את־מצרים. The piel of נצל occurs four times in the Hebrew Bible: twice in the context of the Exodus (Exod 3:22; 12:36), once in the setting of holy war (2 Chr 20:25), and once in Ezekiel (14:14), where the meaning is not

clear. See Coats ("Despoiling the Egyptians," 454) concerning the translation of the piel of נצל as "to despoil."

41. The hithpael occurs only in Exod 33:6, yet the connection to the previous texts is clear. The interconnections between Exod 33:1-6 and the development of the despoiling motif in Exod 3:22, 11:2-3, and 12:35-36 go beyond the verb "to despoil" and include also the motif of jewelry on children from Exod 3:22 (see Blum, *Studien*,18-19). Exod 33:1-5 is clearly meant to function as an aetiology for aniconic cultic practice, which is symbolized in deuteronomistic tradition by Mount Horeb. Note how Exod 33:1-6 states explicitly that it is from Mount Horeb on that Israel is characterized as a people who worship without ornamental icons. See Mettinger (*Dethronement of Sabaoth*, 38-79) for discussion of the aniconic *Tendenz* in deuteronom(ist)ic tradition and especially in their theology of the name. See Dozeman (*God on the Mountain*, 37-86) for a description of how Mount Horeb symbolized the deuteronom(ist)ic aniconic theology of the name. Compare Weimar, *Die Berufung des Mose*, 347-349.

42. Compare Th. C. Vriezen ("A Reinterpretation of Exodus 3:21-22 and Related Texts, Exod 11:2f., 12:35f., and Ps. 105:37f. [Gen 15:4b]," *Jaarbericht* 23 [1973-1974]: 390-391), who concludes that Exod 3:22 and 12:35-36 are Yahwistic tradition while 11:2-3 is a shorter version of J added (most likely) within priestly tradition. W. H. Schmidt (*Exodus*, 143), on the other hand, argues that 3:21-22 may perhaps be a later addition to the despoiling motif because only women are mentioned as being required to ask for valuable objects and only here are they told to place them on their children. This contrasts to 11:2, where men and women are included in the command, and 12:35-36, where no distinction is made between men and women. Compare Childs (*Exodus*, 175-177) or Weimar (*Die Berufung des Mose*, 347-349) for arguments in favor of the unity of the motif.

43. The despoiling motif frames the preexilic account of the death to the Egyptian firstborn. Exod 11:2-3 occurs prior to the announcement by Moses to Pharaoh of the impending plague of death (11:4-7a, 8a), while Exod 12:35-36 now functions as the final incident in this episode before Israel leaves Egypt in 12:37.

44. For further discussion on the intrusive character of the despoiling motif see, among others, Noth, *Exodus*, 93-94; Childs, *Exodus*, 201; and Coats, "Despoiling the Egyptians," 451.

45. In addition to focusing the reader's attention back on Moses and Pharaoh, Exod 11:8b also introduces the anger of Moses. This trait is important in deuteronomistic tradition, since it accentuates Moses' strong charismatic leadership to the point where it becomes a flaw. Note, for example, that he breaks the tablets in Exod 32:19 even though he had already successfully interceded for Israel. This larger dimension to the anger of Moses introduces a degree of ambiguity into the story, since it raises the question of whether Exod 11:8b is meant to be read positively or negatively. In either case, it prompts a reading of Moses as a more independent character.

46. But there is debate on this point. Vriezen ("A Reinterpretation of Exodus 3:21-22," 392, 397-399) has argued that the piel of נצל does not mean "to plunder" or "to despoil" but conveys a more positive connotation of "to rescue someone" or "to take back things to which one is entitled." For Vriezen, therefore, the motif signifies the positive relationship that existed between the Egyp-

tians and Israel, which, he argues, is supported by the larger context. A number of scholars have argued that the use of the verb "to request" (שאל as qal in 3:22; 11:2; and 12:35, and as hiphil in 12:36) indicates only a desire on the part of the Israelites to borrow the valuables from the Egyptians. See Noth, *Exodus*, 93; Coats, "Despoiling the Egyptians," 453; Daube, *Exodus Pattern*, 57; and J. Morgenstern, "The Despoiling of the Egyptians," *JBL* 68 (1949): 4. For those who interpret שאל as a request to borrow objects, there is debate whether (1) the Egyptians were tricked by the Israelites (so Coats, "Despoiling the Egyptians," 453); or (2) they simply had high regard for the Israelites, indicated by the formula that "Yahweh had given the people favor in the eyes of the Egyptians" (so Noth, *Exodus*, 94; and D. J. McCarthy, "Plagues and the Sea of Reeds: Exodus 5-14," *JBL* 85 [1966]: 147); or (3) they gave their possessions because it was a legal requirement that released slaves not leave empty handed (so Daube, *Exodus Pattern*, 55-58; M. Greenberg, *Understanding the Exodus*, The Melton Research Center Series 2 [New York: Behrman House, 1969], 86-87, 168; and Cassuto, *Exodus*, 44). Concerning the shift to the hiphil in Exod 12:36, Vriezen ("A Reinterpretation of Exodus 3:21-22," 393 n. 5) writes that it "gives expression to the willingness of the Egyptians to meet the demands of the Israelites."

47. The formula of favor is broken with the verb "to give" (Hebrew נתן) having replaced the expected verb "to find" (Hebrew מצא), and the subject is Yahweh rather than Israel. See Coats, "Despoiling the Egyptians," 453-454.

48. Coats ("Despoiling the Egyptians, 454) writes: "This rarer formulation can be understood as the causative form of the more common idiom. But the formula also shows that the basis for the Israelite's favor in the eyes of the Egyptians does not lie in the object . . . (i.e., the people) but in the initiation of the subject (i.e., God)." Coats is certainly correct, but his insight leads to the conclusion that there is no deception in the despoiling motif because the relationship between Israel and Egypt is not explored. Instead, the favor that the Israelites enjoyed in the eyes of the Egyptians must be interpreted as Yahweh's gift to Israel. It is part of the divine liberation. See the discussion by D. N. Freedman and J. R. Lundbom ("חנן," *TDOT* VI, ed. G. J. Botterweck and H. Ringgren [Grand Rapids: Eerdmans, 1986], 22-36, esp. 23), who in their study of נתן ("to give") also note how the causative construction of the formula concerning favor is restricted in its application to Yahweh.

49. See Vriezen ("A Reinterpretation of Exodus 3:21-22," 392-393), who would favor the setting of voluntary gifts from 1 Kgs 10:25. He also sees the continuing influence of such a setting through Second and Third Isaiah, where the nations are pictured as giving up wealth voluntarily to Israel (see Isa 45:14; 49:22; 54; 60; 61). Vriezen (p. 398) also argues that the use of נצל in 2 Chr 20:25 describes *how* they took booty ("They took away that much, that they could not even carry it with them") rather than the act of plundering itself.

50. See, among others, Noth, *Exodus*, 93; Coats, "Despoiling the Egyptians," 453; Daube, *Exodus Pattern*, 57; Morgenstern, "The Despoiling of the Egyptians," 4; and see note 46.

51. Exod 3:20-22 underscores holy war. Verse 20 describes how Yahweh will attack the Egyptians (נכה). This attack will change the Egyptians' perception of Israel, which will result in the despoiling. The language in Exod 3:21-22 and the larger context of vv. 16-20 looks to be deuteronomistic (e.g., the central role of elders, the nations listed as occupying the land, its description as

flowing with milk and honey, the need to travel three days into the wilderness to sacrifice).

52. So Childs (*Exodus*, 177), who writes: "The point of the tradition focuses on God's plan for the Israelites to leave Egypt as victors from a battle." The need for Israel's active participation in holy war is accentuated through the word play between hiphil and piel forms of נצל, in which despoiling (the piel form of נצל in 11:2-3 and 12:35-36) signifies Israel's participation in Yahweh's deliverance (the hiphil form of נצל in 12:23, 27 [twice]).

53. Note how the elders are directed to select a lamb according to their families (למשפחתיכם) in Exod 12:21 in contrast to Deut 16:5, where local sacrifice is specifically denied in favor of a centralized national festival (Deut 16:2, 6-7). For initial discussion on passover in Deuteronomy 16 see G. von Rad, *Deuteronomy*, OTL, trans. D. Barton (Philadelphia: Westminster, 1966), 110-113; R. Schmitt, *Exodus und Passa: Ihr Zusammenhang im Alten Testament*, OBO 7, 2d ed. (Göttingen: Vandenhoeck & Ruprecht, 1982), 64-69; P. Laaf, *Die Pascha-Feier Israels: Eine literarkritische und überlieferungsgeschichtliche Studie*, BBB 36 (Bonn: Peter Hanstein, 1970), 73-77; and Boorer, *The Promise of the Land as Oath*, 177-185.

54. Arguments for the antiquity of the passover rite in Exod 12:21-23 include: (1) The obscurity of the word "passover." For an overview of the problems see H.-J. Kraus, *Worship in Israel: A Cultic History of the Old Testament*, trans. G. Buswell (Richmond: John Knox Press, 1966), 45-47. (2) The demonic destroyer. For discussion see Laaf, *Die Pascha-Feier Israels*, 156-157; Noth, *Exodus*, 91-92; Schmitt, *Exodus und Passa*, 24. (3) The night setting of the ritual. See M. Haran, "The Passover Sacrifice," in *Studies in the Religion of Ancient Israel*, VTSup 23 (Leiden: E. S. Brill, 1972), 89. (4) The blood rite. It is interpreted either as being apotropaic (so H.-J. Kraus, *Worship in Israel*, 46) or as signifying purification (so Haran, "The Passover Sacrifice," 89). (5) The absence of a particular cultic location. See E. Otto and T. Schramm, *Festival and Joy*, Biblical Encounters Series, trans. J. L. Blevins (Nashville: Abingdon, 1980), 13. (6) Aspects of the ritual, including the roasting of meat instead of boiling it (Haran, "The Passover Sacrifice," 89) and the use of hyssop (Otto, *Festival and Joy*, 13).

55. See L. Rost, "Weideweschsel und altisraelitischer Festkalender," *ZDPV* 66 (1943): 205-215.

56. An interpretation of passover in 12:21-23 as being independent of the exodus requires that the reference to Yahweh passing over to strike the Egyptians in v. 23 be interpreted as part of the deuteronomistic reinterpretation of the rite. In this regard note the contrast between the more general reference to Egyptians in v. 23 and the specific reference to firstborn in 11:5 (see Boorer, *The Promise of the Land as Oath*, 153). The debate over the interrelation of passover and exodus is extensive in contemporary scholarship. Noth (*Exodus*, 87) favored an early interrelationship between the passover and exodus traditions, being influenced partially by Pedersen, "Passahfest und Passahlegende," 161-175; and idem, *Israel: Its Life and Culture*, trans. by A. I. Fansbøll (Copenhagen: Dyva & Jeppesen, 1940),728-737. Noth (*Exodus*, 93) concluded that the merging of passover and firstborn was already well established already by the formation of a preexilic Yahwist. Compare Wellhausen (*Prolegomena*, 83-92), who argued that passover was a later addition to the exodus tradition. In *Composition* (75) Wellhausen argued that Exod 12:21-27 was a late addition to JE. The secondary literature sur-

rounding the issue is vast and wide ranging. For an overview see Laaf, *Die Pascha-Feier Israels,* 19 n. 82 and passim.

57. See J. Schreiner, "Exodus 12:21-23 und das israelitische Pascha," in *Studien zum Pentateuch: Festschrift für W. Kornfeld*, ed. G. Braulik (Wien: Herder, 1977), 78-79.

58. See Schmitt, *Exodus und Passa,* 47; Laaf, *Die Pascha-Feier Israels,* 20. Reference to destruction or to a destroyer occurs in both deuteronomistic (12:23) and priestly (12:13) traditions. There is debate about, first, whether the personification of a "destroyer" is ancient tradition or a later development in Israelite tradition, and second, whether references in both 12:13 and 23 actually personify a destroyer. With regard to the first point, it would appear that the personification of a destroyer is a later development in Israelite religion. The deuteronomistic history shows transition in the use of the term. The destroyer refers to humans (1 Sam 13:17 and 14:15), but it also appears to be mythologized in 2 Kgs 23:13, where the reference to להר־המשחית suggests cosmic mountain imagery. Note the even stronger parallel to the passover story in 2 Sam 24:10-17, where the angel of Yahweh (המלאך) and the destroyer (המשחית) are merged in the punishment resulting from David's census. A movement toward mythologizing the term is also evident in exilic prophets. Jeremiah tradition uses the term to refer both to humans (4:7; 5:26) and perhaps also to divine power (51:1, 25); so too Ezekiel, where human or natural forces are described as destroyers (5:16; 25:15). But note also Ezek 9:1-11, where the context is once again more mythological. Finally, Isa 54:16 could be read either way. With regard to the second point, it is clear that deuteronomistic tradents personify the destroyer. Note the definite article המשחית in Exod 12:23. The priestly reference in Exod 12:13 is more ambiguous, בכם נגף למשחית ולא־יהיה. For additional discussion see Norin, *Er Spaltete das Meer,* 175-176.

59. Childs, *Exodus,* 185; and Wellhausen, *Composition,* 75 n. 1.

60. See Childs, *Exodus,* 191-192; Kohata, *Jahwist und Priesterschrift in Exodus 3-14,* 268; Laaf, *Die Pascha-Feier Israels,* 20. For a discussion of the apotropaic character of the blood rite see Noth, *Exodus,* 88-89; or Schmitt, *Exodus und Passa,* 35-45.

61. See Noth (*Exodus,* 97-98), who concluded that v. 24b was late because of the use of the second person singular. Few have followed Noth's lead with regard to v. 24b, but his assessment of the text as reflecting deuteronom(ist)ic tradition was suggested earlier by Wellhausen (*Composition,* 74-75) and echoed by any number of more recent scholars, including Fohrer, *Überlieferung und Geschichte des Exodus,* 80; Schmitt, *Exodus und Passa,* 21; Laaf, *Die Pascha-Feier Israels,* 21. The limitation of the deuteronomistic addition to 12:24-27a is common. A firm decision on the placement of v. 27b, within deuteronomistic tradition is not possible. See Rudolph (*Der "Elohist,"* 25 n. 3), who suggests that perhaps a reference to the elders lies behind v. 27b, which would then harmonize the verse with the introduction in v. 21. An assessment of Exod 12:27b rests in part on an interpretation of Exod 4:27-31, since v. 31a also describes the response of the people to the speech of Moses (and Aaron) with the same words (ויקדו וישתחוו). On this parallel see most recently Kohata, *Jahwist und Priesterschrift in Exodus 3-14,* 270 n. 42. The phrase also occurs twice in the story of the servant's search for Rebekah (Gen 24:26, 48), once in the account of the meeting between Joseph and his brothers (Gen 43:28), then again during covenant renewal (Exod 34:8), and finally in Balaam's confrontation with the מלאך יהוה (Num 22:31).

62. Lohfink, *Das Hauptgebot*,122.

63. Lohfink (*Das Hauptgebot*, 122) notes other unexpected or pecular forms of words and phrases such as the use of שׁמר ("to observe" in v. 24), the singular use of חק ("statute" in v. 24), the use of Israel as the subject in the reference to the future possession of the land (v. 25), the combination of "to observe" with "service" (v. 25), and the use of אמר ("to say") rather than שׁאל ("to request") in introducing the child's question concerning the meaning of passover. The linguistic analysis of Exod 12:24-27a is usually undertaken in conjunction with Exod 13:3-16 because of the similarities in form and language. Other scholars who also argue that both Exod 12:24-27a and Exod 13:3-16 are predeuteronomic include J. Loza, "Les catéchèses étiologique dans l'Ancien Testament," *RB* 78 (1971): 481-500, esp. 484-487; M. Caloz, "Exode, XIII, 3-16 et son rapport au Deutéronome," *RB* 75 (1968): 5-62; A. Reichert, "Israel, The Firstborn of God: A Topic of Early Deuteronomic Theology," in *Proceedings of the Sixth World Congress of Jewish Studies*, vol. 1, ed. A Shinan (Jerusalem: World Union of Jewish Studies, 1977), 341-349, esp. 345; M. Weinfeld, *Deuteronomy 1-11,* AB 5 (New York: Doubleday, 1991), 328-329. See Brekelmans, ("Die sogenannten deuteronomischen Elemente in Gen.-Num.," 90-96), who outlines three criteria for identifying protodeuteronomic material in the Tetrateuch.

64. The phrases in 12:25 (מה העבדה הזאת), 12:26 (ושמרתם את־העבדה הזאת), and 13:5 (ועבדה את־העבדה הזאת) do not occur in Deuteronomy.

65. Lohfink, *Das Hauptgebot*, 121-122.

66. Boorer (*The Promise of the Land as Oath*, 154-155) notes that the expressions חקת עולם (Exod 12:14, 17) and לחק־עולם (Exod 29:28; 30:21; Lev 7:34; 10:15) occur in priestly material, but because neither term occurs in combination with עד עולם, she concludes that the word falls between Deuteronomy and P. Other examples supporting this conclusion are the singular use of "statute" in v. 24, the cultic use of "service" in v. 25, and the qal use of בוא ("to go or enter") in reference to the future possession of the land in v. 25).

67. The studies by Lohfink, Boorer, and others have certainly underscored a variety of literary tensions that arise when 12:24-27a is compared to an ideal form of rhetoric from Deuteronomy. But whether these tensions justify the attribution of 12:24-27a either to predeuteronomic or to later tradition is less clear. A position in this matter must include not only one's view of flexibility in the use of language within the same tradition, but also one's view of the formation of the Pentateuch, and these two issues cannot, in the end, be separated. For a discussion of these issues with regard to the formation of the Pentateuch see Blum, *Studien*, 166-169; or Boorer, *The Promise of the Land as Oath*, 7-36, 38-99; and with regard to the flexibility of language within the same tradition see the reservations expressed by A. D. H. Mayes, *Deuteronomy*, NCB (London: Oliphants, 1979), 39. The present study has adopted a more flexible view of language, especially when linguistic differences occur in literary settings whose speech forms and narration otherwise resemble a particular tradition. Clearly there is a bias in this position toward harmonizing linguistic and literary differences, and as a partial safeguard against this tendency, two questions with regard to literary context must be asked, each focusing on the distinct qualities of particular texts. First, can distinctive linguistic forms or literary tropes be accounted for by the immediate context of an insertion? Second, can linguistic and formal peculiarities be explained by the function of a text in the larger design of a redaction?

68. See M. Weinfeld (*Deuteronomy and the Deuteronomic School* [Oxford: Clarendon Press, 1972], 10–58, esp. 32–45), who discusses the role of oration in general in deuteronom(ist)ic tradition, and more particularly he describes Exod 12:21–27 as liturgical oration. See R. Polzin (*Moses and the Deuteronomist: A Literary Study of the Deuteronomic History*, Part One [New York: Seabury Press, 1980]) for a more detailed analysis of how oration functions to create point of view in Deuteronomy and in the deuteronomistic history.

69. For a brief review of the role of elders in deuteronom(ist)ic tradition see Dozeman, *God on the Mountain*, 180–183.

70. The instruction signifies the cultic setting of passover (Exod 12:21–27) and *massot*/firstlings (Exod 13:1–16) in the vicinity of Egypt, the importance of law (Deut 6:4–25) in the wilderness, and Yahweh's power over sea and river (Joshua 4) at the crossing of the Jordan. See especially J. A. Soggin, "Kultätiologische Sagen und Katachese im Hexateuch," *VT* 10 (1960): 341–347.

71. See Weinfeld (*Deuteronomy and the Deuteronomic School*, 332–339) for deuteronom(ist)ic phraseology concerning concepts of loyalty that use שמר with various forms of law, including חק as its object. For discussion concerning עד עולם and its possible relationship to intergenerational teaching see Schmitt, *Exodus und Passa*, 70. For the use of this phrase in Deuteronomy see Deut 12:28, 23:3; 29:28, and in the deuteronomistic history see Josh 4:7 and 1 Sam 1:22.

72. See Weinfeld, *Deuteronomy 1–11*, 57–60; and *Deuteronomy and the Deuteronomic School*, 341–343.

73. The distribution of the passover legislation in the larger context of a deuteronomistic history certainly conforms to the demands for a centralized cult in Deuteronomy 12 and 16. The story progresses from a family occurrence in Egypt as the founding aetiology, to the centralized observance at Gilgal under Joshua (Josh 5:10–12), and finally to the centralized observance at Jerusalem under Josiah (2 Kgs 23:21–23).

74. See Weinfeld, *Deuteronomy and the Deuteronomic School*, 332–339.

75. The use of "service" occurs as a designation of passover in Exod 12:25, 26 and for *massot* in 13:5.

76. For a discussion see chapter 2. Include also the phrase "hard labor" (עבדה קשה) in Exod 1:14 and 6:9 (and compare Deut 26:6).

77. J. N. M. Wijngaards (*The Dramatization of Salvific History in the Deuteronomic Schools*, OTS 16 [Leiden: E. J. Brill, 1969], 54) writes of the leitmotiv עבד that it dominates the whole drama and that the divine imperative, "Let my people go that they may serve me" could be freely translated as, "Give up your claim on this slave so that he may be in my service!" See also Durham, *Exodus*, 164; Zenger, "Le théme de la 'sortie d'Egypte'," 303; and G. Sauter, "'Exodus' and 'Liberation' as Theological Metaphors: A Critical Case-Study of the Use of Allegory and Misunderstood Analogies in Ethics," *SJT* 34 (1981): 481–507.

78. The itinerary notice in 12:37 is only part of a larger deuteronomistic insertion, which includes 12:35–39a. The redactional character of Exod 12:35–39a is indicated by resumptive repetition in vv. 33–34 and 39a, where the hasty departure of Israel now frames vv. 35–38 (see C. Kuhl, "Die 'Wiederaufnahme': Ein literarkritisches Princip?" *ZAW* 64 [1952]: 1–11). References to *massot* are part of this repetition. *Massot* is not specifically named in the preexilic narrative, but some activity with regard to unleavened bread is described in v. 34 (וישא העם את־בצקו טרם יחמץ משארתם צררת בשמלתם על־שכמם) as a by-product of the hurried

manner in which the Israelites were driven out of Egypt. The resumptive repetition in v. 39a reads: ויאפו את־הבצק אלן הוציאו ממצרים ענת מצות כי לא חמץ. This repetition includes the word "unleavened bread" (חמץ), but it also adds further interpretation to the text by specifically naming מצות and by making allusion to the exodus motif. The number of people who left Egypt in 12:37b as roughly 600,000 may be an addition by priestly tradents, since the numbers 603,550 (Num 1:46; 2:32) and 601,730 (Num 26:51) occur as the total of Israelites in their first and second censuses. The reference to 600,00 also reappears in a speech of Moses, which may be a priestly addition to Numbers 11 (i.e., vv. 18-23 with the reference to 600,000 in v. 21). The reference to the mixed group (וגם ערב רב) in Exod 12:38 does fit aspects of deuteronomistic tradition and could provide the basis for laws dealing with the resident alien (גר) in deuteronomic law. Priestly tradents supplement the text precisely at this point with extensive legislation concerning the resident alien in vv. 40-51.

79. The effect of the itinerary in structuring the narrative can be summarized in the following manner:

Place	Ramses	Succoth
Event	Death of Egyptian firstborn	Exodus from Egypt
Cultic Celebration	Passover	*Massot*/firstlings

80. For analysis of the exodus motif see Noth, *History of Pentateuchal Traditions*, 47-51; J. N. M. Wijngaards, "הוציא and העלה: A Twofold Approach to the Exodus," *VT* 15 (1965): 92; idem, *The Formulas of the Deuteronomic Creed (Dt. 6/20-23: 26/5-6)*, Pontificia Universitas Gregoriana (Tilburg: Drukkerij A. Reijnen, 1963), 22-27; idem, *The Dramatization of Salvific History in the Deuteronomic Schools*, 32-67; P. Humbert, "Dieu fait sortir: Hiphil de yāṣā avec Dieu comme sujet" *TZ* 18 (1962): 357-361, 433-436; Coats, "The Traditio-Historical Character of the Reed Sea Motif," 258-261; B. S. Childs, "Deuteronomic Formulae of the Exodus Traditions," in *Hebräische Wortforschung: Festschrift zum 80. Geburtstag von W. Baumgartner*, VTSup 16, ed. G. W. Anderson et al. (Leiden: E. J. Brill, 1967), 30-39; W. Richter, "Beobachtungen zur theologischen Systembildung in der alttestamentlichen Literatur anhand des 'Kleinen geschichtlichen Credo,'" in *Wahrheit und Verkundigung: Festschrift für M. Schmaus*, ed. L. Scheffczyk (Paderborn: Schomigh, 1967), 175-212; Daube, *The Exodus Pattern*, 31-35; W. Gross, "Die Herausführungsformel: Zum Verhältnis von Formel und Syntax," *ZAW* 86 (1974): 425-453; H. D. Preuss, "יצא," in *TDOT VI*, ed. G. J. Botterweck and H. Ringgren (Grand Rapids: Eerdmans, 1990), 225-250; idem, *Theologie des Alten Testaments: YHWHs erwählendes und verpflichtendes Handeln*, Band 1 (Stuttgart: W. Kohlhammer, 1991), 43-51; Zenger, "Le thème de la 'sortie d'Egypte'," 303.

81. Wijngaards, "הוציא and העלה: A Twofold Approach to the Exodus," 92-93. See the criticism by Gross ("Die Herausführungsformel," 427) and its reaffirmation by Preuss, "יצא," 228, 237, 238-242.

82. Wijngaards, "הוציא and העלה: A Twofold Approach to the Exodus," 92.

83. See Preuss, "יצא," 233.

84. Yet the antiquity of the confession is difficult to confirm. Wijngaards ("הוציא and העלה: A Twofold Approach to the Exodus," 92) notes the absence of the phrase in early prophets such as Isaiah, Hosea, and Amos. Still he attributes

an early origin to the tradition because of its presence in the historical credos of Deuteronomy, which he judges to be ancient (*The Formulas of the Deuteronomic Creed*, 40-41 and passim), and he also reasons that its juridical function points to an early Sinaitic tradition of covenant ("הוצי״א and העלה: A Twofold Approach to the Exodus," 101). Even though the antiquity of the credos and the Sinaitic tradition of covenant have become less certain (see L. Rost, "Das kleine geschicthliche Credo," in *Das kleine Credo und andere Studien zum Alten Testament* [Heidelberg: Quelle & Meyer, 1965], 11-25; and Perlitt, *Bundestheologie*), the emergence of some kind of confessional formula about the exodus would still appear to be preexilic and northern, when one notes the identification of Yahweh with Egypt in Hos 11:1; 12:10; 12:14, 13:4. Not only is Yahweh identified with Egypt in Hos 11:1 (וממצרים קראתי לבני) and 12:10 (ואנכי יהוה אלהיך מארץ מצרים), but divine leading is also designated with the hiphil form of the verb "to go up" (העלה) in Hos 12:14 (ובנביא העלה יהוה את־ישראל ממצרים). This evidence, however, does not lead to Noth's (*History of Pentateuch Traditions*, 47-51) conclusion that the exodus motif is the "kernel of the whole subsequent pentateuchal tradition," since the word "to bring out" (הוצי״א) does not occur in Hosea. Indeed, the absence of this verb in Hosea has been used as one argument for its secondary character to the verb "to bring up" (העלה), which does occur in Hosea. For arguments in favor of the secondary character of the verb הוצי״א to the verb העלה see Wijngaards, "הוצי״א and העלה: A Twofold Approach to the Exodus," 96; Daube, *The Exodus Pattern*, 31-35; Zenger, "Le théme de la 'sortie d'Egypte'," 303; and Preuss, "יצ״א," 238. These arguments contrast that of Noth (*History of Pentateuchal Traditions*, 49-51), who would appear to reverse the order or else consider the verbs to be of equal antiquity (see p. 52 n. 169). Whether the verb העלה should be considered as signifying the exodus at all is questionable. Wijngaards ("הוצי״א and העלה: A Twofold Approach to the Exodus," 99) has argued that the confession appears to be anchored more in the taking of the land than in the exodus from Egypt.

85. The "March in the South" theophany tradition includes Judg 5:5; Ps 68:9, 18; Deut 33:2; and Hab 3:3-4. In each of these texts Yahweh is described as coming from a southern region in order to rescue Israel at a time of crisis. For arguments in favor of the antiquity of these poems see W. F. Albright, "The Earliest Form of Hebrew Verse," *JPOS* 2 (1922): 69-86; and "A Catalogue of Early Hebrew Lyric Poems," *HUCA* 23 (1950-1951) 14-24. His arguments are expanded by Cross and Freedman, *Studies in Ancient Yahwistic Poetry,* 97-122; by Cross, *Canaanite Myth and Hebrew Epic*, 99-105; and finally, by Miller, *The Divine Warrior in Early Israel*, 74-120.

86. Ps 68:8-9 reads:

אלהים בצאתך לפני עמך
O God, <u>when you went out</u> before your people

בצעדך בישימו ,
<u>when you marched</u> through the desert

ארץ רעשה אף־שמים נטפו . . .
the earth quaked, the heavens poured down . . .

See H.-J. Kraus (*Psalms 60-150*, vol. 2, trans. H. C. Oswald [Minneapolis: Augsburg, 1988], 47-51) for an overview of the different positions concerning the date and setting of Psalm 68, especially with regard to the difference between Albright and Mowinckel. Note the repetition in imagery between Ps 68:8–9 and the Song of Deborah in Judg 5:4–5, where Yahweh is once again described as "going out" (בצאתך) in a military march (בסעדך), which occurs in the larger context of theophany. In both poems the qal form of יצא is used to describe a salvific intervention by Yahweh, conceived as a military march. See also Gen 49:22; 2 Sam 6:13; and Hab 3:10 for other instances of סעד to signify a military march that culminates in theophany.

87. 2 Sam 22:49 reads:

ומוציאי מאיבי
(The God) who <u>brought me out</u> from my enemies

ומקמי תרוממני
you exalted me above my adversaries

מאיש חמסים תצילני
you delivered me from violent men.

For arguments concerning the place of 2 Samuel 22 in the development of Hebrew prosody see W. F. Albright, *Yahweh and the Gods of Canaan: A Historical Analysis of Two Contrasting Faiths,* The Jordan Lectures 1965 (Winona Lake: Eisenbrauns, 1968), 24–25; and Cross and Freedman, *Studies in Ancient Yahwistic Poetry,* 125–160. More recently see P. Kyle McCarter, Jr., *II Samuel,* AB 9B (New York: Doubleday, 1984) for comparison of 2 Samuel 22 to Psalm 18, and analysis of its possible origin as two separate psalms: a song of deliverance (vv. 2–20) and a royal victory song (vv. 29–31, 33–50, 51ab?). He proposes that these psalms originated in the early monarchy period and were brought together perhaps by deuteronomistic editors. See also Zenger, "Le théme de la 'sortie d'Egypte'," 305.

88. Num 23:22 and 24:8 employ the hiphil form of יצא in conjunction with deliverance from Egypt (אל מוציאם/ ממצרים). See H. Rouillard, *La péricope de Balaam (Nombres 22–24): Le prose et les "oracles,"* Fondation Singer-Polignac (Paris: J. Gabalda, 1985), for an overview of the problems concerning date, the relationship of prose to narrative, the shift between first and third person in the use of the formula, as well as the reference to king in the larger context of Num 23:18b–24 and 24:3b–9 (see מלך in 23:21b and 24:7b). He argues that 23:18b–24 is a unified poem, perhaps from preexilic northern tradition (an Elohist) (pp. 273–322 esp. 290–292, 316–322), while 24:3b–9 separates into three parts (vv. 3–4, 5–6, 7–9) consisting of at least two distinct traditions (vv. 5–6 and 7–9) which may be as late as the exile (pp. 345–388, esp. 385–388). See also Zenger ("Le théme de la "sortie d'Egypte'," 304) for a discussion of the royal imagery.

89. See also Wijngaards, "הוציא and העלה: A Twofold Approach to the Exodus," 91–98, esp. 94–95; Childs, "Deuteronomic Formulae of the Exodus Traditions," 30–31; and Preuss, "יצא," 235.

90. ביד הזקה, Deut 6:21; 7:8; 9:26.

91. ביד חזקה ובזרע נטויה, Deut 5:15; 7:19.

92. בפניו בכחו הגדל, Deut 4:37.

93. מכור הברזל, Deut 4:20.

94. מבית עבדים, Deut 5:6; 6:12; 8:14; 13:18.

95. מיד פרעה, Deut 7:8.

96. ממצרים, Deut 4:20, 37; 6:21; 9:26; 23:3; 26:9.

97. מארץ מצרים, Deut 5:6; 6:12; 8:14; 13:5, 10; 20:1.

98. See, for example, the credo in 6:20–25, which begins with the confession: עבדים היינו לפרעה במצרים.

99. Deut 5:6, 15; 10:19; 13:5, 10.

100. The exodus motif occurs three times in an exchange between Moses and Yahweh in Exod 3:10–12. Schmid (*Der sogenannte Jahwist*, 19–43) has noted that the pattern of this exchange follows the form of a prophetic commission: first the commission (3:10), next the objection (3:11), and then reassurance (3:12). The content of the commission is very narrowly defined in v. 10: Moses is "to bring Israel out of Egypt." And his objection in v. 11 is limited to a repetition of this statement. He doubts his ability "to bring Israel out of Egypt." The future orientation of reassurance in v. 12 is not about the conquest of the land; it is only about Israel's exodus from Egypt.

101. Four times the exodus motif is employed during the promulgation of *massot* and firstlings at Succoth. Throughout these references the exodus is viewed as a past event. Three of these occurrences provide motivation for the promulgation of law (13:3, 9, 16), and once the motif is woven into the parent's answer to the child's question concerning the practice of firstlings (13:13).

102. The people state that Moses has taken them into the wilderness to die.

103. See, initially, A. Schart, *Mose und Israel im Konflikt: Eine redaktionsgeschichtliche Studie zu den Wüstenerzählungen,* OBO 98 (Göttingen: Vandenhoeck & Ruprecht, 1990), 47–49.

104. See below for a discussion of the motif of faith in Moses and Joshua within deuteronomistic tradition.

105. Exod 13:3 marks the success of the exodus: "Remember this day on which you came out of Egypt . . ." (יצאתם ממצרים). Exod 13:4 anchors the time of *massot*: "Today you are going out . . ." (היום אתה יצאים). And Exod 13:8 provides instruction for *massot*: "It is because of what Yahweh did for me when I came out from Egypt (בצאתי ממצרים).

106. Thus the exodus motif is narrowly defined in relation to the specific act of Israel's leaving Egypt (an *Auszugstradition*), which must be distinguished from the death of firstborn and confrontation at the sea. This view contrasts to the preexilic narrative, where there is less precision in separating the exodus from the death of the firstborn. Compare Wijngaards ("הוציא and העלה: A Twofold Approach to the Exodus," 101), who is certainly correct in arguing that the exodus motif does not include the taking of land (as compared to Preuss, "יצא", 243), but he has also argued that the motif signifies the deliverance at the sea. For critical evaluation of this position see Childs, "Deuteronomic Formulae of the Exodus Traditions," 30–39. He explores the interrelationship of the exodus motif to the confession that "Yahweh showed signs and wonders" in Egypt, and he concludes that an early use of the motif signified the plagues, exodus, wilderness, and land and that later deuteronomistic tradition defined the motif more narrowly. The present study would not support Child's argument that there is an early use of the exodus motif in deuteronomic tradition, in which the motif is broadly defined.

107. See Wijngaards, *The Formulas of the Deuteronomic Creed*, 28–34; or Boorer, *The Promise of the Land as Oath*, 112–138.

108. The Hebrew reads, והיה כי-יבאך יהוה אל-ארץ. On the syntax see GKC 112y.

109. See Boorer (*The Promise of the Land as Oath*, 36–37, 112–128, and

passim) for an overview of the promise texts with oath. In the Tetrateuch these texts include; Gen 50:24; Exod 13:5, 11; 32:13; 33:1; Num 11:12; 14:23; 32:11; in Deuteronomy; 1:8, 35; 6:10, 18, 23; 7:13; 8:1; 10:11; 11:9, 21; 19:8; 26:3, 15; 28:11; 30:20; 31:7, 20 (21, 23); 34:4; in the deuteronomistic history; Josh 1:6; 5:6b; 21:43; Judg 2:1; and in the deuteronomistic portion of Jeremiah; 11:5; 32:22. She writes, "This distribution indicates that it was not a common expression used universally in Israel but was peculiar to more narrowly defined circles of thought that can be designated as a dtr school" (p. 37). See also Caloz, "Exode, XIII, 3-16," 12-13; and Wijngaards, *The Dramatization of Salvific History in the Deuteronomic Schools*, esp. chap. 3, "The Cultic Occupation of the Land."

110. H. D. Preuss ("בוא," in *TDOT II*, ed. G. J. Botterweck and H. Ringgren [Grand Rapids: Eerdmans, 1975], 28) writes, "Israel is not (from its beginning or by nature) a people of the land into which they come. . . ." For analysis of the verb "to enter" see, Wijngaards, *The Dramatization of Salvific History in the Deuteronomic Schools*, 68-105; G. Braulik, *Die Mittel Deuteronomischer Rhetorik —erhoben aus Deuteronomium 4,1-40*, AnBib 40 (Rome: Pontifical Biblical Institute, 1978), 95; and Preuss, *Theologie des Alten Testaments*, vol. 1, 132-145, esp. 136-137; E. Jenni, "'Kommen' im theologischen Sprachgebrauch des Alten Testaments," in *Wort-Gebot-Glaube: Beiträge zur Theologie des Alten Testaments: Festschrift für W. Eichrodt*, ATANT 59 (Zürich: Zwingli, 1970), 251-261.

111. See Preuss, "יצא," 228; and Gross, "Die Herausführungsformel," 428.

112. Soggin, "Kultätiologische Sagen und Katechese im Hexateuch," 341- 347.

113. The following chart illustrates the distribution of the catechisms, their setting, the speaker, and the content of the instruction, as well as the existence of the exodus motif and promise of land.

Text:	12:21-27	13:1-16	Deut 6:4-25	Joshua 4
Event:	Death of Egyptian firstborn	Exodus from Egypt	Promulgation of law	Entrance into the land
Speaker:	Moses	Moses	Moses	Joshua
Catechetical Instruction				
Question:	Passover	*Massot/* firstlings	Deuteronomic law	Twelve stones
Answer:	Israel spared plague of death	Israel led from Egypt/Egyptian firstborn killed	*Heilsgeschichte* (excluding sea/ river)	Triumph of Yahweh over sea/river
Promise of Land:	X	X	X	—
Exodus Formula:	—	X	X	—

(X) denotes the presence of a motif and (—) its absence.

114. Exod 13:1-2 is frequently attributed to P. A firm decision is difficult to reach. Scholars have noted that the introduction in v. 1 is similar to introductions in priestly literature (Exod 14:1; 25:1; 30:11; etc.) and that the language of sanctification (the hiphil of קדש) also repeats in priestly material (Num 3:13; 8:17). Thus Childs (*Exodus*, 304-305) argues that priestly tradents have added an introduction to a deuteronomic unit (Exod 13:3-16) to bring the material into conformity with Exod 12:1-20. The result, according to Childs, is that vv. 1-2 take on a spiritualized meaning in their present context as a superscription in order to refer to all of Israel. But, as Kohata (*Jahwist und Priesterschrift in Ex 3-14*, 274)

has noted, the hiphil of קדשׁ is also used in Deut 15:19, while Noth (*Exodus*, 101) is less sure of separating vv. 1–2 from vv. 3–16 in spite of changes with regard to singular and pural between vv. 1–2 and vv. 3–16.

115. Boorer (*The Promise of the Land as Oath*, 129–143) argues on the basis of a comparision of Exod 13:3–16 to Exod 34:18–20 that the instruction concerning *massot* in 13:4, 6a and firstlings in 13:12, 13, 15b is older tradition which has been reframed by later tradition (13:3, 5, 6b–9, 11, 14, 16). In contrast to the present study, Boorer argues that this framing is predeuteronomistic and that it occurs independently of the passover legislation in 12:21–27. In view of these literary-critical conclusions, see her three-part reconstruction of the cultic history of the exodus (pp. 189–202) as a progression from (1) unleavened bread/firstborn to (2) passover and unleavened bread loosely connected, with firstborn becoming isolated, and finally (3) passover and unleavened bread as one unified festival with firstborn removed.

116. The deuteronom(ist)ic character of Exod 13:1–16 has long been recognized, yet debate has continued concerning its literary unity and its exact relationship to Deuteronomy. See Wellhausen (*Composition*, 73) who had assigned vv. 1–2 to P and vv. 3–16 to deuteronomistic tradition. For a similar analysis see Hyatt (*Exodus*, 141–142); Childs (*Exodus*, 184, 202–204); or, with slight variation, Fohrer (*Überliererung und Geschichte des Exodus*, 86–89), who assigns vv. 3–16 to D and designates vv. 1–2 as a later redactional addition in the tradition of either D or P. Moving in a somewhat different direction, Noth (*Exodus*, 101–102) argued that the deuteronomistic character of 13:1–16 was the result of a redaction of earlier distinct tradition, while G. Beer (*Exodus*, HAT 3 [Tübingen: J. C. B. Mohr (Paul Siebeck), 1939], 60) takes the analysis of Noth one step further by splitting the unit further into priestly (vv. 11–16) and deuteronomistic (vv. 3–10) traditions. Along these same lines see also Michaeli (*L'Exode*, 111), who describes the unit as ancient tradition in the spirit of J with deuteronomistic additions. Compare, however, J. Van Seters ("The Place of the Yahwist in the History of Passover and Massot," *ZAW* 95 [1983]: 175–176), who argues that the unit is unified and the product of a late (exilic) Yahwist.

The most sustained debated in recent scholarship is whether the unit is proto-deuteronom(ist)ic or deuteronomistic. The arguments once again tend to center on language, as was the case with Exod 12:21–27. Thus Lohfink (*Das Hauptgebot*, 122–123) notes ten peculiarities in style between Exod 13:3–16 and Deuteronomy in arguing for the protodeuteronomic character of this unit. These peculiarities include the phrase "out of Egypt" as opposed to the phrase "out of the land of Egypt"; the predominance of the syntactical form בחזק יד in 13:3, 14, 16 as opposed to the more common phrase in Deuteronomy ביד חזקה, which occurs only in 13:9; the use of "Yahweh" rather than "Yahweh, your God"; the particular form of the table of nations with only five members rather than seven as in Deut 7:1; the form of the reference to the fathers in 13:5, 11, and others. For an expansion of the arguments by Lohfink see Caloz ("Exode, XIII, 3–16," 5–62), who also argues that the unit is protodeuteronom(ist)ic. Compare, however, Fuss (*Die deuteronomistische Pentateuchredaction in Ex 3–17*, 289–290), who argues not only against a protodeuteronomistic reading, but also that the passover instruction (12:21–27) and *massot*/firstlings (13:3–16) are best attributed to the same author. For recent discussion see Blum, *Studien*, 35–36 and esp. 167–168; and Boorer, *The Promise of the Land as Oath*, 130–138.

117. The list of nations occurs seven times in the Tetrateuch (Gen 15:21; Exod 3:8, 17, 13:5; 23:28; 32:3; Num 13:29), three times in Deuteronomy (Deut 1:7; 7:1; 20:17), and four times in the deuteronomistic history (Josh 3:10; 5:1; 9:1; 11:1). Although most scholars would argree that the list of nations predominates in deuteronom(ist)ic tradition, nevertheless, the five-nation list in Exod 13:5 is contrasted to the seven-nation list in Deut 7:1 as a criterion for the protodeuteronomic character of Exod 13:3–16. But the variation in the number and in the order of the lists creates problems for such a fine distinction. The lists range in number from ten (Gen 15:19–21) to seven (Deut 7:1; Josh 3:10), six (Exod 3:8, 17; 32:3; Deut 20:17; Josh 9:1; 11:1), five (Exod 13:5; Num 13:29), three (Exod 23:28; Deut 1:7), and two (Josh 5:1). There are also changes in the ordering. In the six-nation list the Canaanites and Hittites are reversed, creating a contrast between Exod 3:8, 17; 32:3 and Deut 20:17.; Josh 9:1. The Jebusites and Hivites are reversed in Josh 11:1. In the seven-nation list Deut 7:1 and Josh 3:10 have a different order. And in the five-nation list the Hivites in Exod 13:5 are replaced by the Amalekites in Num 13:29. The differences do not lend themselves to clear tradition-historical distinctions.

118. For מבית עבדים see Deut 5:6; 6:12; 8:14; 13:18. See Caloz, "Exode, XIII, 3–16," 11.

119. See the same use of the infinitive absolute (זכור) in Deut 7:18; 24:9; 25:17, as well as finite forms of the verb in Deut 5:15; 8:2, 18; 15:5; 16:3, 12; 24:18, 22. See Weinfeld, *Deuteronomy and the Deuteronomic School*, 41–42, 326–327. For a discussion of the possible tradition-historical roots of the call to remember in deuteronomic tradition see Aurelius, *Der Fürbitter Israels*, 10–40, esp. 18–29.

120. For other examples of זבת חלב ודבש see Deut 6:3; 11:9; 26:6, 15; 27:3; 31:20.

121. For examples of ביד הזקה see Deut 3:24; 4:34; 5:15; 6:21; 7:8, 19; 9:26; 11:2; 26:8; 34:12. Note also the inverted form of the phrase בחזק יד in Exod 13:3, 14, 16. The motif of Yahweh's strong hand was already present in predeuteronomistic tradition (e.g., 6:1; 9:1 [in a somewhat different form]), yet it takes on prominence in deuteronomistic tradition both within the context of the commissioning of Moses (3:19) and in the context of the exodus (13:3, 9, 14, 16). For a discussion of the motif in the larger ancient Near Eastern context see J. K. Hoffmeier, "The Arm of God Versus the Arm of Pharoah in the Exodus Narratives," *Bib* 67 (1986): 380–386.

122. See Deut 16:1, where the older Canaanite calendar is also used to reckon the festivals as compared to the Neo-Babylonian reckoning by priestly tradents in 12:1–20.

123. For examples of טוטפות see Deut 6:8–9 and 11:18–20. For a discussion see N. Sarna, *Exodus: The JPS Torah Commentary* (Philadelphia: Jewish Publication Society, 1991), 270–273.

124. Childs, *Exodus*, 202–204; and Boorer, *The Promise of the Land as Oath*, 139–140.

125. The question-and-answer format can be illustrated in the following manner:

1. Question: והיה כי־ישאלך בנך מחר לאמר מה־זאת
2. Answer: . . . . ואמרת אליו

For a discussion of the form and syntax of the catechism, along with slight differences in language, see, Soggin, "Kultätiologische Sagen und Katechese im Hexateuch," 341–47; Loza, "Les catéchèses étiologique dans l'Ancien Testament, 481–

483; Caloz, "Exode, XIII, 3-16," 43-54, esp. 47-51; Lohfink, *Das Hauptgebot*, 115; B. O. Long, *The Problem of Etiological Narrative in the Old Testament*, BZAW 108; (Berlin: de Gruyter, 1968), 78-79; and Boorer, *The Promise of the Land as Oath*, 137-138. For a discussion of שאל see S. A. Meier, *Speaking of Speaking: Marking Direct Discourse in the Hebrew Bible*, VTSup 46 (Leiden: E. J. Brill, 1992), 161-167, esp. 163-164.

126. Soggin, "Kultätiologische Sagen und Katechese im Hexateuch," 345.

127. Soggin, "Kultätiologische Sagen und Katechese im Hexateuch," 345.

128. For a discussion of the sign formula in general and particularly with the idiom היה לאות see Long (*Etiological Narrative*, 65-69), and for its application to Exod 13:11-16 see pp. 81-83.

129. For a discussion of the sign schema as significative aetiology see Long (*Etiological Narrative*, 69-78), and for its application to Exod 13:11-16 see pp. 81-83.

130. Long (*Etiological Narrative*, 82-83) raises the question of whether 13:8 might not be a fragment from a more complete form.

131. Long (*Etiological Narrative*, 82-83) does not apply Exod 13:10 to his analysis. See Boorer (*The Promise of the Land as Oath*, 142 n. 22) for arguments concerning the secondary nature of v. 10, perhaps from priestly tradition.

132. Long, *Etiological Narrative*, 82-83.

133. See von Rad, *Deuteronomy*, 65; and Long, *Etiological Narrative*, 80-81.

134. von Rad (*Deuteronomy*, 63-65) argues for four separate units: an appeal or confession in vv. 4-9; aspects of a covenant treaty form in vv. 10-15; a sermon in 16-19; and a unit based on tradition in vv. 20-25. Lohfink (*Das Hauptgebot*, 113-131) limits his analysis to Deut 6:10-25. He identifies a "Kleine Gebotsumrahmung" in vv. 10-19. The instruction is in vv. 20-25, where the focus is to pass on the knowledge of covenant. The two sections combine to form a "Grosse Gebotsumrahumung" in which elements of the covenant or treaty formula are accentuated. G. Seitz (*Redaktionsgeschichtliche Studien zum Deuteronomium*, BWANT 13 [Stuttgart: W. Kohlhammer, 1971], 70-74) argues that two units presupposing Israel's present situation in the land (Deut 6:4-9 and 20-24) are supplemented by 5:10-18(19). See also Mayes (*Deuteronomy*, 41-47, 175-176) who follows Seitz.

135. Weinfeld, *Deuteronomy*, 328-329.

136. Boorer, *The Promise of the Land as Oath*, 138-139.

137. The three-part sequence may include: the identification of X (the promulgation of deuteronomic law in 4-6), X as a sign (vv. 8-9), and the meaning of X (vv. 10-19, especially the recounting of the exodus in v. 12 and the characterization of God in vv. 13-15).

138. Weinfeld (*Deuteronomy and the Deuteronomic School*, 301; and *Deuteronomy*, 330) and Boorer (*The Promise of the Land as Oath*, 139 n. 21) use the contrast between a specific cultic occasion and the more general setting of deuteronomic law to argue that Exod 13:1-16 is earlier tradition. Such an argument fails to address adequately the function of the different catechisms within the larger design of a deuteronomistic history.

139. Lohfink, *Das Hauptgebot*, 113-120, esp. 119. See also Wijngaards ("הוציא and העלה: A Twofold Approach to the Exodus," 94-95) for discussion concerning the role of the exodus motif within the historical prologue of the covenant-treaty form in Deuteronomy.

140. In Deut 6:4-25 the exodus motif must also be distinguished from the plagues and the confrontation at the sea. Israel's exodus from Egypt (6:12 and esp. 6:21b and 23a) is a distinct activity from the plagues (6:22), while the confrontation at the sea is absent altogether from the text.

141. Deut 6:10 reads . . . וְהָיָה כִּי יְבִיאֲךָ יהוה [אֱלֹהֶיךָ] אֶל־הָאָרֶץ . . . [כ]אֲשֶׁר נִשְׁבַּע. For a discussion of the syntax see Boorer, *The Promise of the Land as Oath*, 112-128.

142. Even the syntax of the reference to the land is reminiscent of both Exod 13:5, 11 and Deut 6:10: וְהָיָה כִּי־תָבֹאוּ אֶל־הָאָרֶץ אֲשֶׁר יִתֵּן יהוה לָכֶם כַּאֲשֶׁר דִּבֵּר.

143. Long (*Etiological Narrative*, 79-80) notes an etymological aetiology in the word play between the observance (זֶבַח־פֶּסַח) and a past act of Yahweh (פָּסַח), an aetiology of the last night in Egypt, and a significative aetiology "insofar as it summarizes the essential tradition facts which the rite recalls and memorializes." For discussion of etymological aetiologies exhibiting this form see Long, pp. 30-37.

144. The similarities and differences can be illustrated in the following manner.

Event:	Death of Egyptian firstborn	Exodus from Egypt	Promulgation of law
Location:	Ramses	Succoth	Beth-Peor east of Jordan
Catechism:	12:21-27	13:1-16	Deut 6:4-25
	Passover	*Massot*/firstlings	*Heilsgeschichte*
Exodus Formula:	—	X	X
Promise of Land:	X	X	X

(X) denotes the presence of a motif and (—) its absence.

145. The question in 12:26 reads: מָה הָעֲבֹדָה הַזֹּאת לָכֶם, to which the answer in v. 27 is: זֶבַח־פֶּסַח הוּא לַיהוה אֲשֶׁר פָּסַח עַל־בָּתֵּי בְנֵי־יִשְׂרָאֵל בְּמִצְרַיִם בְּנָגְפּוֹ אֶת־מִצְרַיִם וְאֶת־בָּתֵּינוּ הִצִּיל.

146. The first passover in the land occurs at Gilgal in the deuteronomistic history. How early the association of passover at Gilgal occurred is difficult to determine. See G. von Rad, "The Form-Critical Problem of the Hexateuch," in *The Problem of the Hexateuch and Other Essays*, trans. E. W. T. Dicken (New York: McGraw-Hill, 1966): 3-13, 41-48; H.-J. Kraus, "Gilgal: Ein Beitrag zur Kultusgeschichte Israels," *VT* 1 (1951): 181-199; and *Worship in Israel*, 152-165; E. Otto, *Das Mazzotfest in Gilgal*, BWANT 7 (Stuttgart: W. Kohlhammer, 1975), 4-25 and passim; and most recently Batto, *Slaying the Dragon*.

The role of Gilgal in the structure of the deuteronomistic history can be summarized as follows. It has been inserted into Deut 11:30 as the location for blessing and cursing, which is traditionally associated with Shechem. In the history from Joshua-Kings, Gilgal is Israel's final itinerary stop (Josh 4:19, but see Judg 2:1); it is the initial location for cultic observance (circumcision, passover, *massot* in Josh 5:2-12, which will be superseded by Jerusalem); it is the location from which Israel wages holy war (Josh 9:9; 10:6, 7, 9, 15, 43; 1 Sam 13:4, 7, 8, 12, 15; 15:12, 21, 33) and from where Israel is also judged for not waging holy war (Judg 2:1); it is the location for distributing the land (Josh 14:6) and for anointing or renewing kings (Saul in 1 Sam 10:8; 11:14-15; and David in 2 Sam 19:16). Finally, Gilgal is also associated with Elijah and Elisha (2 Kgs 2:1; 4:38).

In spite of its prominence within the story, its precise geographical location has eluded scholars. Gilgal may have been a defeated city (Josh 12:23), it may be located near Jericho (Josh 4:19), near Bethel (2 Kgs 2:1), on the northern border of Judah (Josh 15:7), or even near Shechem (Deut 11:30). For an overview of the geographical problems see J. Muilenburg, "The Site of Ancient Gilgal," *BASOR* 140 (1955): 11-27; or W. R. Kotter, "Gilgal," in *The Anchor Bible Dictionary*, vol. 2, ed. D. N. Freedman (New York: Doubleday, 1992), 1022-1024.

147. Exod 10:1b-2a is a divine speech to Moses rather than parenetic instruction of Moses to Israel, as is the case with the other instances of the catechism. The reason for this change is that the addition occurs at the outset of the plague of locust, where the pattern is such that Yahweh presents instruction to Moses. The instruction provides commentary on the hardening motif. Yahweh has hardened Pharaoh's heart (10:1ba) for two reasons: first, to multiply signs in the midst of the Egyptians (v. 1bb), and second, to instruct Israel. Blum (*Studien*, 15-17) has also seen the connection between Exod 10:1b-2a and later passover instruction, but he emphasizes the recognition formula in 10:2b as the central aspect of the addition in deuteronomistic tradition. For a more detailed interpretation of the recognition formula within priestly tradition see chapter 4.

148. See Blum (*Studien*, 15-16) for possible functions of this text as a sign for Israel.

149. The absence of the more developed motif concerning the promise of land in Exod 12:25 may be due to the separation of passover from the exodus in the larger structure of the deuteronomistic history.

150. For discussion on the relationship between Moses and Joshua in the book of Joshua see Polzin, *Moses and the Deuteronomist*, 73-85.

151. The Jordan River crossing is usually confined to Josh 3:1-5:1 as an activity distinct from the preceding account of the spies (Joshua 2) and the later cultic activity at Gilgal (Josh 5:2-12) or conquest of Jericho (Joshua 6), even through there are clear temporal and geographical links between these sections in the present form of the text. For a general discussion concerning these boundaries see, for example, M. Noth, *Das Buch Josua*, HAT 7 (Tübingen: J. C. B. Mohr (Paul Siebeck), 1938), 11; Kraus, *Worship in Israel*, 154-159; A. Soggin, *Joshua*, OTL, trans. R. A. Wilson (Philadelphia: Westminster, 1970), 50-54; Otto, *Das Mazzotfest in Gilgal*, 26-57; T. C. Butler, *Joshua*, WBC 7 (Waco: Word Publishing, 1983), 41-44; or Polzin, *Moses and the Deuteronomist*, 91-110.

152. On the role of Joshua, see Noth, *History of Pentateuchal Traditions*, 175-177; Soggin, *Joshua*, 14-18; K. Möhlenbrink, "Josua im Pentateuch," *ZAW* 59 (1942-1943): 140-158. For a discussion of the possible role of Gilgal in ancient liturgy see, among others, Kraus, *Worship in Israel*, 154-165. For a review of the geographical problems assocated with Gilgal see Kotter, "Gilgal," 1022-1024; or R. G. Boling and G. E. Wright, *Joshua*, AB 6 (New York: Doubleday, 1982), 136-138, 177-181. For a review of past interpretations concerning the role of the ark see J. Maier, *Das altisraelitische Ladeheiligtum*, BZAW 93 (Berlin: A. Töpelmann, 1965), 19-32. For arguments favoring as many as nine recensions in the transmission of this tradition into its present form see F. Langlamet, *Gilgal et le récit de la traversée du Jourdain* (Jos. III-IV), CahRB 11 (Paris: J. Gabalda, 1969); for six, see J. Dus, "Die Analyse zweier Ladeerzählungen des Josuabuches (Jos 3-4 und 6)," *ZAW* 72 (1960): 107-134; and Maier, *Ladeheiligtum* 19-32, 76-80. There is also debate concerning the nature of the literature. For arguments in favor of sources see Wellhausen, *Composition*, 118-122; K. Möhlenbrink, "Die Landnahmesagen des Buches Josua," *ZAW* 15 (1938) 254-258; Dus, "Die Analyse

zweier Ladeerzählungen des Josuabuches," 107-134; Maier, *Ladeheiligtum*, 18-32, 76-80; E. Vogt, "Die Erzählung vom Jordanübergang," *Bib* 46 (1965) 125-148; Otto, *Das Mazzotfest in Gilgal*, 26-57; Butler, *Joshua*, 41-44. For a more supplemental view see Noth, *Josua*, 11-16; Soggin, *Joshua*, 50-67; Long, *Etiological Narrative*, 83-84; or T. W. Mann, *Divine Presence and Guidance in Israelite Traditions: The Typology of Exaltation*, JHNES (Baltimore: Johns Hopkins University Press, 1977), 196-206. For a review of scholarship see A. R. Hulst, "Der Jordan in den alttestamentlichen Überlieferungen," *OTS* 14 (1965): 168-177; or Otto, *Das Mazzotfest in Gilgal*, 26-57, 120-186 and passim.

153. Note that the motif of crossing occurs in Josh 4:6b-7 and 4:21-24. But this point of similarity should not mask the profound difference between the two texts. In Josh 4:6b-7a the focus is on the ark, which, when it crossed the Jordan, cut off the water. The stones, therefore, point back to this action of the ark, and Israel is not mentioned. In Josh 4:21-24, by contrast, the focus is on Israel crossing the Jordan as a result of Yahweh's having dried up the water. In spite of these differences, the catechisms are frequently not distinguished from each other in the tradition-historical development of the text. See Wellhausen, (*Composition*, 122), who concludes that 4:6-7 and 20-24 are deuteronomistic, as does Rudolph (*Der "Elohist,"* 178), assigning 4:4-8a and 21-24 to deuteronomistic tradents. Noth (*Josua*, 11) sees the difference in content not only between the catechisms but also in their larger contexts of Josh 4:6-7, 9, 10a and 4:1-3, 8, 20-24. Still he concludes that they are distinct narrative elements being brought together by a collector. So too, apparently, Möhlenbrink, "Die Landnahmesagen des Buches Josua," 256. Compare, however, Soggin (*Joshua*, 66-67), who argues for three stages of tradition, with 4:6-7 being the original instruction, 4:20-23 a later recension, and 4:24 an expansion by the deuteronomistic redactor. Otto (*Das Mazzotfest in Gilgal*, 44-45) attributes 4:6-7 to a predeuteronomistic A Source and 4:21-24 to a deuteronomistic B Source. Along somewhat different lines Vogt ("Die Erzählung vom Jordanübergang,"129-130) speaks of two parallel accounts of catechetical instruction associated with the stones: the first being Josh 4:4-7, 9-10a and the second, 4:1*, 2, 3, 8, 11, 20-24. Butler (*Joshua*, 41) contrasts the two catechetical texts in the following manner. Josh 4:6-7 centers upon the ark cutting off the waters and the memorial stones, while 4:21-23 centers upon the miracle that Israel crossed on dry ground. He then attributes each text to a separate source. Finally, H.-J. Fabry ("Spuren des Pentateuchredaktors in Jos 4,21ff: Anmerkungen zur Deuteronomismus-Rezeption," in *Das Deuteronomium: Entstehung, Gestalt und Botschaft*, BETL 68, ed. N. Lohfink [Leuven: Uitgeverij Peeters, 1985], 351-356) assigns Josh 4:6b-7 to deuteronomistic tradents and 4:21-24 to a postdeuteronomistic Rp redactor. Even when the catechisms are viewed as separate tradition, questions of interpretation remain with regard to the relationship of both texts to a more original account of the crossing of the Jordan. For a description of such a narrative see, among others, Vogt ("Die Erzählung vom Jordanübergang," 129-130), who isolates Josh 3:1, 7, 14a, 16; 4:10b, 12, 13, 14; or Mann (*Divine Presence and Guidance in Israelite Traditions*, 196-197), who specifies Josh 1:10-11; 3:1-14, 9-11, 13-15a, 16.

154. Otto (*Das Mazzotfest in Gilgal*, 44-45) notes a variety of expansions in 4:21-24 from 4:6b-7, both in the question of 4:21 (the addition of אבותם as the object of the verb שאל and the replacement of את בניכם for להם) and in the answer of 4:22-24 (especially the connection between the Red Sea and the Jor-

dan River in 4:23). On the basis of comparisons like Josh 4:24 and 1 Kgs 8:60
למען דעת כל־עמי הארץ Otto concludes that Josh 4:21–24 is deuteronomistic. Fabry
("Spuren des Pentateuchredaktors in Josh 4,21ff," 252–253) has built on the work
of Otto by noting that the reference to the ancestors in v. 21 is characteristic of
deuteronomistic tradents and that the syntax of the question (the use of אשר rather
than כי) could not be predeuteronomistic.

155. The separation of two accounts on the basis of the location of the stones
has been clearly argued by Wellhausen (*Composition*, 122) and expanded upon
by Möhlenbrink ("Die Landnahmesagen des Buches Josua," 254–258), who
describes a Jordan version of the stones (Josh 3:2a, 5, 11, 12b–17a,bα; 4:4–7, 9f,
17–19, [21–24?]) and a Gilgal version (3:1ab, 9; 4:3b, 12, 13, 20). Although precise literary distinctions are debated, the separation of the two accounts is fairly
standard among scholars. There is debate, however, concerning the tradition-historical relationship of the two locations of the stones and their symbolic significance. Many scholars advocate that the stones at Gilgal represent the older version of the story, which is either early Israelite in origin or even pre-Israelite (see,
for example, Kraus, "Gilgal," 181–199; and *Worship in Israel*, 50–51, 152–159).
A presupposition underlying this argument is that the crossing of the Jordan is
considered to be part of an ancient Gilgal festival. See the general argument by
von Rad, *The Form-Critical Problem of the Hextateuch*, 3–13, 41–48. This presupposition has given rise to the argument that the movement of the stones is
from the west bank at Gilgal to the middle of the Jordan and that the symbolic
significance of this movement is from a concrete memorial (something visible
at Gilgal) to a spiritualized memorial (something out of sight in the middle of
the Jordan). Yet the instruction would suggest just the reverse: that the stones
at Gilgal have acquired the more abstract significance by indicating Yahweh's
activity throughout salvation history, as compared to the stones in the middle
of the Jordan, which symbolize more concretely Yahweh's power over this
particular body of water.

156. See C. A. Keller, "Über einige alttestamentliche Heiligtumslegenden II,"
ZAW 68 (1956): 90–94.

157. Yahweh's possession of the land is clearly stated in the older version of
the narrative (Josh 3:11, 13), where his lordship over the land is proclaimed
(אדון כל־הארץ). For discussion see Langlamet, *Gilgal*, 113; and Mann, *Divine Presence and Guidance in Israelite Traditions*, 197.

158. For a discussion of the interrelationship between Josh 4:21–24 and the
crossing of the Red Sea as a basis for attributing the catechism to deuteronomistic
tradition, see Mann, *Divine Presence and Guidance in Israelite Traditions*,
197–206.

159. The restructuring of the narrative is undertaken at the expense of narrative logic. Problems of internal logic include at least the following topics: prepa-
ration for the crossing, the crossing of the river, the priests leaving the river, the
selection of men to carry the stones, the setting up of the stones in different locations, as well as the catechisms. For an overview see, Butler, *Joshua*, 41; Otto,
Das Mazzotfest in Gilgal, 27; or Polzin, *Moses and the Deuteronomist*, 91–92.

160. The presence of signs in the midst of Israel (Josh 4:6, קרב) also occurs
in assocation with the plagues (Exod 10:1b) and in the promulgation of deuteronomic law (Deut 6:15). The memorial function of the stones (Josh 4:7, זכרון)

also appears in association with *massot* (Exod 13:9). Finally, the enduring character of the stones (Josh 4:7, עַד־עוֹלָם) is also applied to the passover (Exod 12:24).

161. Yahweh's possession of the land is reaffirmed in Josh 4:24; 5:1.

162. Norin (*Er Spaltete das Meer*, 23-41, 93-94) has argued that the reference to the בְּיַם־סוּף in 15:4 is a later addition to the poem.

163. See Exod 2:3, 5, where Moses is put in a basket and placed among the reeds (בַּסוּף). See also Isa 19:6.

164. For arguments in favor of the translation "Reed Sea" on the basis of the Egyptian *twf(y)* see J. Bright, *A History of Israel*, 3d ed. (Philadelphia: Westminster, 1981), 122-123; or W. A. Ward, "The Semitic Biconsonantal Root SP and the Common Origin of Egyptian CWP and Hebrew SûP: 'March (-Plant),'" *VT* 24 (1974): 339-349.

165. See J. R. Huddlestun, "Red Sea," in *The Anchor Bible Dictionary*, vol. 5, ed. D. N. Freedman (New York: Doubleday, 1992), 633-642.

166. N. H. Snaith, "יַם־סוּף: The Sea of Reeds: The Red Sea," *VT* 15 (1965): 395-398.

167. Snaith, "יַם־סוּף: The Sea of Reeds: The Red Sea," 397.

168. Snaith, "יַם־סוּף: The Sea of Reeds: The Red Sea," 397.

169. Snaith, "יַם־סוּף: The Sea of Reeds: The Red Sea," 395. See Qoh 3:11; 7:2; 12:13; 2 Chr 20:16; Joel 2:20 for examples of Hebrew סוּף meaning "end."

170. B. F. Batto, "The Reed Sea: Requiescat in Pace," *JBL* 102 (1983): 30-31.

171. Batto ("The Reed Sea: Requiescat in Pace," 32-34) noted that in the Song of Jonah (Jonah 2:2-9) the prophet's prayer in the fish includes the threatening imagery of being engulfed by the sea (vv. 4, 6), and more precisely, that the use of סוּף (v. 6) in the context of this primeval chaos (including imagery of the underworld, the sea-dragon, the abyss, and so forth) would require that the word have "something to do with a cosmic battle against chaos."

172. Batto, "The Reed Sea: Requiescat in Pace," 34-35.

173. Of its twenty-three occurrences, eight are in Deuteronomy or the deuteronomistic history (Deut 1:40; 2:1; 11:4; Josh 2:10; 4:23; 24:6; Judg 11:16; 1 Kgs 9:26), five in late historiographic psalms reflecting deuteronomistic influence (Pss 106:7, 9, 22; 136:13, 15), one occurrence each in Nehemiah (9:9) and Jeremiah (49:21), leaving eight references in Exodus and Numbers, where the term is associated primarily with Israel's wilderness march (Exod 10:19; 13:18; 15:22; 23:31; and Num 14:25; 21:4; 33:10, 11).

174. See Deut 11:4, where Yahweh is described as causing the waters of the Red Sea to flow over the Egyptians (הֵצִיף אֶת־מֵי יַם־סוּף עַל־פְּנֵיהֶם). Compare also Josh 24:6-7 and perhaps Ps 106:22.

175. Note that in the story of the spies, Rahab does not recount the event at the Red Sea as a destruction of the Egyptian army, but only as a miracle that allowed Israel to cross the water on dry ground (Josh 2:10). The same is true for the second catechism in Josh 4:23.

176. Batto, "The Reed Sea: Requiescat in Pace," 35.

177. Batto, "The Reed Sea: Requiescat in Pace," 35.

178. The transfer of the confrontation at the sea from Egypt to the wilderness is evident from an examination of the itinerary notices. Exod 13:20 states that after the promulgation of *massot*/firstlings at Succoth, Israel journeyed to Etham, located on the "edge of the wilderness." This is the new setting for the

confrontation at the sea. The itinerary notice in Exod 15:22 is also noteworthy in determining the location of the confrontation at the sea. It states that Israel journeyed not from Etham, as we would expect from the previous itineraries, but from the Red Sea to the Wilderness of Shur, and it also states that this location is "three days into the wilderness." The use of the Red Sea as a geographical notice underscores that the sea has acquired a precise geographical function as a doorway into the wilderness. The result of this restructuring is that sea tradition is becoming historicized both as the body of water marking a boundary between Egypt and the wilderness (Exod 15:4, 22) and as an ongoing road that extends into the wilderness (Exod 13:18a; see also Num 14:25; 21:4; Deut 1:40; 2:1).

179. The syntax of Exod 13:18a includes the sequence of "road" + "wilderness" and "Red Sea" (דרך המדבר ים־סוף). This syntactical relationship has presented problems to past translators. See, for example, the NRSV ("so God led the people by the roundabout way of the wilderness *toward* the Red Sea") or the New American ("Instead, he rerouted them *toward* the Red Sea by way of the desert road"). Both versions translate Red Sea as though it had a directive *he*, which it does not. Childs' (*Exodus*, 217) conclusion that "[t]here is a syntactical ambiguity in respect to the relation of the 'wilderness way' to the 'sea'" fits the larger design of deuteronomistic redactors to merge these two traditions in their restructuring of the story, since the Red Sea becomes a location within the larger sequence of itineraries. For other occurrences of the identification of the Red Sea as an itinerary stop in the wilderness (דרך המדבר ים־סוף) see Num 14:25; 21:4; 33:10, 11; Deut 1:40; 2:1; Judg 11:16.

180. The itinerary in Exod 15:22a is often attributed to P along with v. 27 (see, for example, Noth, *Exodus*, 127-128). The reference to the Red Sea, the motif of Israel's journeying (יצא), and the specific reference to a location three days into the wilderness correspond to the deuteronomistic restructuring of the exodus and thus provide the basis for our interpretation of this story within deuteronomistic tradition. See Davies ("The Wilderness Itineraries and the Composition of the Pentateuch," 8-10) for a discussion of Exod 15:22 within deuteronomistic tradition. There is also debate concerning the larger structure of the story in Exod 15:22-27, especially whether 15:27 is a continuation of deuteronomistic tradition or a priestly addition to include the story of manna. See the recent study by Schart (*Mose und Israel im Konflikt*, 172-178, 184-185), who identifies at least two levels of tradition in Exod 15:22-26(27): a Jehowistische-Stratum (consisting of 15:22-25a) and a later D-Stratum (15:25b-26).

181. Twice the wilderness is mentioned in Israel's complaint, and twice it is described as a place of death. In v. 11 the Israelites question whether Moses had brought them into the wilderness in order to kill them (למות במדבר), and in v. 12 the people state that slavery in Egypt was better than death in the wilderness (ממתנו בבדבר). The formulation of their complaint to Moses—especially in the second question, "What have you done to us in bringing us from Egypt?"—brings to mind the earlier instruction of *massot* and firstlings with regard to the syntax of the question (מה־זאת) and its content (the exodus motif). The language of slavery (עבד) in v. 12 also interrelates this complaint with the instruction of passover and *massot*/firstlings. The dichotomy between slavery in Egypt and risk of death in the wilderness underscores yet again how liberation in deuteronomistic tradition is not freedom but rather transferred slavery (so also Ska, *Le passage de la mer*, 66). The close parallels in syntax and in content between Israel's murmur-

ing and Yahweh's preceding instruction concerning the exodus underscore how Israel's complaint represents a lack of faith in Yahweh's power to save, even though it is expressed indirectly as a challenge to Mosaic authority.

182. The murmuring motif reappears in Exod 15:22-27; 16; 17:1-7; Num 11:1-3, 4-31; 14; 16; 20:2-13; 21:4-9. For a form-critical study of the phraseology of the murmuring motif see Coats, *The Murmuring Motif in the Wilderness Traditions of the Old Testament*, 29-43; and M. Vervenne, "The Protest Motif in the Sea Narrative (Ex 14,11-12): Form and Structure of a Pentateuchal Pattern," *ETL* 63 (1987) 259-263. For arguments suggesting that the larger structure of the murmuring stories fits two distinct patterns see Childs, *Exodus*, 258-260; or Vervenne, "The Protest Motif," 265-267; as compared to three distinct patterns, see P. Buis, "Les conflits entre Moïse et Israël dans Exode et Nombres," *VT* 28 (1978): 257-261. For tradition-historical analysis of possible predeuteronomistic tradition in the formation of the murmuring stories see Coats, *The Murmuring Motif in the Wilderness Traditions of the Old Testament*, 45-191; S. J. DeVries, "The Origin of the Murmuring Tradition, *JBL* 87 (1968): 51-58; or Fritz, *Israel in der Wüste*, 107-122. For more redaction-critical arguments concerning the formation of the murmuring stories see Vervenne ("The Protest Motif," 270), who favors a protodeuteronomic JE redactor; Aurelius (*Die Fürbitter Israels*, 141-160), who looks to deuteronomistic tradition; Blum (*Studien*, 111-164), who argues for a postdeuteronomistic D-Komposition; or Schart (*Mose und Israel im Konflikt*, 58-241), who traces three levels of tradition: a preexilic Jehowistic-Stratum, a D-Stratum, and P.

183. Deuteronomistic additions to the confrontation at the sea can be summarized around two themes. First, the holy-war character of the confrontation at the sea is played down with the addition of Exod 13:17-18a, 20; 14:11-12; 15a*b*. Second, the emphasis on Israel's entering the sea is achieved with the addition of Exod 14:15b, 16b, 19a, 20a*a*, 22a, 23, 28-29a, 31; 15:19.

184. Exod 13:17b introduces a section consisting of Exod 13:17-22 and 14:1-4, in which Israel's march out of Egypt is described. This section begins with a description of how God initially led the Israelites on a roundabout journey on the Red Sea road because they were not yet ready for holy war (13:17-18a). This description is contradicted in the following statement, where Israel is characterized as being more than ready for battle (13:18b). Then what follows is the mention of the bones of Joseph (13:19), an itinerary notice that Israel journeyed from Succoth to Etham, on the edge of the wilderness (13:20), a description of the pillar of cloud leading the Israelites on their march (13:21-22), and finally, new directions for travel in which Yahweh instructs Moses to turn Israel around in order to camp at Piharhiroth (14:1-4). The contrasting profiles of the Israelites in 13:17-18a and in 13:18b with regard to their preparedness for holy war and the abrupt change in their route in Exod 13:17-18a, 20 and 14:1-4 make it clear that there is a history of tradition in the present form of the text. Past studies have presumed the early rise of historiography in the formation of the Pentateuch. Thus references to the wilderness (vv. 18 and 20), the historicizing of the Red Sea (v. 18), the itinerary notice (13:20), and the role of the cloud to lead Israel through the wilderness (vv. 21-22) were frequently attributed to early preexilic tradition (see, for example, Noth, *Exodus*, 104-105). The central argument of the present study, that the rise of the wilderness tradition in the Pentateuch is an exilic innovation by deuteronomistic tradents, calls into question the attribution of wilderness motifs to preexilic

tradition. As a result, the leading of the Israelites along the Red Sea road (Exod 13:17-18a) and the itinerary notice that places them at the edge of the wilderness (13:20) are being interpreted within deuteronomistic tradition, while the more militant march of Israel (13:18b) behind the pillar of cloud (13:21- 22) will be examined as priestly additions which accompany their itinerary notice (14:1-4). The bones of Joseph in 13:19 could fit in either deuteronomistic or priestly tradition.

185. The redactional design of the framing can be illustrated in the following manner:

PRE-DTR—The cry of Israel to Yahweh (v. 10)
    DTR—The complaint of Israel to Moses (vv. 11-12)

PRE-DTR—The war oracle of Moses (vv. 13-14)
    DTR—The complaint of Yahweh to Moses (v. 15ab)

The framing gives rise to a problem of logic. In the predeuteronomistic text Israel cried to Yahweh at the approach of the Egyptians (14:10), whereas in the deuteronomistic text Yahweh responds in v. 15ab as though it were Moses who cried to God. The problem of logic is certainly not unique to the larger context, since in 13:17-19 Israel has already been described as leaving Egypt both looking for battle and trying to avoid it. At the very least the divine response in Exod 14:15ab highlights the mediatorial role of Moses that is characteristic of deuteronomistic tradition (e.g., Exod 15:25; 32:11-14, 30-32; Num 12:13; 14:13-19; Deut 9:25-29, etc.), which in the context of the confrontation at the sea will result in Israel's having faith in him (Exod 14:31). For an overview of the problems, see Ska (*Le passage de la mer*, 113-114), who looks to ancient patterns of storytelling as a possible solution to the inconsistent logic.

186. Although most scholars have seen that these verses are interrelated, they are usually attributed to a priestly source (see Noth, *Exodus*, 105, 126; or Childs, *Exodus*, 220). The closest parallels in language, however, appear in the deuteronomistic history rather than in priestly tradition. They include the speech by Rahab to the spies (Josh 2:10), the catechism associated with the crossing of the Jordan (Josh 4:21-24), and the farewell speech by Joshua (Josh 24:6-7).

187. The command-and-fulfillment cycle of the older narrative yields two cycles of action as a result of the action of Moses with his hand/staff. In the first cycle the sea is dried up (divine command in 14:15aa, 16aa and its fulfillment in 14:21a, 24aa, 24b-25), and in the second cycle it is brought back as a destructive force against the Egyptian army (divine command in 14:26 and its fulfillment in 14:27). The deuteronomistic insertion of the motif of escape is part of the command-and-fulfillment structure of the first cycle (command in 14:16b and fulfillment in 22a); it provides a summary conclusion to the second cycle (Exod 14:29a) and returns one last time after the Song of the Sea (Exod 15:19) to provide a connection between the confrontation at the sea and Israel's march to the wilderness of Shur (Exod 15:22-26).

188. The fear (ירא) of God is central to deuteronomistic tradition. See Weinfeld (*Deuteronomy and the Deuteronomic School*, 332-323 *and passim*) for its distribution in deuteronomic and deuteronomistic literature. For a discussion of its role in Exodus, especially in relation to the Sinai tradition, see Dozeman, *God on the Mountain*, 49-50, 83-85. Belief (אמן) in Moses also plays a prominent role

in the deuteronomistic redaction of both the exodus and Sinai traditions. Belief in Moses (or the potential lack of it) is explored in the call of Moses in Exod 4:1-31 (see vv. 1, 5, 8, 9, 31). This unit ends with a description of Israel believing (אמן), which results in worship. It occurs two other times, at crucial junctures in both the exodus and Sinai stories. It returns at the close of the sea event in 14:31 (where Israel believes in Yahweh and Moses), which is followed by worship in the singing of the Song of the Sea in Exod 15:1-18. Belief in Moses then returns in Exod 19:9 as one of the purposes for theophany in deuteronomistic redaction of the Mountain of God tradition, where it is followed by theophany (the deuteronomistic revelation of the Decalogue in Exod 19:19; 20:1-17*) resulting in Israel's choice of Moses and fear of God (20:18-20). In all of these instances faith in Moses is associated with worship or cultic activity. For an overview of the motif of faith (אמן) see H. Wildberger, "'Glauben' im Alten Testament," *ZTK* 65 (1968) 129-159, esp. 153-154. See Dozeman (*God on the Mountain*, 45-50) for a discussion of Exod 19:9, 19; 20:18-20 as deuteronomistic tradition. Also compare H.-C. Schmitt ("Redaktion des Pentateuch im Geiste der Prophetie," *VT* 32 [1982] 171-189) for arguments in favor of a postexilic dating for the inclusion of this motif in the Pentateuch.

189. The tradition-historical roots of the מלאך האלהים are difficult to trace. Attempts to sort out the tradition-historical development of the מלאך within the Pentateuch by tracing terminological differences have yielded little success. The term מלאך is used twice in the parenetic conclusion to the Book of the Covenant (Exod 23:20, 23) and twice in the context of the golden calf (Exod 32:34; 33:2) in association with either wilderness leading or conquest. The מלאך יהוה appears to Moses in the burning bush (Exod 3:2), whereas the מלאך האלהים leads Israel at the Red Sea (Exod 14:19a). Yet when the leading at the sea is recounted in Num 20:16, only the word מלאך is used. Thus no discernible patterns emerge. When study is expanded beyond the Pentateuch, it is clear that some form of the messenger certainly preceded deuteronomistic tradition, perhaps functioning in settings of theophany associated with holy war. See Judg 5:23, where the מלאך יהוה is called upon to curse Meroz for not coming to the aid of Yahweh in a situation of war. T. H. Gaster (*Myth, Legend, and Custom in the Old Testament* [New York: Harper & Row, 1969], 419) argues that this reference is ancient and that it represents a professional diviner rather than the mythological personification of God as in the account of the exodus.

190. The holy-war function of the מלאך occurs when the land is mentioned as future promise (Exod 23:20, 23), when Israel is in the vicinity of the land (Numbers 22), and when Israel is settled in the land (Judg 2:1-17; 1 Sam 29:9; 2 Sam 24:15-17 = 1 Chr 21:14-17; 2 Kgs 19:35 = 2 Chr 32:21). The מלאך wages war against Israel (2 Sam 24:15-17) and against Israel's enemies (2 Kgs 19:35), and it also punishes Israel by not completing holy war against Israel's enemies (Judg 2:1-17).

191. Mann (*Divine Presence and Guidance in Israelite Traditions*, 253) has demonstrated that the language of leading (הלך + לפני) is used "exclusively in connection with the Wilderness March." The function of the מלאך as leading Israel in the wilderness would appear to be an innovation within deuteronomistic tradition. It is introduced in the Hagar narrative, when she is rescued in the wilderness and given food (Gen 16:7-17; 21:17). It continues in the account of Israel's journey through the wilderness (Exod 3:2; 14:19a; 32:34; 33:2; Num 20:16). And

it reappears in the Elijah narrative when he too is rescued by the מלאך in the wilderness. The introduction of the מלאך האלהים as leading Israel at the Red Sea certainly fits in with this latter pattern. Yet the leading of Israel in the wilderness is never divorced from conquest imagery in deuteronomistic tradition. References to the מלאך in Exod 23:20, 23; 33:2 show that divine leading is meant to culminate in a future conquest of the land, which is characterized by the act of "driving out" (גרש in Exod 23:28, 29, 30, 31; 33:2) the other nations. For an overview of the different functions of the מלאך see G. von Rad, "αγγελος," in *TDNT 1*, ed. G. Kittel (Grand Rapids: Eerdmans, 1964), 76-80; Noth, *Exodus*, 105; Fohrer, *Überlieferung und Geschichte des Exodus*, 124; Childs, *Exodus*, 221; Kohata, *Jahwist und Priesterschrift in Exodus 3-14*, 372; Weimar, *Die Meerwundererzählung*, 251-253; and Blum, *Studien*, 58-60, 361-382, esp. 365-378.

192. See also Deut 11:4; Josh 24:6.

193. A. Lauha, "Das Schilfmeermotiv im Alten Testament," in *Congress Volume Bonn 1962*, VTSup 9, ed. G. W. Anderson (Leiden: E. J. Brill, 1963), 44.

194. Coats, "The Reed Sea Motif," 260-261. The speech of Rahab in Josh 2:9-13 separates into two parts: first, she recounts the miraculous drying up of the Red Sea when Israel left Egypt (v. 10a, אשר־הוביש יהוה את־מי ים־סוף מפניכם בצאתכם ממצרים), and second, she notes Israel's initial holy war victories against Sihon and Og immediately across the Jordan (v. 10b, אשר עשיתם לשני מלכי האמרי אשר בעבר הירדן לסיחן ולעוג אשר החרמתם אותם). Her speech mirrors the deuteronomistic interpretation of the exodus, wherein the Red Sea does not symbolize holy war as much as it does Israel's miraculous escape from Egypt. This interpretation is also carried through in Josh 4:22-23, where the stones symbolize Yahweh's drying up (יבשה) the Red Sea and the Jordan River in order for Israel to cross over (עבר) both bodies of water.

195. See Cross (*Canaanite Myth and Hebrew Epic*, 112-120) for a discussion of Yamm-Nahar in Ugaritic mythology.

196. See Coats ("The Traditio-Historical Character of the Reed Sea Motif," 253-265; and "The Song of the Sea," *CBQ* 31 (1969):16-17) for application of this mythic structure to the exodus tradition. The present study has followed Coats' conclusions ("The Traditio-Historical Character of the Reed Sea Motif," 264-265) that, first, the event at the sea is not the center of the exodus, and second, that it is actually embedded in the wilderness. But in contrast to Coats, these conclusions are being applied here to deuteronomistic tradition instead of to a predeuteronomistic Yahwist.

197. The differences can be illustrated in the following manner:

	Red Sea	Jordan River
Setting	Exodus from Egypt	Conquest of the land
Holy War	Absent	Present
Divine Leading	At the rear of Israel	In front of Israel
Focus	Israel	Nations
Key Language	To enter (בוא) into the midst of the sea (בתוך הים) on dry ground (יבשה)	To cross (עבר) the Jordan River on dry ground (הובש)

198. The ark occurs seventeen times in Joshua 3-4. It is referred to simply as the ark (הארון) in Josh 3:15 [twice]; 4:10); as the ark of the covenant (of Yahweh your God) (הארון־הברית) in Josh 3:3, 6 [twice], 8, 11, 13, 14, 17; 4:7, 9, 16, 18), and

as the ark of Yahweh (הארון־יהוה in Josh 4:5, 11). It is difficult to discern a tradition-historical development on the basis of the distinct terminology. What is clear is that the ark functions in the role of leading a procession for war in order to possess the land (Josh 1:10-11, 15), and, in the process, it cuts off the Jordan River. See Kraus, (*Worship in Israel*, 164), who describes three functions of the ark: as guidance, holy war, and processional shrine. The war imagery is made explicit in relation to the tribes east of the Jordan. In Josh 1:14 only the warriors (גבורי החיל) are commanded to cross over the Jordan, which they do in Josh 4:12-13 in order to wage war (למלחמה). For more general discussion concerning the holy war function of the ark see Miller, *The Divine Warrior in Early Israel*, 145-155, 157-158.

199. The outward focus on the nations is clear at many points in the story. It is suggested by the language of possession (Josh 1:10-11, 15) and then explicitly expressed in the speech of Rahab, who describes the fear of the nations (2:10-11); in the report of the spies, who also describe the same fear (2:24); in the speech of Joshua, where he describes the dispossession of the Canaanites as the goal of crossing the Jordan (3:10); in the symbolic meaning of the stones within the second catechism, where the nations are described as fearing Yahweh as a result of the crossing of the Jordan (4:24); and in the narrative conclusion to the events, when the nations are described as fearing Israel after they cross the Jordan (5:1). See Polzin (*Moses and the Deuteronomistic*, 99-103), who argues that there is a changing perspective in the narrative from Israel to the nations within the land in the present composition of Josh 3:1-5:1.

200. A. R. Hulst ("Der Jordan in den Alttestamentlichen Überlieferungen," 166-168) notes that frequently the motif of crossing is used in Deuteronomy in relationship to the Israelites' need to enter the land (e.g., 4:26; 9:1) with Yahweh leading them (9:3), and that the motif is used negatively to underscore the inability of Moses to enter the land (4:21).

201. Twice, in Josh 3:11 and 4:11.

202. Fifteen times, in Josh 1:11; 3:1, 4, 14, 16, 17 (twice); 4:1, 7, 10, 11, 13, 22, 23 (twice).

203. Once, in Josh 4:5.

204. Twice, in Josh 1:14 and 4:12.

205. Twice, in Josh 4:3, 8.

206. Exod 14:19a.

207. The framing includes the repetition of cultic activity from the exodus by the second generation of Israelites in Josh 5:2-12.

208. Compare Van Seters with regard to the institutional setting of history writing. He concludes that history writing is the product of an intellectual elite group, that it is transmitted in scribal traditions, and that the institutional settings of older traditions are not carried over into these new literary creations. As a consequence, cultic interests are entirely secondary. The most important work on historiography by Van Seters is *In Search of History*. This research has recently been extended in *Prologue to History* and *The Life of Moses: The Yahwist as Historian in Exodus-Numbers* (Louisville: Westminster/John Knox Press, 1994). For a complete bibliography of Van Seters' work see T. B. Dozeman, "The Institutional Setting of the Late Formation of the Pentateuch in the Work of John Van Seters," SBLSP 30 (1991): 253-264.

209. Mettinger, *The Dethronement of Sabaoth*, 38-79, esp. 67-77. For a broader discussion see Wellhausen, *Prolegomena*, 272-294; Cross, *Canaanite*

Myth and Hebrew Epic, 274 -298; R. Schmitt, *Exodus und Passa*. 74-78; and Weinfeld, *Deuteronomy 1-11*, 65-84.

210. Exod 12:22.

211. For a discussion of remembrance within deuteronom(ist)ic tradition see R. Schmitt, *Exodus und Passa*, 70-74; and for its influence in cultic worship see Mettinger, *The Dethronement of Sabaoth*, 74.

212. See Exod 12:21-23 and 13:6.

213. Exod 12:27.

214. Exod 13:8 states that *massot* commemorates "what Yahweh did for me when I came out of Egypt." The identification of *massot* as being a pilgrimage feast in 13:6 picks up the motif from the deuteronomistic introduction to the plague cycle, where a חג was associated with the wilderness in 5:1: Here Yahweh demanded that Israel ויחגו לי במדבר. See also the insertion of the motif in 10:9. Such language once again reinforces the history-of-salvation perspective of the deuteronomistic school. For a discussion of חג see B. Kedar-Kopfstein, "חג," *TDOT IV*, ed. G. J. Botterweck and H. Ringgren (Grand Rapids: Eerdmans, 1980), 201-213.

215. Exod 13:14-15 recounts the death of the Egyptian firstborn before concluding, "Therefore I sacrifice to Yahweh all the males that first open the womb, but all the firstborn of my sons I redeem." A closer look at the instruction associated with *massot* and firstborn reveals that each festival focuses on different aspects of the exodus motif. *Massot* celebrates Israel's journeying out of Egypt. To be sure the journey was the result of God's liberation, as is indicated by the exodus formula in v. 9. Yet the specific answer underscores Israel's "journeying out" (v. 8, בצאתי ממצרים), as does the designation of *massot* as a pilgrimage feast on the seventh day (v. 6, חג ליהוה). The demand for firstborn, on the other hand, focuses on God's deliverance. The instruction in vv. 14-15 is not about Israel's going out, but about God's intervention. Verse 14 introduces the teaching on firstlings with the exodus motif, which, when viewed from the point of view of God's action, is not about Israelite pilgrimage but about the death of the Egyptian firstborn. It is a sacrifice to Yahweh (זבח ליהוה), which is meant to signify that Yahweh "brought out" Israel by killing all the Egyptian firstborn. The different points of view of the two feasts lead to the conclusion that the sacrifice of firstborn is more sacramental than the commemorative act of *massot*. The sacramental character means that all firstborn males born in the land must be either dedicated to God through sacrifice or redeemed (פדה). For uses of redemption (פדה) in Deuteronomy see 7:8; 9:26; 13:5; 15:15; 24:18.

216. The interrelationship between the apotropaic character of the blood in the passover rite and Yahweh's claim on the firstborn ties these events in with the divine attack on Gershom in Exod 4:18-26, where the elements of apotropaic blood and Yahweh's claim on firstborn are present. Exod 4:18-26 also underscores how circumcision functions in the orbit of Yahweh's claim on firstborn for deuteronomistic tradents. The interrelationship of circumcision, passover, and firstlings is made explicit in Josh 5:2-12 with regard to the second generation of Israelites who enter the land and encamp at Gilgal.

4

Exodus and Creation

Scholars have long recognized that Israel's exodus from Egypt was an important subject within priestly tradition.[1] The call of Moses in Exod 6:2-7:7, with its distinctive account of the revelation of the divine name; the plagues of snakes (7:8-13), gnats (8:12-15), and boils (9:8-12), with their unique focus on a confrontation between Aaron and the Egyptian magicians; the passover legislation in Exod 12:1-20; and such motifs as the recognition formula aimed at the Egyptians (e.g., 14:18) and the splitting of the sea (e.g., 14:21b) have provided a strong basis for identifying a priestly voice in the account of the exodus. And this consensus continues into the present time.[2]

The study of priestly tradition in the Pentateuch is also undergoing a renaissance in recent scholarship, which has raised new questions concerning its interpretation. Fueling this rebirth is a rejection of past judgments concerning the minimal value of priestly tradition both as literature and as an innovative force in the formation of ancient Israelite religion.[3] Indeed, more recent studies have underscored the creativity of priestly tradents by exploring how their historiography and legislation combine to form a coherent symbol system that is meant to give structure and definition to Israelite culture and cultic practice.[4] Such renewed interest has also given rise to debate concerning the character and antiquity of priestly law and narrative, as well as the relation of the two in the formation of the Pentateuch.

Priestly tradition in the Pentateuch is made up of an interconnected web of law and narrative. Although both can be studied in isolation, proper interpretation of the whole requires that the two be interrelated.[5] The exodus provides ample illustration of this point. The priestly account of the plagues and the confrontation at the sea cannot be undertaken independently of the passover legislation, since this legislation is essential to the design of the narrative. As a consequence, both the content of the passover legislation and its position in the plot structure of the priestly account of the exodus are essential for an overall interpretation. The present study, therefore, will seek to interpret both priestly law and narrative, but from a limited perspective. The study of priestly law will be undertaken primarily from the point of view of its function within the structure of the priestly narrative.

There is growing evidence from tradition-historical and more linguistically based studies that priestly law was in formation long before the exile,[6] which is the earliest possible date for the priestly narrative.[7] Consequently, the presupposition of the present study is that, on the whole, priestly narrative is later than the earliest forms of priestly law, and that the narrative is meant to give authority to legislation by placing it in Israel's wilderness period as revelation to Moses.[8] Such a view of the development of law and narrative in priestly tradition does not assume that priestly law is fixed when it acquires a narrative setting. Indeed, that there was a continuing history of interpretation with regard to passover well into the post-exilic period is evident from the Passover Papyrus from Elephantine.[9] And such debate could certainly have influenced pentateuchal legislation. But the placement of the passover legislation in the framework of the priestly narrative most likely did not undergo significant change, and it is the placement of law within the plot structure of the exodus that is important for the present study.

One result of studying priestly law from this limited perspective is that many of the issues concerning its origin and development, especially the interrelationship between the Holiness Code and other priestly legislation, will enter into our study only indirectly.[10] In addition, if we limit interpretation of priestly legislation to its position within a larger literary context, it becomes clear that our primary focus of study will be the priestly narrative account of the exodus and its function within the larger structure of a priestly historiography.

Several questions have emerged in recent interpretation of priestly narrative that bear on the present study. The most pressing question concerns the relationship of P to prior tradition. Is priestly narrative an independent source or a supplementation of earlier material? Distinctive blocks of priestly material such as the introduction to the plague cycle in Exod 6:2–7:7 and the confrontation between Aaron and the magicians during the plagues have lent support to an interpretation of priestly narrative as an independent source, and this has been the dominant position in modern scholarship.[11] Yet there have been dissenting voices.[12] Cross argued "that P was never an independent narrative, but a tradent who shaped and supplemented the received Epic tradition of Israel."[13] He based his conclusion primarily on the omissions that arise if P is read independently. For example, he noted that if P is read in isolation, there is no account of primordial human rebellion, even though the priestly account of the flood assumes such an event. Omissions become even more striking with regard to the exodus, according to Cross, since an independent priestly source would contain no account of the birth of Moses, his early years in Egypt, or his flight into the desert, even though Moses is the central figure in priestly tradition. Cross counters these problems by noting that such omissions present no problem if P is viewed as being a supplement that is dependent on prior tradition.[14] Blenkinsopp has built on the work of Cross by noting that when the growth of tradition is viewed as a process of supplementation, a new interpretation emerges both from the material that is added and "from the ways in which the earlier material is re-edited, represented and, most important of all, restructured."[15]

The prehistory of priestly narrative must remain an open question. The focus of the present study concerns the incorporation of priestly tradition into the deuteronomistic history. For this purpose the work of Cross and Blenkinsopp provides a starting point. Their work underscores that when the incorporation of priestly tradition into the Pentateuch is viewed as a supplementation (regardless of whether it existed as an independent document), its relationship to prior tradition must constantly be kept in the foreground. The central task of this chapter, therefore, must be to describe the ways in which the earlier accounts of the exodus and priestly tradition have been combined to present yet another interpretation of the exodus.

Three interrelationships between P and prior tradition will emerge from our study. First, it will become clear that the introduction of the wilderness within deuteronomistic tradition continues to play a central role in the priestly interpretation of salvation, even though the history-of-salvation perspective of the deuteronomistic school is qualified when priestly tradents play down the conquest. The result of this subordination is that the priestly history accentuates the death of Moses over the account of the crossing of the Jordan River. And such a refashioning of the deuteronomistic history necessarily influences the priestly interpretation of the exodus.

Second, we will see that priestly tradents qualify the deuteronomistic account of the exodus by returning to the structure of the preexilic narrative, where salvation consisted primarily of two events: the death of the Egyptian firstborn and the destruction of the Egyptian army at the sea. Such a reaffirmation of older tradition should not lead one to the conclusion that priestly tradition is simply a repetition of the preexilic account of the exodus. The role of the wilderness in priestly tradition cautions one against such a conclusion from the outset.

This leads to a third point, namely, that priestly tradents add their own distinctive voice to the story of the exodus. Of particular note is the addition of the recognition motif (so that you may know that I am Yahweh).[16] The insertion of this motif into the story of the exodus results in a polemic aimed primarily at the Egyptians, thereby qualifying the more exclusive focus on Israel that dominated deuteronomistic tradition.

SALVATION INTO THE WILDERNESS
AND THE QUEST FOR A NEW CREATION

The Priestly History

Priestly tradents tell their story of salvation in and through the deuteronomistic account of salvation history, even though their understanding
of salvation history is very different. Therefore it is important that we
determine the larger structure of the priestly historiography at the outset,
since changes in their design of salvation history will provide important
clues for interpreting the details of their account of the exodus. A study of
priestly history requires that two interrelated problems be addressed; the
extent of the literature, and its central theme. Scholars have responded to
these problems in a variety of ways, from arguing that the land is a central
theme in P and that consequently its history must include some form of
conquest to proposing that the land plays no role in P because its history
ends with the death of Moses.[17] A more detailed examination of the priestly
history will reveal that a decisive choice between these options is not possible, even though the structure of P suggests that the conquest is subordinated in its account of salvation history.

What is the overall design of the priestly history, and, more precisely,
does it extend into the Book of Joshua? This question is essential for interpreting the priestly account of the exodus, since it brings into stark focus
the problem of whether priestly tradents have followed the deuteronomistic history by interpreting the exodus in conjunction with a conquest
or have separated the two events, in which case the priestly history provides the framework for the Pentateuch. The problem is complicated
because there are clear indications of priestly editing in the Book of Joshua
with regard to the chronological notice of Israel's crossing the Jordan on
Month 1, Day 10 (Josh 4:19)[18] and the distribution of land at Shiloh in Joshua
18–19.[19] Such editing underscores the dependency of priestly tradents on
the deuteronomistic history, and it also cautions against identifying the
priestly history too closely with the canonical Pentateuch.[20]

The chronological notices are especially important for determining the
extent of the priestly history. In his assessment of the narrative style of P,
McEvenue notes the importance of dating. Dates are used to begin and end
units, to form inclusions, and to recall previous events in the story line,
with the result that dates establish a control and objectivity of tone. Yet
McEvenue adds that this objective tone is deceiving because priestly
tradents are less concerned about what a modern reader would consider
historical dating than they are about using chronology as a stylistic device
to mark significant events and to underscore divine control in the unfolding story.[21] The result of this tendency is that history is run like a liturgical
calendar,[22] which gives it a repetitive or paradigmatic quality.[23]

Our goal is to sketch a broad outline of the priestly history that emerges
from its system of chronology. But even here qualifications are necessary

at the outset. The secrets of the priestly dating system, especially with regard to its absolute chronology, will not be a point of focus.[24] Instead, the insight that the liturgical calendar influences priestly history will provide a point of departure for examining its organization, for it suggests that references to the first month should mark important events regardless of where they occur in the absolute chronology of the history. Five references to the first month occur in the priestly history. These mark the end of the flood on Month 1, Day 1 (Gen 8:13); the death of the Egyptian firstborn at evening on Month 1, Day 14 (Exod 12:1); the completion of the Tabernacle on Month 1, Day 1 (Exod 40:17); the death of Miriam on Month 1, which is the first death of the three leaders of the exodus and thus marks the beginning of the death cycle for the leaders of the wilderness generation (Num 20:1); and finally, the crossing of the Jordan on Month 1, Day 10 (Josh 4:19). If the priestly account of creation in Gen 1:1–2:3a is included (as it most likely should be),[25] then chronological references to the beginning of a new liturgical year could be extended to six, even though each event does not occur specifically on New Year's Day: creation, life after the flood, the exodus, the tabernacle cult in the wilderness, the death of the wilderness generation; and entrance into the land of Canaan.

Other references to specific months and days confirm the importance of references to the first month in the priestly history, since such notices tend to provide an anchor for more detailed dating. For example, the dates of the flood, with its beginning on Month 2, Day 17 (Gen 7:11), the resting of the ark on Mount Ararat on Month 7, Day 17 (Gen 8:4), and the appearance of mountain tops on Month 10, Day 1 (Gen 8:5) could be read sequentially as one liturgical year from creation (i.e., Month 1, Day 1). The end of the flood on Month 1, Day 1 (Gen 8:13) provides a reference point for the exiting of the ark on Month 2, Day 27 (Gen 8:14), and the Toledot of Shem suggests that it may provide a new beginning for an absolute chronology, since the birth of Arpachshad is noted as taking place two years after the flood (Gen 11:10).

The exodus from Egypt on Month 1, Day 14 (Exod 12:1–3) becomes the starting point for marking Israel's travel, first to the wilderness of Sin on Month 2, Day 15, where the Israelites receive the revelation of Sabbath (Exod 16:1),[26] and second to the wilderness of Sinai on Month 3, where the revelation of the cult takes place (Exod 19:1).[27] At the same time, it may also signify a new beginning in absolute chronology, since the construction of the Tabernacle is noted as taking place in the second year after the exodus (Exod 40:17).[28]

The construction of the Tabernacle on Month 1, Day 1 (Exod 40:1–2, 17) inaugurates a series of actions by the first generation of Israelites who left Egypt. They observe passover on Month 1, Day 14 (Num 9:1), they are numbered on Month 2, Day 1 (Num 1:1), and they travel to the wilderness of Paran on Month 2, Day 20 (Num 10:11–12). The death of Miriam in Month 1 (Num 20:1) inaugurates the death of the first generation, which takes an entire year, with Aaron dying on Month 5, Day 1 (Num 20:22-29; 33:38-39) and Moses on Month 11, Day 1 (Deut 1:3)[29] followed by thirty days of mourning (Deut 34:8), which leads into the account of the entry into the land of Canaan on Month 1, Day 10 (Josh 4:19) by the second generation.

Thus P knows the deuteronomistic account of salvation history and follows it by presenting a liturgical history of six cycles, which accentuate: (1) creation; (2) flood; (3) exodus; (4) Tabernacle; (5) death of the wilderness generation, and (6) Canaan. Even such a minimal outline provides enough information to address the problem of theme in the priestly history. The framing of this history with creation and Canaan makes it clear that, although the flood and tabernacle are significant points of transition and the exodus from Egypt is certainly a pivotal event, nevertheless the land of Canaan remains a central theme in P history. As Elliger has argued, the promise of land occurs at key points in its story, including the divine covenant with Abraham in Genesis 17 and the call of Moses in the introduction to the exodus in Exod 6:2-7:7.[30] These promise texts alone undercut the thesis of Noth that P has no interest in the land.[31] Furthermore, Elliger has also illustrated how the absence of land provides a point of tension and direction throughout the priestly history, and how the tension escalates with the exodus. The reason for this intensification is that the promise of land is no longer allowed to develop freely at this juncture in P's story but is actively opposed by Pharaoh, who exercises his opposing power through both his magicians and his army.[32] And, as will become clear later in our study, these two poles of opposition become important structuring points for priestly tradents in probing the character of divine power in the exodus.

The central role of the theme of land still leaves open the question of the structure of the priestly history. Elliger, for example, has argued against extending priestly tradition into Joshua–Kings, even though he stressed the central role of land in the priestly history.[33] Furthermore, editorial additions in Joshua–Kings may function to add a priestly perspective to significant events such as land distribution because of the dependence of priestly tradents on the deuteronomistic history, even though such events are no longer of a primary focus in the priestly history itself. The decisive event in resolving the matter is the conquest. And although priestly tradents have incorporated the crossing of the Jordan into their chronology, there are no clear indications that they claim this tradition in the central way that it functioned for deuteronomistic tradents.[34] Blenkinsopp, for example, notes that P may never have had a conquest tradition and that, in any case, "the focus of the P historiography has shifted from military conquest to the reestablishment of the sanctuary and its cult as a precondition for holy living in the land."[35]

Indeed, hints of a more subordinate role of the conquest emerge from the chronology, where the reference to Month 1, Day 10 in marking the crossing of the Jordan functions more as a conclusion to a year of death inaugurated by Miriam than it does a new beginning that is meant to take the priestly history into a holy war against Canaanite city-states. The reference to the first month in Josh 4:19, for example, does not prompt a series of more precise dates, as was the case with the exodus and construction of the Tabernacle. The one subsequent date of passover on the fourteenth day (Josh 5:10) departs in form by lacking a reference to the month, and although there are signs of priestly editing in the context of this verse, this date was most likely already fixed in the deuteronomistic account.[36]

The less significant role of the reference to Month 1 in Josh 4:19 as marking a new and significant progression in the priestly history is further strengthened when it is seen as following the thirty days of mourning for Moses after his death on Month 11, Day 1 (Deut 1:3; 34:8),[37] which ends a year of death that began with Miriam on Month 1 (Num 20:1) and included Aaron on Month 5, Day 1 (Num 20:22-29; 33:38-39). When viewed in this way the date of Month 1, Day 10 for Israel's crossing the Jordan certainly pushes the story ahead, making sure that the theme of land is not lost, but it also is firmly focused on the death of Moses. And from a different literary vantage point, the framing of the Book of Deuteronomy with the death of Moses in the pattern of announcement (Num 27:12-23; 31:1-2) and fulfillment (Deut 32:48-52; 34:1) further reinforces the suspicion that the death of Moses is more significant than conquest in the priestly history,[38] and that the last two references to a new year in the priestly history (death of Miriam and crossing of the Jordan) play a subordinate role to the preceding four (creation, flood, exodus, tabernacle) by framing of the death of the first generation within the time span of one liturgical year.

When the contours of the priestly history are sketched in this way, signs of priestly editing in the Book of Joshua provide insufficient evidence to conclude that priestly tradents follow the deuteronomistic interpretation of salvation as an exodus and conquest. As a consequence, a modified form of the literary argument of Noth begins to acquire strength, namely, that the priestly history provides the framework or at least lays the groundwork for the Pentateuch—not because priestly material is absent from the Book of Joshua, but because these events are of secondary concern to priestly tradents. Such a conclusion has implications for interpreting the exodus. In particular, it suggests that, although the exodus is a pivotal event for priestly tradents in constructing their theology of salvation with its promise of land, its importance does not arise from its relationship to a conquest in the Book of Joshua. Thus, other interrelationships must be explored in order to establish the proper hermeneutical perspective for interpreting the exodus in the priestly history.

There are indications within the internal structuring of the priestly history that suggest that its account of salvation history was oriented more toward creation than toward a conquest. Illustration of this point requires more detailed description of the interaction between the four most significant events that signify a new liturgical year: creation, flood, exodus, and Tabernacle. Although these events present a four-part sequence of action, they can be divided into pairs by the way in which priestly tradents have organized their history. For example, creation and the flood are interrelated by genealogies or "histories" (the Toledot form), which dominate through the end of the Book of Genesis.[39] Over against this, the exodus and the construction of the Tabernacle are organized predominately around geographical (itinerary) notices, which continue through the death of Moses.[40] The change in organizing devices invites a two-part reading of the priestly history: between Genesis and Exodus–Deuteronomy.[41]

The liturgical structure of the priestly history with its references to Month 1 indicates that the two halves themselves are meant to be divided. The major break in the first half of the priestly history is between the Toledot of Adam and those of Noah, each of which marks the beginning of new liturgical year, rather than the story of Abram in Genesis 12, who is introduced within the larger context of other post-flood nations through the Toledot of Terah. The first half of the priestly history, therefore, focuses on the creation and the flood.[42] The scope is universal, yet within this panorama the focus narrows from creation to the post-flood nations, who provide the stage for priestly tradents to trace the early development of Israel on a small scale—as a family tree of three generations, who live and migrate among the other post-flood nations.[43] The universal perspective of Genesis suggests that the first half of the priestly history is best characterized as the prehistory of the Israelite Nation.

Israel emerges as a nation at the outset of the Book of Exodus over against the family stories of Genesis, and this change in its status marks the second half of the priestly history.[44] The scope of this story is much narrower. It is national history rather than world history. Yet it too progresses in two parts, as did the account of Israel's prehistory. Only this time the decisive event is the exodus from Egypt rather than the flood, suggesting that Israel's national history be divided between a pre-exodus and a post-exodus stage. Each half is once again marked by a new liturgical year. The celebration of passover signifies the conclusion of Israel's preexodus story, while the construction of the Tabernacle inaugurates its post-exodus history. Within this progression there is once again a narrowing of scope, from Israel in Egypt to its separate existence in the wilderness, where the revelation of the Tabernacle defines more precisely the boundaries of the cultic community, before narrowing even further to distinguish two generations of post-exodus Israelites. The two-part history of creation–flood and exodus–Tabernacle can be illustrated in the following manner:

I. The Prehistory of the Israelite nation
    A. Creation and the pre-flood history of humanity (Gen 1:1-6:8)
            Creation (1:26-27)   Year 1
    B. The Post-flood history of humanity (Gen 6:9-50:26)
            End of flood (8:13)   Month 1, Day 1
II. The history of the Israelite nation
    A. The pre-exodus history of Israel and the exodus from Egypt as a new creation (Exod 1:1-18:27)
            Death of the Egyptian firstborn (12:1)   Month 1, Day 14
    B. The post-exodus history of Israel in the wilderness (Exod 19:1-Deut 34:12)
            Tabernacle (40:1-2, 7)   Month 1, Day 1
            1. The death of the first generation
               in the wilderness—Miriam   Month 1
            2. The second generation
               in the land—Crossing the Jordan   Month 1, Day 10

Although the liturgical structure of the priestly history stands out clearly, the warning of McEvenue of P's tendency to subvert its owns structures cautions against a too rigid approach in determining the contours of the priestly history.[45] Indeed, any number of scholars have demonstrated that the contrasting pairs of creation–flood and exodus–Tabernacle are inter-related in a variety of ways by priestly tradents, or even subsumed within other organizing structures such as covenant.[46] Yet even with this warn-ing, the loose symmetry between the two halves of the priestly history, with their further bifurcation into liturgical years, invites comparison of Israel's prehistory and national history in general, and, for purposes of the present study, comparison of the creation and the exodus in particular. Such a comparison is encouraged by the most cursory reading of the priestly interpretation of the exodus—with its unmistakable echoes of the origi-nal creation—when Yahweh splits the sea, allowing Israel to march out of Egypt.[47] The inner-biblical relationship suggests that, in the priestly his-tory the exodus is oriented more toward the original creation than toward the conquest—as the occasion of a new creative act of God, which holds the potential for universal significance.

Fishbane's work on typology within the Hebrew Bible provides help-ful guidelines for summarizing more precisely the character of the priestly history. He defines inner-biblical typology as a "literary-historical phenom-enon which isolates perceived correlation between specific events, per-sons or places early in time with their later correspondents."[48] Given this definition, typology reflects a certain degree of historical consciousness and, as such, it can be appropriated as an important feature of biblical his-toriography.[49] In addition, Fishbane distinguishes two varieties of typologies with regard to history: typologies of a historical nature and typologies of a cosmogonic-historical nature.[50] This distinction is useful in contrasting deuteronomistic and priestly histories, and it will also provide a hermeneutical lens for interpreting the latter.

In "typologies of a historical nature," Fishbane notes how one historical occurrence serves as the prototype for another, so that there is emphasis on the linear relationship between events in time.[51] The deuteronomistic history is an example of such a typology, where the exodus and the conquest, the Red Sea and the Jordan River, and Moses and Joshua are historically interrelated as partial repetitions of each other.[52] "Typologies of a cosmogonic-historical nature," by contrast, relate key events in history to a primordial cosmology, with the result that there is a more cyclical dimension in the sequencing of events, since "salvific moments partake of prototypical patterns."[53] The result of this form of typology is, according to Fishbane, that "historical redemption becomes a species of world restoration and the dynamics of history reiterate creative acts of divine power."[54] Fishbane notes that the oracles of Second Isaiah reflect this form of historical consciousness, where the primordial defeat of the sea-monsters gives rise to the prophet's prayer for a new exodus (Isa 51:9-11).[55] The priestly historiography is also an example of the cosmogonic-historical typology, since, for priestly tradents, the exodus begins a process of rediscovering the original creation, where the secrets of the future promise of land are buried in the past and must be found anew.[56] Within this structure, Genesis 1 emerges as a central text in displacing the conquest. It stands outside of the sequence of the Toledot. And to a certain degree Genesis 1 stands outside of all chronology of the priestly history.[57] The result is that Genesis 1 provides both a paradigm of the beginning (*Urzeit*) and a vision of the end (*Endzeit*).[58] Such a design underscores the eschatological character of the priestly history.[59]

The overview of chronology in the priestly history sets the stage for a more detailed interpretation of the exodus. Three hermeneutical guidelines stand out. First, the exodus is not tied closely to a conquest, even though the land remains a central theme. Second, the two-part structure of salvation history that emerges from references to new liturgical years (creation–flood and exodus–Tabernacle) invites comparison between the exodus and the creation in the priestly reading of the exodus. And third, the tendency in the two-part structure of the priestly history to begin broadly and then to narrow in focus suggests that the priestly interpretation of the exodus, as an act of creation, is also broad in its focus, in which case the universal implications of the exodus would be an important topic of reflection for priestly tradents. We will explore such a perspective by paying close attention to the role of Pharaoh and the Egyptians in the priestly account of the exodus, especially the repeated demand that they come to a knowledge of God from these events.

The Plague Cycle

Signs of priestly editing of the exodus begin with the extensive introduction in Exod 6:2-7:7. There has been little debate in assigning Exod 6:2-7:7

to priestly tradition, since, as Noth concluded, the section displays all the linguistic, stylistic, and conceptual characteristics of priestly tradition in the Pentateuch.[60] The introduction includes a new revelation of the divine name (6:2-8),[61] as well as a commission to Moses and Aaron (6:9-13, 26-7:7), which frames a Levitical genealogy (6:14-25).[62] Two aspects of Exod 6:2-7:7 require interpretation. One is how this text relates to the deuteronomistic account of the commissioning of Moses and revelation of the divine name in Exod 3:1-4:17, since this new introduction results in a striking repetition within the present form of the Book of Exodus. The other is how this text is meant to function within the priestly history.

The insertion of a second commissioning of Moses and Aaron in Exod 6:2-7:7 results in a repetition of Exod 3:1-4:17. Both texts narrate the call of Moses (and Aaron), the revelation of the divine name, and a commission that Moses and Aaron deliver Israel from their Egyptian bondage.[63] The repetition is intensified when it is noted that both texts tend to follow the same pattern of a commission, objection, divine response, and sign,[64] and that Exod 6:2-7:7 virtually takes no notice of Exod 3:1-4:17 with regard to its placement in the present context of the Book of Exodus.[65] One solution to this problem has been source-critical, namely that Exod 6:2-7:7 is part of a P document that included, among other texts, Genesis 17 and Exod 2:23-25, which when combined by a pentateuchal redactor resulted in the present doublet.[66] In this case the repetition lacks significance, since it is merely the result of bringing together distinct documents. Yet the distribution of motifs presents a problem for a source-critical solution, since, as Noth already recognized, it would appear that priestly writers were well aware of the earlier version, because of, among other things, the placement of Aaron in both texts (Exod 4:13-16; 7:1).[67] Such a literary interrelationship suggests that the present arrangement of the two accounts is indeed purposeful. But for what end?

The differences between the two accounts may provide a clue to the function of Exod 6:2-7:7. These differences naturally include many of the motifs within Exod 6:2-7:7 that will be noted below. But a more significant overall difference between the two concerns geography. Priestly tradents locate the call of Moses and Aaron explicitly in Egypt (6:28), in contrast to the deuteronomistic version, which places the event in the setting of the wilderness in Midian (3:1).[68] The change in geography is significant, since it restructures the introductory events of the exodus by qualifying the central role of the wilderness in the deuteronomistic historiography, and it emphasizes, instead, the setting of Egypt. Furthermore, the change in setting is certainly not arbitrary, since a similar tendency reappears at the confrontation at the sea, when priestly tradents once again shift the setting from the wilderness to Egypt with the introduction of an itinerary notice in Exod 14:1-2.[69]

The change in geography for the call of Moses and for the confrontation at the sea locates the events of the exodus solely in Egypt in the priestly interpretation. The central role of the setting of Egypt signals a different role for the wilderness in the priestly history. In chapter 3 we saw that the placing of the confrontation at the sea in the wilderness provided the basis for deuteronomistic tradents to reinterpret divine deliverance in the framework of an exodus and a conquest as the events that frame the wilderness period. The confinement of the central features of the exodus story within the boundaries of Egypt lays the groundwork for priestly tradents to separate the exodus from a conquest. For priestly tradents, the confrontation at the sea once again becomes the final event in Egypt rather than the initial event in the wilderness. As a result, the significance of the wilderness is not so much its role in connecting the exodus and the conquest, as its being the location for rediscovering the lost creation of Genesis 1 through the revelation of the Tabernacle cult.

Exod 6:2–7:7 also plays a pivotal role within the priestly history, where it functions within two different horizons. On the one hand, it looks back in order to interrelate the two parts of the priestly history, Israel's pre-history and national history. From this perspective the unfulfilled promise of land to the ancestors stands out as a point of continuity between the two parts of Israel's history. This promise is recounted in Exod 6:4 and applied to the Israelites in Egypt in 6:8.[70] Yet on the other hand, the transfer of the divine promise of land from the ancestors to the Israelites in Egypt also gives Exod 6:2–7:7 a future orientation so that it functions as an introduction to a new phase in Israel's history. And when read as an introduction, Exod 6:2–7:7 signals disjuncture between the two parts of the priestly history, which is accentuated with the revelation of a new name for God, from the name El Shaddai revealed to Abraham in Gen 17:1 to Yahweh.[71] Thus there is continuity between the two parts of the priestly history with regard to the promise of land, as well as a sense of a new beginning conveyed through the new revelation of the divine name, Yahweh, at the outset of the exodus.

On a smaller scale, the introductory function of Exod 6:2–7:7 is especially important for interpreting the exodus, since many of the motifs in this unit provide clues to the central features of the priestly interpretation of the exodus.[72] These motifs include: the formula of divine self-disclosure or introduction, "I am Yahweh";[73] the divine recollection of covenantal obligations;[74] a collection of salvific terms including the exodus motif;[75] the recognition motif (. . . so that you may know that . . .) used with Israel as a subject and, more important, with the Egyptians as a subject;[76] the motif of "not listening" to indicate resistance to the divine claim on Israel;[77] the inclusion of Aaron in the call of Moses, and his designation as one functioning in a prophetic role within the plague cycle;[78] the description of Israel as being Yahweh's host;[79] and the designation of plagues as being "wonders."[80] These motifs combine to form a hermeneutical perspective in which the exodus becomes an event of revelation, of divine self-disclosure, that arises from past obligations rooted in covenant. The effects of this divine activity are cosmic in proportion, and as a consequence,

Israel's birth as a nation is also understood by priestly tradents to have implications for the Egyptians themselves. The cosmic scope of the priestly
interpretation of the exodus turns P's history back toward the creation itself, rather than toward a future conquest of the land, in order to place
Israel's salvation within the most universal setting possible.

Priestly tradents restructure the plague cycle significantly. The clearest
signs of priestly supplementation to the plague cycle include the addition
of three plagues: snakes (7:8–13),[81] gnats (8:12–15), and boils (9:8–12).
All three plagues occur in the following stereotyped manner: (1) Yahweh
addresses Moses and Aaron and (2) commands one or the other to perform a miraculous sign with his staff, (3) which they do, (4) prompting
(initially) a similar action by the Egyptian magicians, (5) before each plague
ends with a summary of how Pharaoh would not listen to the sign, thus
fulfilling a divine prediction.[82] It is also noteworthy that there are no
conditions presented to Pharaoh in any of these plagues; instead they
focus on magical powers produced by Aaron or Moses and at least initially
by the Egyptian magicians.[83] Distinctive priestly motifs include the role of
Aaron,[84] the designation of plagues as being wonders,[85] the role of the
magicians,[86] and the concluding summary that Pharaoh would "not listen"
to the wonder and that his not listening fulfilled a divine prediction.[87]

The distinctive motifs in the stereotyped plagues provide a basis for
locating priestly additions throughout the prepriestly plague cycle. The
structure of the prepriestly plague cycle consists of three pairs of plagues:

1. Blood (7:14–24) and frogs (7:25–8:11)
2. Flies (8:16–28) and cattle (9:1–7)
3. Hail (9:13–35) and locust (10:1–20)

The priestly supplementation of the prepriestly plague cycle can be summarized here briefly. With respect to the first pair of plagues (blood and
frogs), to the plague of blood (7:14–28) priestly tradents add an acknowledgment that Pharaoh has not listened up to this point (7:16b), the recognition motif aimed at Pharaoh (7:17a*a*), the magical competition between
Aaron and the magicians (7:19–20a*a*), a conclusion that the magicians could
perform the same wonder (7:22a) and that Pharaoh would not listen, which
fulfilled divine prediction (7:22b). To the plague of frogs (7:25–8:11)
priestly tradents add the competition between Aaron and the magicians
(8:1–3) and then again the addition of Aaron (in 8:4a*a* and 8:8a*a*), the recognition motif aimed at Pharaoh (8:6b*b*) and the conclusion that Pharaoh
would not listen and that this fulfilled divine prediction (8:11b). With
respect to the second pair of plagues (flies and cattle), to the plague of
flies (8:16–28) priestly tradents add only the recognition motif aimed at
Pharaoh (8:18b*b*) and the addition of Aaron (8:21a*a*). Priestly tradents make
no additions to the plague of cattle (9:1–7). With respect to the third pair
of plagues (hail and locust), to the plague of hail priestly tradents add the
recognition motif aimed at Pharaoh (9:14b*b*), Aaron (9:27a), a second rec-

ognition motif aimed at Pharaoh (9:29b*b*), and a concluding notice of how Pharaoh's refusal to listen fulfilled divine prediction (9:35b*b*). To the plague of locust (10:1-20) priestly tradents may have added the recognition motif aimed at Israel (10:2b*b*);[88] and Aaron (10:3a*a*, 8a*a*, 16a*a*).

The distribution of the three additional plagues within the prepriestly plague cycle, in combination with the additions by priestly tradents to the previous plagues, provides insight into the way in which priestly tradents have restructured not only the plague cycle but the entire account of the exodus. When the distinctive motifs from the stereotyped plagues of snakes, gnats, and boils are located in the prepriestly plague cycle, it becomes clear that the priestly editing of the cycle is very uneven. Both the plagues of blood (7:14-24) and frogs (7:25-8:11) have been extensively expanded by priestly tradents to include a confrontation between Aaron and the Egyptian magicians,[89] a refusal of Pharaoh "to listen" to the sign,[90] and a notice of how Pharaoh's obstinacy fulfilled divine predictions.[91] It is noteworthy that after the extensive priestly redaction of the first pair of prepriestly plagues, similar signs of priestly redaction are, for the most part, absent in the remaining prepriestly plague cycle.[92] The only other distinctive priestly motif added to the plague cycle that does not occur in the stereotyped pattern of snakes, gnats, and boils is the recognition formula (perhaps directed once toward Israel [10:2], but for the most part toward Pharaoh or the Egyptians), and it is woven into all the prepriestly plagues except the death of cattle in 9:1-7.[93]

Priestly supplementation of the plague cycle brings into focus that three distinctive plagues (snakes, gnats, boils) are added to the plague cycle and that the first pair of plagues (blood and frogs) are brought into conformity with the stereotyped pattern. More detailed interpretation will bring to light three aims of priestly tradents in creating this new structure. The first is that the stereotyped plagues function as introductions to the pairs of plagues in the prepriestly plague cycle. The second is that, as introductions, these plagues provide the hermeneutical perspective from which the prepriestly cycle of plagues must now be interpreted. And the third is that the new structure ties the events of the exodus more closely into the plague cycle by the way in which they restructure the entire account, with the result that the reader is encouraged to interpret the events of the exodus as additional signs that are now directed toward the Egyptians.

The insertion of snakes, gnats, and boils results in a structure in which these three plagues function as introductions to the paired plagues in the prepriestly plague cycle.[94] The result of this three-part addition is that the entire plague cycle is fashioned into similar, repetitive sequences, consisting of four cycles of action, each of which begins with an introduction followed by two distinct plagues. This structure can be illustrated in the following manner:

Intro to the Plague Cycle (6:2–7:7)	First Cycle (Aaron)	Second Cycle (Aaron)	Third Cycle (Moses)	Fourth Cycle (Exodus) (Moses)
	Intro: Snakes	Intro: Gnats	Intro: Boils	Intro: Darkness
	Blood	Flies	Hail	Death of firstborn
	Frogs	Cattle	Locust	Defeat of Egyptians at sea

What becomes immediately apparent is that the extensive editing of the first pair of prepriestly plagues (blood and frogs) was done for the purpose of bringing all the plagues in the first cycle into conformity, so that the confrontation between Aaron and the magicians continues throughout the cycle. In conjunction, it also becomes clear that there is no such editing beyond the initial prepriestly plagues of blood and frogs because the paridy between Aaron and the Egyptian magicians in performing miracles ceases after the first cycle, since the magicians are not able to produce gnats as Aaron does at the outset of the second cycle. In addition, the structure also shows that there is design in the manner in which Aaron has been edited into the plague cycle. Note how the four cycles divide evenly between Aaron and Moses, with Aaron functioning in the introductory plagues in the first and second cycles (snakes and gnats) and Moses in the introductory plagues in the third and fourth cycles (boils and darkness). This development plays out the divine prediction of characters from the introduction (7:1), where Aaron was designated as a prophet (functioning in the first two, less intensive cycles of plagues—and even here only where the Egyptian magicians are also present),[95] while Moses was described as one who appears as God (now functioning in the more severe actions of the last two cycles, where the magicians no longer play a role).

Once the structure is brought into focus, it also becomes clear that the new introductions provide the hermeneutical lens from which the entire plague cycle must now be read. These plagues are signs of divine power that must be recognized by the Egyptians, rather than being confrontational displays of divine strength accompanied by conditions whose primary aim is to free Israel from Pharaoh. Indeed, there are no conditions in the plagues of snakes, gnats, and boils, and with the absence of this motif, the drama of opposing powers (as a confrontation of wills) gives way to a more abstract polemic in which divine power must be recognized by the other. The change in focus from liberation to polemic is already indicated in the priestly introduction to the plague cycle in 6:2–7:7. Ska's conclusions concerning the priestly introduction are helpful at this point, especially his noting that the focus in 7:1–5 (esp. 7:4) is less on Yahweh's relationship with Israel than on Yahweh's relationship with the other nations.[96] The divine prediction in 7:1–5 concerning the impending events makes it clear that Israel will indeed be brought out of Egypt but that it is no longer sufficient simply to defeat or to destroy the Egyptians. Instead, priestly tradents underscore that the Egyptians must come to an awareness of Yahweh from this act of judgment (7:4–5),[97] and as a consequence, the plagues become polemical signs for the nations.

The plague cycle carries the polemical character of the priestly plague/ signs further. We have already noted that the conflict between Pharaoh and Yahweh is played down in the plagues of snakes, gnats, and boils in favor of a focus on divine wonder or power displayed through either Aaron or Moses. Several additional features of these plagues underscore that the development in the priestly restructuring of the plague cycle is not for the purpose of control or defeat of the other as much as for a polemical display of divine power in order to bring insight or understanding. This point is accentuated initially when we note that Pharaoh's refusal to send out Israel results from his not perceiving ("not hearing") the divine power behind the plague, rather than his simply refusing to send out Israel.[98]

The role of the magicians underscores the polemical and potentially apologetical function of the plagues event more poignantly. They function in the introductory plagues of the first three cycles (snakes, gnats, boils), as well as in the two additional plagues within the first cycle (blood and frogs).[99] In the first cycle the magicians are presented as those who are able to display the same power as Aaron. They too turn their staffs into snakes, they turn water into blood, and they produce frogs, thus making the first cycle of plagues more or less a standoff with regard to the manipulation or manifestation of power. Yet even here, the way in which Aaron's staff (turned snake) swallows those of the magicians in the opening plague (7:8–13) indicates Yahweh's superior power from the outset.[100] The magicians continue to appear in the introductions to the second and third cycles, but their role begins to change. In the second cycle the reader is told that they could not produce gnats as Aaron had done. Their inability to display the same power as Aaron brings insight, and they inform Pharaoh that the power of Aaron is, in fact, the "finger of God" (8:19). With this new insight they leave the story for the remainder of the second cycle and, indeed, for the remainder of the plague cycle. The magicians are referred to one last time in the introduction to the third cycle, where it is noted that they could not even stand before Moses because of the boils that afflicted them. Thus we see development in the priestly structuring of the plague cycle from a certain degree of shared cosmic or divine power between Egyptians and Israelites (the first cycle of plagues) to an ever-increasing differentiation of power (from the second cycle of plagues onward), which is meant to bring insight to the Egyptians. Aaron possesses this power to a certain degree (he functions like a prophet), but not to the extent of Moses (who appears divine to the Egyptians). The function of the magicians certainly supports the conclusion by Zevit that these plagues are best interpreted as heuristic tools meant for the purpose of teaching.[101]

The reason for the polemical quality of the plagues in priestly tradition is to emphasize the power of God as creator, which requires universal acknowledgment. Indication of this focus in priestly tradition arises from the recognition motif, where three times the power of Yahweh over the land of Egypt and the entire creation is stated as something that the Egyptians must know (Exod 8:18; 9:14, 29).[102] The connection between the plagues and creation is also underscored in the priestly additions of blood and frogs, where, as Zevit has noted, language from Genesis 1 is introduced to stress the cosmic import of these actions and the primordial power of God at work in bringing them about.[103] Thus, for example, priestly tradents expand the plagues of blood and frogs from their localized association with the Nile in the prepriestly plague cycle to stress how these plagues contaminate the primeval elements of creation.[104] Fretheim summarizes well the relationship of the plagues to the created order. He writes that "[t]he deliverance of Israel is ultimately for the sake of the entire creation." He continues: "The issue . . . [in the power of the plagues] . . . is not that God's name be made known in Israel; the scope of the divine purpose is creation-wide, for all the earth is God's."[105]

The restructuring of the plague cycle also merges the events of the exodus more closely with the plagues than had been the case in either of the earlier accounts.[106] The preexilic account of the exodus clearly separated the exodus from the plague cycle by providing a distinct introduction to the events of the exodus (darkness) and by reversing the expected order of paired actions, so that Yahweh's strongest manifestation of power occurred at the sea rather than during the death of the Egyptian firstborn. Deuteronomistic editors separated the events of the exodus even more thoroughly from the plague cycle by restructuring the exodus from two to three events and by placing the destruction of the Egyptian army in the wilderness rather than maintaining its setting in Egypt.

In contrast to the previous accounts, priestly tradents bring the exodus into conformity with the plague cycle. The events of the exodus must be interpreted as the fourth cycle of plagues or signs, and as the second cycle of actions performed by Moses. There are also indications *within* the priestly account that the exodus is meant to be an extension of the plagues. Most noteworthy is the addition of an itinerary notice in Exod 14:1–2, which relocates Israel back into Egypt for the confrontation at the sea, thus separating this event from the wilderness. With the addition of this itinerary notice, the defeat of the Egyptian army at the sea becomes once again the final event in Yahweh's deliverance of Israel from Egypt rather than the initial event in the wilderness, and as a result the exodus is severed from the conquest.

The Death of the Egyptian Firstborn

Priestly additions to the death of the Egyptian firstborn include perhaps the partial form of the recognition motif aimed at Pharaoh or the Egyptians

(11:7b), the divine prediction of Pharaoh's obstinance, which is described as "not hearing" (11:9b), a description of plagues as wonders (11:9b), and the inclusion of Aaron into the events (11:10). Priestly tradents also include their own interpretation of passover and *massot* in Exod 12:1-20, before they close the scene with a concluding summary in 12:28.[107]

From Liberation to Polemic

Moses states in Exod 11:7b that when the Egyptian firstborn die, Pharaoh and the Egyptians would come to the knowledge that Yahweh makes a distinction between Israelites and Egyptians. The theme of knowledge of God in Yahweh's opponent may have been part of the preexilic story. The syntax of the phrase does not conform to the recognition formula in the plague cycle, and a distinction between ethnic groups is indeed a central feature of the older liturgy. The polemical aim of bringing an opponent to knowledge of God is also a central goal of priestly writers. Interpretation of the recognition formula throughout the exodus will illustrate how the recognition of divine action in Exod 11:7b has been incorporated into the polemic of priestly writers that Pharaoh acknowledge the power of God in the acts of the exodus.

The recognition motif consists of two distinct parts: divine self-introduction and the demand for recognition. Self-introduction consists of a short form, "I am Yahweh," (אני יהוה).[108] It is part of Israel's cultic life at least as early as Hosea, where it occurs in 12:10 and 13:4 as a theophany of the name within a polemical context that stresses Yahweh's exclusive claims on Israel over against other deities.[109] Recognition consists of the verb "to know" (ידע) used in conjunction with the causal particle "that" (כי), resulting in the phrase, "so that you/they may know that. . . ."[110] Its cultic roots are more difficult to locate. Knowledge of God may have arisen from the priestly response to prayer in the cult (1 Samuel 1) or as a prophetic proclamation (1 Kings 18).[111] In any case recognition is always preceded by concrete divine action that is public and momentary, which actively prompts and even provides the basis for recognition. Divine action, therefore, is both the occasion and the content of knowledge.[112]

Zimmerli has argued that the combination of divine self-introduction and the demand for recognition intensifies both.[113] The demand for recognition expands divine self-introduction beyond the confines of the cult, so that theophany embraces all aspects of creation and even other nations.[114] Divine self-introduction intensifies the demand for recognition because Yahweh alone becomes the goal of recognition and this demand impinges on all nations.[115] Thus the combination of self-introduction and recognition in the priestly interpretation of the exodus introduces a universal polemic. It is meant to emphasize the power of God over creation and other nations. We have already seen how it transforms the plagues into signs that are meant to bring knowledge not so much to Israel as to the Egyptians.

The motif also transforms the exodus into a polemical story whose goal is to confront Pharaoh and the Egyptians with Yahweh's power as a creator God, who controls all land, including Egypt.

Recognition of God is central throughout the priestly interpretation of the exodus.[116] Knowledge of Yahweh is introduced in the introduction and it occurs in all four cycles of the exodus.[117] In fact, the motif has been inserted in all of the prepriestly plagues except the death of cattle.[118] The most striking feature in the distribution of the recognition motif is how it focuses the events of the exodus on Pharaoh and the Egyptians rather than Israel. To be sure, Israel must recognize the power of Yahweh from the exodus, as is indicated at the outset of events in Exod 6:7, but the near absence of this formula with Israel as its object provides an initial clue that, for priestly tradents, the exodus is not the primary place where the people of God must acknowledge Yahweh. A more broadly based reading of the priestly history confirms this suspicion. Their history underscores that, although the exodus is a significant event for Israel, nevertheless, Israel's recognition of Yahweh will come through the cultic system of the Tabernacle in the wilderness (Exod 29:46) and not the confrontation in Egypt.

The events of the exodus are manifestations of Yahweh's power over creation, which are potentially recognizable by all people. Thus the exodus becomes an occasion for a polemic aimed at Pharaoh and the Egyptians in priestly tradition. The polemical character of the exodus is indicated in the second half of the introduction, where the divine commission to Moses and Aaron is aimed at the Egyptians (7:5). They will recognize the power of Yahweh, when Israel is brought out of Egypt. The fact that the Egyptians are not the intended object of the recognition motif until the confrontation at the sea (Exod 14:4b, 18) suggests that this event marks the end of the polemical focus of the exodus for priestly tradents.

Pharaoh is the object of repeated demands to recognize the power of Yahweh throughout the events of the plagues and exodus.[119] Three times the inauguration of a plague (blood—7:17a; flies—8:18b; and hail—9:14b) and twice the cessation of a plague (frogs—8:6b; hail—9:29b) are meant to provide the occasion for Pharaoh to come to knowledge of Yahweh. The content of this knowledge is carefully delineated. The plague of blood is meant to provide a manifestation of Yahweh's character: "by this you (Pharaoh) will know that I am Yahweh" (7:17a). The remainder of the occurrences provide insight into the sphere of Yahweh's power: Pharaoh must know that there is no God like Yahweh (frogs—8:6b); that Yahweh dwells in the midst of the land (flies—8:18b); that there is no power like Yahweh in the land (hail—9:14b); and finally, that the land is indeed Yahweh's (hail—9:29b). By inserting the recognition motif into the plague cycle, priestly tradents underscore that Yahweh is incomparable and that all of creation belongs to Yahweh, even the land of Egypt.[120] But the polemic toward Pharaoh fails. Repeatedly the reader is told that he did not perceive (hear) the power of the sign.

The recognition motif is directed to the Egyptians in the priestly introduction to the plagues (7:5b) and in the account of the destruction of the Egyptian army at the sea (14:4b,18). These instances frame the plague cycle, and they also give reason for Pharaoh's obstinance. It was not the result of any lack of divine power manifest through the signs themselves, but actually part of a larger polemic aimed at the Egyptians. This larger focus is presented at the outset of the plague cycle in 7:3–5, when Yahweh foretells the forthcoming events to Moses: Yahweh will harden Pharaoh's heart, causing the signs to multiply, which will eventually lead to Israel's liberation and a great act of judgment on Egypt, the result of which would bring knowledge of Yahweh to the Egyptians (not Pharaoh).[121] And the events of the exodus fulfill this prediction at least with regard to divine judgment. The ambiguity in the intended audience of Moses' address in 11:7b, where the context suggests only Pharaoh while the syntax points to others, prepares the way for the explicit shift in focus from Pharaoh to the Egyptians in the event at the sea (14:4b, 18). The recognition motif in 11:7b provides an interpretation of the death to the Egyptian firstborn as an occasion when Egyptians must realize that God makes a distinction between peoples. The occurrence of the motif at the sea in 14:4b and 18 illustrates the full consequences of this fact, since Pharaoh and his army are destroyed there. But the destruction of Pharaoh is not simply an occurrence of divine judgment,[122] nor is it a celebration of divine power in priestly tradition. Instead, it is a polemic and potentially an apologetic for the remaining Egyptians, since the destruction of Pharaoh is the clearest manifestation of divine glory in the entire plague cycle.[123]

Passover and Massot

Priestly tradents also include their own interpretation of passover with the insertion of 12:1–20. Although there is debate concerning the precise details of the tradition-historical development of this unit, scholars are agreed that the instruction belongs to priestly tradition (broadly conceived), since it includes a range of distinctively priestly terms and phrases.[124] In its present form the unit separates into two parts. Verses 1–14 provide detailed instruction concerning the celebration of passover. These instructions include: (1) matters of date in vv. 1–4, 6 (the celebration of passover takes place in the first month of the year and the lamb is taken on the tenth day and killed at evening on the fourteenth day); (2) a range of details on how and where the passover is to be celebrated in vv. 5, 7–11 (the lamb must be roasted whole, eaten in the context of the family, in haste, and not preserved); (3) a theological interpretation of the feast in vv. 12–13 (when Yahweh judges the Egyptian gods by killing the firstborn in the land of Egypt, the blood will provide a sign whereby the destroyer will pass over these houses); and (4) a concluding formula in v. 14 (the passover is a festival [Hebrew, חג] that must be observed forever). Verses 15–20 provide the priestly interpretation of *massot*, which includes: (1) matters of date in vv. 15-16 and 18 (*massot* lasts for seven days, from the evening of the fourteenth day of the first month to the twenty-first day, and it begins and ends with a sacred assembly); (2) a theological interpretation of the feast in v. 17 (it signifies the day that Yahweh liberated Israel from Egypt [the exodus motif]); and (3) instructions concerning who must observe it in vv. 19-20 (both natives in the land and resident aliens [בגר ובאזרח]).[125]

The central place of passover in the death of the Egyptian firstborn indicates the strong influence of the deuteronomistic history on priestly editors. This influence is further reinforced by the use of the exodus motif in conjunction with *massot* in 12:17. These strong points of correlation underscore how priestly tradents have accepted the deuteronomistic interpretation of the death to the Egyptian firstborn over the predeuteronomistic account. Thus, for priestly tradents also the death of the firstborn is not simply a national story which automatically runs its course independent of Israel. Instead priestly tradents too require cultic participation by Israel to ensure their own safety during the midnight attack. And they also place these instructions prior to the slaughter of the firstborn, a placement that once again opens the possibility for non-Israelites to participate in the protective cultic events. With regard to the latter point, note in particular the inclusion of resident aliens into the instructions for *massot* (12:20), which will be expanded in 12:40-51 in relationship to passover.[126]

In spite of the strong influence of deuteronomistic tradition, priestly tradents depart from the earlier tradition in a number of important ways. In P there is an emphasis on the land of Egypt in contrast to the Egyptians.[127] In the deuteronomistic interpretation of the passover (12:23a*a*, 27) the death of the firstborn was an attack against the Egyptians themselves, and not their land.[128] In contrast, priestly tradents shift the focus from the Egyptians to their land, with the result that the divine attack is a judgment against humans, animals, and gods (v. 12), thus partially fulfilling the divine prediction from 6:6 and 7:4. The shift in focus to the land of Egypt corresponds well with the tendency of priestly tradents to interpret the exodus within the framework of creation. But this shift in focus also lays the groundwork for an additional contrast with the deuteronomistic history; the subordination of the act of leaving Egypt with its close ties to conquest. To be sure, the exodus motif is introduced in 12:17 in conjunction with *massot*, but it plays a far more subordinate role than in the deuteronomistic history, where Israel's need to journey with God into the future toward a promised land was repeatedly emphasized.[129] The lack of reference to any future promised land (as compared to 12:25, where it enjoyed a central role in the instructions for passover in deuteronomistic tradition) is an initial indication of the more subordinate role of the exodus from Egypt in the priestly history.[130]

The subordinate role of the exodus is reinforced by a final point of contrast between priestly and deuteronomistic accounts of the passover instruction. In the deuteronomistic history, the exodus from Egypt was clearly separated from the death of the Egyptian firstborn both geographically (by means of an itinerary notice in 12:37) and culticly (with passover functioning in association with the death of the Egyptian firstborn, while *massot* and firstlings were tied to the exodus and promise of land). Over against this structure, priestly tradents merge passover and *massot* in the setting of the death to the Egyptian firstborn.[131] By moving *massot* back into the events of the death to the Egyptian firstborn, priestly tradents play down the distinction between the two feasts and with it the central role that the exodus from Egypt acquired in the deuteronomistic history. By separating *massot* from firstlings, they also lay the groundwork for severing the relationship between exodus and conquest in deuteronomistic tradition.[132]

The Exodus from Egypt

The priestly interpretation of Israel's exodus from Egypt includes Exod 12:40-51. Israel is described as leaving the land of Egypt at the outset of the unit, where the noncausative form of the verb "to go out" (יצא) is employed. In addition, the exodus motif occurs twice: in v. 42 Yahweh is described as bringing Israel out of the land of Egypt, and v. 51 repeats the motif in providing the concluding summary. Exod 12:40-51 separates into two distinct parts. Verses 40-42 provide a concluding summary of the events surrounding the death of the Egyptian firstborn. This summary includes a precise date of how long Israel was in Egypt (430 years), and it emphasizes that the events occurred during one night, which is characterized as a night of vigil.[133] Although the passover is not mentioned in these verses, the implication of this summary is that it provides more information on the character of this feast. Passover commemorates Yahweh's night of vigil (ליל שמרים הוא ליהוה) in bringing Israel out of Egypt.[134] Verses 43-51 turn the focus even more explicitly on passover in order to describe in detail who is allowed to participate in the ritual. Foreigners (נכר) as well as clients (תושב) and hired (שכיר) slaves are not allowed to participate in the Passover. All of the congregation of Israel (כל־עדת ישראל) must participate in passover, while any purchased slave (עבד) and resident alien (גר) may also participate in passover, if having undergone circumcision. Furthermore, if a resident alien (גר) undergoes circumcision, that person must be treated as a native (אזרח).

The location of the priestly insertion is important for a proper interpretation of its content. It has been inserted between the itinerary notice (12:37-39a) and cultic legislation for *massot* and firstling (13:1-16) of the deuteronomistic account.[135] The act of leaving Egypt played a subordinate role to the death of the Egyptian firstborn in the oldest form of the narrative, where as a consequence of Yahweh's attack, first Pharaoh (vv. 31-32) and then the Egyptians (vv. 33-34, 39b) drive Israel out in haste. The action is devoid of geography and does little more than hold together the death of the Egyptian firstborn and the confrontation at the sea. The story changes significantly when deuteronomistic tradents introduce a journey motif complete with geographical locations (Exod 12:37-39a) and new cultic instructions concerning *massot* and firstlings (Exod 13:1-16). With these additions in place the act of leaving Egypt emerges as a central feature of the story and it is accentuated with the exodus motif. The priestly interpretation of the exodus from Egypt falls somewhere between the two earlier accounts. The content of 12:40-51 suggests that a process of inner-biblical commentary is taking place, especially with the deuteronomistic insertion of 12:37-39a.

Deuteronomistic tradents emphasized three points with the addition of 12:37-39a: that Israel journeyed from Ramses to Succoth (v. 37); that a "mixed multitude" left Egypt (v. 38); and that the exodus was the result of divine leading or liberation, expressed with the exodus motif (v. 39a). Priestly tradents react in slightly different ways to each of these points. They affirm through repetition (12:42a) the deuteronomistic teaching from 12:39a, that the exodus from Egypt was the result of divine leading. Thus priestly tradents also use the exodus motif to describe the liberation from Egypt, and they emphasize that the exodus launched Israel on a wilderness journey by referring back to this event throughout the Pentateuch (Exod 16:1; 19:1; Num 1:1; 9:1; 33:38).[136] They also reaffirm, and indeed develop in some detail, the more inclusive interpretation of the exodus by providing an extensive midrash on the deuteronomistic notice in v. 38 that a "mixed multitude" left Egypt with Israel. Priestly tradents provide detailed information concerning the character of this "mixed group" as well as precise boundaries with regard to who might participate in the passover.[137] Such detailed information concerning the requirements for incorporating non-Israelites into the cult is a natural outgrowth of the more universal focus of priestly tradents that has been evident throughout the plagues and exodus.

Priestly tradents play down the itinerary notice in 12:37, where Israel's exodus out of Egypt was traced from Ramses to Succoth. In deuteronomistic tradition this itinerary provided a clear separation between the death of the firstborn and the exodus from Egypt, and between passover and *massot/* firstlings. In contrast, priestly tradents reaffirm the structure of the preexilic liturgy, where the exodus functioned in a subordinate role to the death of the Egyptian firstborn and destruction of the Egyptian army at the sea. Priestly tradents do not negate the deuteronomistic itinerary notice in 12:37, as they will in the subsequent notice of 13:17-18a, 20, where they specifically place Israel back in the land of Egypt in 14:1-2. Instead they emphasize how the passover and exodus from Egypt are closely related in Yahweh's night of vigil. The result of this focus is twofold: first, the clear temporal and geographical distinction between passover and *massot* that was established with the deuteronomistic itinerary notice in 12:37 is blurred; and second, the merging of passover and *massot* that was already noted in the instructions of 12:1–20 is carried over into the exodus from Egypt, where the focus continues to be on passover for priestly tradents, rather than *massot*, as was the case in deuteronomistic tradition.

Salvation by the Sea

Priestly tradents follow the story line of the deuteronomistic history, in which an itinerary notice in 13:17–18a, 20 locates Israel at Etham, a site at the edge of the wilderness. But they restructure the story by means of their own itinerary notice in 14:1–2, so that the event at the sea once again takes place in Egypt as the final act of Yahweh's salvation, in much the same way as it functioned in the preexilic account.[138] This restructuring provides the basis for priestly tradents to present their own interpretation of Yahweh's victory at the sea.

Supplementation to the confrontation at the sea includes the new setting at Pihahiroth (14:1–2, 9b); an emphasis on Israel as being prepared for war (13:18b; 14:8b); the designation of the cloud as the means by which Yahweh led Israel from Egypt and waged holy war against the Egyptian army (13:21–22; 14:19b, 20ab, 24ab); a sequence of divine predictions and their fulfillment, including the hardening motif, Egyptian pursuit of Israel, destruction of the Egyptian army, and the recognition motif with Egypt as the object (14:3–4, 8a, 17–18); the motifs of splitting the sea with the resultant walls of water as the consequence of Yahweh's action against the sea (14:16ab, 21b, 22b, 29b); and finally, a separate victory hymn with the addition of the Song of Miriam (15:20–21).[139] Interpretation of the priestly version will be in two parts: first, the emphasis on the cloud both at the confrontation at the sea and in the wilderness in 13:18b-19, 21–22; 14:19b, 20ab, 24ab; and second, the refashioning of the account of Yahweh's victory at the sea in 14:1–4, 8, 9b, 16ab, 17–18, 19b, 22b, 20abb, 21b, 24ab, 29b.

The Cloud and the Wilderness

The itinerary notice in Exod 13:17–18a, 20 located Israel at the edge of the wilderness, which became the setting for the events at the sea. Although priestly tradents shift the setting of the sea back to Egypt in Exod 14:1–2, they maintain the setting of the wilderness momentarily in order to provide their own initial interpretation of Yahweh's leading and of Israel's march through the wilderness. In so doing, they qualify the deuteronomistic interpretation of these events in two ways with the addition of Exod 13:18b-19, 21–22.

An initial point of contrast to the deuteronomistic historiography is the reemergence of holy war. An emphasis on the holy-war character of the confrontation at the sea had already begun in the previous section, where Israel was described as Yahweh's "host" as they marched out of

Egypt (Exod 12:41, 51), and it continues in Exod 13:18b, when priestly tradents go out of their way to underscore that Israel marched out of Egypt ready for war.[140] This emphasis contrasts sharply with Exod 13:17, where Yahweh was described as leading Israel in such a way as to avoid battle. The shift in focus underscores that for priestly tradents the conflict at the sea is a central and even climactic event in Yahweh's holy war to liberate Israel, and not merely an introductory episode pointing to a distant and future conquest of the land, as was the case for deuteronomistic tradents.

Another point of contrast to the deuteronomistic history is the cloud. It too accentuates holy war. Priestly tradents emphasize that Yahweh led Israel out of Egypt by means of a pillar of cloud (13:21-22), as opposed to direct divine leading (13:17-18a) in deuteronomistic tradition. The identification of the pillar of cloud with priestly tradition requires caution, since the motif is not an innovation by priestly tradents. It is anchored in an ancient Tent of Meeting tradition, wherein a divine descent in a cloud or a pillar of cloud is described for the purpose of delivering oracles. Mettinger has noted that such an ancient tradition is most clearly reflected in three texts: Exod 33:7-11; Num 11:14-17, 24-30; 12;[141] while Clifford and Mann have demonstrated that this tradition may reach back to Canaanite religion.[142]

The antiquity of the Tent of Meeting tradition has provided one reason for attributing the motif of the pillar of cloud in 13:21-22 to a prepriestly Yahwist.[143] But the close ties between the pillar of cloud and the wilderness argue against this identification, regardless of its tradition-historical roots. Two of the texts cited by Mettinger (Exod 33:7-11 and Num 11:14-17, 24-30) suggest that the Tent of Meeting tradition was already incorporated in the deuteronomistic historiography, where its original function (of a divine descent for oracular purposes) was maintained. Such a conclusion is reinforced by Deut 31:14-15, where the oracular tradition of the Tent of Meeting reappears to confirm Joshua as the successor of Moses.[144] It is equally clear that the Tent of Meeting tradition is also central to priestly tradents, since reference to it occurs nearly one hundred times in association with the Tabernacle cult, where the cloud (either in conjunction with a theophany or as cultic incense) also plays an important role.[145]

The Tent of Meeting tradition undergoes a significant transformation at the hands of priestly tradents, which helps to account for the new role of the cloud from medium of divine communication to wilderness guide. Although priestly tradents retain aspects of the ancient Tent of Meeting tradition in Numbers 12, where Yahweh is described as descending in a pillar of cloud for oracular purposes, they tend to substitute the Kabod Yahweh (glory of Yahweh) for the cloud in connection with the Tent of Meeting.[146] The Kabod Yahweh is associated with the Tent of Meeting/Tabernacle during the revelation of the cult at Sinai (Exod 24:16, 17; 29:43; 40:34, 35; Lev 9:6, 23), where its function is to sanctify the priesthood and Israel, allowing Yahweh to dwell in a mediated way with the people of

God.[147] Divine presence as the Kadob Yahweh turns into judgment, however, after Israel's failure at Paran.[148] Thus in the spy story (Num 14:10, 21), in the Korah rebellion (Num 16:19), in the subsequent murmuring story (Num 17:7), and in the disobedience of Moses (Num 20:7) priestly tradents repeatedly emphasize that the Kabod Yahweh descended on the Tent of Meeting to execute divine judgment.[149]

The substitution of the Kabod Yahweh for the cloud in the Tent of Meeting is coupled with an expansion of the function of the cloud as a wilderness guide in Exod 13:21-22 and even as a means for waging holy war.[150] Thus, in addition to leading Israel in Exod 13:21-22, the cloud plays a role throughout the priestly account of the confrontation at the sea in 14:19b, 20ab, 24ab. The insertion of the (pillar of) cloud in 14:19b and 20ab contrasts to the Messenger of God in deuteronomistic tradition, in order to describe how God separated the Israelite and Egyptian camps and, in the process, how the cloud of fire lit up the night. The insertion of 14:24ab emphasizes the role of the cloud in God's holy war against the Egyptian army.[151]

The cloud does not leave the orbit of the Kabod Yahweh and the Tent of Meeting tradition in the priestly account of the confrontation at the sea. This fact is evident when we broaden our focus from the confrontation at the sea to the larger priestly history. Note in particular that the cloud/pillar of cloud is tied to three locations (Pihahiroth, Sinai, and Paran) in its function as Israel's guide through the wilderness. These locations follow the priestly itinerary notices.[152] At Pihahiroth the pillar of cloud is first described as leading Israel from Egypt and as waging holy war against the Egyptian army (13:21-22; 14:19b, 20ab, 24ab). At Sinai the function of the cloud in guiding Israel is spelled out in Exod 40:35-36/Num 9:15-23, and the action is narrated in the priestly itinerary notice of Num 10:11-12, where the cloud is described as leading Israel to Paran.[153] Finally, at Paran Moses recounts the events of the exodus to Yahweh in his intercession for the Israelites after they reject the land of Canaan (Num 14:10, 25-35). All references to the cloud leading Israel cease at this point, which is also where the Kabod Yahweh changes its role from one of purification to judgment.[154]

Confronting the Egyptians at the Sea

Priestly tradents reinterpret the narrative account of Yahweh's victory at the sea with the addition of Exod 14:1-4, 8, 9b, 16ab, 17-18, 19b, 20ab, 21b, 22b, 24ab, 29b. Once the setting for the event at the sea is reestablished in Egypt (14:1-2), the priestly additions tend to follow a pattern of divine prediction and fulfillment.[155] Twice Yahweh predicts to Moses the coming events at the sea, first at the outset of the story in 14:3-4, and once again when the Egyptian army is approaching Israel in 14:17-18.[156] These predictions include some motifs that have occurred throughout the plague cycle (e.g., the hardening motif, the recognition motif), but they also indicate a degree of intensification. This time Yahweh will gain glory (כבד) over Pharaoh and his army, which will result in Pharaoh's destruction and create the possibility of knowledge for the Egyptians.[157] The predictions are fulfilled when Pharaoh approaches the Israelites in 14:8 at Pihahiroth, prompting Yahweh first to separate the two camps by means of his cloud (14:19b, 20ab) before waging a holy war on the Egyptians through it (14:24ab).[158] In addition to this action against Pharaoh and his army, priestly writers also add the mythological motif of Yahweh's splitting the water (14:16ab, 21b), which results in two walls (14:22b, 29b), giving the event strong overtones of being a story of creation, as Batto has demonstrated.[159]

The emphasis on the creative power of Yahweh over the sea is accentuated by divine prediction for polemical purposes.[160] The prominence given to divine prediction plays down the drama of the confrontation between Yahweh and Pharaoh, while it also brings to conclusion a perspective on the exodus that began at the outset of the priestly interpretation. In the introduction (7:1-5) Yahweh had already provided a detailed account of how the plagues and exodus would develop and what the eventual outcome would be—Yahweh would harden Pharaoh's heart in order to bring about more plagues (signs), which would eventually result in Israel's exodus from Egypt and create the possibility of knowledge for the Egyptians. Then Yahweh's control over the development of the events was continually reaffirmed throughout the plague cycle with the concluding phrase that all things were, indeed, proceeding as Yahweh had said (7:13, 22; 8:11, 15; 9:12, 35). The central role of prediction throughout the priestly account of the plagues and exodus would certainly indicate a despotic view of God if the only purpose of the plagues were to free the Israelites from Egypt, since their liberation is a foregone conclusion from the outset. But the plagues are not primarily about Israel's liberation. They are signs, whose multiplication is meant to display Yahweh's power as creator and thus confront the Egyptians with this fact. The emphasis on the exodus as a sign of Yahweh's power as creator is actually intensified in the confrontation at the sea, with the result that the destruction of Pharaoh and his army takes on a didactic function to bring the Egyptians to a knowledge of Yahweh.

A CELEBRATION OF THE NEW CREATION

The Plot Structure of the Exodus as a Passover Legend

The wilderness continues to play a central role in the plot structure of the priestly interpretation of the exodus. But journey through the wilderness does not lead to a conquest of the land. In fact priestly tradents critically evaluate the exodus-conquest perspective of the deuteronomistic school by reaffirming the plot structure of the preexilic liturgy. Thus salvation once again becomes a two-part action by Yahweh, consisting of the death of the

Egyptian firstborn and the destruction of the Egyptian army in the sea, with the emphasis on the latter event. Priestly tradents underscore this structure by playing down the itinerary notice in 12:37, which in deuteronomistic tradition served to separate the exodus from the death of the Egyptian firstborn. The result is that in the priestly history these events are merged more closely by means of cultic observance (passover and *massot* are combined). In addition the priestly itinerary notice in 14:1–2 places the confrontation at the sea back in Egypt, so that this event becomes once again Yahweh's final act of liberation against the Egyptians, as it was in the preexilic account.

The changes in plot transform the exodus into a passover legend. It is Pedersen who first advanced this interpretation, and his description of it still catches the imagination.[161] He argued for the cultic character of the exodus story by stating that "the whole narrative aims at glorifying the god of the people at the paschal feast through an exposition of the historical event that created the people."[162] Such glorification is accomplished through a grand drama in which "the mythical fight between Yahweh and his enemies" is described. "Here the events have been re-lived in the Paschal night by the whole of the festival legend being reviewed. Therefore the night that is passed in the crossing of the Reed sea is for the participants identical with the Paschal night itself, the night they experienced in the holy place, and which was not of course different from its archetype in Egypt."[163] "[T]he keynote of the whole story is that Israel as well as her enemies [are] entirely in the hands of her God."[164]

Many aspects of the priestly refashioning of the exodus conform to Pedersen's interpretation. Priestly tradents have indeed emphasized the passover as the cultic setting of the exodus. They have accentuated its observance through dating (Exod 12:1–3) and by combining it with *massot* (Exod 12:1–20). The result is that in the priestly interpretation it is the passover that dominates the cultic instructions during the night of death to the Egyptian firstborn (Exod 12:1–20) and during the exodus from Egypt (12:40–51). The relocation of both the death of the Egyptian firstborn and the confrontation at the sea within the boundaries of Egypt also supports Pedersen's argument that the events of the exodus should not be separated but read as a unity.[165] But even when a unified reading of the exodus is undertaken, the focus of the priestly interpretation is not on Israel's crossing, as Pedersen has argued, but on the splitting of sea, with its overtones of creation.[166] And this act of creation is two-sided. It is both a new creation and an instance of divine judgment resulting in the death of the Egyptian army.

The meaning of the passover in priestly tradition also supports Pedersen's thesis that the "keynote" of the legend is Yahweh's control of events with regard to both Israelites and the Egyptians.[167] The passover embodied polemical characteristics already in deuteronomistic tradition, since the more universal power of God over Israelites and non-Israelites was also central to their interpretation. The focus of deuteronomistic interpretation, however, tended to be more exclusive in order to emphasize Israel's need to participate in cultic action in order to avoid the plague of death.[168] Priestly tradents expand the polemical character of passover by accentuating the power of Yahweh as creator in their interpretation of the rite. Thus, for priestly tradents Yahweh no longer strikes simply the Egyptians, but now their land, a shift that gives the action a larger dimension. As a result, the passover signifies Israel's exemption from an act of divine judgment that would inevitably be felt by humans, animals, and gods (Exod 12:17–18).[169]

The plot structure of the priestly history is determined by the priestly cultic calendar, as was the case in the deuteronomistic version of salvation history. The passover legend of the priestly tradents is an event of creation, which has universal implications of potential judgment and salvation. Priestly tradents locate these events in Egypt and place the observance of passover in the spring, where it is set apart from the fall festivals of trumpets, atonement, and tabernacles.[170] Once this separation is noted, additional contrasts come to light in the placement of these festivals within the priestly history. The fall festivals take place in the wilderness, they presuppose the revelation of the Tabernacle cult, and they focus more exclusively on Israel. Here we see that the spring and fall festivals follow the process of narrowing in scope that is characteristic of the priestly history. Yet this progression is more than a literary device. It also signals that although the passover is important to priestly tradents, it does not retain the preeminent place that it enjoyed in the deuteronomistic history, where the focus of the rite was more exclusively on Israel. Instead the festival has acquired more universal and polemical overtones, which, however necessary for the salvation of Israel and God's re-creation, now function as a prerequisite for cultic atonement in the fall, where the focus turns more exclusively on Israel.

The Character of God in the New Creation

Holy war continues to play an important role in the priestly understanding of salvation. Many of the motifs from the deuteronomistic redaction are carried over into priestly tradition, but, as the preceding literary analysis would suggest, priestly tradents shift the emphasis of holy war away from the death of the Egyptian firstborn and the exodus from Egypt, and back to the confrontation at the sea, as was the case in the preexilic narrative. Furthermore, priestly tradents tend to cluster the holy-war imagery around this event. Thus, in contrast to the deuteronomistic interpretation in 13:17–18a that Israel was not yet ready for holy war when they left Egypt, priestly tradents insert in 13:18b that the people left Egypt specifically prepared for war. This interpretation is amplified in the larger context of the exodus by the repeated description of Israel as being Yahweh's "host"

(Exod 6:26; 7:4; 12:17, 41, 51), itself a term with militaristic overtones. The holy-war imagery is carried forward into the confrontation at the sea, when the Israelites are described in 14:8 as going out with their "hands raised."[171] Other holy-war images associated with the confrontation at the sea include the cloud,[172] which evokes ancient Near Eastern imagery associated with divine warfare, perhaps also the intensification of the hardening motif,[173] and the Song of Miriam.[174]

The concentration of holy war motifs around the confrontation at the sea encourages, upon first reading, a unilateral interpretation of divine power, in which strength is measured by the degree to which one party is able to produce intended effects on the other. This definition of power is, in fact, taken to an extreme point, since, according to priestly tradents, God is the active force in both resistance and its breakdown in an opponent. In addition, the absence of Israel as an independent and active character throughout the priestly interpretation adds further support to the unilateral view of divine power, as does the dominant role of divine prediction from the outset of the plagues right through to the destruction of the Egyptian army. The God of the priestly history is certainly in absolute control of the sequence of events, so much so, that the outcome of the exodus fades into the background. The result of these changes to the story is that whatever drama and suspense might have been present in early accounts are removed. All of these points suggest a close correspondence between the preexilic liturgy and the priestly history.

The extreme rhetoric of divine power, however, must be tempered by an examination of the structure of the priestly history. Indeed, a more careful reading of the plot of the priestly interpretation of the exodus underscores that it is not simply a reaffirmation of preexilic tradition. The use of the exodus motif, the inclusion of the passover, the absence of divine enthronement, the central role of the wilderness, and the future promise of land all point to the influence of deuteronomistic tradition, in which divine power was conceived of relationally rather than unilaterally.

Priestly tradents fashion yet another view of divine power by merging both preexilic and deuteronomistic accounts of the exodus—a view that, in the end, must be interpreted as being a relational view of divine power. The predominant role of divine prediction provides a point of entry into the priestly view of divine power, and it illustrates how unilateral and relational views of power have been interwoven. The God of the exodus is certainly in control of all events for priestly tradents. Nearly every event that is predicted by God is fulfilled within the boundaries of the story of the exodus. Thus there is an orderliness to the priestly history that is reminiscent of the preexilic narrative. What remains unfulfilled is the divine promise of land and the prediction that humans will come to a knowledge of Yahweh from the events of the exodus.

Although the future promise of land is important to priestly tradents, it is not conceived in the open-ended way of deuteronomistic tradents, whereby events evolve in the wilderness toward a conquest of Canaan. Instead, for priestly tradents the secrets of the future promise of land are buried in the past and must be found anew. The priestly history, therefore, is more circular than linear, more paradigmatic than sequential, and hence more mythopoeic, since it emphasizes how Israel's salvation from Egypt begins a process of rediscovering the original creation. Within this structure, Genesis 1 emerges as a central text, standing outside of P's chronology. It provides both a paradigm of the beginning (*Urzeit*) and a vision of the end (*Endzeit*). As the beginning, Genesis 1 is a polemical account of origins, stressing the power of Yahweh to control chaos (Gen 1:1–2) and to bring forth creation in six days (Gen 1:3–31) before resting on the seventh (2:1–3). When Genesis 1 is read as the end of the priestly history, it once again underscores that creation has replaced conquest and that the promise of land is now conceived in a more eschatological perspective, by priestly tradents, as a new creation. In spite of the differences in the structuring of a cosmic history, the unfulfilled promise of land places the priestly account of the exodus squarely in deuteronomistic tradition, thereby creating a point of tension between the rhetoric of divine control in the priestly account of the exodus and the more open-ended structure of the story.

The rhetoric of divine control is qualified both by the plot of the exodus and by the motif of recognition. For priestly tradents, Yahweh, as the creator God, can certainly control all events (a unilateral view of divine power), and in so doing the divine is able to confront humans with inescapable choice (the recognition motif). But such confrontation cannot control the content of human knowledge (a relational view of divine power). Instead Yahweh can create only the possibility for human knowledge of God. As a consequence, only humans, in the end, can determine whether acts of divine recognition are occasions of judgment or salvation. This is true for both Israel and Egypt, although the focus in the exodus is on Egypt.[175]

The inability of God to determine the specific content of knowledge in humans concerning the divine is a relational view of divine power, since persuasion is required over dominance. On the one hand, God *produces* effects by controlling the course of events. Yet on the other hand, God can also *undergo* effects depending on how humans respond to different situations. For priestly tradents, God's active effects are the events of the exodus. These events are clear, unambiguous, and closed off in the past. How humans may respond to these events is not clear.

What is most striking about the exploration of divine power in the priestly account of the exodus is that the relationship receiving the most attention is that between God and the other nations (Egypt), rather than between God and Israel. The relationship between God and Egypt is not explored in the open-ended and ambiguous manner of deuteronomistic tradition, wherein Israel could actually change the course of the exodus at a number of different junctures in the story. For priestly tradents the events of the exodus are locked into place. What remains open-ended is whether these events will be a source of judgment for the Egyptians or lead to a more positive form of recognition of Yahweh. This ambiguity is never resolved in the telling of the story, and it gives rise to the polemical emphasis in priestly tradition, with its apologetical overtones. The uncertainty of the Egyptians' response to the events of the exodus continues to influence Israel's history long after Egypt. The Egyptians' need to recognize the power of God in the exodus returns when Moses mediates with God during the affair of the golden calf (Exodus 32) and the spy story (Numbers 14). In these instances the uncertainty of how the Egyptians might respond to divine judgment on Israel even changes Yahweh's behavior toward the people in the wilderness.

The description of the priestly interpretation of the exodus as being an apologetic aimed at other nations is somewhat misleading, since priestly tradition is certainly not a missionary movement.[176] Rather the apologetic is meant to address an aspect of divine power that arises from the confession that Yahweh is not only Israel's savior but, indeed, the creator of all things. This strong emphasis on creation gives the priestly interpretation of the exodus a more universal and potentially inclusive character, and this focus is evident throughout the priestly reading. The plagues are refashioned into signs aimed primarily at Egyptians, the magicians are inserted into the plague cycle to illustrate what such signs can accomplish when they detect the power of God behind the actions of Aaron. The incorporation of non-Israelites is explored in detail within the priestly passover legislation. Finally, the confrontation at the sea is fashioned into a polemic aimed at the Egyptians in general.

Thus, in the end priestly tradition adheres more to the perspective of deuteronomistic than to preexilic tradition. Both advocate a relational view of divine power, and, in so doing, both reject the national theology of preexilic tradition, where the rule of Yahweh was celebrated as a present reality in the land. Yet priestly tradents also provide a counterpoint to deuteronomistic tradition, especially with their emphasis on the relationship between Yahweh and the nations, as opposed to the deuteronomistic focus on Yahweh and Israel. The result is that, in the end, although both adhere to a relational view of divine power, they explore the implications of such a confession in two somewhat different directions. The influence of Israel on the outcome of salvation history is explored by deuteronomistic tradents through the exodus–conquest pattern of their history. The influence of the nations on divine action comes into greater focus for priestly tradents, whose pattern of exodus and creation provides a more expansive and eschatological vision of salvation history.

NOTES

1. This consensus holds regardless of methodological orientation and the more specific details of what constitutes priestly tradition in the exodus. See, for example, the recent and very different studies by Kohata, *Jahwist und Priesterschrift in Exodus 3–14*; and Blum, *Studien*, 229-262.

2. See, for example, Wellhausen (*Prolegomena*, 347), who writes: "In the Priestly code the work of Moses lies before us clearly defined and rounded off. . . . It is detached from its originator and from his age: lifeless itself, it has driven the life out of Moses and out of the people, nay, out of the very Deity." For criticism see J. Blenkinsopp, "The Structure of P," *CBQ* 38 (1976): 291. For a brief cataloguing of this attitude with regard to past evaluations of the narrative style of P see S. E. McEvenue, *The Narrative Style of the Priestly Writer*, AnBib 50 (Rome: Biblical Institute, 1971), 1–8.

3. With regard to law see, for example, M. Douglas, "The Abominations of Leviticus," in *Purity and Danger: An Analysis of Concepts of Pollution and Taboo* (London: Routledge & Kegan Paul, 1966), 41–57; M. Haran, *Temples and Temple-Service in Ancient Israel: An Inquiry into the Character of Cult Phenomena and the Historical Setting of the Priestly School* (Oxford: Clarendon Press, 1978); D. P. Wright, *The Disposal of Impurity*, SBLDS 101 (Atlanta: Scholars Press, 1987); F. H. Gorman, Jr., *The Ideology of Ritual: Space, Time and Status in the Priestly Theology*, JSOTSup 91 (Sheffield: Academic Press, 1990); B. A. Levine, *In the Presence of the Lord*, SJLA 5 (Leiden: E. J. Brill, 1974); and J. Milgrom, *Leviticus 1–16*, AB 3A (New York: Doubleday, 1991). With regard to the priestly history see, K. Elliger, "Sinn und Ursprung der priesterlichen Geschichtserzählung," *ZTK* 49 (1952) 121–143; Cross, *Canaanite Myth and Hebrew Epic*, 293–325; W. Brueggemann, "The Kerygma of the Priestly Writers," in *The Vitality of Old Testament Traditions* (Atlanta: John Knox, 1976), 101–113; Blenkinsopp, "The Structure of P," 275; N. Lohfink, "Die Priesterschrift und die Geschichte," in *Congress Volume: Göttingen 1977*, VTSup 29, ed. J. A. Emerton et al. (Leiden: Brill, 1978), 189–225; M. Saebø, "Priestertheologie und Priesterschrift: Zur Eigenart der priesterlichen Schicht im Pentateuch," in *Congress Volume: Vienna 1981*, VTSup 32, ed. J. A. Emerton et al. (Leiden: E. J. Brill, 1982), 357–374; P. Weimar, "Struktur und Komposition der priesterschriftlichen Geschichtsdarstellung," *BN* 23 (1984): 81–134; and 24 (1984): 138–162; V. Fritz, "Das Geschichtsverständnis der Priesterschrift," *ZTK* 84 (1987): 426–439; and R. B. Coote and D. R. Ord, *In the Beginning: Creation and the Priestly History* (Minneapolis: Fortress Press, 1991), esp. 39–47.

4. See especially Milgrom, *Leviticus*.

5. For an examination of the interrelationship between law and narrative in the tradition-historical development of the Pentateuch in general and the wilderness tradition in particular see T. B. Dozeman, "Horeb/Sinai and the Rise of Law in the Wilderness Tradition," *SBLSP* 28 (1989): 282–290.

6. See the arguments in favor of the antiquity of priestly law based on a linguistic comparision with Ezekiel by A. Hurvitz, *A Linguistic Study of the Relationship Between the Priestly Source and the Book of Ezekiel: A New Approach to an Old Problem*, CahRB 20 (Paris: J. Gabalda, 1982), and the extension of his work by Milgrom, *Leviticus*, 13–35. For additional studies arguing for an early date to priestly (primarily legal) tradition see Haran, *Temples and Temple-Service in Ancient Israel*, 146–147; and "Behind the Scenes of History: Determining the Date of the Priestly Source," *JBL* 100 (1981): 321–333; Z. Zevit, "Converging Lines of Evidence Bearing on the Date of P," *ZAW* 94 (1982): 481–511; and G. Rendsburg, "Late Biblical Hebrew and the Date of P," *JANESCU* 12 (1980): 65–80.

7. The starting point for dating priestly narrative must be its dependence on the deuteronomistic history. For arguments in favor of an exilic date for priestly narrative see, among many others, Elliger, "Sinn und Ursprung der priesterlichen Geschichtserzählung," 121–143; P. R. Ackroyd, *Exile and Restoration: A Study*

of Hebrew Thought of the Sixth Century B.C., OTL (Philadelphia: Westminster, 1968), 85 and passim; B. A. Levine, "Priestly Writers," in *IDBSup*, ed. K. Crim (Nashville: Abingdon, 1976), 683-687; Brueggemann, "The Kerygma of the Priestly Writers," 101-113; Blenkinsopp, "The Structure of P," 275; Lohfink, "Die Priesterschrift und die Geschichte," 189-225. Compare J. G. Vink ("The Date and Origin of the Priestly Code in the Old Testament," *OTS* 15 [1969]: 1-144), who favors a postexilic date.

8. This position is the reverse of previous source-critical arguments that a priestly narrative (Pg) was supplemented later by legislation. See, for example, Noth (*History of Pentateuch Traditions*, 8-19), whose distinction was foreshadowed by Wellhausen with his contrast between Q (a narrative source) and the *Priesterkodex* (a legal corpus).

9. See B. Porten and A. Yardeni, *Textbook of Aramaic Documents from Ancient Egypt*, vol. 1 (Winona Lake: Eisenbrauns, 1986), 54; P. Grelot, "Etudes sur la 'Papyrus Pascal' D'Eléphantine," *VT* 4 (1954): 349-384; and T. Eves, "The Role of Passover in the Book of Chronicles: A Study of 2 Chronicles 30 and 35" (Ph.D. diss., Annenberg Research Institute, 1992), chap. 6, pp. 18-22.

10. For a reevaluation of the relationship between the Holiness Code and other priestly legislation see I. Knohl, "The Priestly Torah Versus the Holiness School: Sabbath and the Festivals," *HUCA* 58 (1987): 65-117; and Milgrom, *Leviticus*, 13-51.

11. See, for example, Wellhausen, *Composition*, 331, 333; *Prolegomena*, 295; Noth, *History of Pentateuchal Traditions*, 8-19; Elliger, "Sinn und Ursprung der priesterlichen Geschichtserzählung," 9; Childs, *Exodus*, 138-141, 219, 221, and passim; Brueggemann, "The Kerygma of the Priestly Writers," 101-113. Compare G. von Rad (*Die Priesterschrift im Hexateuch* [Stuttgart: W. Kohlhammer, 1934]), who advocated two parallel priestly sources. For more recent discussion in favor of a priestly source see Lohfink, "Die Priesterschirft und die Geschichte," 196-197; K. Koch, "P—Kein Redaktor! Erinnerung an zwei Eckdaten der Quellenscheidung," *VT* 37 (1987): 446-467; Fritz, "Das Geschichtsverständnis der Priesterschrift," 426-439; E. W. Nicholson, "P as an Originally Independent Source in the Pentateuch," *IBS* 10 (1988): 192-206; and J. A. Emerton, "The Priestly Writer in Genesis," *JTS* 39 (1988): 381-400. For arguments in favor of reading P as a source because of its absolute chronology see J. Hughes, *Secrets of the Times: Myth and History in Biblical Chronology*, JSOTSup 66 (Sheffield: Academic Press, 1990), 5-54, esp. 49-51.

12. Among recent scholars see Rendtorff, *Problem des Pentaeuch*, 141-142; J. Van Seters, *Abraham in History and Tradition* (New Haven: Yale University Press), 281-282 and passim; Cross, *Canaanite Myth and Hebrew Epic*, 293-325; M. Greenberg, "The Redaction of the Plague Narrative in Exodus," in *Near Eastern Studies in Honor of W. F. Albright*, ed. H. Goedicke (Baltimore: Johns Hopkins University Press, 1971), 243-252; Z. Zevit, "The Priestly Redaction and Interpretation of the Plague Narrative in Exodus," *JQR* 66 (1975): 193-211; and the modified argument by Blum (*Studien*, 229-285) in which he advocates both an independent source and supplementation. For an overview of the debate and further arguments in support of the redactional character of priestly tradition see J.-L. Ska, "Quelques remarques sur Pg et la dernière rédaction du pentateuque," in *Le pentateuque en question: Les origines et la composition des cinq premiers livres de la Bible à la lumière des recherches récentes,* Le monde de la Bible, ed. A. de

Pury (Genève: Labor & Fides, 1989), 95-128; with regard to Exodus 14 see M. Vervenne, "The 'P' Tradition in the Pentateuch: Document and/or Redaction? The 'Sea Narrative' (Exod 13,17-14,31) as a Test Case," in *Pentateuchal and Deuteronomistic Studies: Papers Read at the XIIIth IOSOT Congress, Leuven 1989*, BETL 94, ed. Chr. Brekelmans and J. Lust (Leuven: University Press, 1990), 67-90.

13. Cross, *Canaanite Myth and Hebrew Epic*, 306.

14. Cross, *Canaanite Myth and Hebrew Epic*, 306-318. See also Blum, *Studien*, 231-232; but especially H. Utzschneider, *Das Heiligtum und das Gesetz: Studien zur Bedeutung der Sinaitischen Heiligtumstexts (Ex 25-40; Lev 8-9)*, OBO 77 (Göttingen: Vandenhoeck & Ruprecht, 1988), 19-35, esp. 31-35. These problems are also noted by Lohfink, "Die Priesterschrift und die Geschichte," 199 n. 31.

15. Blenkinsopp, "The Structure of P," 280.

16. See W. Zimmerli, "Erkenntnis Gottes nach dem Buche Ezechiel," in *Gottes Offenbarung*, Theologische Bücher 19 (München: Chr. Kaiser, 1963), 41-119 = "Knowledge of God According to the Book of Ezekiel," in *I am Yahweh*, ed. W. Brueggemann, trans. D. W. Stott (Atlanta: John Knox, 1982), 29-98. The term "recognition formula or motif" is a translation of the German *Erkenntnisformel* and follows the translation of Stott. See the "Translator's Preface" (p. vii) concerning the problems of rendering the German into English.

17. The debate is central to the modern interpretation of the Pentateuch. For the sharpest form of the debate compare here S. Mowinckel (*Tetrateuch-Pentateuch-Hexateuch: Die Berichte über die Landnahme in den Drei Altisrael- itischen Geschichtswerken* [Berlin: A. Töpelmann, 1964], 51-76), who argues for the presence of P in Joshua; and Noth (*History of Pentateuchal Traditions*, 8-19 and passim), who rejects any influence of P in Joshua. For a review of the debate through the work of Rendtorff (*Problem des Pentateuch*) and S. Tengström (*Die Hexateucherzählung: Eine literaturgeschichtliche Studie*, ConBOT 7 [Lund: Gleerup, 1976]) see A. G. Auld, *Joshua, Moses and the Land: Tetrateuch-Pentateuch- Hexateuch in a Generation Since 1938* (Edinburgh: T & T Clark, 1980). The debate is not confined to source-critical approaches to the Pentateuch but continues in more redaction-critically oriented studies of P, as is clear from a comparison of Cross (*Canaanite Myth and Hebrew Epic*, 301-325), who follows Noth, and Blenkinsopp ("The Structure of P," 275-292), who argues for priestly tradition in Joshua.

18. The itinerary notice in Josh 4:19 describing Israel's crossing the Jordan and encampment at Gilgal is deuteronomistic, but the precise date is priestly.

19. Especially the framing of the account in Josh 18:1 and 19:51. See Blenkinsopp, "The Structure of P," 276, 288. The influence may go beyond framing to include the very structure of the larger text in Joshua 18-19. See D. G. Schley (*Shiloh: A Biblical City in Tradition and History*, JSOTSup 63 [Sheffield: Academic Press, 1989], 110-118), who offers a source-critical solution; and most recently E. Cortese, *Josua 13-21: Ein priesterschriftlicher Abschnitt im deuteronomistischen Geschichtswerk*, OBO 94 (Göttingen: Vandenhoeck & Ruprecht, 1990). Furthermore, signs of priestly editing may extend into the Book of Kings, where the construction of the Jerusalem temple is also dated (1 Kgs 6:1) 480 years after the exodus, in a manner that is reminiscent of priestly chronology, and interrelates this event with Exod 12:40. See Hughes, *Secrets of the Times*, 32-33.

20. So also Blenkinsopp, "The Structure of P," 275-292.

21. McEvenue, *The Narrative Style of the Priestly Writer*, 56-59.

22. McEvenue, *The Narrative Style of the Priestly Writer*, 59, 182, 184-185 and passim. For an overview of the calendrical system, including the priestly system of dating, see J. C. VanderKam, "Calendars: Ancient Israelite and Early Jewish," in *The Anchor Bible Dictionary*, vol. 1, ed. D. N. Freedman (New York: Doubleday, 1992), 814-820.

23. See Lohfink ("Die Priesterschrift und die Geschichte," 214, 215) for a discussion of the paradigmatic character of the priestly history, and also note the use of this term by Fritz ("Das Geschichtsverständnis der Priesterschrift," 427) to underscore that the priestly history is oriented toward the past.

24. For an initial discussion see Blenkinsopp, *Pentateuch*, 47-50; and for more detail, Hughes, *Secrets of the Times*, 3-54.

25. See Blenkinsopp, *Pentateuch*, 48; and "The Structure of P," 283-283.

26. See Childs, *Exodus*, 275.

27. See Dozeman, *God on the Mountain*, 90-93.

28. Note also the reference to an absolute chronology in Exod 12:40 with regard to Israel's time in Egypt as consisting of 430 years.

29. For arguments in favor of reading Deut 1:3 as a priestly addition see Mayes, *Deuteronomy*, 115; Weinfeld, *Deuteronomy*, 128; Seitz, *Redaktionsgeschichtliche Studien zum Deuteronomium*, 27-29.

30. Elliger, "Sinn und Ursprung der priestlichen Geschichtserzählung," 121-143, esp. 134-143. See also Blenkinsopp, "The Structure of P," 289; Brueggemann, "The Kerygma of the Priestly Writers," 101-113; and Lohfink, "Die Priesterschrift und die Geschichte," 215-225.

31. Noth, *History of Pentateuchal Traditions*, 9; see also Cross, *Canaanite Myth and Hebrew Epic*, 318-230.

32. Elliger, "Sinn und Ursprung der priestlichen Geschichtserzählung," 138.

33. Elliger, "Sinn und Ursprung der priestlichen Geschichtserzählung," 121-122.

34. There are no signs that P claims or restructures the account of the crossing of the Jordan in Josh 3:1-5:1. The only indication of priestly language outside of the references to chronology in Josh 4:19 and the highlighting of passover in 5:11 (בעצם היום הזה) is the description of the ark in Josh 4:16 as being the ark of testimony (ארון העדות). The significance of this reference as a basis for asserting P's interest in the crossing of the Jordan River and the conquest of the land of Canaan is lessened when one realizes that the ark is referred to no less than seventeen times in Josh 3:1-5:1: in addition to 4:16, it occurs eleven times as the "ark of the covenant." (ארון הברית, Josh 3:3, 6 [twice], 8, 11, 13, 14, 17; 4:7, 9, 18); three times as "the ark" (הארון, Josh 3:15 [twice]; 4:10); and twice as the ark of Yahweh (הארון־יהוה, Josh 4:5, 11).

35. Blenkinsopp, "The Structure of P," 287. See Brueggemann ("The Kerygma of the Priestly Writers," 108, 110), who argues that creation is expressed in conquest language in P through the imagery of subduing the earth and having dominion.

36. See note 34.

37. See Mayes (*Deuteronomy*, 411-413) and von Rad (*Deuteronomy*, 209-210) for discussion of Deut 34:8 as part of a priestly addition that includes Deut 34:1 (or part of it) and 7-9.

38. The main texts dealing with the death of Moses include Num 27:12-23;

Deut 32:48-52; 34:1-12, but these could be expanded to include texts in which Joshua is commissioned as the successor of Moses (such as Deut 3:21-29; 31:1-8, 14, 15, 23), as suggested by M. Rose, "Empoigner le pentateuque par sa fin! L'investiture de Josué et la mort de Moïse," in *Le pentateuque en question: Les origines et la composition des cinq premiers livres de la Bible à la lumière des recherches récentes*, Le monde de la Bible, ed. A. de Pury (Genève: Labor & Fides, 1989), 129-147. For a discussion of the tradition-historical development of these texts, and their possible function in shaping the priestly history and/or the canonical Pentateuch see Noth (*History of Pentateuchal Traditions*, 16-17), who speaks of both the priestly writer and a pentateuchal redactor in describing the development of these texts. Blenkinsopp (*Pentateuch*, 229-232) describes a process in which Deuteronomy is amalgamated with the priestly history. Rose ("Empoigner le pentateuque par sa fin!," 140-147) describes a three-part process of growth from a deuteronomistic account that emphasized, first, the succession of Joshua to replace Moses in a military context (Deut 1:37; 3:21-29; 31:1-8; 34) which continued into the Book of Joshua; second, a Yahwistic redaction (Deut 31:14, 15, 23) which supplemented the deuteronomistic history backwards, thus making connection with Exodus 33 and Numbers 11-12; and third, the incorporation of P (Num 27:12-23; Deut 32:48-52; and 34:7-9).

39. The division between Genesis and Exodus is not absolute, since the eleven Toledot texts continue into Numbers: Gen 2:4a (heaven and earth), 5:1 (Adam), 9:8 (Noah), 10:1 (Sons of Noah), 11:10 (Shem), 11:27 (Terah), 25:12 (Ishmael), 25:19 (Isaac), 36:1, 9 (Esau), 37:2 (Jacob), and then Moses and Aaron in Num 3:1. For an analysis of the Toledot texts with regard to their form/syntax and their distribution see among many others, Cross, *Canaanite Myth and Hebrew Epic*, 301-305; G. J. Wenham, *Genesis 1-15*, WBC (Waco: Word Books, 1987), xxi-xxii, 49-51; J. Scharbert, "Der Sinn der Toledot-Formel in der Priesterschrift," in *Wort-Gebot-Glaube: Beiträge zur Theologie des Alten Testaments. Festschrift für W. Eichrodt*, ATANT 59, ed. J. J. Stamm et al. (Zürich: Zwingli, 1970), 45-56; P. Weimar, "Die Toledot-Formel in der priesterschriftlichen Geschichtsdarstellung," *BZ* 18 (1974): 65-93; and S. Tengström, *Die Toledotformel und die literarische Struktur der priesterlichen Erweiterungsschicht im Pentateuch*, ConBOT 17 (Lund: Gleerup, 1981). See Weimar ("Die Toledot-Formel in der priesterschriftlichen Geschichtsdarstellung," 93), who argues for the secondary character of Num 3:1. But compare Tengström (*Die Toledotformel*, 55-56), who is most likely correct in arguing that there are no literary grounds for excluding Num 3:1 from the basic Toledot structure.

40. Once again priestly tradents illustrate that they are not bound by their own structures, since geographical notices reach back and also function in an important (although subordinate) manner in Genesis. Especially noteworthy is the framing of geographical notices concerning the ancestors: with the migration of Abram from Haran in Gen 12:4 and the migration of Jacob to Egypt (Goshen) in Gen 46:5-6.

41. For a discussion of the division between Toledot and itinerary notices in the priestly history see also Cross, *Canaanite Myth and Hebrew Epic*, 302-317; Lohfink, "Die Priesterschrift und die Geschichte, 204-205; or Fritz, "Das Geschichtsverständnis der Priesterschrift," 428. The contrast between Genesis and Exodus-Deuteronomy brings into relief the thesis of R. Knierim ("The Composition of the Pentateuch," SBLSP 24 [1985]: 393-415) that the Pentateuch is struc-

tured into a life of Moses, with Genesis providing the introduction to his life. Such a focus for interpretation would invite comparison between Noah and Moses (especially in the birth story of Moses), since each plays a central role in the two halves of the priestly history.

42. For a discussion of the central role of the flood in the priestly history see Tengström, *Die Toledotformel*, 39–43; or Blenkinsopp, *Pentateuch*, 59. Blenkinsopp's argument is limited to the first five Toledot, which he argues are structured in a pentad, with the flood functioning in the center.

43. Thus, in spite of the universal perspective in the way in which the Toledot texts organize Genesis, there is also a narrowing process which progresses from the widest possible categories of heaven and earth (Gen 2:4a) and Adam (Gen 5:1) in the preflood history of humanity to the survivor Noah (Gen 6:9) and eventually to the family of Jacob (Gen 37:2) at the close of the postflood history of humanity.

44. Exod 1:1–5, 7 is an insertion by priestly tradents. Verses 1–5 create a connection between the Israelite prehistory and national history with the opening words of Exodus (1:1, "These are the names of Israelites . . ."), which is reminiscent of the Toledot form ("These are the generations of . . .") and repeats language from Gen 46:8. See Childs (*Exodus*, 1–3) for discussion and compare W. H. Schmidt, *Exodus*, 7–12. But v. 7 underscores the contrast between the two parts of the history by emphasizing that Israel had evolved into a nation. Their greatness harkens back to creation (Gen 1:28), since Israel has been fruitful (פרה) and has increased in numbers (רבה). Yet the language of this verse also conveys threatening (or perhaps better, subversive) overtones, since they are also now strong (עצם). See especially Brueggemann, "The Kerygma of the Priestly Writers," 101–113, esp. 107.

45. McEvenue, *The Narrative Style of the Priestly Writer*, 183–185.

46. For interpretations of P that accentuate the important role of covenant see Wellhausen, *Prolegomena*, 352; or Cross, *Canaanite Myth and Hebrew Epic*, 295–300. Scholars have also underscored the importance of divine presence; the relationship of creation to the Tabernacle; the central role of Abraham; Sabbath; the interrelationship of creation, Tabernacle, and land distribution; promise and fulfillment, etc.

47. Batto, *Slaying the Dragon*.

48. M. Fishbane, *Biblical Interpretation in Ancient Israel* (Oxford: Clarendon Press, 1985), 351.

49. Fishbane, *Biblical Interpretation*, 351–352.

50. Fishbane, *Biblical Interpretation*, 354–368.

51. Fishbane, *Biblical Interpretation*, 358–364.

52. Fishbane (*Biblical Interpretation*, 358–359) discusses Joshua 3–5 within this framework.

53. Fishbane, *Biblical Interpretation*, 357.

54. Fishbane, *Biblical Interpretation*, 357.

55. Fishbane, *Biblical Interpretation*, 354–356.

56. On the hiddenness of the original structures of creation and Israel's need to rediscover them see Elliger, "Sinn und Ursprung der priesterlichen Geschichtserzählung," 135–137. For a discussion of the focus on the past original creation as providing the paradigm for the future see Fritz, "Das Geschichtsverständnis der Priesterschrift," 426–439.

57. The present study assumes that the Toledot in Gen 2:4a functions as an introduction to the next section rather than as a summary conclusion to Gen 1:1-2:3. See Wenham (*Genesis 1-15*, 49-50 and passim) for a discussion.

58. See Lohfink, "Die Priesterschrift und die Geschichte," 216-225; and Fritz, "Das Geschichtsverständnis der Priesterschrift," 434-439.

59. See Lohfink, "Die Priesterschrift und die Geschichte," 217.

60. Noth, *Exodus*, 58-62. See also Childs, *Exodus*, 111-120; W. H. Schmidt, *Exodus*, 269-312. Compare Kohata (*Jahwist und Priesterschrift in Exodus 3-14*, 28-41), who argues that at least 6:8 is a later addition to the text; or P. Weimar (*Untersuchungen zur priesterschriftlichen Exodusgeschichte*, Forschung zur Bibel 9 [Würzburg: Echter Verlag, 1973], 77-164) for arguments supporting prepriestly tradition in Exod 6:2-8, including vv. 2, 5a, 6a, 6b, 7b.

61. For a recent analysis of the literary structure of Exod 6:2-8 see J. Magonet ("The Rhetoric of God: Exodus 6.2-8," *JSOT* 27 [1983]: 56-67), who follows the work of N. Leibowitz, *Studies in Shemot*: Part 1, trans. A. Newman (Jerusalem: The World Zionist Organization, 1981), 114-131, esp. 116-117. See the response by P. Auffret, "Remarks on J. Magonet's Interpretation of Exodus 6.2-8," *JSOT* 27 (1983): 69-71. For a form-critical analysis focusing on comparison to disputation texts in Ezekiel see Ska, "Quelques remarques sur Pg," 98-99.

62. The genealogy in Exod 6:14-27 appears to be a Zadokite document that traces the authority of Phinehas through Eleazar-Aaron-Amran-Kohath-Levi. See R. R. Wilson (*Genealogy and History in the Biblical World* [New Haven: Yale University Press, 1977], 40-45, 69-72 and passim) for a discussion of the function of the Levitical genealogies within priestly tradition. For arguments that Exod 6:14-25 is a redactional insertion see Childs, *Exodus*, 111. For a detailed interpretation of Exod 6:14-25 see W. H. Schmidt, *Exodus*, 293-312.

63. See, for example, Noth, *Exodus*, 58.

64. See Childs, *Exodus*, 111.

65. There have been attempts to harmonize the two accounts or to interpret the two in some form of developmental sequence. See Childs (*Exodus*, 114) and Noth (*Exodus*, 58), who suggest that Exod 6:2-7:7 now confirms the commission of Exod 3:1-4:17; or T. E. Fretheim (*Exodus*, 88-89), who suggests that the emphasis is changed between the two. Yet even with such arguments, the contrast between the two texts is striking, requiring a more inner-biblical (and hence less harmonized) interpretative solution.

66. See, for example, W. H. Schmidt, *Exodus*, 270-276.

67. Noth, *Exodus*, 58; and Ska, "Quelques remarques sur Pg," 95-125, esp. 123..

68. So also Noth, *Exodus*, 58; and Childs, *Exodus*, 111. The elimination of the call of Moses from Midian requires further study concerning the negative attitude of priestly tradents toward Midianites throughout the Pentateuch.

69. See also Childs, "A Traditio-Historical Study of the Reed Sea Tradition," 407-410.

70. See Elliger ("Sinn und Ursprung der priesterlichen Geschichtserzählung," 137), who writes: "Der Bund mit den Vätern steht unverrückbar fest. Sein Inhalt ist—wieder erscheint es als eigentlicher Kernpunkt—, 'ihnen das Land Kanaan zu geben' (Ex 6 4 8)."

71. For discussion of El Shaddai in priestly tradition and the relationship between Genesis 17 and Exod 6:2-7:7 see, among others, Noth, *Exodus*, 59-61;

Childs, *Exodus*, 114-115; W. H. Schmidt, *Exodus*, 282-283. See Ska ("Quelques remarques sur Pg," 95-125), who broadens the discussion of interrelated texts in priestly tradition to include Gen 17; 35:9-12; Exod 1:13; 2:23-25; 6:2-8; 12:43-51; 14; 29:45-46, focusing not only on the progressive revelation of divine names, but also on the important motifs of covenant and promise of land.

72. For a discussion of the introductory function of 6:2-7:7 to the priestly account of the plagues and exodus, with particular focus on 7:1-5, see J.-L. Ska, "Les plaies d'Egypte dans le récit sacerdotal (Pg)," *Bib* 60 (1979): 23-26. See also, among others, Kegler, "Zu Komposition und Theologie der Plagenerzählungen," 58-59; and Wilson, "The Hardening of Pharaoh's Heart," 23, 29-32.

73. The formula of divine self-disclosure ("I am Yahweh," אני יהוה) occurs fives times in Exod 6:2-7:7 (6:6, 7, 8, 29; 7:5) and also repeats in three plagues (blood—7:17a*a*; flies—8:18b; and locust—10:2b*b*) and twice during the destruction of the Egyptian army at the sea (14:4b, 18). The tradition-historical roots of this phrase certainly precede priestly tradition, as is evident by its use in Hosea (see, for example, Hosea 12:9; 13:4). Nevertheless, the frequent use of this phrase in Leviticus (for example, 11:45; 19:34, 35-36; 22:31-33; 23:43; 25:38, 55; 29:46) as well as in priestly portions of Numbers (such as 3:11; 15:41) underscores how the phrase has also become central to priestly tradents. Note the slightly different form of self-disclosure in Exod 3:6, 14-15; 4:11. For a discussion of the formula see Zimmerli, "I am Yahweh," 1-28. See Sarna (*Exodus*, 31) and N. Lohfink ("Die priesterschriftliche Abwertung der Tradition von der Offenbarung des Jahwenamens an Moses," *Bib* 49 [1968]: 1-8) for discussion of divine self-disclosure being not so much the introduction of a previously unknown name as the revelation of the essential character and power of God and thus an affirmation of the promises made earlier to the ancestors.

74. In Exod 6:4 Yahweh recounts the past establishment of a covenant (את־בריתי הקמתי), and in 6:5 these covenant obligations are remembered (אזכר את־בריתי). See also the important role of covenant in the introduction of the Book of Exodus in 2:23-25, where the recollection of past covenantal obligations provides the divine motivation for the exodus, which extends backward to Abraham (Genesis 17) and even into the the flood story (Gen 8:1; 9:16). For a discussion of covenant in priestly tradition with a focus on Genesis 17; Exod 2:23-25; and 6:2-8 see Ska, "Quelques remarques sur Pg," 102, 108-112, 119-120.

75. Exod 6:6 is a compendium of important terms for salvation from earlier exodus traditon. Here Yahweh states that he will deliver (נצל) the Israelites from their slavery and redeem (גאל) them by leading them out (הוציא) of Egypt. The exodus formula continues to be an important motif throughout Exod 6:2-7:7, both to commission Moses and Aaron (Exod 6:13; 26, 27) and to signify divine liberation in Israel's exodus (Exod 6:6, 7; 7:4, 5). See below for discussion.

76. The recognition motif frames Exod 6:2-7:7. It is used with Israel as a subject in 6:7 and with Egypt as its subject in 7:5. This motif plays an important role in the priestly introduction to the plague cycle (for discussion see Zevit, "The Priestly Redaction and Interpretation of the Plague Narrative in Exodus," 197), and it also functions as a unifying device in the larger structure of the plague cycle (see here J. Krasovec, "Unifying Themes in Ex 7,8-11,10," in *Pentateuchal and Deuteronomistic Studies: Papers Read at the XIIIth IOSOT Congress, Leuven 1989*, BETL 94, ed. Chr. Brekelmans and J. Lust [Leuven: University Press, 1990], 52-55).

77. The motif of "hearing" or "not hearing" is carefully developed in Exod 6:2-7:7. The introductory unit begins with the notice that God has heard Israel's cry (וגם אני שמעתי את־נאקת בני ישראל, 6:5). In contrast, both Israel (Exod 6:9, 12) and Pharaoh (Exod 6:12, 30; 7:4) are described as not hearing. Furthermore the distribution of the references to "not hearing" provides insight into the design of Exod 6:2-7:7. As Childs (*Exodus*, 111) has noted, there is a repetitive structure in the present arrangement of this text. The genealogy (Exod 6:14-25) is framed, first, by commission texts which use the exodus motif (6:13 and 26-27) and second, by the objection of Moses to his commission (6:9-12 and 29-30). The objection of Moses in 6:9-12 and 29-30 is not simply an instance of resumptive repetition after the insertion of the genealogy. Rather the repetition narrows the scope of Moses' objection from Israel and Pharoah not listening (6:9-12) to only Pharoah (6:29-30). This narrowing in scope provides insight into the focus on Pharoah and the Egyptians that will be central to priestly tradents. For a discussion of the motif of "not listening" in priestly tradition see Wilson, "The Hardening of Pharoah's Heart, 31-33.

78. The references to Aaron in Exodus 1-15 include: in Moses' call in Exodus 3-4 (4:28, 29, 30); in the first encounter with Pharoah (5:1, 4); in the priestly introduction to the plague cycle (6:23, 25, 26, 27; 7:1, 2); unevenly throughout the plague cycle (snakes—7:8, 9, 10, 12; blood—7:19, 20; frogs—8:1, 2, 4, 8; gnats—8:12, 13; flies—8:21; absent in cattle; boils—9:8; hail 9:27; locust—10:3, 8, 16); and in the exodus (death of firstborn and passover—11:10; 12:28, 31; leaving Egypt—12:43; and the victory at the sea—15:20). The distribution suggests the work of redactors, who are transforming a story line that is already in place. Several aspects concerning the insertion of Aaron into the story of the exodus are particularly noteworthy. First, he is included in both of the accounts of Moses' commission, even though he functions more prominently in the priestly commission of 6:2-7:7. Second, his primary role occurs in the earlier phase of the plague cycle (when he functions over against the Egyptian magicians), and he is only loosely redacted into the concluding plagues. Third, although Aaron plays a minimal role in the events of the exodus, priestly tradents have included him into each of the three distinct actions: death of firstborn, leaving Egypt, and victory at the sea.

79. The designation of Israel as Yahweh's host (צבאה) is limited to priestly tradition and occurs in the Levitical genealogy (6:26) and the priestly introduction to the plague cycle (7:4), as well as in the priestly account of the passover instructions (12:17) and the exodus from Egypt (12:41, 51). For a brief discussion of the holy-war implications in the use of this term see Wilson, "The Hardening of Pharoah's Heart," 34.; and C. J. Labuschagne, "The Meaning of *běyād rāmā* in the Old Testament, in *Von Kanaan bis Kerala: Festschrift für J. P. M. van der Ploeg,* AOAT 211, ed. W. E. Delsman et al. (Neukirchen-Vluyn: Neukirchener, 1982), 143-148, esp. 147.

80. Scholars have long noted that priestly tradents reinterpret the plagues as wonders or miracles (מופת). The term appears first as divine instruction to Moses in 4:21-23, where the death of the Egyptian firstborn is referred to, then in the priestly introduction to the plague cycle (7:3), again in the first plague of snakes (7:9), and finally in the concluding summary to the death of the Egyptian firstborn (11:9-10).

81. See D. J. McCarthy ("Moses' Dealings with Pharoah: Ex 7,8-10,27," *CBQ* 27 [1965]: 336-347); T. E. Fretheim ("The Plagues as Ecological Signs of Histori-

cal Disaster," *JBL* 110 [1991]: 388); and Childs (*Exodus*, 131-132) for arguments supporting an interpretation of snakes as the first plague in the cycle rather than as part of the priestly introduction, in which case it is interpreted as functioning in parallel to Exod 3:1-4:17 (so, for example, Fohrer, *Überlieferung und Geschichte des Exodus*, 59

82. For further discussion of the internal structure of snakes, gnats, and boils see, among others, Childs, *Exodus*, 111-112; Wilson, "The Hardening of Pharoah's Heart," 30-31; Greenberg, "The Redaction of the Plague Narrative in Exodus," 243-252; Kegler, "Zu Komposition und Theologie der Plagenerzählungen," 58-59; and L. Schmidt, *Plagenerzählung*, 77-80.

83. For a discussion of the shift from direct confrontation with conditions in prepriestly tradition to the emphasis on wonder in the priestly account see, Kegler, "Zu Komposition und Theologie der Plagenerzählungen," 60; or L. Schmidt, *Plagenerzählung*, 77-80.

84. Snakes—7:8, 9, 10, 12; gnats—8:12, 13; and boils—9:8.

85. Snakes—7:9.

86. Snakes—7:11-12; gnats—8:12-13; boils—9:11.

87. Snakes—7:13; gnats—8:15; boils—9:12.

88. The overall emphasis on Pharaoh and Egypt as the subject of recognition and the deuteronomistic context of Exod 10:1-2a raise a question of whether the recognition motif with Israel as a subject in 10:2b*b* is a deuteronomistic or priestly addition to the text. A firm decision is difficult to establish and not essential to an overall interpretation of the exodus in either deuteronomistic or priestly tradition. The general absence of this motif in deuteronomistic tradition (see, however, Deut 29:5) in contrast to its central role in the priestly history favors attributing it to priestly tradition. Compare Blum (*Studien*, 16-17) for interpretation of the motif within a prepriestly D-Komposition.

89. Blood—7:19-20a*a*, 22a; frogs—8:1-3, 4* (Aaron).

90. Blood—7:22b; frogs—8:11b.

91. Blood—7:16b, 22b*b*; frogs—8:11b*b*.

92. See L. Schmidt (*Plagenerzählung*, 77-80), who arrives at a very similar conclusion concerning the distribution of priestly tradition, even through he advocates an interpretation of the tradition as an independent source. He concludes that P consists of the following: snakes (7:8-13), blood (7:19, 20a*a*, 21b, 22), frogs (8:1-3, 11ag, b), gnats (8:12, 13*, 14a, 15), and boils (9:8-12), with 11:9-10 providing a conclusion to the plague cycle. Compare also Greenberg (*Understanding the Exodus*, 182-184) with regard to his analysis of a B narrative (= P?).

93. See blood—7:17b; frogs—8:6b; flies—8:18b; hail—9:14b, 29b*b*; and locust—10:2b. The recognition formula occurs eight times in the plague cycle, twice with Israel as the subject (6:7; 10:2) and six times with Pharaoh as the subject (7:5, 17; 8:6, 18; 9:14,29).

94. Scholars have offered a variety of solutions to the present structure of the plague cycle. Perhaps the most notable interpretation is the long tradition of structuring the priestly (or present) form of the plague cycle in groups of three, with the death of the Egyptian firstborn providing a climax. See, for example, Cassuto, *Exodus*, 92-93; Greenberg, *Understanding the Exodus*, 171-172; S. E. Loewenstamm, *The Evolution of the Exodus Tradition*, trans. B. J. Schwartz, Perry Foundation for Biblical Research in the Hebrew Universtiy (Jerusalem: Magnes

Press, 1992), 35; Zevit, "The Priestly Redaction and Interpretation of the Plague Narrative in Exodus," 193; Kegler, "Zu Komposition und Theologie der Plagener-zählungen," 61. See Blum, *Studien*, 242-256 for the most recent discussion of this structure. According to this argument the priestly additions function as conclu-sions to the pairs of prepriestly plagues, resulting in the following structure: group one (blood, frogs, gnats); group two (flies, cattle, boils); and group three (hail, locust, darkness), which yields the pattern 3 + 3 + 3 + 1 when the death of the Egyptian firstborn is added. Two problems arise with this structure: it presupposes that darkness is a priestly addition to the plague cycle even through it lacks all the stereotyped motifs of the other priestly additions, and it does not account for the plague of snakes within the plague cycle, even though this plague clearly includes many of the motifs from both gnats and boils.

Compare, here, Ska ("Les plaies d'Egypte dans le récit sacerdotal (Pg)," 23-35), who argues that a division within 7:1-5 (1-4a*a* and 4a*b*-5) provides the clue to a two-part structure of the plague cycle and exodus (7:7-11:10 and 12:1-14:28). First 7:1-4a*a* introduces the function of plagues as signs or wonders in priestly tradition, which are illustrated in 7:7-11:10, and then 7:4a*b*-5 shifts the focus to judgment, which is played out in 12:1-14:28. Ska's analysis offers many strengths: he recognizes that the plague of snakes must be included in the plague cycle and that the priestly plague cycle is meant to include the events of the exodus. In addition he has uncovered many interesting correlations in this structure, espe-cially the verbal links between 7:1-4a*a* and 11:9-10. However, two problems remain: the division does not accentuate the introductory role of snakes, gnats, and boils; and the structure does not account adequately for the tradition-histori-cal development of the material.

Finally, see L. Schmidt (*Plagenerzählung*, 77-80 and passim) for a recent source-critical approach to priestly tradition. He concludes that P presents a five-plague sequence which emphasizes competition between Aaron/Moses and the Egyptian magicians: snakes (7:8-13), changing of water into blood (7:19, 20a*a*, 21b, 22), frogs (8:1-3, 11a*g*, b), gnats (8:12, 13*, 14a, 15), and boils (9:8-12), with 11:9-10 providing a conclusion to the plague cycle. Although P used the Jehowistic account as a *Vorlage*, its version of the plagues is a new history written in the early postexilic period, but not the final redaction to the cycle. Schmidt concludes that a final redactor harmonized the different accounts at a number of places by adding Aaron where he was absent (8:4, 8, 21; 9:27; 10:3, 8, 16) and by changing the number of verbs or pronominal suffixes. The redactor, according to Schimdt, also expanded hail and locust and added the plague of darkness to make a sequence of ten plagues. Although this analysis takes seriously the tradition-historical development of the plague cycle, the designation of P as an independent source and the subsequent need to posit yet another pentateuchal redactor overly com-plicate the analysis.

95. Aaron functions over against the magicians in priestly tradition only in a prophetic role: throughout the first cycle (in the introductory plague of snakes [7:8-13, see especially 7:10-12], in the confrontation with the magicians in the plague of blood [see especially 7:19-20a], and in the plague of frogs [see espe-cially 8:1-3]) and in the introduction to the second cycle (gnats, 8:12-15). Once the Egyptian magicians are unable to perform the same sign as Aaron (in the plague of gnats), they recognize the power of Yahweh, and Aaron's prophetic role is completed. Thus it becomes clear that when the magicians leave the narrative,

Aaron also ceases to function as an independent character. Moses becomes the main character in the introduction to the third cycle (boils, [9:8-12), and he maintains his singular role in the prepriestly plague of darkness (10:21-27). For an initial discussion on the prophetic function of the priestly account of the plagues see J.-L. Ska, "La sortie d'Egypte (Ex 7-14) dans le récit sacerdotal (Pg) et la tradition prophétique," *Bib* 60 (1979): 191-215. For a discussion of the polemical role of Aaron over against the magicians see Blum, *Studien*, 249.

96. Ska, "Les plaies d'Egypte dans le récit sacerdotal (Pg)," 25-26.

97. For more detailed interpretation concerning the structure of 7:1-5 see Weimar, *Untersuchungen zur priesterschriftlichen Exodusgeschichte*, 195-233; and compare Ska, "Les plaies d'Egypte dans le récit sacerdotal (Pg)," 24-26.

98. See, for example, Wilson, "The Hardening of Pharaoh's Heart," 32.

99. See also Kegler, "Zu Komposition und Theologie der Plagenerzählungen," 66; and Greenberg, *Understanding the Exodus*, 152-156.

100. Greenberg (*Understanding the Exodus*, 152) is correct in noting that the actions of Aaron and the magicians are not equal in their intensity and that Aaron's signs are, in fact, stronger, thus already serving a polemical purpose in the first cycle. See also Blum, *Studien*, 252.

101. Zevit ("The Priestly Redaction and Interpretation of the Plague Narrative in Exodus," 198) is certainly correct when he concludes that the description of plagues as signs or wonders was meant to have a didactic function. See his discussion of how this didactic function was meant to inform a creation theology. For a somewhat similar emphasis on creation theology in the priestly construction of the plague cycle see Fretheim, "The Plagues as Ecological Signs of Historical Disaster," 385-396. Fretheim writes concerning the function of the plagues as signs: "As signs/portents the intent of the plagues is not finally to leave observers with mouths open in amazement. Having gotten people's attention, they point beyond themselves toward a disastrous future, while carrying a certain force in their own terms" (p. 387). See also Ska ("La sortie d'Egypte [Ex 7-14] dans le récit sacerdotal [Pg] et la tradition prophétique," 192-193) for a detailed analysis of the function of "signs and wonders" in priestly tradition as opposed to deuteronomistic tradition (see p. 193 n. 4 for the full listing of deuteronomistic references).

102. Exod 8:18, כי אין שמני בכל־הארץ; Exod 9:14, למען תדע כי אני יהוה בקרב הארץ; Exod 9:29, למען תדע כי ליהוה הארץ; בעבור תדע. See also Fretheim, "The Plagues as Ecological Signs of Historical Disaster," 392.

103. Zevit, "The Priestly Redaction and Interpretation of the Plague Narrative in Exodus," 198.

104. Zevit's strongest example of an explicit connection between the priestly redaction of the plague cycle and Genesis 1 is in the plague of blood: the term מקוה in Exod 7:19 picks up the same term from Gen 1:10. On the more universal scope of the plagues in P see Zevit, "The Priestly Redaction and Interpretation of the Plague Narrative in Exodus," 199-202; L. Schmidt, Plagenerzählung, 79; and Coote and Ord, *In the Beginning*, 46-47.

105. Fretheim, "The Plagues as Ecological Signs of Historical Disaster," 392.

106. The arguments of McCarthy ("Plagues and the Sea of Reeds: Exodus 5-14," 137-158) concerning the close interrelationship between the plagues and the Red Sea are particularly important at this point. See also Ska, "Les plaies d'Egypte dans le récit sacerdotal (Pg)," 32.

107. The additions by priestly tradents are localized primarily in one place within the text, which can be illustrated in the following manner:

DTR Announcement to Israel—Despoiling of Egyptians (11:2-3)
PRE-DTR Announcement to Pharaoh—Death of Egyptian firstborn (11:4-7a, 8a)
PR Announcement to Pharaoh—Polemical Character of the Event (11:7b, 9-10)
PR Announcement to Israel—Passover and *massot* (12:1-20)
DTR Announcement to Israel—Passover (12:21-27)
PR Summary—(12:28)
PRE-DTR Fulfillment—Death of Egyptian firstborn (12:29-34)
DTR Fulfillment—Despoiling of Egyptians (12:35-36)

The structure underscores how the two priestly additions are meant to qualify the announcements both to Israel (11:2-3) and to Pharaoh (11:4-7a, 8a) concerning the death of the Egyptian firstborn, while the summary in 12:28 serves to pull the deuteronomistic account of the passover (12:21-27) into the orbit of the priestly account in 12:1-20. The partial form of the recognition motif intensifies the announcement to Pharaoh by adding a polemic and by transforming a prophetic announcement of Moses into a proof-saying, while the priestly reinterpretation of passover underscores that this event must be combined with *massot* rather than being separate as it was in deuteronomistic tradition.

108. Self-introduction ("I am Yahweh") can also include the phrase, "your God" to signify the relationship between Yahweh and Israel. It can also be expanded to include actions (exodus, land, etc.) and attributes (sanctifying, leading, dwelling, etc.) of God. It occurs alone five times in the story of the Exodus: three times in the revelation of the divine name to Moses in Exod 6:2-8 (vv. 2, 6, 8), once in the divine commission that Moses go to Pharaoh in Exod 6:28-7:5 (6:28), and once during the instructions for passover in Exod 12:1-20 (12:12). See Zimmerli, "I am Yahweh," 1-7.

109. The cultic use of self-introduction is expanded significantly in Second Isaiah, where its polemical character is intensified with the result that, according to Zimmerli, "Yahweh's self-exaltation is spoken as a delimitation against potential rival gods" (e.g., Isa 42:8). Yahweh's self-introduction occurs in two distinct contexts: in the setting of disputation, when the deity answers trial questions (e.g., 41:4; 44:6; 45:5); and in the context of supplication, when Yahweh responds to a cry of help (e.g., 43:11; 45:21; 49:23). Both contexts emphasize the power of God as creator, since recognition results from the power of God as being the holy one of Israel, or the first and the last force in creation (Isa 41:4; 42:8; 44:6; 45:5, etc.). Zimmerli writes: [Y]ahweh's entire predication in his self-statements is directed decisively toward the Creator's activity. . . ." See Zimmerli, "I am Yahweh," 17-20, esp. 20.

110. The demand for recognition occurs alone four times: in the plague of frogs (8:6b), twice in the plague of hail (9:14b, 29b), and in the announcement of the death to the Egyptian firstborn (11:7b).

111. W. Zimmerli, "Knowledge of God According to the Book of Ezekiel," 71-87 and passim.

112. W. Zimmerli, "Knowledge of God According to the Book of Ezekiel," 32-33, 53-56.

113. The combination occurs seven times: in the revelation of the divine name (6:7); at the close of the priestly introduction to the plagues (7:5); in the

plagues of blood (7:17), flies (8:18b), and locust (10:2b); and twice during the confrontation at the sea (14:4b, 18).

114. Zimmerli, "Knowledge of God According to the Book of Ezekiel," 83–87; and W. Zimmerli, "The Word of Divine Self-Manifestation (Proof-Saying): A Prophetic Genre," in *I am Yahweh*, 99–110 = "Das Wort des göttlichen Selbsterweises (Erweiswort), eine prophetische Gattung," in *Gottes Offenbarung*, Theologische Bücherei 19 (München: Chr. Kaiser, 1963), 120–132.

115. See especially the use of the "recognition motif" in Second Isaiah and Ezekiel.

116. The following chart lists the occurrences of the recognition formula and to whom the call for recognition is directed: Pharaoh, Egypt, or Israel.

Intro to the Plague Cycle (6:2–7:7) *Israel (6:7)* *Egypt (7:5)*	First Cycle (Aaron) Intro: Snakes Blood *Pharaoh (7:17a)*	Second Cycle (Aaron) Intro: Gnats Flies *Pharaoh (8:18b)*	Third Cycle (Moses) Intro: Boils Hail *Pharaoh (9:14b)* *Pharaoh (9:29b)*	Fourth Cycle (Exodus) (Moses) Intro: Darkness Death of firstborn *Pharaoh/Egypt (11:7b)*
	Frogs *Pharaoh (8:6b)*	Cattle	Locust *Israel (10:2b)*	Sea confrontation *Egypt (14:4b)* *Egypt (14:18)*

117. This polemic is a response to Pharaoh's opening comment to Moses and Aaron in 5:2: "Who is Yahweh that I should listen to him and let Israel go? I do not know Yahweh, and I will not let Israel go."

118. There is a wide variation in how the formula is introduced. למען in 8:6b, 18b; 9:29b; 11:7b; בזאת in 7:17a; בעבור in 9:14b. See Zimmerli ("Recognition of God According to the Book of Ezekiel," 36–39) for a discussion of the syntax, especially the matter-of-factness that is presupposed in divine actions by the preposition ב. There is also variation in the person and number of the verbs. Second person plural suffix forms occur in 6:7 and 10:2; a second person plural prefix form is used in 11:7b; second person singular prefix forms occur in 7:17a; 8:6b; 8:18b; 9:14b; 29b; and finally, third person plural suffix forms occur in 7:5; 14:4b, 18. Yet no distinctive patterns emerge that would signal different traditions. This conclusion also includes the instances where the recognition motif (". . . so that you may know that . . .") functions independently of the motif of self-introduction (". . . I am Yahweh"), since these occurrences (frogs—8:6b; hail—9:14b, 29b; and death to firstborn—11:7b) tend to enhance the interpretation of the exodus in relation to creation and thus fit best within priestly tradition. Such a conclusion is further supported by the central use of the recognition formula in the priestly introduction to the plague cycle and at other important locations in the Book of Exodus and in the priestly legislation within the Pentateuch. The recognition motif occurs in the priestly introduction to the plague cycle in 6:7 and 7:5. Other instances in Exodus are tied closely to cultic events, including manna/ Sabbath (16:6, 12), the confession by Jethro (18:11); the revelatory function of the tabernacle cult (29:46), and Sabbath (31:13). The recognition motif is associated with the Feast of Booths in Leviticus 23:42–43. Compare Zimmerli ("Knowledge of God According to the Book of Ezekiel," 42–53), who argues for a history of tradition to the motif within the formation of the exodus.

119. See Greenberg, *Understanding the Exodus*, 169–170.

120. See C. J. Labuschagne, *The Incomparability of Yahweh in the Old Testament (Leiden: E. J. Brill)*, 11, 74-76, 92-95.

121. See Ska, "Les plaies d'Egypte dans le récit sacerdotal (Pg)," 23-35.

122. Note the repetition of judgment in Exod 12:12. For a discussion see Ska, "Les plaies d'Egypte dans le récit sacerdotal (Pg)," 23-35.

123. Twice the destruction of Pharaoh is designated as an occurrence of divine glory (14:4, 18), both times in the context of the recognition motif.

124. For arguments concerning the attribution of Exod 12:1-20 to priestly tradition see, among others, Noth, *Exodus*, 94-96; and Childs, *Exodus*, 184-185, 196-199. For a review of past arguments concerning the formation of Exod 12:1-20, especially concerning the problems with regard to second and third person speech, see Laaf (*Die Pascha-Feier Israels*, 11-18), who distinguishes initially between Pg (12:1-14) and Ps (12:15-20) and separates 12:1-14 further into three levels of tradition, including a *Vorlage* (12:3b, 6b-8, 11bb) which underwent two revisions: a first redaction inserted direct divine speech, and a second expansion clarifed cultic concerns. See also Kohata, *Jahwist und Priesterschrift in Exodus 3-14*, 262-267. Compare Knohl ("The Priestly Torah Versus the Holiness School: Sabbath and the Festivals," 77-79), who separates 12:1-20 into three parts: passover (vv. 1-14), and two laws concerning *massot* (vv. 15-17 and 18-20). He argues that the entire unit (12:1-20) is part of the Holiness School (= holiness code) and not the Priestly Torah (= priestly source). Knohl's aim is to reserve the historical relationship of these schools. Knohl also argues that there are two levels of tradition concerning *massot*: an original law in vv. 15-17 and a later supplementation in vv. 18-20.

125. Compare Childs (*Exodus*, 196-197), who separates the text into two parts, vv. 1-13 and 14-20, and interprets the reference to "this day" in v. 14 as an introduction rather than a summary conclusion. Compare Knohl, "The Priestly Torah Versus the Holiness School: Sabbath and the Festivals," 78, 113-115.

126. See Knohl ("The Priestly Torah Versus the Holiness School: Sabbath and the Festivals," 77-81), who argues that the detailed instructions concerning resident aliens is a later addition to the text.

127. The divine speech to Moses and Aaron in 12:1 is located in the land of Egypt (בארץ מצרים), in v. 12 Yahweh crosses over the land of Egypt (בארץ־מצרים והכיתי כל־בכור בארץ מצרים), and strikes all firstborn in the land of Egypt (ועברתי), which is echoed in v. 13 (ולא־יהיה בכם נגף למשחית בהכתי בארץ מצרים).

128. Exod 12:23aa describes Yahweh crossing over to strike the Egyptians (ועבר יהוה לנגף את־מצרים), and in the answer portion of the catechism in Exod 12:27 it is noted a second time that Yahweh passed over the houses of the Israelites in Egypt (במצרים) when he struck the Egyptians (את־מצרים).

129. See chapter 3 for a discussion.

130. Although the promise of land plays no role in the priestly legislation of passover, the land of Canaan is most likely presupposed in 12:19, where the law concerning the participation of resident aliens in passover is mentioned. The reference to land (הארץ) in this verse is Israel's land and not Egypt.

131. See Knohl ("The Priestly Torah Versus the Holiness School: Sabbath and the Festivals," 78) on the tendency to fuse passover and *massot* in Exod 12:1-20; and Childs (*Exodus*, 197), who writes of Exod 12:1-20: "The passage views passover and *massot* as part of the one redemptive event." The fusion of festivals is also indicated by the mention of *massot* in conjunction with passover in Exod 12:8.

132. See Num 3:11-13, 40-43, and 8:14-19, where the Levites fulfill Yahweh's claim on firstborn rather than future sacrifices in the land, as was stressed in deuteronomistic tradition (Exod 13:11-16 and Deut 26:1-15).

133. See Fishbane (*Biblical Interpretation in Ancient Israel*, 146-151) concerning problems of precise dating in the priestly account, especially with regard to the notice in Num 33:3 that Israel marched out of Egypt the day after the passover (the fifteenth day of the first month) on the morrow of the paschal offering.

134. See Noth, *Exodus*, 99-101.

135. The placement of the insertion can be illustrated in the following manner:

DTR—Itinerary notice, mixed multitude, *massot* (12:37-39a)
PRE-DTR—Israel is driven out (12:39b)
PR—The night of vigil and instructions concerning who may take the passover (12:40-51)
DTR—*Massot* and firstlings (13:1-16)

136. Yet the exodus motif undergoes a change of interpretation in the priestly history. It occurs in the revelation of the divine name (6:6-7); in the commissioning of Moses and Aaron (6:13, 26-27); in the instructions for *massot* (12:17); in the instructions for passover (12:41, 42, 51); and in priestly legislation (Exod 29:46; Lev 11:45 [where the verb "to bring up" is used]; 19:36; 22:32-33; 23:42-43; 25:38, 42, 55; 26:13, 45; Num 15:41). The tendency of priestly tradents to emphasis that Yahweh's liberation was from the land of Egypt rather than from the power of the Egyptians was noted earlier. More significant is an additional tendency to separate the exodus motif from a promise of land, in comparison with the way in which these two motifs were held together in the deuteronomistic history. Although the future prospect of land is interwoven with the exodus motif in the priestly introduction to the exodus (6:2-7:7, esp. vv. 7-8), such a combination does not occur again in the exodus, or, for that matter, in the priestly material throughout the Pentateuch, with the one exception of the Jubilee Law (Lev 25:38). In its place, priestly tradents show a preference for combining the self-introduction and exodus formulas, which are often followed by some form of predication (e.g., I am Yahweh, your God, who brought you out of the land of Egypt *to be your God* . . ."). For examples of the combination of the self-introduction and exodus motif see Lev 19:36; 25:55; with additional predication see Lev 11:45; 22:32-33; Num 15:41; and with the recognition formula see Exod 29:46; Lev 23:42-43.

137. See Knohl, "The Priestly Torah Versus the Holiness School," 79-80; J. Milgrom, "Religious Conversion and the Revolt Model for the Formation of Israel," *JBL* 101 (1982): 169-176, esp. 170-171; and C. van Houten, *The Alien in Israelite Law*, JSOTSup 107 (Sheffield: JSOT Press, 1991), 109-157.

138. For a discussion of the itinerary notices in priestly tradition see Davies, "The Wilderness Itineraries and the Composition of the Pentateuch," 1-13.

139. The interpretation of priestly material in Exodus 14 has shifted in modern scholarship from an earlier conclusion that there was very little priestly influence to the position that the priestly source was, indeed, a significant voice in the narrative. For illustration of this shift note the earlier study by Wellhausen (*Composition*, 76), who designates parts of 13:20; 14:1, 2, 4, 8, 9, 10, 16, 28(?) to a P source; it was expanded by Gressmann (*Mose und seine Zeit*, 108 n. 1), who assigns 13:20; 14:1, 2, 4, 8, 9, 10a.c, 15-18*, 21ac-23, 26, 27a, 28 to P; and even further by Noth (*Exodus*, 105), who concludes that P is the most obvious source

in Exodus 14, including Exod 14:1-4, 8, 9abb, 10abb, 15-18, 21aab, 22ff., 26, 27aa, 28ff. Noth's assessment is followed in the main by Childs (*Exodus*, 220): 13:20; 14:1-4, 8, 9abb, 15-18, 21aab, 22-23, 26, 27a, 28-29. More recent work has begun to distinguish between a priestly source and a final pentateuchal redaction, with both being designated as significant influences in Exodus 14. See H.-Chr. Schmitt ("'Priesterliches' und 'prophetisches' Geschichtsverständnis in der Meerwundererzählung Ex 13,17-14,31: Beobachtungen zur Endredaktion des Pentateuch," in *Textgemäss: Aufsätze und Beiträge zur Hermeneutik des Alten Testaments. Festschrift für E. Würthwein*, ed. A. H. J. Gunneweg and O. Kaiser [Göttingen: Vandenhoeck & Ruprecht, 1980], 139-155), who argues that a priestly source (Exod 13:20; 14:1-4, 8, 9aa,b, 10*, 15-18, 21aa,b, 22, 23, 26, 27aa, 28, 29) was supplemented and restructured by a postexilic redaction with a prophetic perspective, which included the framing of Exod 13:17-19 and 14:30-31, as well as 14:5ff., 11ff., 13ff., 19ff., 24, 25. Compare F. Kohata (*Jahwist und Priesterschrift in Exodus 3-14*, 277-279; and "Die Endredaktion (Rp) der Meerwundererzählung," *AJBI* 14 [1988]: 10-37), who designates 13:20; 14:1-4, 8-9, 10abb, 15-18, 21aa, 22, 23, 26, 27aa, 28a, 29 to a priestly source and only 13:21ff; 14:25, 29, 31 to a pentateuchal redaction; or Weimar (*Meerwundererzählung*, 165-184, 239-240), who designates 14:1, 2, 4, 8, 10a,bb, 15aa,b, 16, 17, 18a, 21aa,b, 22, 23aa,b, 26*, 27aa, 28a, 29 to a priestly source (which itself is built off a prepriestly account) and who expands significantly the role of a pentateuchal redaction to include 13:17abb, 18, 20, 21b; 14:2b, 3, 7aab, 8aa*, 9ab,*ag,b, 11a*, 12, 13abb, 15ab, 17bb, 18b, 19a, 20aa, 23abg, 26bb, 30a*, 31aa. Finally, note also the recent work that advocates a reading of priestly tradition as being redactional in character. See here especially Vervenne ("The 'P' Tradition in the Pentateuch," 85), who designates Exod 13:20; 14:1-4, 8ab, 9b*, 10a, 11-12, 15-18, 21a, 21bc, 21d, 22-23, 26, 27a, 27b-d, 28ab, 29, 31* to a priestly redaction.

140. The Hebrew reads, וחמשים עלו בני-ישראל מארץ מצרים. On the holy-war posture of Israel in both 13:18b and 14:8b see Labuschagne, "The Meaning of *bĕyād rāmā*," 143-148.

141. Mettinger, *The Dethronement of Sabaoth*, 81-87. See pp. 83-85 for a review of past scholarship. Although the reference to the pillar of cloud is prominent in these texts, the degree to which it must be distinguished from the cloud descending on the Tent of Meeting is not clear, since only the cloud is referred to in Num 11:25. Part of the ambiguity may be the result of later tradition, where priestly tradents frequently interchange the cloud (e.g., Exod 14:20; Num 9:15-23) and the pillar of cloud (Exod 13:21-22; 14:19, 24) in the setting of the wilderness. The ambiguity suggests that a study of the pillar of cloud in the Pentateuch must also include references to the cloud. See note 154 for a listing of texts.

142. See R. J Clifford ("The Tent of El and the Israelite Tent of Meeting," *CBQ* 33 [1971]: 221-227) for a comparison of priestly tradition and a Canaanite tent tradition, where the divine assembly met under the leadership of El. T. W. Mann ("The Pillar of Cloud in the Reed Sea Narrative," *JBL* 90 [1971]: 19-24), on the other hand, compares the cloud that accompanies Yahweh with the *'nn*, "messengers" or "servants" who function in association with Canaanite storm deities.

143. See especially Mann, "The Pillar of Cloud in the Reed Sea Narrative," 24-30.

144. The function of the Tent of Meeting may not be limited to divine communication in the deuteronomistic history but may also take on aspects of holy

war by being associated with the ark. For possible connections between the cloud, Tent of Meeting, and ark in prepriestly tradition see Mann ("The Pillar of Cloud in the Reed Sea Narrative," 24-25), who describes two functions of the ark and by extension the cloud as, first, military palladium, and second, migratory guide.

145. See a concordance for references to the Tent of Meeting in priestly cultic legislation. The cloud functions in association with theophany in Exod 24:15-18 and appears as incense in Lev 16:2, 13. See Mettinger, *The Dethronement of Sabaoth*, 80-87; Dozeman, *God on the Mountain*,126-136; or J. Plastaras, *The God of the Exodus: The Theology of the Exodus Narratives* (Milwaukee: Bruce Publishing, 1966) 185-186; and *Creation and Covenant* (Milwaukee: Bruce Publishing, 1968), 151-153.

146. Numbers 12 addresses at least two issues. One is a problem of inclusivity, which is addressed with the tradition about Moses' Cushite wife. The other is a problem of prophetic authority. The two problems are woven together in the present text: v. 1 presents a complaint by Miriam and Aaron about Moses' Cushite wife; vv. 2-5 shift the focus to prophetic authority, which shows signs of being influenced from the murmuring stories that presently run throughout the account of Israel's wilderness travel; vv. 6-8 are a poem about Mosaic oracular authority over against prophecy in general; and vv. 9-15 conclude the narrative with an account of Miriam's leprosy, of Aaron's confession of sin, and of Moses' successful mediation for Miriam. See M. Noth (*Numbers*, OTL, trans. J. D. Martin [Philadelphia," Westminster, 1968], 91-97) for discussion of the possible traditionhistorical background; Mettinger (*The Dethronement of Sabaoth*, 85-86 and n. 32) for influence of priestly tradents in the present structure of the chapter; and J. Milgrom (*Numbers*, The JPS Torah Commentary [Philadelphia: Jewish Publication Society, 1990], 376-380) on the interrelation of Numbers 11-12 as three complaint stories (the complaint at Taberah in Num 11:1-3, the complaint at Kibroth-Hattaavah in Num 11:4-35, and the complaint at Hazeroth in Numbers 12) surrounding the prophetic function of Moses.

147. For a discussion of the Kabod in conjunction with Israel's wilderness journey and the Sinai tradition see Mettinger (*The Dethronement of Sabaoth*, 80-87), who builds on the research of R. Rendtorff, "The Concept of Revelation in Ancient Israel," in *Revelation as History*, ed. W. Pannenberg, trans. D. Granskou (New York: Macmillan, 1968), 32-37.

148. See Dozeman, *God on the Mountain*, 131-133.

149. See note 154 for distribution of references to the Kabod.

150. On the holy-war background of the cloud see Mann, "The Pillar of Cloud in the Reed Sea Narrative," 22-23.

151. Mann, "The Pillar of Cloud in the Reed Sea Narrative," 26.

152. See Davies, "The Wilderness Itineraries and the Composition of the Pentateuch," 1-13.

153. The cloud is also referred to in the deuteronomistic itinerary notice of Num 10:33-34 and in the recounting of both this event and Exod 13:21-22 in Deut 1:33. The association of the cloud (Num 10:34) with the ark in Num 10:33, 35-36 could certainly be deuteronomistic in origin, since, as Mann has noted, the cloud embodies holy-war characteristics. But the additional emphasis of the cloud leading Israel would simply repeat the role of the Messenger of God and contrast to the oracular function of the cloud at other places in deuteronomistic tradition, suggesting, instead, that references to the cloud in Num 10:34 and Deut 1:33b

are priestly additions. In this regard note the similarity in language of Exod 13:21–22 and Deut 1:33b. See Mayes, *Deuteronomy*, 130–131.

154. The following is a listing of the most significant references to the cloud/pillar of cloud and Kabod.

	Cloud	Pillar of Cloud/Fire	Kabod
1. Exodus	Exod 14:20	13:21, 22; 14:19, 24	—
2. Travel to Sinai	16:10	—	16:7, 10
3. Sinai			
A. Mountain theophany	19:9, 16	—	—
	24:15–18	—	24:16, 17
B. Priests/sacrifice	—	—	29:43
C. Tent of Meeting	—	33:9, 10	—
D. Mountain theophany	34:5	—	—
E. Tabernacle	40:35–38	—	40:34, 35
F. Priests/sacrifice	—	—	Lev 9:6, 23
	Lev 16:2, 13	—	—
G. Travel preparation Tabernacle/tent	Num 9:15–23	—	—
4. Travel from Sinai			
A. Itineraries	Num 10:11–12	—	—
	10:34	—	—
B. Tent of Meeting Seventy elders	11:16, 25	—	—
C. Tent of Meeting Moses/Aaron/Miriam	12:10	12:5	—
D. Tent of Meeting Spy story	14:14	14:14	14:10, 21
E. Tent of Meeting Korah rebellion	—	—	16:19
F. Tent of Meeting Murmuring story	17:7	—	17:7
G. Tent of Meeting Sin of Moses	—	—	20:7

See also Deut 1:33 where reference is also made to the fire by night.

155. The structure of announcement and fulfillment has been explored by a number of scholars, although with slightly different distributions of priestly tradition. See, for example, Weimar, *Meerwundererzählung*, 175–184; or Vervenne, "The 'P' Tradition in the Pentateuch," 82.

156. Compare Weimar (*Meerwundererzählung*, 175–184), who would include yet a third sequence of prediction (4:26) and fulfillment (27–28) with the the motif of Moses' stretching his hand over water. See chapter 3 for an interpretation of this motif in preexilic tradition.

157. See Ska, *Le passage de la mer*, 97–98.

158. See Mann, "'The Pillar of Cloud in the Reed Sea Narrative," 26.

159. See Batto, *Slaying the Dragon*, 110, 135–136. The action of splitting (בקע) the sea suggests a relationship between the priestly interpretation of the exodus and the Babylonian myth *Enuma Elish*, where the god Marduk splits Tiamat in combat, prompting creation. The motif does not appear in the Canaanite mythology, although Anat is described as splitting Mot in CTA 6 ii 31–32. The motif

is associated with the exodus primarily in late texts, including Isa 63:12; Pss 74:15; 78:13; and in Neh 9:9-11, where the action of splitting the sea must be distinguished from crossing the Red Sea. The juxtaposition of the Red Sea and the splitting of sea in Neh 9:9-11 is the result of a late conflation, yet even here the two traditions are kept separate.

160. Compare Vervenne ("The 'P' Tradition in the Pentateuch," 79) or L. Schimdt (*Plagenerzählung*, 78), who argue that the central focus of priestly tradition is the authentication of Moses. Moses certainly functions in a central role within priestly tradition, as someone who appears like a God. Yet in priestly tradition this role is so secure that it needs no authentication. The focus on the legitimation of Moses plays a stronger role in deuteronomistic tradition, where the event at the sea results in Israel's fearing God and believing in Moses (14:31).

161. Johs. Pedersen, "Passahfest und Passahlegende," *ZAW* 52 [1934]: 161-175; and *Israel*, 728-737.

162. Pedersen, *Israel*, 728.

163. Pedersen, *Israel*, 730.

164. Pedersen, *Israel*, 729.

165. Pedersen, *Israel*, 731.

166. Pedersen (*Israel*, 729) writes, "The most important point is the crossing itself."

167. Pedersen, *Israel*, 729-730.

168. Note, however, Exod 12:38, where a mixed multitude is described as leaving with Israel. This emphasis is a result of the polemical emphasis of the deuteronomistic account of the passover.

169. See also the instructions with regard to non-Israelites in Exod 12:19, 43-49.

170. See Leviticus 23 and Numbers 28-29.

171. See Labuschagne, "The Meaning of *bĕyād rāmā*," 143-148.

172. See Mann, "The Pillar of Cloud in the Reed Sea Narrative," 15-30.

173. See Weimar, *Untersuchungen*, 207-208; and Wilson, "The Hardening of Pharoah's Heart," 33. Note in particular the use of קשׁה in the priestly introduction to the plague cycle (7:3-5) to describe the hardening of Pharoah's heart. This term also appears in Deut 2:30 in the context of holy war to describe the destruction of an enemy and the victory of Israel.

174. S.-M. Kang, *Divine War in the Old Testament and in the Ancient Near East*, BZAW 177 (Berlin: de Gruyter, 1989), 114-115. See chapter 5 for a discussion of the Song of Miriam in priestly tradition.

175. The revelation of the cult is the place where Israel must come to knowledge of Yahweh (see Exod 29:46).

176. See in particular the recent study by S. McKnight (*A Light Among the Gentiles: Jewish Missionary Activity in the Second Temple Period* [Minneapolis: Fortress Press, 1991]), who argues against interpreting even later Jewish tradition as being mission oriented.

5

The Hymns of the Exodus

The liturgy of the exodus is not limited to narrative. Two voices emerge in Exodus 15 in celebration of the event. Moses and the Israelites sing a hymn in Exod 15:1–18, and it is followed by Miriam and all the women singing a hymn in Exod 15:21. The two hymns celebrate the same event, yet they provide very different interpretations of salvation. Moses interprets the exodus as an event of salvation history that will lead to Israel's future conquest of the land. Miriam does not share this point of view. Salvation and a future conquest are not interrelated in her song. Such a striking repetition raises questions concerning the tradition-historical relationship between the two hymns[1] as well as their function in the canonical Pentateuch.[2]

An interpretation of the poems in relation to the narratives will provide an avenue for addressing the questions of the formation of the hymns and their present function in the canon. The Song of the Sea will be interpreted in two stages of development, and these interpretations will provide comparision with the preexilic liturgy of the exodus and the deuteronomistic reinterpretation of it. An early form of the hymn consisting of Exod 15:1–12, 18 will provide comparison with the preexilic liturgy, and the expansion of the hymn into an account of salvation history with the addition of vv. 13–17 will be compared with the deuteronomistic reinterpretation of the exodus as requiring a conquest for its completion. Finally, the Song of Miriam (Exod 15:20–21) will be interpreted within the context of priestly tradition as a qualification of the exodus-conquest model in deuteronomistic tradition.

THE SONG OF THE SEA

The Song of the Sea is the cornerstone of any tradition-historical study of the exodus, and, indeed, of the Pentateuch in general. Although Noth

argued for a late date to the poem in Exod 15:1–18 (limiting the nucleus
of the exodus tradition to the poetic couplet in 15:21b), his hypothesis
that the exodus was always conceived as an event of salvation history,
encompassing the theme of land (i.e., conquest), has tended to over-
shadow much of the discussion of the Song of the Sea, because it has cast
debate concerning the antiquity and original unity of the poem within
the hermeneutical framework of salvation history.[3] Over against this position I will argue that the Song of the Sea has gone through a history of
composition in which a hymn celebrating Yahweh's victory at the sea
and kingship (Exod 1–12, 18) has been expanded into a prototype of salvation history with the addition of the wilderness and conquest motifs
(Exod 15:13–17).

From Divine Kingship to Salvation History

The most striking contrast within the Song of the Sea concerns the content of vv. 1–12, 18, and 13–17. As Jeremias has recently noted, the first
half of the poem focuses on (1) Yahweh alone, (2) in a battle event, (3)
where the enemy is destroyed in the sea, (4) culminating in Yahweh's victory and kingship. This sequence of events contrasts sharply with vv. 13–17,
where the focus is on (1) Israel (2) being lead on a journey by Yahweh (3)
through nations that are specifically named, (4) culminating in Israel's
arrival at the cult.[4]

   The contrasts in content are accentuated by problems with regard to
genre.[5] What begins as a hymn of the individual celebrating Yahweh's victory at the sea and kingship in vv. 1–12, 18 shifts abruptly both in topic
and in time in vv. 13–17 to describe Israel's wilderness journey and eventual arrival at Yahweh's cult. Exod 12:1–12, 18 could be characterized as
a victory hymn that celebrates a past event of salvation. Motifs supporting
this conclusion include Yahweh's destruction of the Egyptians (vv. 1b, 4a)
with the use of his right hand (vv. 6b, 12), images of Yahweh as a warrior
(v. 3a), God's fierce anger (vv. 7, 8a) and destroying breath (v. 10), as well
as the contrasting imagery of the enemies' anticipation of victory and the
sudden reversal brought about by Yahweh (v. 9). All of these images
encourage the reader to envision a past concrete context, which, upon comparison with other similar songs (e.g., the song of Deborah in Judges 5),
would appear to be a common trait in the victory song.[6]

   Exod 15:13–17, however, does not fit in well with the victory hymn.
Imagery of holy war remains, but the divine leading becomes more dominant, while a future orientation replaces the emphasis on the past in
vv. 1–12.[7] Thus Zenger concludes: "If v. 1b is thought of as the summary
or as the title of a hymn that follows, then vv. 13–17 could scarcely have
been original to the stated theme."[8] Coats saw the problem of shifting
temporal perspectives and attempted to deal with it by introducing
Westermann's language of declarative and descriptive praise into the song

in order to account for the different styles of speech. He concluded that there was a transition in genre between the event at the sea and the wilderness-conquest material, the former being characterized as declarative praise (praise of God for a specific deed) and the latter as descriptive praise (more general praise of God in all times and in all places).[9]

An additional point of contrast between vv. 1–12, 18 and vv. 13–17 is the lack of verbal contact between the two sections. This contrast could simply be the result of the difference in subject matter, as some scholars have argued,[10] especially since there is repetition of certain motifs between vv. 1–12 and 13–17 (e.g., "like a stone" in vv. 5, 16; "hand" in vv. 9, 17; "strength" in vv. 2, 13; and "holy" in vv. 11, 13, 17).[11] Yet the distinctive deuteronomistic language within the limited boundaries of vv. 13–17 suggests that the points of contact between the two sections are the result of redactional interweaving rather than an inherent unity.

One of the clearest indicators of the deuteronomistic interpretation of the sea tradition is the word "dry ground" to indicate that Yahweh dried up the sea and the word "to cross" (e.g., Josh 2:10; 4:23; 5:1) to describe how they crossed the Red Sea and the Jordan River.[12] All of these motifs are absent in vv. 1–12, and furthermore there is no focus whatsoever on Israel in vv. 1–12, which is a strong argument against attributing this section of the hymn to deuteronomistic tradition. The absence of the deuteronomistic interpretation of the sea in vv. 1–12, 18, however, contrasts sharply to vv. 13–17, where the central motifs—one, of divine leading (vv. 13, 17);[13] two, of the fear of the nations (vv. 14–16a);[14] and three, of Israel's crossing (v. 16b)[15]—all reflect a deuteronomistic point of view. In addition, as Brenner has most recently underscored, the description of salvation in these verses as a divine act of "redemption" (גאל in v. 13) or as an act of divine "purchase" (קנה in v. 16) also points to exilic reinterpretations of the exodus.[16]

An examination of content (the striking change of focus from Yahweh's battle at the sea vv. 1–12, 18 to the pastoral leading of Israel in vv. 13–17), genre (especially the shift from a specfic past event of divine victory at the sea to the future leading and conquest), and language (the predominance of deuteronomistic and exilic images for the exodus in vv. 13–17) suggests that the Song of the Sea is not an originally unified poem. The original form of the Song of the Sea is a victory hymn that separates into three parts: an introduction (vv. 1–3), the body (vv. 4–11), and a conclusion (vv. 12, 18).[17] Clear divisions concerning the structure must remain tentative, however, since, as Coats has noted, "suggested patterns of bicola or tricola as strophic units produce no satisfactory results, no consensus."[18] Although there is debate whether vv. 2, 12, 18 fit the context of the hymn, each has been retained.[19] Verses 13–17 are an addition, which reinterprets the confrontation at the sea from a singular event of divine victory in battle to an account of salvation history.[20] The primary motifs in this transformation are divine leading in the wilderness and conquest of the land.

Mythological Patterns

The Plot Structure of the Song of the Sea

The conflict between Baal and Yamm/Nahar provides important mythological comparison for interpreting the plot structure of the Song of the
Sea.[21] The Canaanite myth separates into a conflict between the gods (CTA
2) and the construction of Baal's palace (CTA 3 and 4).[22] CTA 2 recounts,
first, Baal's conflict with the enthroned god Yamm/Nahar; second, his subsequent victory; and third, the proclamation of Baal's kingship. The clos-
ing proclamation of kingship (CTA 2.IV.32) should not be interpreted as
an enthronement, since at this point in the cycle of stories Baal is not
described as having either a temple, a throne, a dominion, or a land of possession, all of which appear to be necessary to complete a god's enthronement in the mythology.[23]

CTA 3 and 4 complete the process of Baal's enthronement by developing the theme of Baal's need for a temple, which includes the motifs of
enthronement, dominion, and a land that Baal can possess. Notice that twice
in CTA 3 and 4 Baal's kingship is proclaimed in the context of his not yet
having a temple, and that the implication in both of these contexts is that
a temple must be built to complete his enthronement (CTA 3.E.40–47;
4.IV.43–62).[24] The plot structure of CTA 4 is especially important, since it
describes the actual construction of the temple and the sequence of events
that result in Baal's enthronement. It can be summarized in three parts:
(1) the construction of a temple with an initial feast, (2) conquest of cities
and the formation of an empire over which Baal can rule, and (3) Baal's
enthronement, when he sits on his throne (CTA 4.VII.13–52), with the
thought that no one could now challenge his kingship or think of taking
over the land of his possession (CTA 4.VII.43–44).[25]

The tradition-historical development of the Song of the Sea echoes the
separation between conflict and temple construction that is evident in CTA
2 and 3–4. The form of the Song of the Sea in Exod 15:1–12, 18 follows
the same three-part structure of CTA 2, namely, conflict, victory, and proclamation of Yahweh's kingship. In addition, the proclamation of an eternal kingship at the end of each liturgy is identical.[26] Indeed, the parallels
end abruptly at this point. Exod 15:1–12, 18 does not include the motifs
of temple construction, conquest, or the establishment of a kingdom that
accompanies divine enthronement in CTA 3–4.

The deuteronomistic expansion of the Song of the Sea in Exod 15:13–
17, however, does include motifs that are central in CTA 3–4; temple
building (Exod vv. 13,17),[27] conquest of surrounding peoples (vv. 14–16),
and divine enthronement in an established kingdom (v. 17). Once again
the verbal parallels are striking. Particularly noteworthy is Exod 15:17,
where Yahweh's temple is located "on the mount of possession" and where
Yahweh's enthronement is described as "the place of abode." When one
examines the Ugaritic parallels in their larger context, it becomes clear that

the two motifs are part of a larger network of related terms, which describe a god's enthronement as including not only a "mountain of possession" won in battle and the establishment of a throne, but also a "land of possession" and a "domain" or "kingdom."[28]

Comparison between the Song of the Sea and the mythology of Baal reinforces indirectly the tradition-historical arguments that were proposed earlier. Not only do Exod 15:1-12, 18, and 13-17 contrast to each other in content, genre, and language, they also explore separate (but related) features of Canaanite mythology, which when combined transform the plot structure of the Song of the Sea. The original form of the Song of the Sea is a celebration of divine victory over chaos or evil and a proclamation of Yahweh's rule as a result of his victory. This victory hymn refrains from describing Yahweh's kingship with the more monarchical imagery associated with enthronement in CTA 3-4, a fact that raises questions about ancient Israel's cultic ideology, especially whether the absence of monarchical imagery is intentional. The elevation of a historical monarch (v. 6) as Yahweh's opponent does indeed suggest that the exodus is here a celebration of divine victory against the kind of social structures that make enthronement possible.[29] Such a conclusion regarding the cultic and social ideology of early Israelite celebration of the exodus must remain tentative.

What is clear is that Israel plays no role in this celebration either by participating in the conflict or by journeying with Yahweh through a wilderness march. Instead, salvation is explored in the framework of unilateral power, with the result that the destruction of Pharaoh and the kingship of Yahweh are a singular event, in much the same way as in Baal's conflict with Yamm/Nahar, where the death of Yamm and the kingship of Baal were also proclaimed simultaneously in a single line (CTA 2.IV.32).[30] Such a construction of salvation implies that the land is a present reality for Israel and that the content of Yahweh's victory is life in the land. A journey in the wilderness toward a promised land is absent from the plot structure.

The deuteronomistic addition to the Song of the Sea in Exod 15:13-17 is not a free literary creation. Rather it expands the early version of the victory hymn along the lines of Canaanite mythology by including the imagery of temple building, conquest, and enthronement from CTA 3-4. As Mettinger has demonstrated, the deuteronomistic additions, especially with regard to the establishment of enthronement, presuppose Zion tradition.[31] But Exod 15:17 is not simply an affirmation of Zion tradition, where Yahweh's enthronement was celebrated as a present reality.[32] In contrast, the enthronement of Yahweh is placed in the future, as the end result of salvation history. Deuteronomistic tradents achieve this by historicizing the mythology of Baal's conflict with Yamm/Nahar. In their version of the Song of the Sea, Yahweh's initial victory over Yamm is no longer part of a single event that results in Yahweh's kingship. Instead this victory propels Israel on a journey with God (v. 13) through other nations (vv. 14–16a), which eventually leads to the crossing of Nahar (v.16b) before Israel arrives at Yahweh's cult and celebrates divine enthronement (vv. 17–18).[33] Such historicizing transforms the plot structure of the hymn by introducing a salvation history hermeneutic that was not part of the early version of the Song of the Sea.

The Character of God in the Song of the Sea

The transformation in the plot structure of the Song of the Sea gives rise to differing conceptions of divine power. Exod 15:1–12, 18 is a celebration of Yahweh's salvific power conceived as a holy-war event. This fact is made explicit from the overall setting of the hymn as one of potential oppression from the Egyptian threat, in the introduction with reference to the defeat of the enemy at the sea (v. 1b), through the confession that Yahweh is strength, protection, and salvation to the psalmist (v. 2), and hence a warrior (v. 3), with the account of the destruction of the Egyptian army (v. 4a), and with the clear declaration of victory as a result of Yahweh's intervention.[34] Finally, the holy-war setting is further reinforced by the form-critical assessment that the poem includes aspects of the victory song. However one divides the body of the hymn (vv. 4–11), the two refrains (vv. 6 and 11a) underscore that Yahweh's holy war is a victory not only over earthly forces (v. 6) but also over cosmic forces (v. 11a). Indeed, it would appear that the two are not meant to be separated, in order to celebrate Yahweh's incomparability.[35] Verses 4–5 and 7 describe the defeat of Pharaoh and the Egyptian army, which is accentuated with the refrain: "Your right hand, Yahweh, glorious in power; Your right hand, Yahweh, shattered the enemy" (v. 6). Verses vv. 8–10 shift the focus from the confrontation between Yahweh and Pharaoh to underscore Yahweh's power over the sea.[36] Such power over sea prompts the second refrain, where the incomparability of Yahweh is expressly stated with the words, "Who is like you among the gods, Yahweh?" (v. 11a).[37] The conclusion of the hymn turns the focus back to the historical enemy by describing the destruction of the Egyptian army (v. 12) before the proclamation of Yahweh's present kingship (v. 18).

The holy-war imagery underscores that Exod 15:1–12, 18 is a celebration of divine power conceived unilaterally. Yahweh is worthy of praise because he possesses the ability to produce intended or desired effects on the other. Opposing powers to Yahweh never emerge as independent characters, while Israel is absent altogether. Even the arrogant "I" statements by Pharaoh in v. 9,[38] where his own self-perceived power is stated, is meant only to provide background and striking contrast to the real power of Yahweh that surrounds him, first by holding the sea at bay (v. 8), thus giving him opportunity to boast, and second by letting the sea loose again

(v. 10). Pharaoh and the sea function only as impersonal gauges to measure Yahweh's power. The defeat of the enemy brings about a clear ending, in which Israel celebrates the power of God from the perspective of the land. This vision of salvation is a static one, in which the oppression of Egypt and life in the land are pitted against each other in a dialectical relationship, with the result that Yahweh's destruction of Pharaoh is part of a single act which includes Yahweh's present rule.

The deuteronomistic editing of the Song of the Sea parallels the transformation of the exodus liturgy of the Day of Yahweh in the narrative. Deuteronomistic tradents disrupt the static vision of the older hymn by historicizing the confrontation at the sea into the framework of an exodus and a conquest. This larger design is evident with the inclusion of wilderness and conquest material in vv. 13–17. This strophe emphasizes that Israel must march (presumably) in the wilderness (v. 13) and, more important, that they must cross over (עבר) into the land (vv. 14–16) in order for Yahweh to be enthroned (vv. 17–18). Once the event at the sea is merged with the wilderness, Yahweh's enthronement in the land (vv. 17–18) becomes a future hope, a shift that disrupts the genre of the older hymn. Thus what had been a celebration of a past event must now be read as prophecy.[39] As a result, the prophetic voice of Moses interprets the exodus in relation to a future conquest, and in the process, he provides a blueprint for the larger structure of the deuteronomistic history.

THE SONG OF MIRIAM

There is a long history of debate concerning the antiquity of the poetic couplet in 15:21. Scholars have argued that it is ancient tradition—so ancient, in fact, that it may have given rise to the entire hymn form—while others argue that it is a late literary repetition of the opening couplet in 15:1.[40] A resolution to this debate is not crucial to the present study. Regardless of how one evaluates the antiquity of the Song of Miriam, it contrasts sharply with the deuteronomistic version of the Song of Moses (Exod 15:1–18). The Song of Miriam lacks any reference to the wilderness or the future conquest of the land that are so central to the deuteronomistic hymn of salvation history.

The juxtaposition of two hymns in the present form of Exodus 15 forces the reader to make a choice concerning the priority of the exodus–conquest perspective of the Song of Moses (15:1–18) or the more focused celebration of Yahweh's victory at the sea in the Song of Miriam (15:20–21). There are indications in the introduction to the Song of Miriam (v. 20) that priestly tradents have forced this decision upon the reader by inserting the hymn into its present position, and that by so doing they intend to separate the exodus from the conquest, thus providing a competing interpretation to the deuteronomistic history and to its refashioning of the Song of the Sea in 15:1–18. Three aspects of v. 20 are important for its interpretation within priestly tradition: that Miriam is the singer, that she is the "sister of Aaron," and that she is a "prophetess."

Miriam is frequently judged to be an obscure character in the Pentateuch whose meaningful function in the ancient Israelite cult has either been long forgotten or intentionally obscured by later priestly tradents.[41] In either case the result is that her presence in the Pentateuch is now, for the most part, unexplainable. Yet this conclusion immediately runs into obstacles, for Miriam is one of only three characters (along with Moses and Aaron) explicitly associated with the exodus. In addition, she is actually given the final word of prophetic commentary on the event at the sea. Such a prominent position in what must be judged to be one of the more central pentateuchal texts is not obscurity.

Nor does there appear to be a concerted effort by late tradents to obscure her role in the Pentateuch. Even though one might wish for more detailed information on the tradition-historical development of Miriam within the Israelite cult, nevertheless Miriam remains a central character within priestly tradition in the Pentateuch. Of the five pentateuchal texts in which she is explicitly named, four show clear markings of priestly interests.[42] Exod 15:20–21 and Numbers 12 link her specifically with Aaron either as "sister" in Exod 15:20–21 or as one who shares his interests over against Moses in Numbers 12.[43] Num 26:59 goes even further to assign her a prominent place as the "sister" of Aaron and Moses in a Levitical genealogy.[44] Her death notice in Num 20:1 also appears to be a priestly creation aimed at presenting the "death of the three family members, Miriam, Aaron, and Moses . . . at the three final stations [of the priestly itinerary]."[45] Exod 2:1–10 may be an allusion to Miriam without specifically mentioning her, in which case this story would add still further support to the conclusion that she has become a prominent character in priestly tradition. As the "sister" of Moses in this story, she too is a Levite, who functions as the primary agent in her brother's salvation.[46] The only text that might challenge the conclusion that Miriam is a central character within priestly tradition is Deut 24:9, until one considers that this reference to Miriam occurs in a section of late miscellaneous laws and that it presupposes the existence of Leviticus 13–14 and Numbers 12, which prompts the conclusion that Deut 24:9 is not a competing or distinct tradition concerning Miriam, but simply late commentary arising from priestly tradition.[47]

The central problem in interpreting the function of Miriam within priestly tradition concerns the two descriptions of her in Exod 15:20–21 as "sister of Aaron" and as "prophetess." These titles have been judged to be conflictual if not contradictory, and as a consequence, scholars have tended to advocate one role over the other in order to interpret her function in Exod 15:20–21, but never both roles together.[48] Yet it is the combination of priestly and prophetic roles that provides the key for interpreting her function within the priestly interpretation of the exodus.

Recent research in the development of prophecy in later priestly tradition suggests that the titles "prophet" and "priest" underwent creative transformation in the second temple period, a change particularly evident in the Chronicler's work, where there is a marked intention to confer prophetic status on Levites. Tournay has most recently underscored again that the Book of Chronicles is best viewed as prophetic history. Not only do prophetic figures play a central role throughout the work, but it would also appear that the Chronicler actually roots his authority to recount history in prophecy.[49] In addition, as Petersen has demonstrated, prophecy undergoes significant redefinition at the hands of the Chronicler, which is most evident when one examines the prophetic role of Levitical singers.[50] Such an examination reveals that Levitical singers are prophets, that the content of their prophecy is cultic song, and that they assume their central prophetic role in at least three distinct contexts: in narratives about the ark (1 Chronicles 15–16), holy war (2 Chr 20), and passover (2 Chronicles 29).[51]

The prophetic claims for Levitical singers by priestly groups in the second temple period provide background for interpreting the function of Miriam in Exod 15:20–21. The reinterpretation of prophecy as cultic song suggests that the description of Miriam as "sister of Aaron" and as "prophetess" need not be contradictory, nor that the title "prophetess" be judged meaningless because of the absence of a traditional oracle.[52] On the contrary, Miriam's primary activity in this narrative of making music and of singing mirrors exactly the prophetic role of Levitical singers, while the immediate context of holy war also finds a close analogy to the prophetic role of Levites in 2 Chronicles 20.[53] These parallels suggest that regardless of her prior history in Israelite tradition, Miriam is functioning as a prophetic ideal within priestly tradition much like Levitical singers in Chronicles. She is the counter-voice to Moses.

The content of the Song of Miriam gives voice to the priestly interpretation of the confrontation at the sea. Her song underscores that Yahweh's triumph at the sea is a climactic and hence final event in which the Egyptian army is destroyed. The destruction of the Egyptians does not lead to a conquest as in the deuteronomistic form of the Song of Moses (Exod 15:1–18), nor does it result in divine rule as in the original form of the hymn (Exod 15:1–12, 18). The Song of Miriam falls in between these two interpretations as did the priestly narrative account.

The placement of the Song of Miriam in Exodus 15 provides further insight into how this hymn is meant to function within priestly tradition. The most noteworthy feature of the insertion is the striking repetition that dominates the canonical text. Moses is no more finished singing about the future conquest of the land in Exod 15:1–18 before Miriam enters the stage to focus the reader's attention back on the event at the sea in Exod 15:21. Her song creates a repetition that is spatial in form.[54] Spatial form devices subvert the chronological sequence inherent in narrative, and such techniques are common in priestly tradition.[55] The repetition created by the

Song of Miriam is spatial in form because it disrupts the plot structure of the Song of Moses in Exod 15:1-18, since the content of Exod 15:21 separates the exodus from the conquest and, in the process, turns the reader's attention back to Egypt and the sea. In this way the Song of Miriam reinforces the change in geography that was evident in the priestly narrative account of the exodus, whereby the confrontation at the sea was also relocated from the wilderness in the deuteronomistic history back into Egypt with the insertion of the itinerary notice in Exod 14:1-2. Thus the priestly narrative and the Song of Miriam work in tandem to present an interpretation of the confrontation at the sea as the final salvific event in Egypt, rather than as the first event in the wilderness as was the case in the deuteronomistic interpretation.

NOTES

1. For arguments in favor of the antiquity of Exod 15:21 see, for example, F. Crüsemann (*Studien zur Formgeschichte von Hymnus und Danklied in Israel*, WMANT 32 [Neukirchener-Vluyn: Neukirchener, 1969], 19-38 and passim), who anchors the tradition-historical development of the hymn form in Exod 15:21. Other representatives of this position include O. Kaiser, *Die mythische Bedeutung des Meeres in Ägypten, Ugarit und Israel*, 2d ed., BZAW 78 (Berlin: A. Töpelmann, 1962), 130-131; F. M. Cross and D. N. Freedman, "The Song of Miriam," *JNES* 14 (1955): 237-250; Fohrer, *Überlieferung und Geschichte des Exodus*, 111; Smend, *Yahweh War and Tribal Confederation*, 110; R. J. Burns, *Has the Lord Indeed Spoken Only Through Moses? A Study of the Biblical Portrait of Miriam*, SBLDS 84 (Atlanta: Scholars Press, 1987), 12-16; and P. Trible, "Subversive Justice: Tracing the Miriamic Traditions," in *Justice and the Holy: Essays in Honor of Walter Harrelson*, Scholars Press Homage Series, ed. D. A. Knight and P. J. Paris (Atlanta: Scholars Press, 1989), 102. For a recent summary of the different positions with regard to date see Kang, *Divine War in the Old Testament and in the Ancient Near East*, 114-116.

2. The function of both songs in their present narrative context has not received nearly as much attention as attempts to date the two hymns in order to determine which is older. For a departure from past method see B. W. Anderson, "The Song of Miriam Poetically and Theologically Considered," in *Directions in Biblical Hebrew Poetry*, JSOTSup 40, ed. E. R. Follis (Sheffield: Sheffield Press, 1987), 285-296; J. W. Watts, *Psalm and Story: Inset Hymns in Hebrew Narrative*, JSOTSup 139 (Sheffield: JSOT Press, 1992), 41-62; and J. G. Janzen, "Song of Moses, Song of Miriam: Who Is Seconding Whom?" *CBQ* 54 (1992): 211-220.

3. Noth, *A History of Pentateuchal Traditions*, 46-62; *Exodus*, 104-105, 121-123. The influence of a salvation history hermeneutic is especially evident with the reassessment of early Israelite tradition by the Albright school, whose comparison with Ugaritic literature provided the basis for isolating a corpus of archaic poetry, of which Exod 15:1-18 was considered a central example. This innovative approach to the origin of Israelite literature positioned early representatives of the school, such as Cross and Freedman (*Studies in Ancient Yahwistic Poetry*, 45-65), over against Noth in arguing that the complete version of the Song

of the Sea in Exod 15:1–18 (rather than just the couplet in 15:21b) constituted the earliest account of the exodus, and furthermore that the song was part of an epic of salvation history, which formed the basis for all subsequent pentateuchal tradition. Even though this thesis presented a strong point of debate concerning the literary character of early Israelite tradition, on a hermeneutical level it served to intensify Noth's thesis that the exodus was an event of salvation history from its inception, since now the entire sequence of exodus, wilderness, and conquest could be shown to be embedded in an archaic poem.

4. J. Jeremias, *Das Königtum Gottes in den Psalmen: Israels Begegnung mit dem kanaanäischen Mythos in den Jahwe-König-Psalmen*, FRLANT 141 (Göttingen: Vandenhoeck & Ruprecht, 1987), 99. Scholars who note the abrupt change of topic but favor in the end an essentially unified poem (at least with regard to the joining of exodus and wilderness-conquest traditions) include Cross, *Canaanite Myth and Hebrew Epic*, 121–144; J. Muilenburg, "A Liturgy of the Triumphs of Yahweh," in *Studia Biblica et Semitica*, ed. W. C. van Unnik and A. S. van der Woude [Wageningen: H. Veenman en Zonen, 1966]), 233–251 = *Hearing and Speaking the Word: Selections from the Works of James Muilenburg*, Scholars Press Homage Series, ed. T. F. Best (Chico: Scholars Press, 1984), 151–169; D. N. Freedman, "Strophe and Meter in Exodus 15," in *Potter, Poetry, and Prophecy: Studies in Early Hebrew Poetry* (Winona Lake: Eisenbrauns, 1980), 187–227; Childs, *Exodus*, 251–252; H. Strauss, "Das Meerlied des Mose: Ein 'Siegeslied' Israels?" *ZAW* 97 (1985): 106–107; M. Rozelaar, "The Song of the Sea: Exodus XV, 1b–18," *VT* 2 (1952): 221–228; R. Alter, *The Art of Biblical Poetry* (New York: Basic Books, 1985), 50–54; M. Howell, "Exodus 15,1b-18: A Poetic Analysis," *ETL* 65 (1989): 9, 34–35, 42; R. J. Tournay, *Voir et entendre Dieu avec les Psaumes ou la liturgie prophétique du second temple à Jérusalem*, CahRB 24 (Paris: J. Gabalda, 1988), 68; and M. L. Brenner, *The Song of the Sea: Ex 15:1–21*, BZAW 195 (Berlin: de Gruyter, 1991), 26–34. Scholars who suggest some form of tradition-historical development in the joining of the two parts of the poem include J. D. W. Watts, "The Song of the Sea—Ex. XV," *VT* 7 (1957): 371–380; Coats, "The Song of the Sea," 1–17; E. Zenger, "Tradition und Interpretation in Exodus XV 1–21," in *Congress Volume: Vienna 1980*, VTSup 32 ed. J. A. Emerton et al. (Leiden: E. J. Brill, 1980), 452–482; T. C. Butler, "'The Song of the Sea': Exodus 15:1–18: A Study in the Exegesis of Hebrew Poetry" (Ph.D. diss., Vanderbilt University, 1971),102–199; Norin, *Er Spaltete das Meer*, 77–107; and H. Spieckermann, *Heilsgegenwart: Eine Theologie der Psalmen*, FRLANT 148 (Göttingen: Vandenhoeck & Ruprecht, 1989), 96–115.

5. Form-critical assessments include hymn (Rozelaar, "The Song of the Sea," 222; Fohrer, *Überlieferung und Geschichte des Exodus*, 110–116; Watts, "The Song of the Sea—Ex. XV," 372 and passim); victory song (Cross and Freedman, *Ancient Yahwistic Poetry*, 45; Brenner, *The Song of the Sea*, 36–38.); enthonement hymn (Mowinckel, *Psalms I*, 126); liturgy (H. Schmidt, "Das Meerlied: Ex 15 2–19," *ZAW* 49 [1931]: 63; Muilenburg, "Liturgy of the Triumphs," 236); hymn with elements of thanksgiving (Noth, *Exodus*, 123); hymn of praise (Rylaarsdam, *Exodus*, 942); a developed reporting style in the hymn (Crüsemann, *Studien*, 191–199, esp. 193–194); and simply mixed (Westermann, *Praise and Lament in the Psalms*, 141; Coats, "The Song of the Sea," 7–8). For a review of scholarship on genre see Butler, "'The Song of the Sea,'" 4–60, 79–101, or more recently Strauss, "Das Meerlied des Mose," 103–109.

6. A. J. Hauser ("Two Songs of Victory: A Comparison of Exodus 15 and Judges 5," in *Directions in Biblical Hebrew Poetry,* JSOTSup 40, ed. E. R. Follis [Sheffield: Sheffield Press, 1987], 280) concludes that, although no set genre of a victory song is recoverable in the Hebrew Bible, a comparison of Exodus 15 and Judges 5 suggests several common features: focus on a specific name of God; application of specific terms to God; description of God's use of forces of nature; mocking of the enemy; and a description of the enemy's fall. References to the future are not part of such a genre. See also Westermann, *Praise and Lament in the Psalms*, 92.

7. Cross (*Canaanite Myth and Hebrew Epic*, 121-132) has sought to address the problem of time by arguing that vv. 1b-18 are an archaic victory song and that all the prefixed forms of the verbs in vv. 13-17, including the refrain in v. 16b and the approach to the sanctuary in v. 17, must be read as preterites on analogy to Ugaritic *yaqtul* forms. Once this decision is made, Cross concludes that the poet wrote "from the point of view of one re-enacting the Conquest, including both the episode of the sea and the passing over into the land to a Palestinian sanctuary" (p. 128 n. 59). A consistent reading of the prefixed verb forms as preterites in vv. 13-17 already runs into difficulty in vv. 14-16a, where the fear of Israel's neighbors need not be read as a singular past event. It becomes even more difficult to maintain in the refrain of v. 16b: here the syntactical construction of the word "until" with an imperfect form of the verb nearly always has future meaning. Compare Brenner (*The Song of the Sea*, 36-39), who takes yet another approach by arguing that vv. 13-17 are indeed future in their orientation but that "the defeat of the future enemies and the security of the friends of God" is a developed form of the victory song from Judg 5:31a.

8. Zenger, "Tradition und Interpretation," 468-469.

9. Coats, "The Song of the Sea," 9. See Westermann (*Praise and Lament in the Psalms*, 15-164) for a discussion of declarative and descriptive modes of speech in hymns. The distinctive types of speech may also be reflected in problems of meter. The problem is that the 2 + 2 meter which predominates in vv. 1-12 is difficult to maintain in vv. 14-16a, a difficulty that prompts some scholars to scan lines in 3 + 4 (v. 14) and 4 + 4 (vv. 15a and 16a), and Zenger ("Tradition und Interpretation," 464) goes so far as to conclude that v. 15b is prose rather than poetry. For discussion of the problems of meter see Watts ("The Song of the Sea," 376- 377), who scans vv. 14-16a: 3:4; 4:4; 4:4; Muilenburg ("Litergy of the Triumphs," 155, 163), who notes the problems of meter but fails to provide an analysis; Cross and Freedman ("Song of Miriam," 242), who scan vv. 14-16a: 3:3; and then 2:2 throughout, an analysis that is also followed by Cross in *Canaanite Myth and Hebrew Epic*, 126, although Freedman ("Strophe and Meter in Exodus," 211-212) suggests that v. 14 may be 3:4 while vv. 15 and 16ab could be either 2:2 or 4:4. See also Jeremias, *Königtum Gottes*, 99; and Spieckermann, *Heilsgegenwart*, 106-107; or finally, Howell ("Exodus 15,1b-18," 34-35), who scans v. 14 (3:3), v. 15 (3:3:3 or 2:2/2:2/2:2), and v. 16a (2:2/2:2/2:2).

10. See most recently Brenner, *The Song of the Sea*, 28-29.

11. See, for example, Muilenburg, "Liturgy of the Triumphs," 155-156; Freedman, "Strophe and Meter in Exodus," 187-189 and passim; Alter, *The Art of Biblical Poetry*, 51-54; Brenner, *The Song of the Sea*, 30-31.

12. See the exhaustive study by Butler ("'The Song of the Sea,'" 107-149), who also attributes the motif of Israel's crossing (עבר) on dry ground (יבשׁ) to deuteronomistic tradition but in addition concludes from Deut 11:4 that another

primary motif in the deuteronomistic interpretation of the sea is the covering over of the Egyptians, which occurs in Exod 15:2, 12. In contrast to Butler, the present study is advocating that the motif of the Egyptians' being covered over by the water is predeuteronomistic. There are two aspects of the sea tradition in deuteronomistic interpretations: first, the destruction of the Egyptians, and second, the salvation of Israel. The deuteronomistic description of the destruction of the Egyptians is not innovative but follows the traditional material from Exod 15:2,12 (as is reflected in Deut 11:4 and Josh 24:6). They make their account innovative by adding a second focus to the event at the sea, namely, the detailed account of Israel's actions during this event. This focus on Israel crossing over the sea is absent in preexilic tradition, and it provides the framework to connect the exodus with the wilderness tradition—which reaches its conclusion in the crossing of the Jordan. For further tradition-historical study of the Song of the Sea within deuteronomistic tradition see Coats, "The Song of the Sea," 1-31; Norin, *Er Spaltete das Meer*, 77-107; Jeremias, *Königtum Gottes*, 93-106; Spieckermann, *Heilsgegenwart*, 96-115; or F. Foresti, "Composizione e redazione deuteronomistica in Ex 15,1-18," *Lateranum* 48 (1982): 41-69. See also chapter 3.

13. The motif of divine leading in vv. 13 and 17 includes the verbs נהל, נחה, and בוא. This motif is part of the larger focus on Israel that is introduced in deuteronomistic tradition. Note here especially בוא in v. 17, which is used frequently throughout deuteronomistic conquest traditions to describe both Yahweh's promise of land and divine leading into the land. For a discussion of בוא within divine land promises see Boorer, *The Promise of the Land as Oath*,133-135; and as a description of Israel's possession of the land see Braulik, *Die Mittel Deuteronomischer Rhetorik*, 95; Butler, "'The Song of the Sea,'" 156-162. For more general studies see Jenni, "'Kommen' im theologischen Sprachgebrauch des Alten Testaments," 251-261; Pruess, "בוא," 20-49; and Brenner, *The Song of the Sea*, 139-140.

14. The fear of the nations in vv. 14-16a includes the words אימה, מוג, חיל, רגז, פחד. The fear of the nations occurs in the same context as in the Jordan crossing (note the use of מוג and אימה in Josh 2:9, 24), and it even has closer parallels in Deut 2:25, where three of the terms occur in the context of conquest (חיל, רגז, פחד). For further discussion of this motif in deuteronomistic tradition see Butler, "'The Song of the Sea,'" 162-199. Note also the study by W. L. Moran, "The End of the Unholy War and the Anti-Exodus," *Bib* 44 (1963): 333-342. For comparison to similar descriptions of fear in Ugaritic literature see N. Waldman, "A Comparative Note on Exodus 15:14-16," *JQR* 66 (1975): 189-192.

15. עבר in v. 16b is best explained as a secondary addition to the sea event originating in the deuteronomistic description of the Jordan crossing in Josh 2:10; 4:23. See, among others, Coats, "The Song of the Sea," 1-17; and Butler, "'The Song of the Sea,'" 112-113. See also chapter 3.

16. Brenner, *The Song of the Sea*, 127-130.

17. By describing the hymn as predeuteronomistic, I am assuming that it is preexilic. A more exact dating of the predeuteronomistic song is difficult to determine because of the wide range of methodologies that have been applied. Norin (*Er Spaltete Das Meer*, 77-107) argues for an original form of the song, perhaps as old as the twelfth century B.C.E., which was then expanded by deuteronomistic editors to include at least vv. 1b, 2, 4, 5, 8, 14, 15b, 16b. Few have followed his lead on this point, but nearly all scholars concede minor redactional additions or textual corruptions in vv. 1-12, 18. Cross and Freedman ("Song of

Miriam," 237-250) have emphasized archaic orthography and comparison to Ugaritic prosody to argue for a premonarchical date. At the other end of the spectrum, Brenner (*The Song of the Sea*, 54-92) has most recently argued for a postexilic date to the psalm because of similarities in language in vv. 1-12 to postdeuteronomistic tradition. The more nuanced comparison of language in vv. 1-12 as evidence of postdeuteronomistic rather than predeuteronomistic tradition is more difficult to confirm, since a clear correspondence between the song and any one narrative tradition does not exist. See Noth (*History of Pentateuchal Traditions*, 30 n. 107), who concluded, "The hymn in Ex. 15:1-19 is so isolated that it can no longer be classified in a literary manner and presumably does not belong to any source at all." A number of scholars, including Spieckermann (*Heilsgegenwart*, 113); Jeremias, (*Königtum Gottes*, 103); and Mettinger (*The Dethronement of Sabaoth*, 26-27), have argued that the poem should be dated sometime in the late monarchy period, during the time of the Josianic reform, while Day (*God's Conflict with the Dragon and the Sea*, 99) favors an earlier monarchical period. The results of the present study of Exod 15:1-12, 18 certainly favor a preexilic date.

18. Coats, "The Song of the Sea," 2. For a review of past interpretations concerning the structure of the hymn see, among others, Coats, "The Song of the Sea," 2 n. 9; Butler, "'The Song of the Sea,'" 56; Zenger, "Tradition und Interpretation," 454-455; and the detailed work of Howell, "Exodus 15,1b-18," 5-42.

19. Two reasons support the presence of v. 2: one, the first person praise is carried through both v. 1b and v. 2; and two, as Muilenburg ("Liturgy of the Triumphs," 157) has noted, vv. 2-3 work in consort to provide elaboration concerning the meaning of the divine name. Even though the imagery of the earth swallowing the enemy in v. 12 is repeated in the story of Korah's rebellion (Num 16:30-31), the meaning of "earth" as "underworld" as well as the repetition of "your arm" from v. 6b suggest that this verse is referring to Yahweh's victory at the Sea and not to Israel's wilderness travels. See Cross (*Canaanite Myth and Hebrew Epic*, 129) for an interpretation of v. 12 as a coda to the previous description of the sea event. Verse 18 presents the most problems for interpretation, since the prefixed form of the verb "to rule" certainly refers to the future in the present form of the hymn. Yet there are no firm literary or linguistic reasons for excluding this exclamation of Yahweh's kingship from the predeuteronomistic form of the hymn, where the proclamation would take on a more durative meaning in light of Yahweh's victory over sea and Pharaoh. The evaluation of v. 18 is complicated by its close relationship to the enthronement psalms (Pss 93:1; 96:10; 97:1; and 99:1) with regard to vocabulary and syntax. Where Exod 15:18 contrasts to the enthronement hymns is in the use of the prefixed form of the verb "to rule," which has only one parallel, in Ps 146:10.

20. Three aspects of v. 17 underscore how closely this verse is tied to vv. 13-16. First, the suffixes on the initial verbs "you brought them in and planted them" must be interpreted as referring to Israel rather than Pharaoh or the Egyptians, signaling how intimately connected v. 17 is with the motif of Yahweh's leading Israel that dominates vv. 13-16. Second, v. 17 actually repeats language from v. 13 with regard to Yahweh's holy abode. And third, the future tense of the verbs in v. 17 follows the future orientation of vv. 13-16. Not only does the syntax of v. 17 encourage its reading with the deuteronomistic addition in vv. 13-16, but the imagery in this verse also corresponds well with deuteronomistic tradition. Mettinger (*The Dethronement of Sabaoth*, 27) has argued that the imagery of

Yahweh's dwelling place presupposes the influence of Zion tradition, which alone does not argue for deuteronomistic authorship, but it does preclude a premonarchical date, and the same holds true for the description of Yahweh's abode as a "mountain of inheritance." See also Blenkinsopp (*The Pentateuch,* 159-160), who also concludes that both מכון לשבתך in v. 17a (see 1 Kgs 8:13 and also Isa 4:5; Dan 8:11) and מקדש אדני in v. 17b (see Pss 48:9; 87:5) presuppose Zion tradition. Ambiguity remains concerning the meaning of "mountain of your inheritance" (בהר נחלתך) in v. 17 (is it the temple, the land, or both?). For a discussion of these problems see Wijngaards, *The Dramatization of Salvific History in the Deuteronomic Schools,* 82-84; or Brenner (*The Song of the Sea,* 141), who argues that the reference designates the land and that such use is late, occurring first in Jer 2:7; 16:18; and 50:11. Whether the usage is deuteronomistic is difficult to confirm, even though the use of נחלה is frequent in deuteronomistic tradition (both in the deuteronomistic history [e.g., 1 Sam 26:19; 2 Sam 14:16; 20:19; 21:3] and in Jeremiah [e.g., Jer 12:7-9; 50:11]). For a complete listing see F. Horst, "Zwei Begriffe für Eigentum (Besitz)," in *Verbannung und Heimkehr: Festschrift für Wilhelm Rudolph,* ed. A. Koschke (Tübingen: J. C. B. Mohr (Paul Siebeck), 1961), 140. Horst (p. 141) also argues that uses of inheritance in reference to God (as in Exod 15:17) most likely presuppose Zion tradition.

21. See the studies by Cross, *Canaanite Myth and Hebrew Epic,* 112-120 and passim; Jeremias, *Königtum Gottes,* 93-106; Kaiser, *Die mythische Bedeutung des Meeres,* 40-77; Spieckermann, *Heilsgegenwart,* 88-113; Norin, *Er Spaltete das Meer,* 42-77 and passim; Day, *God's Conflict with the Dragon and the Sea;* Mettinger, *The Dethronement of Sabaoth,* 27, 67-75; Coats, "The Traditio-Historical Character of the Reed Sea Motif," 253-265; and "The Song of the Sea," 1-17; P. C. Craige, "The Poetry of Ugarit and Israel," *TynBul* 22 (1971): 3-31; C. Kloos, *Yhwh's Combat with the Sea: A Canaanite Tradition in the Religion of Ancient Israel* (Leiden: E. J. Brill, 1986), 127-212; M. S. Smith, *The Early History of God,* 41-79.

22. For a discussion of the relationship between the Ugaritic tablets see R. J. Clifford, "Cosmogonies in the Ugaritic Texts and in the Bible," *Or* 53 (1984): 188-198.

23. Baal is encouraged in CTA 2.IV.10 to sieze his throne and to take over his rightful kingdom (*tqh.mlk.'lmk//drkt.dt.drkrk*), but the fulfillment of the second part of this statement, where Baal must take over his kingdom, does not occur in CTA 2. There are a number of examples that suggest that a god's rule must be accompanied by the possession of a kingdom (*arṣ nḫlt*) or a domain (*drkt*). Note, for example, how the descriptions of enthroned gods tend to mention both their possession of a throne (*ksu ṯbt*) and the description of the land over which they rule (*arṣ nḫlt*). See here the description of Yamm in CTA 1.III.1, of Kothar-and-Khasis in Memphis (CTA 3.C.27 and 3.F.16), of Mot in his underworld palace (CTA 4.VIII.14 and 5.II.16), or of Keret (CTA 16.VI.22-24). In other instances when a god is overthrown, the loss of his throne (*ksu.mlk*) is accompanied by the description of the loss of his domain (*kht.drkt*). Examples include Baal's overthrowing of Yamm (CTA 2.IV.13, 20) and Anat's recounting of her victories (CTA 3.D.47). The same language is used at other places in the Baal-Yamm/Nahar myth (CTA 1.IV.24-25), in the Keret epic (CTA 14.I.42-43), and in the description of Baal's enthronement over Mot (CTA 6.V.6).

24. In both CTA 3.E.40-45 and 4.IV.43-62 Baal's rule is affirmed (*mlkn.aliyn.b'l//ṯptn.in.d'lnh*), an event that provides the basis for the further proclamation that

he needs a temple (*wn.'in.bt[.]lb't.km.ilm* in CTA 3.E.46–47 or *ybn.bt.lb'l* in CTA 4.IV.62).

25. See Mann (*Divine Presence and Guidance in Israelite Traditions*, 99) concerning traces of the motif of the divine warrior with his vanguard in this material.

26. Hebrew יהוה ימלך = Ugaritic: *b'lm ymlk*. See Cross, *Canaanite Myth and Hebrew Epic*, 112–120; Jeremias, *Königtum Gottes*, 99–100, 103; and Spieckermann, *Heilsgegenwart*, 110.

27. The deuteronomistic addition in Exod 15:13–17 is framed with images of temple contruction in v. 13 (אל־נוה קדשך) and in v. 17 (בהר נחלתך, מכון לשבתך, אדני, מקדש). See Norin (*Er Spaltete das Meer*, 84–92) for a discussion of אל־נוה קדשך in v. 13 within the larger context of Canaanite mythology. The verbal parallels in Exod 15:17 to the Baal mythology are Hebrew בהר נחלתך = Ugaritic *bġr nḥlt* in CTA 3.C.27; 3.D.64; and Hebrew מכון לשבתך = Ugaritic *ksu tbt* in CTA 1.III.1; 3.F.16; 4.VIII.14; 5.II.16.

28. The Ugaritic motif *arṣ nḥlt* ("land of possession") occurs four times in combination with *ksu tbt* ("the throne on which [he] sits," CTA 1.III.1; 3.F.16; 4.VIII.14; 5.II.16), while the two additional occurrences are associated with Baal's holy mountain, *bġr nḥlt* ("mountain of possession," CTA 3.C.27; 3.D.64). Forms of *drkt* ("domain" or "kingdom") occur frequently in the context of enthronement (CTA 1.IV.25(?); 2.IV.10, 13, 20; 3.D.47; 4.VII.44; 6.V.6; 14.I.42; 16.VI.24, 38, 53).

29. Thus the predeuteronomistic form of the Song of the Sea is certainly not a replication of the Baal–Yamm/Nahar myth, where the conflict is solely cosmological. The inclusion of a historical monarch as representing Yahweh's enemy has given rise to a debate concerning myth and history in the early formation of Israel's cult. See Kloos (*Yhwh's Combat with the Sea*, 158–190) for a brief overview of the many positions that have been advanced. The potential for historicizing Canaanite mythology is certainly evident in the early victory song, but in regard to its present form Spieckermann (*Heilsgegenwart*, 110–111) is certainly correct when he cautions against demythologizing the song too quickly, since the opponent shifts rapidly between Pharaoh and a more general "enemy."

30. See Spieckermann, *Heilsgegenwart*, 110.

31. Mettinger, *The Dethronement of Sabaoth*, 27.

32. See, Mettinger (*The Dethronement of Sabaoth*, 1–19) for a discussion of the permanent presence of Yahweh in the Zion cult tradition. See also Spieckermann, *Heilsgegenwart*, 110–111.

33. See here especially Jeremias (*Königtum Gottes*, 100–106) for a discussion of the historicizing tendency in the deuteronomistic form of the Song of the Sea.

34. For a further discussion of holy-war imagery in Song of the Sea see Miller, *Divine Warrior*, 113–117.

35. Labuschagne, *The Incomparability of Yahweh*, 77, 96, 98 and passim.

36. מים and ים in vv. 8, 10.

37. Sea maintains a quasi-independent status in the hymn, a fact that suggests that it is personified, but under Yahweh's control. Note in particular that sea functions as the subject of verbs in vv. 8 and 10, but again only to provide a gauge for measuring Yahweh's strength, which leads to a celebration of Yahweh's power among the gods (v. 11a). For similar conclusions see Ollenburger, *Zion, the City of the Great King*, 58–59; and Spieckermann, *Heilsgegenwart*, 110–111. Compare here Cross (*Canaanite Myth and Hebrew Epic*, 131), who concludes that

the sea is neither hostile nor personified but simply a passive instrument in Yahweh's control.

38. Note that the quotation of the enemy in v. 9 is not the focus of this section. See also the discussion by Jeremias (*Königtum Gottes*, 97) concerning the ring structure of vv. 6-12, where the power of Yahweh over the enemy is accentuated through the literary device of framing: the enemy (C, v. 9) is framed both by Yahweh's actual (B, v. 8 and B', v. 10) and more general (A, vv. 6-7 and A' 11-12) power.

39. See Childs (*Exodus*, 248-251) on the emerging prophetic function of the psalm in its present context.

40. See note 1.

41. For example, Noth (*History of Pentateuchal Traditions*, p. 181) acknowledges her role in later priestly tradition but concludes that it is now meaningless and that perhaps lost stories might provide clarity; Trible ("Subversive Justice: Tracing the Miriamic Traditions," 102) would attribute sinister motive to late redactors who attempted to cover up the central cultic role of Miriam; while Burns (*Has the Lord Indeed Spoken Only Through Moses?* p. 84) argues that Miriam is meant to give status to later priestly characters through her association with Aaron.

42. Miriam appears outside of the Pentateuch in Mic 6:4 with Moses and Aaron as one of the three heroes of the exodus and in the Levitical genealogy of 1 Chr 5:29, where she is also listed with Aaron and Moses.

43. See Noth, *Numbers*, 92-97; Milgrom, *Numbers*, 376-380.

44. The Levitical genealogy in Num 26:57-65 is composed of at least two distinct traditions. Verse 58a preserves an older list of five Levitical families: Libnites, Hebronites, Mahlites, Mushites, and Korahites. This list has been framed in vv. 57 and 58b-62 with later material, which reinterprets the older list and thus brings it into conformity with the standard priestly genealogy of Levi in Exod 6:14-27 and 1 Chr 5:27-6:15. Verse 57 is a segmented genealogy which redefines the Levitical families from five to three: Gershonites, Kohathites, and Merarites, while vv. 58b-62 is a linear genealogy, which traces the Kohathites through three generations: first Amran and his wife Jochebed; then Aaron, Moses, and Miriam; and finally the four sons of Aaron: Nadab, Abihu, Eleazar, and Ithamar.

45. Noth, *A History of Pentateuchal Traditions,* 182-183. Compare Burns (*Has the Lord Indeed Spoken Only Through Moses?* 119-120), who argues that the death notice of Miriam is early and authentic. Even if Burns is correct, that fact would not preclude the reworking of this tradition by priestly tradents, something that would certainly appear to be the case from the present form of the text. Note that the deaths of the three heros are dealt with together (Miriam and Aaron in Numbers 20 and Moses in Numbers 20 and 27). It is as though the breakup of this relationship of characters with the death of Miriam in v. 1 marks the downfall of all.

46. See Noth, *Exodus*, 25.

47. von Rad (*Deuteronomy,* 151) writes concerning this text, "In the section about leprosy in vv. 8-9 the passage about the Levitical priests must be judged to be a secondary addition, not only because it passes into the second person plural, but particularly because it changes abruptly into the form of direct speech by God which is quite alien to Deuteronomy."

48. For the most recent example of this dichotomy, see Trible ("Subversive Justice," p. 101), who emphasizes Miriam's prophetic role in Exod 15:20-21, over

against Burns (*Has the Lord Indeed Spoken Only Through Moses?* pp. 46–48), who would not emphasize the title in intepreting the role of Miriam. For a review of past scholarship on these two titles see Burns (pp. 41–79).

49. Tournay, *Voir et entendre Dieu avec les Psaumes*, 19–28.

50. D. L. Petersen, *Late Israelite Prophecy: Studies in Deutero-Prophetic Literature and in Chronicles*, SBLMS 23 (Missoula: Scholars Press, 1977), 55–87. See also Tournay, *Voir et entendre Dieu avec les Psaumes*, pp. 19–28; and J. Blenkinsopp, *A History of Prophecy in Israel: From the Settlement of the Land to the Hellenistic Period* (Philadelphia: Westminster, 1983), 252–255.

51. The Chronicler's concern with conferring prophetic status on Levites is starkly evident in the substitution of Levites for prophets when 2 Kgs 23:2 is reworked in 2 Chr 34:30. Yet this substitution does little more than alert the reader to the prophetic claims of priestly groups that run throughout the Chronicler's presentation of Levites. Although Jahaziel, a Levite from the family of Asaph, in 2 Chr 20:14–17 assumes the traditional prophetic role of presenting a divine oracle to Jehoshaphat concerning the outcome of an impending battle, the Chronicler appears to be more concerned with redefining the function of prophecy itself in relation to Levites. Thus more traditional prophetic oracles give way to cultic singing as the primary prophetic activity of Levites. This shift is evident two verses later in the same story of Jahaziel and Jehoshaphat, for when Levites begin singing to Yahweh in v. 19, Jehoshaphat responds in v. 20 by calling them prophets and by encouraging the people to believe in them (the Levites). The primary function of prophecy as song is underscored further in the Levitical genealogy of 1 Chronicles 25 where the reader is told in the opening verse that the purpose of the Levitical families of Asaph, Heman, and Jeduthun is to "prophesy with lyres, with harps, and with cymbals" and that this prophetic function originated with David (1 Chr 25:1), who in turn was given divine advice in the matter through the prophets Gad and Nathan (2 Chr 29:25). H. G. M. Williamson (*1 and 2 Chronicles,* NICOT [Grand Rapids: Eerdmans, 1982], 358) writes concerning 2 Chr 29:25, "[T]he Chronicler was anxious to stress that these arrangements [the instruments for Levitical song] followed a word of commandment . . . from the Lord, and for his readers this would be accepted as most authoritative if it was understood as having been mediated through his prophets." For additional secondary discussion of the prophetic role of Levites in Chronicles see Petersen (*Late Israelite Prophecy*, pp. 69–77), who ends his study of 2 Chronicles 20 by concluding that this narrative "presents us with a glimpse of how post-exilic prophecy was conceived by the hierocratic elements," which was to "substantiate the Levitical singers' claim to cultic authority as prophets in post-exilic society." For a discussion of the prophetic role of David within the Chronicler's work see Tournay, *Voir et entendre Dieu avec les Psaumes*, pp. 26–27.

52. For elaboration of this argument see Burns, *Has the Lord Indeed Spoken Only Through Moses?* pp. 46–48.

53. The parallels in cultic context between Levitical singers in Chronicles and Miriam in Exod 15:20–21 could also include passover if the context of Miriam's song were expanded to include Exodus 12, as it most likely should be.

54. T. B. Dozeman, "Spatial Form in Exod 19:1–8a and in the Larger Sinai Narrative," *Semeia* 46 (1989): 88–89.

55. See Dozeman, *God on the Mountain*, 159–173.

6

Divine Power and Presence
as Themes in the Formation
of the Pentateuch

The perspective will change in this chapter from reading individual traditions within the Pentateuch to looking more broadly at the formation of
the canonical Pentateuch as a whole. The aim in broadening the scope of
study is to inquire what the organizing theme or themes of the Pentateuch
might be. A quick reading of the canonical Pentateuch in conjunction with
even the most recent interpretations of it suggests that the organization of
Torah eludes a single solution with regard to its central theme or themes.
Indeed, there are any number of successful modern interpretations that
describe the organization of the Pentateuch. Martin Noth's organization
of it into five themes (Patriarchs, Exodus, Wilderness, Sinai, Land) is perhaps the best known.[1] But there are others. There is Hugo Gressmann's
organization of the Pentateuch around the life of Moses,[2] which is echoed
in the recent work of John Van Seters.[3] There is the emphasis of D. J. A.
Clines on promise as the organizing theme in relation to fertility, divine–
human relationship, and land,[4] which has also been examined by a number of scholars including Rolf Rendtorff.[5]

The aim of this chapter is to look at the formation of the Pentateuch
from yet another perspective. The point of focus will not be the themes
that make up the story line of the Penateuch, as important as these are for
interpreting the canonical Pentateuch. Instead, the chapter will explore
how the formation of pentateuchal tradition addresses two fundamental
aspects of Yahwism: the character of divine power and the quality of
divine presence. The present study has sought to outline how the power
of God as both savior and creator is developed in Israel's cultic traditions
of the exodus. But the confession concerning the power of God can never
be separated from the issue of divine presence. The prominent role of the
cultic presence of Yahweh throughout the Pentateuch, the central place

of cosmic mountains as locations for the revelation of law, and indeed, the vision of the land as the necessary culmination of the exodus provide ample illustration of the need for God to be present with Israel in this world.

The power of God to effect change and the presence of God to concretize such change among the people of God and throughout creation are so interdependent that a modification in one necessarily forces changes in the other. Such complementarity underscores how inadequate a study of the exodus tradition alone is for constructing a theology of the Pentateuch, since the power of God exercised in the exodus requires the presence of God at Sinai as its counterpart. Or to state the point within the imagery of the Pentateuch: The warring of God is never far removed from the divine mountain. It is to this relationship that we turn in the final chapter.

THE RELATIONSHIP OF EXODUS AND SINAI IN THE FORMATION OF THE PENTATEUCH

The relationship of the exodus and Sinai traditions has been and continues to be one of the central problems in the study of the formation of the Pentateuch. The reason is that this one problem incorporates a variety of related concerns, including the rise of historiography in ancient Israel and with it a history-of-salvation perspective in theology, the relationship between narrative and law in the history of Israelite religion, the role of deuteronomistic and priestly authors or editors in the formation of the Pentateuch, as well as changing conceptions of the cult. As a consequence, how one accounts for the interrelationship of the exodus and Sinai traditions tends to influence one's view of the tradition-historical development of the Pentateuch.[6] Since the present study on the exodus tradition is a continuation of an earlier work on the Sinai tradition, *God on the Mountain*, we are in a position to reexamine this most central question and, with it, to offer a tentative hypothesis concerning the formation of the Pentateuch.[7] The tentative nature of the proposal arises not only from the complexity of the literature under study, but also from its narrow scope. A firmer hypothesis with regard to the formation of the Pentateuch would require a more broadly based study including the formation of Genesis in relation to Exodus–Deuteronomy and a more focused study of law.

Preexilic Tradition

Preexilic tradition has been conceived in this study as the cultic mythology that supported the various monarchies in ancient Israel. Although there has been occasional reference to Zion tradition, for the most part the study has not sought a more precise historical or social location than this general category. Indeed, the question has been left open as to whether preexilic exodus tradition was rooted in northern or southern tradition. A central question has been to determine the literary character of early exodus tradition, especially with regard to the role of salvation history in the formation of the material.

The absence of the wilderness in preexilic exodus tradition is strong confirmation of Rendtorff's hypothesis that in its earliest formation the Pentateuch consisted of separate and independent units of tradition (*Grösse Einheiten*).[8] Although Rendtorff's hypothesis provided the starting point for *God on the Mountain*, the textual base of that work was too narrow to reach a firm conclusion with regard to the nature of preexilic tradition in the Pentateuch. The study supported the presence of a preexilic account of the Sinai tradition (a Mountain of God tradition), yet the research was not able to confirm whether this Mountain of God tradition was one episode in a larger preexilic epic (a JE source) or an independent tradition, as Rendtorff has advocated.[9] The present study of the exodus tradition provides a broad enough textual base to address the character of preexilic pentateuchal tradition with more precision at least with regard to historiography.

The exodus and the Sinai traditions do not participate in a larger epic at a preexilic stage of development. Instead, each is a self-contained and independent cultic legend. The basis for this conclusion is in the Song of the Sea (Exod 15:1–12, 18) and the liturgy of the Day of Yahweh. The Song of the Sea celebrates salvation as the simultaneous defeat by Yahweh of Pharaoh and kingship, while the liturgy of the exodus shows signs of being a legend for the cult of the monarchy, in which the focus remained on Yahweh's present rule. The exact dating of these traditions will vary according to how early one dates the Song of the Sea, but they are certainly preexilic.

Preexilic Sinai tradition (the Mountain of God) is an account of theophany that celebrates the static and permanent presence of Yahweh in the cult, conceived in the larger framework of cosmic mountain mythology.[10] Although such a conception of divine presence certainly corresponds with Zion tradition, the preexilic Mountain of God tradition may have had its roots in northern tradition.[11] Regardless of the exact provenance of the earliest Sinai tradition, two aspects of this tradition are clear: it is preexilic, and it is not connected to the exodus by means of the wilderness tradition. It is noteworthy that despite their independence from each other, both the exodus and Sinai traditions share a similar confession of Yahweh's permanent rule in the cult. The exodus tradition describes what such rule means from the point of view of power, whereas the Mountain of God tradition explores the spatial implications of such divine rule.

Deuteronomistic Tradition

Deuteronomistic tradents are the architects of the earliest formation of the Pentateuch. They are responsible for interrelating the preexilic exodus and

Sinai traditions so that each becomes an episode in a larger historiography. The primary means for creating an account of salvation history is the introduction of the wilderness as a constitutive component in Israel's initial encounter with God. The presence of wilderness traditions in preexilic prophets, and perhaps also the itinerary list in Numbers 33, would suggest that deuteronomistic tradents are expanding upon tradition that is already in formation rather than creating the material themselves.[12] Just how developed the wilderness tradition is by the time of the deuteronomistic literary activity during the exile would require a more detailed study of these traditions in the Pentateuch and in preexilic prophets.

That some form of the wilderness tradition was in formation would not be surprising, since deuteronomistic tradents tend to build off prior tradition. Such supplementation and radical reformulation was certainly evident in both the exodus and Sinai traditions. In the account of the exodus, deuteronomistic tradents followed the structure of the preexilic account even while they significantly reinterpreted the events by adding the despoiling motif, passover, firstlings, an emphasis on journeying with God, the wilderness, the future promise of land, and so forth. The same interaction with prior tradition is also evident in the Sinai material. Here also deuteronomistic tradents followed the three-part structure of the Mountain of God tradition even while they significantly reinterpreted the earlier account with the introduction of law around the theme of covenant.[13]

What is clear at this juncture is that the interweaving of wilderness stories and larger independent traditions such as exodus and Sinai by means of itinerary notices is the result of deuteronomistic tradents, and it creates historiography in the Pentateuch for the first time as a framework for interpreting the exodus. The present study, therefore, would support the work of Van Seters, who has argued that historiography is not located in the earlier levels of Israelite tradition (as was presupposed in previous source-critical theories), but that it is an innovation of deuteronomistic tradents.[14] Comparison of the catechisms and sea/river events would also support Van Seters' argument that historiography in the Tetrateuch (Genesis through Numbers) is a later supplementation to some form of the deuteronomistic history of the monarchy (Deuteronomy through 2 Kings), since the tradition of the Jordan crossing appears to be influencing that of the Red Sea. Where the present study has departed from Van Seters' work is, first, in the conclusion that historiography within the Tetrateuch is deuteronomistic rather than a postdeuteronomistic Yahwist and, more important, that historiography is directly influenced by cultic tradition and is meant to serve cultic purposes.

The exact boundaries of the deuteronomistic account of salvation history are difficult to determine, especially with regard to the role of creation. Yet it would appear that deuteronomistic tradents created a history that spans Genesis through 2 Kings.[15] Within this construction Deuteronomy must be conceived of as the central book, with the Tetrateuch

(Genesis–Numbers) providing an introduction by recounting Israel's primary experiences of God, and with the history of the monarchy (Joshua–2 Kings) providing a critical recounting of Israel's life in the land based on deuteronomic law.

The deuteronomistic refashioning of both the exodus and Sinai traditions reinforces this structure. In the exodus tradition it was clear that deuteronomistic tradents merged the event at the sea with the wilderness, giving this event a future orientation that required the conquest traditions at the outset of the Book of Joshua for its conclusion. In the Sinai tradition deuteronomistic tradents refashioned a theophany tradition into an occasion for the promulgation of deuteronomic law, whose progression from public (Decalogue) to private (Book of the Covenant) revelation anticipated the more detailed revelation of deuteronomic law at Mount Horeb in the Book of Deuteronomy.[16] In addition, the introduction of law in the wilderness gives the legislation a future orientation which provides a framework for evaluating Joshua–2 Kings, since the law is meant to function in the context of the land. In both the exodus and Sinai traditions, it is the introduction of the wilderness that provides the setting for the deuteronomistic reinterpretation of these events and interrelates previously independent traditions into a larger history.

Priestly Tradition

Priestly narrative is brought into the Pentateuch through a process of supplementation. Whether there existed an independent version of a priestly history prior to its incorporation into the deuteronomistic history is certainly possible, but difficult to determine.[17] The process of supplementation is evident throughout the Sinai material by the way in which priestly tradents interacted with both preexilic and deuteronomistic material. Priestly tradents tended to follow the structure of the preexilic Mountain of God tradition with regard to outline and imagery, even while they incorporated many of the deuteronomistic readings of divine presence (e.g., the metonymic presence of God on the mountain as opposed to the metaphoric presence of God in preexilic tradition, the incorporation of law as a channel of divine revelation, and an emphasis on the mediatorial role of Moses). In the process priestly tradents constructed a theology of the Kabod Yahweh, which functioned as a channel for the revelation of priestly law.[18] The same complex interaction between traditions is evident in the exodus material. Again priestly tradents tended to favor the structure of preexilic tradition (an emphasis on death of Egyptian firstborn and the confrontation at the sea as opposed to the deuteronomistic emphasis on the exodus from Egypt as the basis for interrelating it with a conquest), even while they incorporated many specific features of the deuteronomistic interpretation of salvation (e.g., the wilderness, passover).

The question still remains whether priestly tradents created the

Pentateuch. When the focus is on the Sinai tradition, it appears for all prac-
tical purposes that priestly tradents provided the canonical shaping of this
material, in the sense that they introduced the final significant restructuring of the traditions.[19] In the Sinai tradition, the priestly redaction not only
provided the final significant reshaping of this material, but it also influenced the larger structure of the Pentateuch. The restructuring of the Sinai
tradition included the designation of the mountain as being Mount Sinai
(which dominates in the present form of the text) and the introduction of
the priestly legislation (which includes most of the material from Exodus
35–Numbers 10).

Priestly restructuring had implications beyond the Sinai tradition, since
it provided a springboard for priestly tradents to interact with deuteronomistic tradition so that the central role of Deuteronomy within the deuteronomistic history (Genesis–2 Kings) was displaced with the addition of
priestly law now revealed on a distinct cosmic mountain. Such displacement did not negate deuteronomic law, but created an interrelationship
between two distinct voices, with the result that the revelation of deuteronomic law on Mount Horeb in the Book of Deuteronomy could no longer
be read as the apex in a larger history.[20] In place of the singular focus of
the deuteronomistic history, priestly tradents appeared to fashion the
present form of the Pentateuch, in which there are two law codes (priestly
and deuteronomic law) on two distinct cosmic mountains (Sinai and
Horeb), which were held in a complementary relationship by the one setting of the wilderness.[21]

In the exodus tradition the identification of priestly tradents with the
formation of the Pentateuch is less clear, since priestly supplementation is
evident in the distribution of land at Shiloh in Joshua. Nevertheless, the
overall design of priestly tradents in refashioning the exodus to emphasize
creation instead of conquest still provides the basis for a more modest
conclusion: that the priestly history provides the framework for the Pentateuch. Support for this conclusion from the story of the exodus is the clear
shift of location for the confrontation at the sea. Priestly tradents move this
event from the wilderness back into the land of Egypt. As a consequence,
the defeat of the Egyptian army functions once again as the final event of
salvation from Egypt rather than as the initial event in the wilderness. This
interpretation is punctuated with the Song of Miriam, which also limits its
focus to the event at the sea. The result of the priestly editing is that the
merging of exodus and conquest in deuteronomistic tradition is severed.
This separation lays the groundwork for the literary boundaries of the
Pentateuch, where the story of the exodus (Exodus–Deuteronomy) is also
isolated from the story of the conquest in the Book of Joshua.

A similar tendency of priestly tradents to separate the exodus from the
conquest is evident in the larger structure of the priestly history. It comes
into focus in the account of the death of Moses, which frames the Book of
Deuteronomy. It is announced in Num 27:12–23 and fulfilled in Deut 32:

48-52 and 34.[22] Such framing reinforces the separation between exodus and conquest by punctuating the wilderness wandering with the death of Moses. In addition the emphasis on primeval creation throughout the exodus and wilderness gives Israel's journey from Egypt a new direction, from conquest to rediscovery of an ideal but lost past. In fact, when the Israelites' turning back into Egypt at Pihahiroth in Exod 14:2 is read in the large context of the priestly history, their change of direction continues to the original creation in Genesis 1, rather than to conquest in Joshua 3–5. This change of emphasis from conquest to creation certainly lays the groundwork for the present form of the Pentateuch, even though its formation as Torah is most likely the work of subsequent canonical editors.

The Canonical Pentateuch

The reason for separating the canonical text here as a distinct development in the formation of the Pentateuch is that priestly tradition is a history, while the present form of the Pentateuch is not. It is a Torah of five books. The stark contrast brings into sharp relief the fact that the exodus undergoes one additional and significant restructuring, which cannot be harmonized with priestly tradition, because this final transformation turns salvation history into its opposite, an eternal law.

A distinctive voice with its own social development unique from that of priestly tradition must be posited to account for the canonical Pentateuch. The distinctive voice is identifiable because of the transformation of genre in the Pentateuch from history to law. The social implications of turning history into law requires a separate study in its own right, since such a transformation is no less significant than the original historicizing of the preexilic cult by deuteronomistic tradents. Law already played an important role in both the deuteronomistic and priestly histories. The transformation of genre from salvation history to Torah, however, changes the relationship of law and narrative. In the deuteronomistic and priestly histories law was historicized and, to a certain degree, subordinated to the larger plot structure of salvation history. One suspects that each corpus of law was open to revision as the story progressed. With the formation of Torah, history is subordinated to law, making revision through time a more difficult proposal, since law is given an eternal status.

Momigliano captures the radical character of this final change in genre. He notes that the creation of Torah out of salvation history in the second temple period meant that "[t]he Jews, to whom history meant so much, abandoned the practice of historiography." All the history that mattered was already written.[23] The social and religious implications of this development were significant. New histories were no longer required to discern the ongoing power and presence of God in the wilderness. Instead, canonical editors turned the reader's attention to the two paradigmatic examples from the past. What stands out in this process is how the two histories become law upon which even God now meditates.[24] Such an eternal Torah encourages the community of faith to replace the writing of history with a history of interpretation. This change in perspective already comes into focus in the late development of Torah, when an emerging midrashic form of editing replaces the less constrained restructuring of tradition by deuteronomistic and priestly tradents.[25]

THE RELATIONSHIP OF EXODUS AND SINAI FOR A THEOLOGY OF THE PENTATEUCH

The Central Role of the Wilderness for a Theology of the Pentateuch

The most significant transformation of the exodus and Sinai traditions is the rise of the wilderness. It interrelates the two traditions into a larger story, making each part of a history of salvation. But the importance of the wilderness exceeds its role as a bridge between once independent traditions. It is also a theological symbol in its own right. The incorporation of the wilderness into Israel's cultic tradition critically evaluates previous conceptions of divine power and divine presence. Earlier we noted that, despite the independent nature of the exodus and the Mountain of God traditions in preexilic Israel, both shared a similar confession of Yahweh's permanent rule in the cult. The exodus tradition described what such rule means from the point of view of power. In both the Song of the Sea and in the liturgy of the Day of Yahweh divine power was conceived as being unilateral. Both accounts of salvation explored how Yahweh was able to produce intended effects on Pharaoh, resulting in God's present rule in the cult and possession of the land. The Mountain of God tradition explored the spatial implications of such divine rule by evoking an immanent theology of divine cultic presence. The Mountain of God tradition underscored the belief that God's rule was premanent and unchanging. The preexilic account of the exodus and the Mountain of God tradition combined to support a theology of the kingdom in which the divine warrior's defeat of the enemy signaled salvation for the nation.

The wilderness transforms both the character of divine power and the nature of divine presence in Israel's cultic tradition. In deuteronomistic tradition the introduction of the wilderness turns Yahweh's holy war against Egypt into an incomplete story of salvation history, in which Israel is required to journey with God into an unknown future toward a distant conquest, rather than celebrate God's present rule in the land. Such a transformation of the plot redefines divine power from being unilateral to relational at least with regard to God and Israel, because Israel's active participation throughout the wilderness is now required for the story to reach its conclusion. The Israelites must decide repeatedly to journey with God, and it is only in the process of their making decisions of faith in the wilderness that the story of the exodus is able to evolve into a conquest of the land and thus reach its culmination. The murmuring stories illustrate that Israel is able to stop the story at any point, and as a consequence, divine power shifts from control or dominance over Israel to influence or persuasion. The wilderness also transforms the cultic presence of God in deuteronomistic tradition from conceptions of immanence to a more qualified view in which the divine is mediated into the cult through the name. Thus the introduction of the wilderness not only transforms the character of divine power, but at the same time it gives rise to the Deuteronomic Name Theology that is symbolized by Horeb.

The wilderness remains a central feature of the priestly refashioning of the exodus. Even though the rhetoric of the priestly account of salvation history emphasizes the power of God as creator who controls all events, in the end the priestly tradents too reject a unilateral view of divine power by separating the event of the exodus from their ideal view of creation by means of the wilderness. For priestly tradents the exodus and the wilderness provide a sequence of events in which both the nations and Israel are confronted with the self-manifestation of Yahweh, and such signs provide an inescapable challenge for both parties to recognize divine power. But the content of recognition is determined, in the end, by the human participants in the story of salvation history and not by God. This inability of God to determine the content of knowledge in humans is a relational view of power, since God can undergo change depending on how humans respond. Such a transformation in divine power is carried over into the setting of the wilderness, when the priestly view of divine presence is symbolized by Mount Sinai, where the Kabod Yahweh in the Tabernacle cult replaces the permanent and static presence of God in the temple. In the priestly Kabod Theology Yahweh's mediated cultic presence is neither static nor singular in its function. Instead, it is able to confront all the nations of the world, to wage holy war, to lead the Israelites in the wilderness, to purify them for worship, and to judge them when they fail to recognize the power of God in their midst.

Relational Power as a Hermeneutic for the Canonical Pentateuch

The preceding overview of transmission within pentateuchal tradition is certainly not meant to be exhaustive. Rather the aim has been more suggestive in order to illustrate that the rise of the wilderness is not a subordinate development in the Pentateuch but rather its most significant addition for constructing theology. We have seen how the changing theologies of divine power in the growth of the exodus tradition correspond to changing views of divine presence in the Sinai/Horeb traditions, and how the introduction of the wilderness is the unifying factor in the transformation of both divine power and divine presence. The significance of the wilder-

ness, however, exceeds its important role in the tradition-historical development of the Pentateuch. It also provides an avenue for interpreting the
Pentateuch in its canonical form. The key to this hermeneutic is, once again,
the prominence of relational power that is inherent in the setting of the
wilderness. Thus we end our study where it began by returning to the work
of Loomer concerning the ideology of power.

The dominance of the wilderness in the canonical Pentateuch and its
significance as a symbol of relational power provide a framework for
interrelating deuteronomistic and priestly histories in a theology of Torah.
A central characteristic of the wilderness throughout this study is that it has
tended to complicate the accounts of salvation in the Song of the Sea and in
the preexilic liturgy by introducing ambiguity with regard to the outcome
of events. Whether the goal of salvation was conceived as a conquest of the
land of Canaan or a return to a pristine form of creation, the wilderness en-
sured that each remained a distant hope toward which Israel journeyed.
Although such ideal goals informed Israel's march in the wilderness through
the symbols of Horeb and Sinai, the images of a future divine rule in a new
land or in a new creation were mediated and, at best, only partially clear.

Two important conclusions follow from this, both of which have theological and social implications for constructing biblical theology. First, the
canonical form of Torah would oppose any form of national religion in
which national power and security are merged with divine power and
presence. The absence of land in the Pentateuch as realized promise is a
form of self-criticism within ancient Israelite religion and culture, in which
national religion is rejected. God, country, and people are never merged
in Torah. In place of a national religion secure in its own land, Torah
offers its adherents a more ambiguous journey through the wilderness,
where God is always on the move three days ahead (Num 10:33–34). Power
in this setting is relational, not unilateral, and this tends to blur boundaries
between people and nations.

Second, blurred boundaries are reinforced even further within
Torah itself by the way in which the two competing interpretations of
salvation history have been interwoven in the present form of the Pentateuch. Deuteronomistic and priestly accounts of salvation history differ
significantly in how each views the past event of the exodus and the
future goal of the land. In spite of this difference, they are brought into
a close orbit with each other through the setting of the wilderness, where
they are meant to function as models for living the life of faith in the
present time. Their separate ideals of the future ensure that neither is
merged into the other in the setting of the wilderness, and thus their
relationship is not characterized by unilateral power. The distinct histories are not harmonized through focusing on one or the other, but rather
both are brought into a mutual relationship. The result is that each history has "the ability to produce and to undergo an effect."[26] Thus relational power not only characterizes each separate account of salvation

history, it also determines how they function together in the canonical Pentateuch. The result is that neither a focus on creation nor a focus on conquest is allowed to dominate the present text. Instead they complement each other in the setting of the wilderness, where difference, ambiguity, and the necessity of choice are constitutive to the ongoing plot of the story. This complementarity gives rise to a canonical hermeneutic in which the competing visions of the exodus both enrich and critically evaluate each other, thus creating an inescapable relationship between the two. As a result, the point of focus is not on one of the two traditions, but on the relationship itself.

The prominence of relational power in the development of the Pentateuch and in its present construction provides the basis for a contemporary hermeneutic. The challenge for a contemporary theology of the Pentateuch is to mirror as closely as possible the interrelationship of the traditions that results from the present arrangement of the text. The goal cannot be to isolate an original voice or any one subsequent voice at the expense of others, since such a hermeneutic is rooted in a unilateral view of power, the rejection of which is clear from the formation of pentateuchal tradition. Instead, the central role of the wilderness in the canonical Pentateuch demands that a contemporary theology of the exodus also be informed by a relational view of power.

The aim of such a canonical hermeneutic is to embrace both priestly and deuteronomistic interpretations of the exodus. Strength in such a hermeneutic is determined by the degree to which a contemporary theology is able to incorporate the full range of internal relationships that result from the present construction of the text. Such a hermeneutic does not deny difference or preference on the part of the interpreter, but preference cannot inform a unilateral view of power, in which an interpreter selectively uses distinct traditions to defend a particular point of view (be it deuteronomistic, priestly, or some other). Instead, a canonical hermeneutic arising from a relational view of divine power measures strength more self-critically by gauging how much of the rejected traditions can be incorporated into one's interpretative stance.

A biblical hermeneutic rooted in relational power implies change through time, since the interpreter both influences the interrelationship of traditions and is influenced by them. And no matter how one's interpretation may change through time, the social effects of a hermeneutic rooted in relational power will inevitably strive toward three goals. First, the aim of any interpreter will always be to strive for the broadest inclusion of canonized traditions. Second, the quest for inclusion implies that a strong interpretation of the Pentateuch will seek to be ecumenical, since, as Loomer noted at the outset of this study, the other will always be viewed personally and concretely. Finally, self-criticism will remain central to any interpretation because of the ambiguous character of the interrelation of traditions in Torah.

NOTES

1. Noth, *A History of Pentateuchal Traditions*.

2. Gressmann, *Mose und seine Zeit*.

3. Van Seters, *Prologue to History*; and *The Life of Moses*.

4. D. J. A. Clines, *The Theme of the Pentateuch*, JSOT Sup 10 (Sheffield: JSOT Press, 1978).

5. Rendtorff, *Problem des Pentateuch*. See, among others, Boorer, *The Promise of the Land as Oath*.

6. The work of Wellhausen (*Die Composition*, and *Prolegomena*), von Rad ("The Form-Critical Problem of the Hexateuch"), and Noth (*A History of Pentateuchal Traditions*) provides ample illustration. The late insertion of the more legalistic Sinai tradition into a preexilic Yahwist source consisting of only narrative was a fundamental hypothesis in Wellhausen's overall source-critical solution to the formation of the Pentateuch. The tradition-historical synthesis of von Rad and Noth, too, rested on a theory of the relationship between the exodus and Sinai traditions. Each tradition (or theme) had a long and independent development that could be traced through preliterary stages until they were first combined by the Yahwist. Noth focused on the preliterary development of the exodus tradition, whereas von Rad emphasized the literary creativity of the Yahwist in combining the two traditions.

7. Dozeman, *God on the Mountain*.

8. Rendtorff, *Problem des Pentateuch*; and "The 'Yahwist' as Theologian? The Dilemma of Pentateuchal Criticism," *JSOT* 3 (1977): 2–9; "The Future of Pentateuchal Criticism," *Hen* 6 (1984): 1–14. Our study would not support the hypothesis that individual complexes of tradition (like the exodus and Sinai material) undergo extended internal revision prior to their incorporation into an account of salvation history.

9. Dozeman, *God on the Mountain*, chap. 2.

10. Dozeman, *God on the Mountain*, chap. 2.

11. For recent arguments in favor of a northern origin for the predeuteronomistic form of the Sinai tradition see B. Renaud, *La Théophanie du Sinaï: Ex 19–24: Exégèse et Théologie,* CahRB 30 (Paris: J. Gabalda, 1991).

12. See here especially the wilderness tradition in Amos and Hosea.

13. Dozeman, *God on the Mountain*, chap. 3.

14. Van Seters, *In Search of History*.

15. Such a hypothesis requires a thorough study of Genesis in relation to Exodus–Deuteronomy, which is lacking in the present work. Our hypothesis, however, is certainly not innovative. A number of scholars advocate an extended deuteronomistic history from Genesis through 2 Kings even though the methodological perspective is often very different. Compare Freedman, Zenger, Weimar, Vermeylen, Mayes, Rendtorff, Blenkinsopp. Nevertheless, there is debate concerning the historical and literary process of how such a history was formed. For example, a distinction between deuteronomistic tradition in the Tetrateuch as compared to Deuteronomy or the DtrG has been advocated in recent research by Van Seters, *Abraham in History and Tradition*; and *In Search of History*; H. H. Schmid, *Der sogenannte Jahwist*; Rose, *Deuteronomist und Jahwist*; and "Empoigner le pentateuque par sa fin!" 129–147; H.-C. Schmitt, "Redaktion des Pentateuch im Geiste der Prophetie," 170–189; and Blum, *Studien*.

16. Dozeman, *God on the Mountain*, chap. 3.

17. See especially the discussion by Blum, *Studien*, 229–285.

18. Dozeman, *God on the Mountain*, chap. 4.

19. There is certainly postpriestly editing within the Sinai tradition, but not of the systematic nature that is evident in deuteronomistic or priestly tradition. One suspects that after priestly tradition, editing within specific traditions becomes more midrashic in character, seeking to clarify points of ambiguity or stating explicitly what is already implicit in the text.

20. For a discussion of displacement see Dozeman, *God on the Mountain*, chap. 5. Note also a similar discussion by Rose ("Empoigner le pentateuque par sa fin!" 133) with regard to a late Yahwist.

21. Dozeman, *God on the Mountain*, chap. 5.

22. See Noth, *History of Pentateuchal Traditions*; and more recently Rose, "Empoigner le pentateuque par sa fin!" 134–147.

23. Momigliano, *The Classical Foundations of Modern Historiography*, 20.

24. See Momigliano (*The Classical Foundations of Modern Historiography*, 23), who quotes 'Abod. Zar 3.b, "God himself sits and studies the Torah."

25. See Fishbane, *Biblical Interpretation in Ancient Israel*.

26. Loomer, "Two Kinds of Power," 20.

Bibliography

Ackroyd, P. R. *Exile and Restoration: A Study of Hebrew Thought of the Sixth Century B.C.* OTL. Philadelphia: Westminster, 1968.

Ahlström, G. W. *The History of Ancient Palestine.* Minneapolis: Fortress Press, 1993.

Albright, W. F. "The Earliest Form of Hebrew Verse." *JPOS* 2 (1922): 69-86.

———. "A Catalogue of Early Hebrew Lyric Poems." *HUCA* 23 (1950-1951): 14-24.

———. *Yahweh and the Gods of Canaan: A Historical Analysis of Two Contrasting Faiths.* The Jordan Lectures 1965. Winona Lake: Eisenbrauns, 1968.

Alter, R. *The Art of Biblical Poetry.* New York: Basic Books, 1985.

Anderson, B. W. "The Song of Miriam Poetically and Theologically Considered." In *Directions in Biblical Hebrew Poetry,* edited by E. R. Follis, pp. 285-296. JSOTSup 40. Sheffield: Sheffield Press, 1987.

Auffret, P. Essai sur la structure littéraire d'Ex 14." *Est Bib* 41 (1983): 53-82.

———. "Remarks on J. Magonet's Interpretation of Exodus 6.2-8."*JSOT* 27 (1983): 69-71.

Auld, A. G. *Joshua, Moses and the Land: Tetrateuch-Pentateuch-Hexateuch in a Generation Since 1938.* Edinburgh: T & T Clark, 1980.

Aurelius, E. *Der Fürbitter Israels: Eine Studie zum Mosebild im Alten Testament.* ConBOT 27. Lund: Almqvist & Wiksell, 1988.

Barré, M. L. "My Strength and My Song in Exod 15:2." *CBQ* 54 (1992): 623-637.

Barth, Chr. "Zur Bedeutung der Wüstentradition." In *Congress Volume: Genève 1965*, edited by G. W. Anderson et al, pp. 14-23. VTSup 15. Leiden: E. J. Brill, 1966.

Batto, B. F. "The Reed Sea: Requiescat in Pace." *JBL* 102 (1983): 27-35.

———. *Slaying the Dragon: Mythmaking in the Biblical Tradition.* Louisville: Westminster/John Knox, 1992.

Beer, G. *Exodus.* HAT 3. Tübingen: J. C. B. Mohr (Paul Siebeck), 1939.

Begrich, J. "Das priesterliche Heilsorakel." *ZAW* 52 (1934): 81-92.

Berge, K. *Die Zeit des Jahwisten: Ein Beitrag zur Datierung jahwistischer Vätertexte.* BZAW 186. Berlin: de Gruyter, 1990.

Blenkinsopp, J. "The Structure of P." *CBQ* 38 (1976): 275-292.

————. *A History of Prophecy in Israel: From the Settlement in the Land to the Hellenistic Period.* Philadelphia: Westminster, 1983.

————. *The Pentateuch: An Introduction to the First Five Books of the Bible.* The Anchor Bible Reference Library. New York: Doubleday, 1992.

Blum, E. *Studien zur Komposition des Pentateuch.* BZAW 189. Berlin: de Gruyter, 1990.

Boling, R. G., and G. E. Wright. *Joshua.* AB 6. New York: Doubleday, 1982.

Boorer, S. *The Promise of the Land as Oath: A Key to the Formation of the Pentateuch.* BZAW 205. Berlin: de Gruyter, 1992.

Boyce, R. N. *The Cry to God in the Old Testament.* SBLDS 103. Atlanta: Scholars Press, 1988.

Braulik, G. *Die Mittel Deuteronomischer Rhetorik—erhoben aus Deuteronomium 4,1-40.* AnBib 40. Rome: Pontifical Biblical Institute, 1978.

————. *Studien zur Theologie des Deuteronomiums.* Stuttgarter Biblische Aufsatzbände Altes Testament 2. Stuttgart: Katholisches Bibelwerk, 1988.

Brekelmans, Chr. "Die sogenannten deuteronomischen Elemente in Gen.-Num.: Ein Beitrag zur Vorgeschichte des Deuteronomiums." In *Congress Volume: Genève 1965,* edited by G. W. Anderson, pp. 89-96. VTSup 15. Leiden: E. J. Brill, 1966.

Brenner, M. L. *The Song of the Sea: Ex 15:1-21.* BZAW 195. Berlin: de Gruyter, 1991.

Bright, J. *A History of Israel.* 3d ed. Philadelphia: Westminster, 1981.

Brueggemann, W. "The Kerygma of the Priestly Writers." In *The Vitality of Old Testament Traditions,* edited by W. Brueggemann, pp. 101-113. Atlanta: John Knox, 1976.

————. "A Response to 'The Song of Miriam' by Bernhard Anderson." In *Directions in Biblical Hebrew Poetry,* edited by E. R. Follis, pp. 297-302. JSOTSup 40. Sheffield: Sheffield Press, 1987.

Buber, M. *Kingship of God.* 3d. ed. New York: Harper & Row, 1967.

Budde, K. "Das nomadische Ideal im Alten Testament." *Preussische Jahrbücher* 88 (1895): 57-79.

Buis, P. "Les conflits entre Moïse et Israël dans Exode et Nombres." *VT* 28 (1978): 257-270.

Burns, R. J. "Red Sea or Reed Sea: How the Mistake Was Made and What *yam sûp* Really Means." *BAR* 10 (1984): 57-63.

————. *Has the Lord Indeed Spoken Only Through Moses? A Study of the Biblical Portrait of Miriam.* SBLDS 84. Atlanta: Scholars Press, 1987.

Butler, T. C. "'The Song of the Sea': Exodus 15:1-18: A Study in the Exegesis of Hebrew Poetry." Ph.D. diss. Vanderbilt University, 1971.

————. *Joshua.* WBC 7. Waco: Word Publishing, 1983.

Caloz, M. "Exode, XIII, 3-16 et son rapport au Deutéronome." *RB* 75 (1968): 5-62.

Case-Winters, A. *God's Power: Traditional Understandings and Contemporary Challenges.* Louisville: Westminster/John Knox, 1990.

Cassuto, U. *A Commentary on the Book of Exodus.* Translated by I. Abrahams. Jerusalem: Magnes Press, 1967.

Cathcart, K. J. "The Day of Yahweh." In *The Anchor Bible Dictionary,* edited by D. N. Freedman, pp. 84-85. Vol. 2. New York: Doubleday, 1992.

Cazelles, H. *Autour de l'Exode.* Sources Biblique. Paris: J. Gabalda, 1987.

Černý, P. L. *The Day of Yahweh and Some Relevant Problems.* Facultas Philosophica Universitatis Carolinae Pragensis 53. Prague: Nakladem Filosofické Fakuty University Karlovy, 1948.

Childs, B. S. "Deuteronomic Formulae of the Exodus Traditions." In *Hebräische Wortforschung: Festschrift für W. Baumgartner*, edited by G. W. Anderson et al., pp. 30-39. VTSup 16. Leiden: E. J. Brill, 1967.

———. "A Traditio-Historical Study of the Reed Sea Tradition." *VT* 20 (1970): 406-418.

———. *The Book of Exodus: A Critical Theological Commentary*. OTL. Philadelphia: Westminster, 1974.

Clifford, R. J. "The Tent of El and the Israelite Tent of Meeting." *CBQ* 33 (1971): 221-227.

———. "Cosmogonies in the Ugaritic Texts and in the Bible." *Or* 53 (1984): 183-201.

Clines, D. J. A. *The Theme of the Pentateuch*. JSOTSup 10. Sheffield: JSOT Press, 1978.

Coats, G. W. "The Traditio-Historical Character of the Reed Sea Motif." *VT* 17 (1967): 253-265.

———. *The Murmuring Motif in the Wilderness Traditions of the Old Testament: Rebellion in the Wilderness*. Nashville: Abingdon, 1968.

———. "Despoiling the Egyptians." *VT* 18 (1968): 450-457.

———. "The Song of the Sea." *CBQ* 31 (1969): 1-17.

———. "The Wilderness Itinerary." *CBQ* 34 (1972): 135-152.

———. "A Structural Transition in Exodus." *VT* 22 (1972): 129-142.

———. "An Exposition for the Wilderness Tradition." *VT* 22 (1972): 288-295.

———. "Conquest Traditions in the Wilderness Theme." *JBL* 95 (1976): 177-190.

———. "An Exposition for the Conquest Theme." *CBQ* 47 (1985): 47-54.

Cohn, R. L. *The Shape of Sacred Space: Four Biblical Studies*. AAR Studies in Religion 23. Missoula: Scholars Press, 1981.

Conrad, E. W. *Fear Not Warrior: A Study of "al tîra" Pericopes in the Hebrew Scriptures*. BJS 75. Chico: Scholars Press, 1985.

Cooper, A., and B. R. Goldstein. "The Festivals of Israel and Judah and the Literary History of the Pentateuch." *JAOS* 110 (1990): 19-31.

Coote, R. B., and D. R. Ord. *In the Beginning: Creation and the Priestly History*. Minneapolis: Fortress Press, 1991.

Cortese, E. *Josua 13-21: Ein priesterschriftlicher Abschnitt im deuteronomistischen Geschichtswerk*. OBO 94. Göttingen: Vandenhoeck & Ruprecht, 1990.

Craige, P. C. "The Poetry of Ugarit and Israel." *TynBul* 22 (1971): 3-31.

———. *The Problem of War in the Old Testament*. Grand Rapids: Eerdmans, 1978.

Croatto, J. S. *Exodus: A Hermeneutics of Freedom*. Translated by S. Attanasio. Maryknoll: Orbis Books, 1978.

Cross, F. M. *Canaanite Myth and Hebrew Epic: Essays in the History of the Religion of Israel*. Cambridge: Harvard University Press, 1973.

Cross, F. M., and D. N. Freedman. "The Song of Miriam." *JNES* 14 (1955): 237-250.

———. *Studies in Ancient Yahwistic Poetry*. SBLDS 21. Missoula: Scholars Press, 1975.

Crüsemann, F. *Studien zur Formgeschichte von Hymnus und Danklied in Israel*. WMANT 32. Neukirchen-Vluyn: Neukirchener, 1969.

Dahood, M. "Exodus 15,2 'anwehu and Ugaritic snwt." *Bib* 59 (1978): 260-261.

Daube, D. *The Exodus Pattern in the Bible*. All Souls Studies 2. London: Faber & Faber. 1963.

Davies, G. I. "The Wilderness Itineraries: A Comparative Study." *TynBul* 25 (1974): 46-81.

———. *The Way of the Wilderness. A Geographical Study of the Wilderness Itineraries in the Old Testament*. MSSOTS 5. Cambridge: University Press, 1979.

———. "The Wilderness Itineraries and the Composition of the Pentateuch." *VT* 33 (1983): 1-13.

———. "The Wilderness Itineraries and Recent Archaeological Research." In *Studies in the Pentateuch*, edited by J. A. Emerton, pp. 161-175. VTSup 41. Leiden: E. J. Brill, 1990.

Day, J. *God's Conflict with the Dragon and the Sea: Echoes of a Canaanite Myth in the Old Testament*. University of Cambridge Oriental Studies 35. Cambridge: Cambridge University Press, 1985.

de Moor, J. C. *The Seasonal Pattern in the Ugaritic Myth of Ba'lu*. AOAT 16. Neukirchen: Kevelaer/Neukirchen, 1971.

———. *New Year with Canaanites and Israelites*. 2 vols. Kampen: J. H. Kok, 1972.

———. *The Rise of Yahwism: The Roots of Israelite Monotheism*. BETL 41. Leuven: University Press, 1990.

DeVries, S. J. "The Origin of the Murmuring Tradition." *JBL* 87 (1968): 51-58.

———. "Temporal Terms as Structural Elements in Holy-War Tradition." *VT* 25 (1975): 80-105.

Dion, P. E. "The 'Fear Not' Formula and Holy War." *CBQ* 32 (1970): 565-570.

Douglas, M. *Purity and Danger: An Analysis of the Concepts of Pollution and Taboo*. London: Routledge & Kegan Paul, 1966.

Dozeman, T. B. *God on the Mountain: A Study of Redaction, Theology and Canon in Exodus 19-24*. SBLMS 37. Atlanta: Scholars Press, 1989.

———. "Horeb/Sinai and the Rise of Law in the Wilderness Tradition." *SBLASP* 28 (1989): 282-290.

———. "Spatial Form in Exod 19:1-8a and in the Larger Sinai Narrative." *Semeia* 46 (1989): 87-101

———. "The Institutional Setting of the Late Formation of the Pentateuch in the Work of John Van Seters." *SBLASP* 30 (1991): 253-264.

Driver, G. R. *Canaanite Myths and Legends*. 2d ed. Edited by J. C. L. Gibson. Edinburgh: T & T Clark, 1977.

Durham, J. I. *Exodus*. WBC 3. Waco: Word Books, 1987.

Dus, J. "Die Analyse zweier Ladeerzählungen des Josuabuches (Jos 3-4 und 6)." *ZAW* 72 (1960): 107-134.

Eakin, F. E. "The Reed Sea and Baalism." *JBL* 86 (1967): 378-384.

———. "The Plagues and the Crossing of the Sea." *RExp* 74 (1977): 473-482.

Eaton, J. H. *Kingship and the Psalms*. 2d ed. The Bible Seminar. Sheffield: JSOT Press, 1986.

Elliger, K. "Sinn und Ursprung der priesterlichen Geschichtserzählung." *ZTK* 49 (1952): 121-143.

Emerton, J. A. "The Priestly Writer in Genesis." *JTS* 39 (1988): 381-400.

Engnell, I. *A Rigid Scrutiny: Critical Essays on the Old Testament*. Translated by J. T. Willis. Nashville: Vanderbilt University Press, 1969.

Eslinger, L. "Freedom or Knowledge? Perspective and Purpose in the Exodus Narrative (Exodus 1-15)." *JSOT* 52 (1991): 43-60.

Eves, T. "The Role of Passover in the Book of Chronicles: A Study of 2 Chronicles 30 and 35." Ph.D. diss., Annenberg Research Institute, 1992.

Fabry, H.-J. "Spuren des Pentateuchredaktors in Jos 4,21ff: Anmerkungen zur Deuteronomismus-Rezeption." In *Das Deuteronomium: Entstehung, Gestalt und Botschaft*, edited by N. Lohfink, pp. 351-356. BETL 68. Leuven: Uitgeverij Peeters, 1985.

Fishbane, M. *Biblical Interpretation in Ancient Israel*. Oxford: Clarendon Press, 1985.

Flight, J. W. "The Nomadic Idea and Ideal in the Old Testament." *JBL* 42 (1923): 158-226.

Fohrer, G. *Überlieferung und Geschichte des Exodus: Eine Analyse von Ex 1-15*. BZAW 91. Berlin: A. Töpelmann, 1964.

Foresti, F. "Composizione e redazione deuteronomistica in Ex 15,1-18." *Lateranum* 48 (1982): 41-69.

Forsyth, N. *The Old Enemy: Satan and the Combat Myth*. Princeton: Princeton University Press, 1987.

Freedman, D. N.. "Pentateuch." In *IDB*, edited by G. A. Buttrick, pp. 711-727. Volume 3. Nashville: Abingdon, 1962.

———. "Canon of the OT," In *IDBSup*, edited by K. Crim, pp. 130-136. Nashville: Abongdon, 1976.

———. "Temple Without Hands." In *Temples and High Places: Proceedings of the Colloquium in Honor of the Centennial of Hebrew Union College-Jewish Institute of Religion*, pp. 21-30. Jerusalem: Nelson Glueck School of Biblical Archaeology, 1977.

———. "Strophe and Meter in Exodus 15." In *Potter, Poetry, and Prophecy: Studies in Early Hebrew Poetry*. Winona Lake: Eisenbrauns, 1980.

———. *The Unity of the Hebrew Bible*. Ann Arbor: University of Michigan Press, 1991.

———, and J. R. Lundbom. "חָנַן." In *TDOT VI*, edited by G. J. Botterweck and H. Ringgren, pp. 22-36. Grand Rapids: Eerdmans, 1986.

Fretheim, T. E. *Exodus*. Interpretation. Louisville: John Knox, 1991.

———. "The Plagues as Ecological Signs of Historical Disaster." *JBL* 110 (1991): 385-396.

Fritz, V. *Israel in der Wüste: Traditionsgeschichtliche Untersuchung der Wüstenüberlieferung des Jahwisten*. Marburger Theologische Studien 7. Marburg: N. G. Elwert Verlag, 1970.

———. "Das Geschichtsverständnis der Priesterschrift," *ZTK* 84 (1987): 426-439.

Fuhs, H. F. "יָרֵא." In *TDOT VI*, edited by G. J. Botterweck and H. Ringgren, pp. 290-315. Grand Rapids: Eerdmans, 1990.

Fuss, W. *Die deuteronomistische Pentateuchredaktion in Exodus 3-17*. BZAW 126. Berlin: de Gruyter, 1972.

Gaster, T. H. *Thespis: Ritual, Myth, and Drama in the Ancient Near East*. 2d ed. The Norton Library. New York: Norton, 1953.

———. *Myth, Legend, and Custom in the Old Testament: A Comparative Study with Chapters from Sir James G. Frazer's Folklore in the Old Testament*. New York: Harper & Row, 1969.

Gnuse, R. *"Heilsgeschichte" as a Model for Biblical Theology: The Debate Concerning the Uniqueness and Significance of Israel's Worldview*. College Theology Society Studies in Religion 4. Lanham: University Press of America, 1988.

Goldin, J. *The Song of the Sea*. New Haven: University Press, 1971.

Good, E. M. "Exodus XV 2." *VT* 20 (1970): 358-359.

————. "The Just War in Ancient Isael." *JBL* 104 (1985): 385–400.

Görg, M. "Mirjam—ein weiterer Versuch." *BZ* 23 (1979): 285–289.

Gorman, F. H. Jr. *The Ideology of Ritual: Space, Time and Status in the Priestly Theology*. JSOTSup 91. Sheffield: Sheffield Press, 1990.

Gottwald, N. K. *The Tribes of Yahweh. A Sociology of the Religion of Liberated Israel, 1250–1050 B.C.E.* Philadelphia: Fortress Press, 1979.

Gray, G. B. *Numbers*. ICC. Edinburgh: T & T Clark, 1903.

Gray, J. *Joshua, Judges and Ruth*. NCB. London: Nelson & Sons, 1967.

————. "The Day of Yahweh in Cultic Experience and Eschatological Prospect." *SEÅ* 39 (1974): 5–37.

————. *The Biblical Doctrine of the Reign of God*. Edinburgh: T & T Clark, 1979.

Greenberg, M. *Understanding the Exodus*. The Melton Research Center Series 2. New York: Behrman House, 1969.

————. "The Redaction of the Plague Narrative in Exodus." In *Near Eastern Studies in Honor of W. F. Albright*, edited by H. Goedicke, pp. 243–252. Baltimore: Johns Hopkins University Press, 1971.

Grelot, P. "Etudes sur le 'Papyrus Pascal' d'Eléphantine." *VT* 4 (1954): 349–384.

————. "Sur le "Papyrus Pascal" d'Eléphantine." In *Mélanges bibliques et orientaux en l'honneur de M. Henri Cazelles*, edited by A. Caquot and M. Delcor, pp. 163–172. AOAT 212. Neukirchen-Vluyn: Neukirchener, 1981.

Gressmann, H. *Mose und seine Zeit: Ein Kommentar zu den Mose-Sagen*. FRLANT 1. Göttingen: Vandenhoeck & Ruprecht, 1913.

Gross, W. "Der Glaube an Mose nach Exodus (4.14.19). In *Wort-Gebot-Glaube: Beiträge zur Theologie des Alten Testaments. Festschrift für W. Eichrodt*, pp. 57–65. ATANT 59. Zürich: Zwingli, 1970.

————. "Die Herausführungsformel: Zum Verhältnis von Formel und Syntax." *ZAW* 86 (1974): 425–453.

Gunn, D. M. "The 'Hardening of Pharaoh's Heart': Plot, Character and Theology in Exodus 1–14." In *Art and Meaning: Rhetoric in Biblical Literature*, edited by D. J. A. Clines, D. M. Gunn, and A. Hauser, pp. 72–96. JSOTSup 19. Sheffied: Sheffield Press, 1982.

Haag, H. "Das 'Buch des Bundes' (Ex 24,7)." In *Das Buch des Bundes: Aufsätze zur Bibel und zu ihrer Welt*, edited by B. Lang, pp. 226–233. Düsseldorf: Patmos, 1980.

Halbe, J. "Passa-Massot im deuteronomischen Festkalender: Komposition, Entstehung und Programm von Dtn 16, 1–8." *ZAW* 87 (1975): 147–168.

————. "Erwägungen zur Ursprung und Wesen des Massotfestes." *ZAW* 87 (1975): 324–346.

Halpern, B. *The Constitution of the Monarchy in Israel*. HSM 25. Chico: Scholars Press, 1981.

Hanson, P. D. "War and Peace in the Hebrew Bible." *Int* 38 (1984): 341–362.

Haran, M. "The Passover Sacrifice." *Studies in the Religion of Ancient Israel*. VTSup 23. Leiden: E. J. Brill, 1972, 86–116.

————. "The Exodus." In *IDBSup*, edited by K. Crim, pp. 304–310. Nashville: Abingdon, 1976.

————. *Temples and Temple-Service in Ancient Israel: An Inquiry into the Character of Cult Phenomena and the Historical Setting of the Priestly School*. Oxford: Clarendon Press, 1978.

———. "Behind the Scenes of History: Determining the Date of the Priestly Source." *JBL* 100 (1981): 321-333.

Hasel, G. "צעק/זעק." In *TDOT IV*, edited by G. J. Botterweck and H. Ringgren, pp. 112-122. Grand Rapids: Eerdmans, 1980.

Hauser, A. J. "Two Songs of Victory: A Comparison of Exodus 15 and Judges 5." In *Directions in Biblical Hebrew Poetry,* edited by E. R. Follis, pp. 265-284. JSOTSup 40. Sheffield: Sheffield Press, 1987.

Herzberg, H. W. *Die Bücher Josua, Richter, Ruth*. ATD 9. Göttingen: Vandenhoeck & Ruprecht, 1959.

Hesse, F. *Das Verstockungsproblem im Alten Testament*. BZAW 74. Berlin: A. Töpelmann, 1955.

Hiers, R. H. "Day of Judgment." In *The Anchor Bible Dictionary*, edited by D. N. Freedman, pp. 79-82. Vol. 2. New York: Doubleday, 1992.

———. "Day of the Lord." In *The Anchor Bible Dictionary*, edited by D. N. Freedman, pp. 82-83. Vol. 2. New York: Doubleday, 1992.

Hoffman, Y. "The Day of the Lord as a Concept and a Term in the Prophetic Literature." *ZAW* 93 (1981): 37-50.

Hoffmeier, J. K. "The Arm of God Versus the Arm of Pharaoh in the Exodus Narratives." *Bib* 67 (1986): 378-387.

Horst, F. "Zwei Begriffe für Eigentum (Besitz)." In *Verbannung und Heimkehr: Festschrift für Wilhelm Rudolph*, edited by A. Koschke, pp. 141-156. Tübingen: J. C. B. Mohr (Paul Siebeck), 1961.

Hosch, H. "Exodus 12:41. A Translational Problem." *HS* 24 (1983): 11-15.

Houten, C. van. *The Alien in Israelite Law*. JSOTSup 107. Sheffield: JSOT Press, 1991.

Houtman, C. *Der Pentateuch: Die Geschichte seiner Erforschung neben einer Auswertung*. Biblical Exegesis and Theology 9. Kampen: Kok Pharos Publishing, 1994.

Howell, M. "Exodus 15,1b-18: A Poetic Analysis." *ETL* 65 (1989): 5-42.

Huddlestun, J. R. "Red Sea." In *The Anchor Bible Dictionary*, edited by D. N. Freedman, pp. 633-642. Vol. 5. New York: Doubleday, 1992.

Hughes, J. *Secrets of the Times: Myth and History in Biblical Chronology*. JSOTSup 66. Sheffield: Sheffield, 1990.

Hulst, A. R. "Der Jordan in den Alttestamentlichen Überlieferungen." *OTS* 14 (1965): 162-188.

Humbert, P. "Dieu fait sortir: Hiphil de *yāṣā'* avec Dieu comme sujet." *TZ* 18 (1962): 357-361, 433-436.

Hurvitz, A. *A Linguistic Study of the Relationship between the Priestly Source and the Book of Ezekiel: A New Approach to an Old Problem*. CahRB 20. Paris: J. Gabalda, 1982.

Hyatt, J. P. *Exodus*. NCB. London: Oliphants, 1971.

Inbody, T. "History of Empirical Theology." In *Empirical Theology: A Handbook*. Edited by R. C. Miller, pp. 11-35. Birmingham: Religious Education Press, 1992.

Isbell, C. "Exodus 1-2 in the Context of Exodus 1-14: Story Lines and Key Words." In *Art and Meaning: Rhetoric in Biblical Literature*, edited by D. J. A. Clines et al., pp. 37-61. JSOTSup 19. Sheffied: Sheffield Press, 1982.

Jacob, B. *The Second Book of the Bible: Exodus*. Translated by W. Jacob. Hoboken: KTAV, 1992.

Janzen. J. G. "Song of Moses, Song of Miriam: Who Is Seconding Whom?" *CBQ* 54 (1992): 211-220.

Jeffers, A. "The Magical Element in Ancient Israelite Warfare." In *Proceedings of the Irish Biblical Association 13*, edited by K. J. Cathcart, pp. 35-41. Dublin: Columba Press, 1990.

Jenni, E. "'Kommen' im theologischen Sprachgebrauch des Alten Testaments." In *Wort-Gebot-Glaube: Beiträge zur Theologie des Alten Testaments: Festschrift für W. Eichrodt*, pp. 251-261. ATANT 59. Zürich: Zwingli, 1970.

Jeremias, J. *Das Königtum Gottes in den Psalmen: Israels Begegnung mit dem kanaanäischen Mythos in den Jahwe-König-Psalmen*. FRLANT 141. Göttingen: Vandenhoeck & Ruprecht, 1987.

Johnson, A. R. *Sacral Kingship in Ancient Israel*. 2d ed. Cardiff: University of Wales, 1967.

Johnstone, W. "The Exodus as Process." *ExpTim* 91 (1979/80): 358-363.

———. 'The Two Theological Versions of the Passover Pericope in Exodus." In *Text and Pretext: Essays in Honour of Robert Davidson*, edited by R. P. Carroll, pp. 160-178. JSOTSup 138. Sheffield: JSOT, 1992.

Jones, Gw. H. "Holy War or Yahweh War?" *VT* 25 (1975): 642-658.

Kaiser, O. *Die mythische Bedeutung des Meeres in Ägypten, Ugarit und Israel*. 2d ed. BZAW 78. Berlin: A. Töpelmann, 1962.

Kang, S.-M. *Divine War in the Old Testament and in the Ancient Near East*. BZAW 177. Berlin: de Gruyter, 1989.

Kearney, P. "Creation and Liturgy: The P Redaction of Ex 25-40." *ZAW* 89 (1977): 375-387.

Kedar-Kopfstein, B. "זבח." In *TDOT IV*, edited by G. J. Botterweck and H. Ringgren, pp. 201-213. Grand Rapids: Eerdmans, 1980.

Kegler, J. "Zu Komposition und Theologie der Plagenerzählungen." In *Die Hebräische Bibel und ihre zweifache Nachgeschichte: Festschrift für Rolf Rendtorff*, edited by E. Blum et al., pp. 55-74. Neukirchen-Vluyn: Neukirchener, 1990.

Keller, C. A. "Über einige alttestamentliche Heiligtumslegenden II." *ZAW* 68 (1956): 85-97.

Kloos, C. *Yhwh's Combat with the Sea: A Canaanite Tradition in the Religion of Ancient Israel*. Leiden: E. J. Brill, 1986.

Knierim, R. "The Composition of the Pentateuch." SBLASP 24 (1985): 393-415.

Knohl, I. "The Priestly Torah Versus the Holiness School: Sabbath and the Festivals." *HUCA* 58 (1987): 65-117.

Koch, K. "P—Kein Redaktor! Erinnerung an zwei Eckdaten der Quellenscheidung." *VT* 37 (1987): 447-467.

Kohata, F. *Jahwist und Priesterschrift in Exodus 3-14*. BZAW 166. Berlin: de Gruyter, 1986.

———. "Die Endredaktion (Rp) der Meerwundererzählung." *AJBI* 14 (1988): 10-37.

Kotter, W. R. "Gilgal." In *The Anchor Bible Dictionary*, edited by D. N. Freedman, pp. 1022-1024. Vol. 2. New York: Doubleday, 1992.

Krasovec, J. "Unifying Themes in Ex 7,8-11,10." In *Pentateuchal and Deuteronomistic Studies: Papers Read at the XIIIth IOSOT Congress, Leuven 1989*, edited by Chr. Brekelmans and J. Lust, pp. 47-66. BETL 94. Leuven: University Press, 1990.

Kraus, H.-J. "Gilgal: Ein Beitrag zur Kultusgeschichte Israels." *VT* 1 (1951): 181-199.

————. *Worship in Israel: A Cultic History of the Old Testament.* Translated by G. Buswell. Richmond: John Knox Press, 1966.

————. *Psalms.* 2 vols. Translated by H. C. Oswald. Minneapolis: Augsburg, 1988.

Kuhl, C. "Die 'Wiederaufnahme': Ein literarkritisches Princip?" *ZAW* 64 (1952): 1–11.

Kutsch, E. "Erwägungen zur Geschichte der Passafeier und des Massotfestes." *ZTK* 55 (1958): 1–35.

Laaf, P. *Die Pascha-Feier Israels: Eine literarkritische und überlieferungsgeschichtliche Studie.* BBB 36. Bonn: Peter Hanstein, 1970.

Labuschagne, C. J. *The Incomparability of Yahweh in the Old Testament.* Leiden: E. J. Brill, 1966.

————. "The Meaning of *bĕyād rāmā* in the Old Testament." In *Von Kanaan bis Kerala: Festschrift für J. P. M. van der Ploeg,* edited by W. E. Delsman et al., pp. 143–148. AOAT 211. Neukirchen-Vluyn: Neukirchener, 1982.

Lang, B. "זבח." In *TDOT IV,* edited by G. J. Botterweck and H. Ringgren, pp. 8–29. Grand Rapids: Eerdmans, 1980.

Langlamet, F. *Gilgal et le récit de la traversée du Jourdain (Jos. III–IV).* CahRB 11. Paris: J. Gabalda, 1969.

Lauha, A. "Das Schilfmeermotiv im Alten Testament." In *Congress Volume: Bonn 1962,* edited by G. W. Anderson et al., pp. 32–46. VTSup 9. Leiden: E. J. Brill, 1963.

Leibowitz, N. *Studies in Shemot: Part 1.* Translated by A. Newman. Jerusalem: The World Zionist Organization, 1981.

Levenson, J. D. "Exodus and Liberation." *Horizons in Biblical Theology* 13 (1991): 134–174.

————. "Zion Traditions." In *The Anchor Bible Dictionary,* edited by D. N. Freedman, pp. 1098–1102. Vol. 6. New York: Doubleday, 1992.

Levine, B. A. *In the Presence of the Lord.* SJLA 5. Leiden: E. J. Brill, 1974.

————. "Priestly Writers." In *IDBSup,* edited by K. Crim, pp. 683–687. Nashville: Abingdon, 1976.

Lind, M. C. *Yahweh Is a Warrior: The Theology of Warfare in Ancient Israel.* Kitchener: Herald Press, 1980.

Loewenstamm, S. E. "The Lord is my Strength and my Glory." *VT* 19 (1969): 464–470.

————. *The Evolution of the Exodus Tradition.* Perry Foundation for Biblical Research in the Hebrew University. Translated by B. J. Schwartz. Jerusalem: Magnes Press, 1992.

Lohfink, N. *Das Hauptgebot: Eine Untersuchung literarische Einleitungsfragen zu Dtn 5–11.* AnBib 20. Rome: Pontificio Instituto Biblico, 1963.

————. "Das Siegeslied am Schilfmeer." In *Das Siegeslied am Schilfmeer: Christliche Auseinandersetzungen mit dem Alten Testament,* pp. 109–110. Frankfurt: Knecht, 1965.

————. "Die priesterschriftliche Abwertung der Tradition von der Offenbarung des Jahwenamens an Moses." *Bib* 49 (1968): 1–8.

————. "Die Priesterschrift und die Geschichte." In *Congress Volume: Göttingen 1977,* edited by J. A. Emerton et al., pp. 189–225. VTSup 9. Leiden: E. J. Brill, 1978.

————. "Die Schichten des Pentateuch und der Krieg." In *Gewalt und Gewaltlosigkeit im Alten Testament,* edited by N. Lohfink, pp. 51–110. Quaestiones Disputatae 96. Freiburg: Herder, 1983.

————. "'Gewalt' als Thema alttestamentlicher Forschung." In *Gewalt und Gewalt-losigkeit im Alten Testament*, edited by N. Lohfink, pp. 15–50. Quaestiones Disputatae 96. Freiburg: Herder, 1983.

————. "Literaturverzeichnis." In *Gewalt und Gewaltlosigkeit im Alten Testament*, edited by N. Lohfink, pp. 225–247. Quaestiones Disputatae 96. Freiburg: Herder, 1983.

————. *Studien zum Pentateuch*. Stuttgarter Biblische Aufsatzbände 4. Stuttgart: Katholisches Bibelwerk, 1988.

Long, B. O. *The Problem of Etiological Narrative in the Old Testament*. BZAW 108. Berlin: de Gruyter, 1968.

Loomer, B. "Two Kinds of Power." *Criterion* 15 (1976): 12–29.

Loretz, O. "Ugarit-Texte und Israelitische Religionsgeschichte: The Song of the Sea." *UF* 6 (1974): 245–247.

Loza, J. Les catéchèses étiologique dans l'Ancien Testament. *RB* 78 (1971): 481–500.

Luyster, R. "Wind and Water: Cosmogonic Symbolism in the Old Testament." *ZAW* 93 (1981): 1–10.

Magonet, J. "The Rhetoric of God. Exodus 6.2–8." *JSOT* 27 (1983): 56–67.

Maier, J. *Das altisraelitische Ladeheiligtum*. BZAW 93. Berlin: A. Töpelmann, 1965.

Mann, T. W. "The Pillar of Cloud in the Reed Sea Narrative." *JBL* 90 (1971): 15–30.

————. *Divine Presence and Guidance in Israelite Traditions: The Typology of Exaltation*. JHNES. Baltimore: Johns Hopkins University Press, 1977.

Martin-Achard, R. *Essai biblique sur les fêtes d'Israël*. Genève: Labor & Fides, 1974.

Mastin, B. A. "Was the *šališ* the Third Man in the Chariot?" In *Studies in the Historical Books of the Old Testament*, edited by J. A. Emerton, pp. 125–154. VTSup 30. Leiden: E. J. Brill, 1979.

Mayes, A. D. H. *Deuteronomy*. NCB. London: Oliphants, 1979.

————. *The Story of Israel Between Settlement and Exile: A Redactional Study of the Deuteronomistic History*. London: SCM Press, 1983.

McCarter, P. Kyle, Jr. *II Samuel*. AB 9B. New York: Doubleday, 1984.

McCarthy, D. J. "Moses' Dealings with Pharaoh: Exodus 7.8–10.27." *CBQ* 27 (1965): 336–347.

————. "Plagues and the Sea of Reeds: Exodus 5–14." *JBL* 85 (1966): 137–158.

McEvenue, S. E. *The Narrative Style of the Priestly Writer*. AnBib 50. Rome: Biblical Institute, 1971.

McKay, J. W. "The Date of Passover and Its Significance." *ZAW* 84 (1972): 435–447.

————. "Psalms of Vigil." *ZAW* 91 (1979): 229–247.

McKnight, S. *A Light Among the Gentiles: Jewish Missionary Activity in the Second Temple Period*. Minneapolis: Fortress Press, 1991.

Meier. S. A. *Speaking of Speaking: Marking Direct Discourse in the Hebrew Bible*. VTSup 46. Leiden: E. J. Brill, 1992.

Mettinger, T. N. D. *The Dethronement of Sabaoth: Studies in the Shem and Kabod Theologies*. ConBOT 18. Lund: Gleerup, 1982.

Michaeli, F. *Le livre de l'Exode*. CAT 2. Paris: Delachaux et Niestle, 1974.

Michel, D. *Tempora und Satzstellung in den Psalmen*. Abhandlungen zur Evangelischen Theologie 1. Bonn: H. Bouvier & Co., 1960.

Miller, Jr., P. D. *The Divine Warrior in Early Israel*. HSM 5. Cambridge: Harvard University Press, 1973.

Milgrom, J. "Religious Conversion and the Revolt Model for the Formation of Israel." *JBL* 101 (1982): 169–176.

———. *Leviticus 1–16*. AB 3A. New York: Doubleday, 1991.

———. *Numbers. The JPS Torah Commentary*. Philadelphia: Jewish Publication Society, 1990.

Möhlenbrink, K. "Die Landnahmesagen des Buches Josua." *ZAW* 15 (1938): 254–258.

———. "Josua im Pentateuch." *ZAW* 59 (1942–1943): 140–158.

Momigliano, A. *The Classical Foundations of Modern Historiography*. The Sather Classical Lectures 54. Berkeley: University of California Press, 1990.

Moran, W. L. "The End of the Unholy War and the Anti-Exodus." *Bib* 44 (1963): 333–342.

Morgenstern, J. "The Gates of Righteousness." *HUCA* 6 (1929): 1–37.

———. "The Despoiling of the Egyptians." *JBL* 68 (1949): 1–28.

———. *The Fire Upon the Altar*. Leiden: E. J. Brill, 1963.

Mowinckel, S. "Die vermientliche 'Passahlegende' Ex. 1–15 in Bezug auf die Frage: Literarkritik und Traditionskritik." *ST* 5 (1951): 66–88.

———. *The Psalms in Israel's Worship*. 2 vols. Translated by D. R. Ap-Thomas. Nashville: Abindgon, 1962.

———. "Drive and/or Ride in O. T." *VT* 12 (1962): 278–299.

———. *Tetrateuch–Pentateuch–Hexateuch: Die Berichte über die Landnahme in den Drei Altisraelitischen Geschichtswerken*. Berlin: A. Töpelmann, 1964.

Muilenburg, J. The Site of Ancient "Gilgal." *BASOR* 140 (1955): 11–27.

———. "The Form and Structure of the Covenantal Formulations." *VT* 9 (1959): 347–365.

———. "A Liturgy of the Triumphs of Yahweh." In *Studia Biblica et Semitica*, edited by W. C. van Unnik and A. S. van der Woude, pp. 233–251. Wageningen: H. Veenman en Zonen, 1966 = *Hearing and Speaking the Word: Selections from the Works of James Muilenburg*, edited by T. F. Best, pp. 151–169. Scholars Press Homage Series. Chico: Scholars Press, 1984.

Müller, H.-P. "חמם." In *TDOT III*, edited by G. J. Botterweck and H. Ringgren, pp. 419–422. Grand Rapids: Eerdmans, 1978.

Nicholson, E. W. "P as an Originally Independent Source in the Pentateuch." *IBS* 10 (1988): 192–206.

Nicolsky, N. M. Pascha im Kulte des jerusalemischen Tempels." *ZAW* 45 (1927): 171–190, 241–253.

Niditch, S. *War in the Hebrew Bible: A Study in the Ethics of Violence*. Oxford: Oxford University Press, 1993.

Norin, S. I. L. *Er Spaltete das Meer: Die Auszugsüberlieferung in Psalmen und Kult des Alten Israel*. ConBOT 9. Lund: CWK Gleerup, 1977.

Noth, M. *Das Buch Josua*. HAT 7. Tübingen: J. C. B. Mohr "Paul Siebeck", 1938.

———. "Der Wallfahrtsweg zum Sinai." *PJ* 36 (1940): 5–28.

———. *Exodus: A Commentary*. Translated by J. S. Bowden. OTL. Philadelphia: Westminster, 1962.

———. *Numbers*. Translated by J. D. Martin. OTL. Philadelphia: Westminster, 1968.

———. *A History of Pentateuchal Traditions*. Translated by B. W. Anderson. Chico: Scholars Press, 1981.

Ollenburger, B. *Zion, the City of the Great King: A Theological Symbol for the Jerusalem Cult*. JSOTSup 41. Sheffield: JSOT Press, 1987.

———. "Introduction: Gerhard von Rad's Theory of Holy War." In *Holy War in Ancient Israel*, translated and edited by M. J. Dawn, pp. 1–33. Grand Rapids: Eerdmans, 1990.

Otto, E. *Das Mazzotfest in Gilgal*. BWANT 7. Stuttgart: W. Kohlhammer, 1975.

———. "Erwägungen zum überlieferungsgeschichtlichen Ursprung und 'Sitz im Leben' des jahwistischen Plagenzyklus." *VT* 26 (1976): 3–27.

Otto, E. and T. Schramm. *Festival and Joy*. Translated by J. L. Blevins. Biblical Encounters Series. Nashville: Abingdon, 1980.

Parker, S. B. "Exodus XV 2 Again." *VT* 21 (1971): 373–379.

Patrick, D. "Traditio-History of the Reed Sea Account." *VT* 26 (1976): 248–249.

Pedersen, Johs. "Passahfest und Passahlegende." *ZAW* 52 (1934): 161–175.

———. *Israel: Its Life and Culture*. Translated by A. I. Fausbøll. Copenhagen: Dyva & Jeppesen, 1940.

Perlitt, L. *Bundestheologie im Alten Testament*. WMANT 36. Neukirchen-Vluyn: Neukirchener, Verlag, 1969.

Petersen, D. L. *Late Israelite Prophecy: Studies in Deutero-Prophetic Literature and in Chronicles*. SBLMS 23. Missoula: Scholars Press, 1977.

Plastaras, J. *The God of the Exodus: The Theology of the Exodus Narratives*. Milwaukee: Bruce Publishing, 1966.

———. *Creation and Covenant*. Milwaukee: Bruce Publishing, 1968.

Polzin. R. *Moses and the Deuteronomist: A Literary Study of the Deuteronomic History*. Pt. 1. New York: Seabury Press, 1980.

Porten, B., and A. Yardeni. *Textbook of Aramaic Documents from Ancient Egypt*. Vol. 1. Winona Lake: Eisenbrauns, 1986.

Preuss, H. D. "בוא." In *TDOT II*, edited by G. J. Botterweck and H. Ringgren, pp. 20–49. Grand Rapids: Eerdmans, 1975.

———. "יצא." In *TDOT VI*, edited by G. J. Botterweck and H. Ringgren, pp. 20–49. Grand Rapids: Eerdmans, 1990.

———. *Theologie des Alten Testaments*. Bände 1–2. Stuttgart: W. Kohlhammer, 1992.

Pury, A. de, and T. Römer. "Le pentateuque en question: Position du problème et brève histoire de la recherche." In *Le pentateuque en question: Les origines et la composition des cinq premiers livres de la Bible à la lumière des recherches récentes,* edited by A. de Pury, pp. 9–80. Le monde de la Bible. Genève: Labor & Fides, 1989.

Rabenau, K. von. "Die Beiden Erzählungen vom Schilfmeerwunder in Exod. 13,17–14,31." In *Theologische Versuche*, edited by P. Watzel, pp. 9–29. Berlin: Evangelische Verlag, 1966.

Rabinowitz, I. "'*az* Followed by Imperfect Verb-Form in Preterite Contexts: A Redactional Device in Biblical Hebrew." *VT* 34 (1984): 53–62.

Rad, G. von. *Die Priesterschrift im Hexateuch*. Stuttgart: W. Kohlhammer, 1934.

———. "The Origin of the Concept of the Day of Yahweh." *JSS* 4 (1959): 97–108.

———. *Old Testament Theology*. 2 vols. Translated by D. M. G. Stalker. New York: Harper & Row, 1962, 1965.

———. "ἄγγελοζ." In *TDNT 1*, edited by G. Kittel, pp. 76–80. Grand Rapids: Eerdmans, 1964.

———. *Deuteronomy*. Translated by D. Barton. OTL. Philadelphia: Westminster, 1966.

———. "The Form-Critical Problem of the Hexateuch." In *The Problem of the*

Hexateuch and Other Essays, translated by E. W. T. Dicken, pp. 1-78. New York: McGraw-Hill, 1966.

——. "Beobachtungen an der Moseerzählung Exodus 1-14." *EvTh* 31 (1971): 579-588.

——. *Holy War in Ancient Israel*. Translated by M. J. Dawn. Grand Rapids: Eerdmans, 1991.

Reichert, A. "Israel, The Firstborn of God: A Topic of Early Deuteronomic Theology." In *Proceedings of the Sixth World Congress of Jewish Studies*, edited by A. Shinan, pp. 341-349. Volume 1. Jerusalem: World Union of Jewish Studies, 1977.

Renaud, B. *La Théophanie du Sinaï: Ex 19-24: Exégèse et Théologie*. CahRB 30. Paris:J. Gabalda, 1991.

Rendsburg, G. "Late Biblical Hebrew and the Date of P." *JANESCU* 12 (1980): 65-80.

Rendtorff, R. "The Concept of Revelation in Ancient Israel." In *Revelation as History*, edited by W. Pannenberg, translated by D. Granskou, pp. 25-53. New York: Macmillan, 1968.

——. *Das überlieferungsgeschichtliche Problem des Pentateuch*. BZAW 147. Berlin: A. Töpelmann, 1976.

——. "The 'Yahwist' as Theologian? The Dilemma of Pentateuchal Criticism." *JSOT* 3 (1977): 2-9.

——. "Pentateuchal Studies on the Move." *JSOT* 3 (1977): 43-45.

——. "The Future of Pentateuchal Criticism." *HEN* 6 (1984): 1-14.

Richter, W. "Beobachtungen zur theologischen Systembildung in der alttestamentlichen Literatur anhand des 'Kleinen geschichtlichen Credo.'" In *Wahrheit und Verkundigung: Festschrift für M. Schmaus*, edited by L. Scheffczyk, pp. 175-212. Paderborn: Schomigh, 1967.

Robertson, D. A. *Linguistic Evidence in Dating Early Hebrew Poetry*. SBLDS 3. Missoula: Scholars Press, 1972.

Rose, M. *Deuteronomist und Jahwist: Untersuchung zu den Berührungspunkten beider Literaturwerke*. ATANT 67. Zürich: Theologischer Verlag, 1981.

——. "Empoigner le pentateuque par sa fin! L'investitute de Josué et la mort de Moïse." In *Le pentateuque en question: Les origines et la composition des cinq premiers livres de la Bible à la lumière des recherches récentes*, edited by A. de Pury, pp. 129-147. Le monde de la Bible. Genève: Labor & Fides, 1989.

Rost, L. "Weidewechsel und altisraelitischer Festkalender." *ZDPV* 66 (1943): 205-215.

——. "Das kleine geschichtliche Credo." In *Das kleine Credo und andere Studien zum Alten Testament*, pp. 11-25. Heidelberg: Quelle & Meyer, 1965.

Rouillard, H. *La péricope de Balaam (Nombres 22-24): Le prose et les "oracles."* Fondation Singer-Polignac. Paris: J. Gabalda, 1985.

Rowley, H. H. *Worship in Ancient Israel: Its Forms and Meaning*. London: SPCK, 1967.

Rozelaar, M. "The Song of the Sea. Exodus XV, 1b-18." *VT* 2 (1952): 221-228.

Rudolph, W. *Der "Elohist" von Exodus bis Josua*. BZAW 68. Berlin: A. Töpelmann, 1938.

Rupprecht, K. עלה מן הארץ (Ex 1 10 Hos 2 2): "sich des landes bemächtigen"? *ZAW* 82 (1970): 442-447.

Rylaarsdam, J. C. *The Book of Exodus.* In *IB*, edited by G. A. Buttrick, pp. 833–1099. Vol.1. Nashville: Abingdon, 1952.

———. "Passover and Feast of Unleavened Bread." In *IDB*, edited by G. A. Buttrick, pp. 663–668. Vol. 3. Nashville: Abingdon, 1962.

Saebø, M. "Priestertheologie und Priesterschrift: Zur Eigenart der priesterlichen Schicht im Pentateuch. In *Congress Volume Vienna 1981*, edited by J. A. Emerton et al., pp. 357–374. VTSup 32. Leiden: E. J. Brill, 1982.

Sanderson, J. E. "War, Peace, and Justice in the Hebrew Bible: A Representative Bibliography." In *Holy War in Ancient Israel by Gerhard von Rad*, translated and edited by M. J. Dawn, pp. 135–166. Grand Rapids: Eerdmans, 1990.

Sarna, N. *Exploring Exodus: The Heritage of Biblical Israel.* New York: Schocken Books, 1986.

———. *Exodus: The JPS Torah Commentary.* Philadelphia: Jewish Publication Society, 1991.

Sauer, G. "Vom Exoduserleben zur Landnahme." *ZTK* 80 (1983): 26–32.

Sauter G. "'Exodus' and 'Liberation' as Theological Metaphors: A Critical Case-Study of the Use of Allegory and Misunderstood Analogies in Ethics." *SJT* 34 (1981): 481–507.

Sawyer, J. F. A. "ישע." In *TDOT VI*, edited by G. J. Botterweck and H. Ringgren, pp. 441–463. Grand Rapids: Eerdmans, 1990.

Scharbert, J. "Der Sinn der Toledot-Formel in der Priesterschrift." In *Wort-Gebot-Glaube: Beiträge zur Theologie des Alten Testaments. Festschrift für W. Eichrodt*, edited by J. J. Stamm et al., pp. 45–56. ATANT 59. Zürich: Zwingli, 1970.

———. "Das 'Schilfmeerwunder' in den Texten des Alten Testaments." In *Mélanges bibliques et orientaux en l'honneur de M. H. Cazelles*, edited by A. Caquot and M. Delcor, pp. 395–417. AOAT 212. Keukirchen-Vluyn: Neukirchener, 1981.

Schart, A. *Mose und Israel im Konflikt: Eine redaktionsgeschichtliche Studie zu den Wüstenerzählungen.* OBO 98. Göttingen: Vandenhoeck & Ruprecht, 1990.

Schley, D. G. *Shiloh: A Biblical City in Tradition and History.* JSOTSup 63. Sheffield: Sheffield Press, 1989.

Schmid, H. *Mose: Überlieferung und Geschichte.* BZAW 110. Berlin: A Töpelmann, 1968.

Schmid, H. H. *Der sogenannte Jahwist: Beobachtungen und Fragen zur Pentateuchforschung.* Zürich: Theologischer Verlag, 1976.

———. "Auf der Suche nach neuen Perspectiven für die Pentateuchforschung." *SVT* 32 (1981): 375–394.

Schmidt, H. "Das Meerlied. Ex 15, 2–19." *ZAW* 49 (1931): 59–66.

Schmidt, J. M. "Erwägungen zum Verhältnis von Auszugs- und Sinaitradition." *ZAW* 82 (1970): 1–31.

Schmidt, L. *Beobachtungen zu der Plagenerzählung in Exodus VII 14–XI 10.* Studia Biblica 4. Leiden: E. J. Brill, 1990.

Schmidt, W. H. *Exodus, Sinai und Moses: Erwägungen zur Ex 1–19 und 24.* Erträge der Forschung 191. Darmstadt: Wissenschaftliche Buchgesellschaft, 1983.

———. *Exodus.* BKAT II/1. Neukirchen-Vluyn: Neukirchener, 1988.

Schmitt, H. Chr. "'Priesterliches' und 'prophetisches' Geschichtsverständnis in der Meerwundererzählung Ex 13,17–14,31: Beobachtungen zur Endredaktion des

Pentateuch." In *Textgemäss: Aufsätze und Beiträge zur Hermeneutik des Alten Testaments. Festschrift für E. Würthwein*, edited by A. H. J. Gunneweg and O. Kaiser, pp. 139-155. Göttingen: Vandenhoeck & Ruprecht, 1980.

———. "Redaktion des Pentateuch im Geiste der Prophetie." *VT* 32 (1982): 171-189.

Schmitt, R. *Exodus und Passa: Ihr Zusammenhang im Alten Testament*. OBO 7. 2d. ed. Göttingen: Vandenhoeck & Ruprecht, 1982.

Schreiner, J. "Exodus 12:21-23 und das israelitische Pascha." In *Studien zum Pentateuch: Festschrift für W. Kornfeld*, edited by G. Braulik, pp. 69-90. Wien: Herder, 1977.

Schwally, F. *Der heilige Krieg im alten Israel*. Semitische Kriegsaltertümer 1. Leipzig: Deiterich, 1901.

Segal, J. B. *The Hebrew Passover from the Earliest Times to A.D. 70*. London Oriental Series 12. London: Oxford University Press, 1963.

Seitz, G. *Redaktionsgeschichtliche Studien zum Deuteronomium*. BWANT 13. Stuttgart: W. Kohlhammer, 1971.

Ska, J.-L. "La sortie d'Egypte (Ex 7-14) dans le récit sacerdotal (Pg) et la tradition prophétique." *Bib* 60 (1979): 191-215.

———. "Les plaies d'Egypte dans le récit sacerdotal (Pg)." *Bib* 60 (1979): 23-35.

———. "La place d'Ex 6,2-8 dans la narration de l'exode." *ZAW* 94 (1982): 530-548.

———. "Ex xiv contient-il un récit de 'guerre sainte' de style deutéronomistique?" *VT* 33 (1983): 454-467.

———. *Le passage de la mer: Etude de la construction, du style et de la symbolique d'Ex 14, 1-31*. AnBib 109. Rome: Biblical Institute Press, 1986.

———. "Quelques remarques sur Pg et la dernière rédaction du pentateuque," in *Le pentateuque en question: Les origines et la composition des cinq premiers livres de la Bible à la lumière des recherches récentes*, edited by A. de Pury, pp. 95-125. Le monde de la Bible. Genève: Labor & Fides, 1989.

Smend, R. *Yahweh War and Tribal Confederation: Reflections upon Israel's Earliest History*. 2d ed. Translated by M. G. Rogers. Nashville: Abingdon, 1970.

Smith, M. S. "Review of *Solare Elemente in Jahweglauben des Alten Testaments*." *JBL* 106 (1987): 513-515.

———. *The Early History of God: Yahweh and the Other Deities in Ancient Israel*. San Francisco: Harper & Row, 1990.

Snaith, N. H. "יַם־סוּף: The Sea of Reeds: The Red Sea." *VT* 15 (1965): 395-398.

Soggin, J. A. "Kultätiologische Sagen und Katechese im Hexateuch." *VT* 10 (1960): 341-347.

———. "Gilgal, Passah und Landnahme: Eine neue Untersuchung des Kultischen Zusammenhangs der Kap. III-IV des Josuabuches.," In *Volume du Congrès: Genève 1965*, edited by G. W. Anderson et al., pp. 263-277. VTSup 15. Leiden: E. J. Brill, 1966.

———. *Joshua*. Translated by R. A. Wilson. OTL. Philadelphia: Westminster, 1970.

———. "Das Wunder am Meer und in der Wüste (Exodus, cc. 14-15)." In *Mélanges bibliques et orientaux en l'honneur de M. Mathias Delcor*, edited by A. Caquot et al., pp. 379-385. AOAT 215. Neukirchen-Vluyn: Neukirchener, 1985.

Spieckermann, H. *Heilsgegenwart: Eine Theologie der Psalmen*. FRLANT 148. Göttingen: Vandenhoeck & Ruprecht, 1989.

Stähli, H.-P. *Solare Elemente in Jahweglauben des Alten Testaments.* OBO 66. Fribourg: Universitätsverlag, 1985.

Steingrimsson, S. O. *Vom Zeichen zur Geschichte: Eine literar- und formkritische Untersuchung von Ex 6,28-11,10.* ConBOT 14. Lund: GWK Gleerup, 1979.

Stek, J. H. "What Happened to the Chariot Wheels in Exodus 14:25?" *JBL* 105 (1986): 293-294.

Stolz, F. *Jahwes und Israels Kriege: Kriegstheorien und Kriegserfahrungen im Glauben des alten Israels.* ATANT 60. Zürich: Theologische Verlag, 1972.

Strauss, H. "Das Meerlied des Mose: Ein 'Siegeslied' Israels?" *ZAW* 97 (1985): 103-109.

Struppe, U. *Die Herrlichkeit Jahwes in der Priesterschrift: Eine semantische Studie zu kebod YHWH.* ÖBS 9. Klosterneuburg: Österreichisches Katholisches Bibelwerk, 1988.

Talmon, S. "The 'Desert Motif' in the Bible and in Qumran Literature." In *Biblical Motifs: Origins and Transformations,* edited by A. Altmann, pp. 31-63. Philip W. Lown Institute of Advanced Judaic Studies, Brandeis University Studies and Texts 3. Cambridge: Harvard University Press, 1966.

———. "Wilderness." In *IDBSup,* edited by K. Crim, pp. 946-949. Nashville: Abingdon, 1976.

———. *King, Cult and Calendar in Ancient Israel.* Jerusalem: Magnes, 1986.

Tengström, S. *Die Hexateucherzählung: Eine literaturgeschichtliche Studie.* ConBOT 7. Lund: Gleerup, 1976.

———. *Die Toldedotformel und die literarische Struktur der priesterlichen Erweiterungsschicht im Pentateuch.* ConBOT 17. Lund: Gleerup, 1981.

Thompson, T. L. *Early History of the Israelite People: From the Written and Archaeological Sources.* Studies in the History of the Ancient Near East 4. Leiden: E. J. Brill, 1992.

———. "Historiography [Israelite]." In *The Anchor Bible Dictionary,* edited by D. N. Freedman, pp. 206-212. Vol. 3. New York: Doubleday, 1992.

Tournay, R. J. "Recherches sur la chronologie des Psaumes." *RB* 65 (1958): 321-357.

———. *Voir et entrendre Dieu avec les Psaumes ou la liturgie prophétique du second temple à Jérusalem.* CahRB 24. Paris: J. Gabalda, 1988.

Towers, J. R. "The Red Sea." *JNES* 8 (1959): 150-153.

Trible, P. "Subversive Justice: Tracing the Miriamic Traditions." In *Justice and the Holy: Essays in Honor of Walter Harrelson,* edited by D. A. Knight and P. J. Paris, pp. 99-109. Scholars Press Homage Series. Atlanta: Scholars Press, 1989.

Utzschneider, H. *Das Heiligtum und das Gesetz: Studien zur Bedeutung der Sinaitischen Heiligtumstexts (Ex 25-40; Lev 8-9).* OBO 77. Göttingen: Vandenhoeck & Ruprecht, 1988.

VanderKam, J. C. "Calendars: Ancient Israelite and Early Jewish." In *The Anchor Bible Dictionary,* edited by D. N. Freedman, pp. 814-820. Vol. 1. New York: Doubleday, 1992.

Van Der Lingen, A. *Les guerres de Yahvé: L'implication de YHWH dans les guerres d'Israël selon les livres historique de l'Ancien Testament.* Lectio Divina 139. Paris: Les Editions du Cerf, 1990.

Van Seters, J. "Confessional Reformulation in the Exilic Period." *VT* 22 (1972): 448-459.

———. *Abraham in History and Tradition.* New Haven: Yale University Press, 1975.

————. "Recent Studies on the Pentateuch. A Crisis in Methods." *JAOS* 99 (1979): 663-673.

————. *In Search of History: Historiography in the Ancient World and the Origins of Biblical History*. New Haven: Yale University Press, 1983.

————. "The Place of the Jahwist in the History of Passover and Massot." *ZAW* 95 (1983): 167-182.

————. "The Plagues of Egypt. Ancient Tradition or Literary Invention." *ZAW* 98 (1986): 31-39.

————. "Tradition and History: History as National Tradition." In *Histiore et conscience historique*, pp. 63-74. Les civilisations du Proche-Orient Ancien 5. Leuven: Editions Peeters, 1986.

————. "The So-Called Deuteronomistic Redaction of the Pentateuch." In *Congress Volume: Leuven 1989*, edited by J. A. Emerton et al., pp. 58-77. VTSup 43. Leiden: E. J. Brill, 1991.

————. *Prologue to History: The Yahwist as Historian in Genesis*. Louisville: Westminster/John Knox, 1992.

————. *The Life of Moses: The Yahwist as Historian in Exodus-Numbers*. Louisville: Westminster/John Knox Press, 1994.

Vater, A. "A Plague on Both Our Houses: Form and Rhetorical Critical Observations on Exodus 7-11." In *Art and Meaning: Rhetoric in Biblical Literature*, edited by D. J. A. Clines et al., pp. 62-71. JSOTSup 19. Sheffield: Sheffield Press, 1982.

Vaux, R. de. *Ancient Israel*. 2 Vols. New York: McGraw-Hill, 1965.

————. *The Early History of Israel*. Translated by D. Smith. Philadelphia: Westminster, 1978.

Vermeylen, J. "La formation du Pentateuque á la lumière de l'exèse historico-critique." *RTL* 12 (1981): 324-346.

Vervenne, M. "The Protest Motif in the Sea Narrative (Ex 14,11-12): Form and Structure of a Pentateuchal Pattern." *ETL* 63 (1987): 257-271.

————. "The 'P' Tradition in the Pentateuch: Document and/or Redaction? The 'Sea Narrative' (Ex 13,17-14,31) as a Test Case." In *Pentateuchal and Deuteronomistic Studies: Papers Read at the XIIIth IOSOT Congress, Leuven 1989*, edited by Chr. Brekelmans and J. Lust, pp. 67-90. BETL 94. Leuven: University Press, 1990.

Vink, J. G. "The Date and Origin of the Priestly Code in the Old Testament." *OTS* 15 (1969): 1-144.

Vogt, E. "Die Erzählung vom Jordanübergang." *Bib* 46 (1965): 125-148.

Volkwein, B. "Masoretisches 'edut, edwot, 'edot: 'Zeugnis' oder 'Bundesbestimmungen'?" *BZ* 19 (1969): 18-40.

Vriezen, Th. C. "A Reinterpretation of Exodus 3:21-22 and Related Texts, Exod 11:2f., 12:35f., and Ps. 105:37f. (Gen 15:4b)." *Jaarbericht* 23 (1973-1974): 389-401.

Waldman, N. "A Comparative Note on Exodus 15:14-16." *JQR* 66 (1975): 189-192.

Walsh, J. P. M. *The Mighty from Their Thrones: Power in the Biblical Tradition*. OBT 21. Philadelphia: Fortress Press, 1987.

Walsh, J. T. "From Egypt to Moab: A Source Critical Analysis of the Wilderness Itinerary." *CBQ* 39 (1977): 20-33.

Waltke, B. K., and M. O'Connor. *An Introduction to Biblical Hebrew Syntax*. Winona Lake: Eisenbrauns, 1990.

Wambacq, B. N. "Les origines de la Pesah israélite." *Bib* 57 (1976): 206-224, 301-326.

——. "Les Massot," *Bib* 61 (1980): 31-53.

——. "Pesah-Massot." *Bib* 62 (1981): 499-518.

Ward, W. A. "The Semitic Biconsonantal Root SP and the Common Origin of Egyptian ČWP and Hebrew SûP: March(-Plant)." *VT* 24 (1974): 339-349.

Watts, J. D. W. "The Song of the Sea–Ex. XV." *VT* 7 (1957): 371-380.

Watts, J. W. *Psalm and Story: Inset Hymns in Hebrew Narrative.* JSOTSup 139. Sheffield: JSOT Press, 1992.

Weber, Hans-Ruedi. "Power: Some Biblical Perspectives." *The Ecumenical Review* 38 (1986): 265-279.

——. *Power: Focus for a Biblical Theology.* Genève: WCC Publications, 1989.

Weber, M. *Ancient Israel.* Translated by H. H. Gerth and D. Martindale. New York: Macmillan, 1952.

Weimar, P. *Untersuchungen zur priesterschriftlichen Exodusgeschichte.* Forschung zur Bibel 9. Würzburg: Echter Verlag, 1973.

——. "Die Toledot-Formel in der priesterschriftlichen Geschichtsdarstellung." *BZ* 18 (1974): 65-93.

——. *Die Berufung des Mose: Literaturwissenschaftliche Analyse von Exodus 2,23-5,5.* OBO 32. Göttingen: Vandenhoeck & Ruprecht, 1980.

——. "Struktur und Komposition der priesterschriftlichen Geschichtsdarstellung," *BN* 23 (1984): 81-134; and 24 (1984): 138-162.

——. *Die Meerwundererzählung: Eine redaktionskritische Analyse von Ex 13,17-14,31.* Ägypten und Altes Testament 9. Wiesbaden: Otto Harrassowitz, 1985.

Weinfeld, M. *Deuteronomy and the Deuteronomic School.* Oxford: Clarendon Press, 1972.

——. *Deuteronomy 1-11.* AB 5. New York: Doubleday, 1991.

Wellhausen, J. *Die Composition des Hexateuchs und der Historischen Bücher des Alten Testament.* 3d ed. Berlin: Georg Reimer, 1899.

——. *Israelitische und Jüdische Geschichte.* 5th ed. Berlin: Georg Reimer, 1904.

——. *Prolegomena to the History of Ancient Israel.* Translated by Menzies and Black. 1883 reprint. New York: Meridian Books, 1957.

Wenham, G. J. *Genesis 1-15.* WBC. Waco: Word Books, 1987.

Westermann, C. *Praise and Lament in the Psalms.* 2d ed. Translated by K. R. Crim and R. N. Soulen. Atlanta: John Knox, 1981.

Wifall, W. "The Sea of Reeds as Sheol." *ZAW* 92 (1980).

Wijngaards, J. N. M. *The Formulas of the Deuteronomic Creed (Dt. 6/20-23: 26/ 5-6).* Pontificia Universitas Gregoriana; Tilburg: Drukkerij A. Reijnen, 1963.

——. "הוציא and העלה: A Twofold Approach to the Exodus." *VT* 15 (1965): 91-102.

——. *The Dramatization of Salvific History in the Deuteronomic Schools.* OTS 16. Leiden: E. J. Brill, 1969.

Wilcoxen, J. A. "Narrative Structure and Cult Legend: A Study of Joshuas 1-6." In *Transitions in Biblical Scholarship,* edited by J. C. Rylaarsdam, pp. 43-70. Essays in Divinity VI. Chicago: University of Chicago Press, 1968.

Wildberger, H. "'Glauben' im Alten Testament." *ZTK* 65 (1968): 129-159.

Williamson, H. G. M. *1 and 2 Chronicles.* NICOT. Grand Rapids: Eerdmans, 1982.

Wilson, R. R. *Genealogy and History in the Biblical World.* New Haven: Yale University Press, 1977.

———. "The Hardening of Pharaoh's Heart." *CBQ* 41 (1979): 18-36.

Winnett, F. V. *The Mosaic Tradition*. Near and Middle East Series 1. Toronto: University of Toronto Press, 1949.

———. "Re-examining the Foundations." *JBL* 84 (1965): 1-19.

Wolff, H. W. *Joel and Amos*. Translated by W. Janzen et al. Hermeneia. Philadelphia: Fortress Press, 1977.

Wolters, A. "Not Rescue but Destruction. Rereading Exodus 15:8." *CBQ* 52 (1990): 223-240.

Wright, D. P. *The Disposal of Impurity*. SBLDS 101. Atlanta: Scholars Press, 1987.

Wright, G. R. H. "The Passage of the Sea." *Göttinger Miscellen* 33 (1979): 55-68.

Wyatt, N. "The Development of the Tradition in Exodus 3." *ZAW* 91 (1979): 437-442.

Zenger, E. *Die Sinaitheophanie: Untersuchungen zum jahwistischen und elohistischen Geschichtswerk*. Forshung zur Bibel. Würzburg: Echter Verlag, 1971.

———. "Tradition und Interpretation in Exodus XV 1-21." In *Congress Volume: Vienna 1980*, edited by J. A. Emerton et al., pp. 452-483. VTSup 32. Leiden: E. J. Brill, 1980.

———. "Le thème de la 'sortie d'Egypte.'" In *Le pentateuque en question: Les origines et la composition des cinq premiers livres de la Bible à la lumière des recherches récentes*, edited by A. de Pury, pp. 301-331. Le monde de la Bible. Genève: Labor & Fides, 1989.

———, and P. Weimar. *Exodus: Geschichten und Geschichte der Befreiung Israels*. SBS 75. Stuttgart: KBW Verlag, 1975.

Zevit, Z. "The Priestly Redaction and Interpretation of the Plague Narrative in Exodus." *JQR* 66 (1975): 193-211.

———. "Converging Lines of Evidence Bearing on the Date of P." *ZAW* 94 (1982): 481-511.

———. "Three Ways to Look at the Ten Plagues." *BRev* 6 (1990): 16-23.

Ziegler, J. "Die Hilfe Gottes 'am Morgen." In *Alttestamentliche Studien: Friedrich Nötscher zum 60. Geburtstag*, edited by H. Junker and J. Botterweck, pp. 281-288. BBB 1. Bonn: Peter Hanstein, 1950.

Zimmerli, W. *Gottes Offenbarung: Gesammelte Aufsätze zum Alten Testament*. TBü 19. München: Chr. Kaiser, 1963 = *I am Yahweh*. Translated by D. W. Stott. Atlanta: John Knox, 1982.

Index of Biblical Citations

Index of Selected
Hebrew Words and Phrases

Index of Authors

Subject Index

2000. 01.25B   49.95 (24.95)